THE NEW
MAMLUKS

Middle East Studies Beyond Dominant Paradigms

Peter Gran, *Series Editor*

The Charter, by 'Abd al-Hadi al-Gazzar.
Courtesy of Elias Modern Publishing House, Cairo.

THE NEW
MAMLUKS
• • •
EGYPTIAN SOCIETY
AND MODERN FEUDALISM

AMIRA EL-AZHARY SONBOL

With a Foreword by
ROBERT A. FERNEA

Syracuse University Press

The paper used in this publication meets the minimum requirements
of American National Standard for Information Sciences—Permanence
of Paper for Printed Library Materials, ANSI Z39.48-1984. ∞™

Library of Congress Cataloging-in-Publication Data

Sonbol, Amira el Azhary.
The New Mamluks : Egyptian society and modern feudalism / Amira el Azhary Sonbol ;
with a foreword by Robert A. Fernea.
p. cm. — (Middle East studies beyond dominant paradigms)
Includes bibliographical references and index.
ISBN 0-8156-2844-7 (cloth : alk. paper) — ISBN 0-8156-2845-5 (pbk. : alk. paper)
1. Egypt—History—1517-1882—Historiography. 2.
Egypt—History—1798—Historiography. 3. Egypt—Social conditions—History. I. Title.
II. Series.
DT97 .S66 2000
962¹.03—dc21   00-035820

Manufactured in the United States of America

*To El-Motaz Sonbol, who did not always agree
but was always there with his support*

Amira el-Azhary Sonbol is associate professor of Islamic history, society, and law at the Center for Muslim Christian Understanding at Georgetown University. She is the author of *The Creation of a Medical Profession in Egypt, 1800–1922* (1992) and editor of *Women, the Family, and Divorce Laws in Islamic History* (1996), both published by Syracuse University Press, and the editor and translator of *The Last Khedive of Egypt: Memoirs of Abbas Hilmi II* (1998).

CONTENTS

FOREWORD

ROBERT A. FERNEA

Histories are ethnographies of the past, penned according to the fashions of scholarship of the time and place in which they are set down. Most histories of Egypt, like other sorts of ethnography from the area, have been written in European languages by Western scholars who have made Egypt an object of their research and constructed narratives for their contemporaries to read and understand. But this is changing. Among books currently being published in contemporary cultural anthropology and history, as well as in economics and sociology, are important texts produced for a Western readership by members of the non-Western community, country, or region that is the subject of study. Does this matter? Will this new indigenous literature affect scholarly discourse? I believe so, and Amira Sonbol's study well demonstrates why it will.

Scholars are persons who do research and write. Our personal identities contribute, directly and indirectly, to our scholarship. What we notice and what we neglect, what we select as the object of our research, the significance we lend to facts and figures, and the feelings we have about our subjects all impinge on what we say, what we want to say, to an academic audience. And of course our personal identities are a cultural construction, formed by the discourses of our own cultural experience.

The most convincing evidence of the scholarly consequences of cultural differences and personal identity is in the contribution of women to both contemporary science and the humanities. As a new category of scholar, women have interests that are the same as that of their male colleagues, but many also have had areas of scholarly interest quite different from that of the men in their fields. Much the same can be said about the increasing presence of scholarship by members of American minorities. How many books and articles have been written by both groups on subjects that would not otherwise have attracted scholarly attention? Can anyone doubt that in the long run they will affect the overall discourse of the various scholarly disciplines? Women,

African Americans, and scholars from other minorities are asking new questions and suggesting new answers. The world of scholarly endeavor will never be the same as it was when it was an exclusive white male domain.

If gender and race matter, so do other forms of cultural difference. In the past decade, cultural anthropologists have been very concerned about the consequences of their own position as outsiders among the people about whom they write. How does this Otherness impose upon ethnographic representations? How can these differences properly be taken into account? If Otherness is important, should we not also wonder what happens when scholars write about their own communities, their own histories? In fact, Western scholars have not always welcomed "native" scholarship, if notice was taken at all.

The term "indigenous scholar" has in many contexts stigmatized scholarly work and implied biases or political positions deemed antithetical to objective scholarship. Such work could be dismissed as "nationalist" in nature. Sometimes, however, opinion has greatly favored "the native's voice," granting it the veracity of "super-informant," a voice that can speak the truth with a natural ability. Both extreme views lack merit.

The significance of indigenous scholarship is far more complex than can be suggested by exaggerated polemics or benign platitudes. Perhaps the most important shift in twenty-first-century scholarly production is going to be that intellectuals from the rest of the world will tell us, westerners, about themselves—and ourselves. Many of these scholars have been, and will be, educated in Western schools. Certainly, they will be part of an intellectual tradition that is becoming just as global as corporations are. That does not mean, however, that they have become Western in outlook and opinion, much less in identity. What this shift in scholarship means cannot be understood just by alluding to a "globalization of knowledge." A more critical inquiry is required. What difference can the work of non-Western scholars writing about their own societies make? What might they notice that outsiders neglect?

The New Mamluks has been written by a mature scholar, a historian, a professor, a colleague of American academics, and a teacher of American students. The author is also a woman, an Egyptian born and raised, a native speaker of Arabic, and a Muslim. The history of modern Egypt she offers here is therefore a history of her own people, her own community. The people and events of which she speaks have been part of a past she has heard about all her life; it is not what happened to "them," but rather what happened to "us." Yet she is also very familiar with Western studies of Egypt, with histories of her country written by non-Egyptians. It is useful to look at some of the ways in which this authorial positioning has infused and shaped the narrative she here presents for us.

Dr. Sonbol has articulated several issues that appear to guide the construction of her text. First, she rejects the unproblematized use of either Marxist or Western progressive-modernist models of analysis in her understanding of modern Egyptian history. Second, she is critical of those who, in studying Egypt, would employ deconstructionist terminology and unquestioningly use models of deconstruction that have been developed in a European context. Instead she proposes an emic vocabulary and, using methods of deconstruction of her own, offers a model of Egyptian social organization that, she argues, better identifies and locates groups in Egypt. These groups have had successive changes in membership but have remained dynamic social forces from Ottoman times to the present. Third, she takes issue with the practice of treating countries that are Islamic as somehow "exceptional," hindered and enframed by the constraints of a medieval religion that refuses to move with the times. Finally, she argues that Egypt was already "modern" under latter-day Ottoman rule, with its own courts and judicial systems, a class structure, political pressure groups—in practice, a society very different from the one that emerged under the French and British colonial rule or from the one that developed in the postrevolutionary period that followed.

The author looks at foreign domination from the point of view of the poorer classes in Egypt—the great majority of its population then and now—and she shows us a society in which, before Western rule, the majority of the people felt they had opportunities to seek redress according to the provisions of *shari'a* law. At least that was hegemonic: Muslims among Muslims took it for granted. One important purpose of Dr. Sonbol's narrative is to demonstrate how this hegemonic understanding changed, perhaps disappeared, under Western rule and, given the foreign institutions that were introduced, has stayed changed until this very day.

I would argue that this questioning of the past cannot help but be based in part on what the author has brought with her to the construction of her narrative: an experience and knowledge of the very different feelings Egyptians still have about the Turkish and Western colonizers and a knowledge of the way the historical differences that account for these feelings have been glossed over by many other historians. Does this Egyptian presence in the narrative mean that it is necessarily a better book? Others more informed than I will attempt to answer this question, judging this text as a history among other histories. Certainly much more is required of a historian than a native's experience, and sound evidence as well as cogent argument must continue to reign supreme. This book accomplishes this, reflecting the author's scholarship as well as her personal insights, for she has not only cited and used other histories, she has also relied extensively on many kinds of written documentation in the construction of the narrative. Archival evidence—manuscripts and other documentation written, often by hand, in five languages: Arabic, Turkish, Old Ottoman, French, and English—is abundant. The court and administrative records are quoted, as are accounts from private libraries and a diversity of (to me) unfamiliar sources. These sources are apparently available to any scholar, foreign or Egyptian. But could a non-Egyptian scholar have found and used such sources so well? Only with exceptional linguistic facility and a well-developed knowledge of how and where to find and use such a diversity of local texts.

Clearly, I have little sympathy for the argument that modern scholarship in foreign lands by Western scholars is but the latest, if not last, phase of Western colonialism. Surely foreign scholarship will always be recognized as valuable: need one recall what de Tocqueville and the many European scholars who have followed have added to our image of American society, for instance? Using national boundaries to mark off the limits of scholarly research is retrogressive at the very least. One thing is certain, however: All scholarship about any country is going to have to meet intellectual standards that scholars from those countries have helped create, and that means historians just as much as anthropologists. In my opinion, Dr. Sonbol has made a significant contribution to this pattern of intercultural discourse, as well as to our understanding of modern Egypt. I am honored that she asked me for this foreword.

FOREWORD

PETER GRAN, SERIES EDITOR

Middle East Studies Beyond Dominant Paradigms books call into question aspects of the dominant paradigm in the field of history. This dominant paradigm has three interdependant parts. One part builds on the assumption of the rise of the West; another part, the one of special concern for this series, builds on the assumption of the stagnation of the so-called oriental societies or oriental despotisms; a third part postulates with regard to Africa regions that are nonstate societies. These ideas appeared as early as the seventeenth century; by the nineteenth century, they constituted a kind of orthodoxy for the field of history. Challenging this orthodoxy has been a slow process.

The present work attempts to recast modern Egyptian history in ways that reject a number of the assumptions of the oriental despotism model. It experiments in so doing with a methodology new to Egyptian studies, that of using contemporary discourse as a window to look at social history. Sonbol notes that in the popular language of contemporary Egypt, one finds a number of terms alluding to institutions and practices hailing from the eighteenth century or before. Among these terms are *tajir* (merchant), *multazim* (tax-farmer), *mamluk* (ruler), *khassa* (the establishment, usually made up of elements of the above) and *'amma'* (the mass population or civil society). The use of these terms, she demonstrates in this book, offers an important indigenous view of modern Egyptian history and society. The broad outline of her study reveals three main phases: first, a highly integrated society in the eighteenth century; second, the rise of a social dualism following the French Invasion and along with it the oriental despotism mode of discourse lasting through the 1960s; third, in the past thirty years, the breakdown of this dualism in fact if not in theory.

The novelty of this study can be discerned first in its inclusion of the eighteenth century as a part of modern secular history. Until now the eighteenth century has been used by most scholars as a period wherein one finds the backwardness from which modern Egypt arose thanks to Muhammad 'Ali and the French or it has been used as a period of religious authenticity, for example, of Wahhabism, or of Islamic Enlightenment. Second, the novelty of this study lies in its discovery of the cultural integration (or reintegration) of contemporary Egypt and in its claim that cultural integration today points toward revolution. Finally, the novelty of this study lies in its redirection of Egyptian political economy studies toward a concern with the power of the state and the control of culture away from international trade and globalism.

To sum up, while popular discourse may not ultimately provide the language of science, its neglect by scholars of history, politics, and culture weakens their studies. This study underscores the contribution of the study of popular discourse.

PREFACE

Ten years ago I began to write an introduction to a book on the modern history of the Egyptian *'ulama'*. The essential purpose of the book was to draw connections between the Islamic reformist movements beginning in the nineteenth century and the Islamic fundamentalism and revivalism evident in Egypt today. Like most historians educated in Western universities, I approached my study with preconceived methodologies and paradigms, which I began to apply to Egypt's contemporary society to determine how much it had changed since the days when the nationalism of Zaghlul and Mustafa Kamil, and later the socialism of Nasser, were the dominant popular ideologies. I soon found myself in trouble. Even though I have studied and worked in the United States since the mid-seventies, I continue to have a home in Cairo, and I visit yearly. Still, I did not seem to conceptualize the transformations taking place. Thus began a process of relearning what the culture was all about: human and social relations as understood by Egyptians, how they view their own relationships with each other and with the state, how they perceive their roles within society, what their expectations of life are, what makes them angry, and what their priorities are. Visiting, talking, and reading were going to be the most useful methods for getting back in gear. But most important was a reevaluation of my own presumptions and ideological beliefs, including my unquestionable acceptance of positivism as an essential part of human existence.

By rereading Hafiz and Shawqi's classical poetry and the *ghazzal*s of Bayram al-Tunsi, listening to good old folklore like *Abu Zeid al-Hillali* and Egypt's version of *Alf Layla Wa Layla (One Thousand and One Nights)*, and watching the five-year TV historical soap opera *Layali al-Hilmiya,* a lot of the continuities and differences experienced by Egypt became more obvious. After all, today Hafiz and Shawqi may be recited in intellectual circles, but it is all the others that are celebrated in coffeehouses and watched avidly on television. Popular theater proved to be another eye-opener. Popular comedy theater is today the only form enjoyed by Egyptians. Some comedies have continued fully booked for five and six years and are still running strong. Changes were to be expected. The mass media, particularly television, together with the population explosion and urbanization, have been transformative in spreading "Egyptian" and "Islamic" revivalism.

The big dilemma in writing an introductory chapter to a book was turning out to be a confrontation with the normative view we have come to accept in academic circles as the "scholarly" method to discuss societies and cultures. The most important issue facing any author is how to make meaning clear to readers, and mine were to be primarily in universities—teachers and students. Using the accepted "scholarly" terminology to explain Egyptian society only led me to "box" the analysis in predetermined concepts and grids of conceptualization. This study of modern Egypt is therefore one effort in the search for new terminologies and methodologies for understanding Islamic societies. It does not give final answers. There are many other scholars who are searching for new methodologies and terminologies; this effort stresses that it must be tried, so that research directed toward clarification of history and social relations, and the specificities of history, should not be lost because of ideologically based "progressive" or other models.

This book has benefited from discussions and suggestions from colleagues in Egypt and America. I am in their debt for their criticisms and encouragement. Afaf Lutfi al-Sayyid Marsot actually read three different versions of the manuscript. Her detailed suggestions, corrections, and comments illustrate why her students respect and admire her. Nelly Hanna listened and discussed; she is a friend who shares my love of history and of Egypt. Peter Gran debated social theory and admonished changes, many of which are included. I am grateful for the long hours and discussions, gallons of coffee later. Dr. Ra'uf Abbas read and criticized helping to make the argument more focused. Many colleagues have offered wise advice; some agreed with me and others did not, but all offered scholarly advice. They include Nick Hopkins, Dina Khouri, Michael Hudson, Hisham Sharabi, and John Ruedy, who advised me that I was on to something and should take the time to develop it—advice I followed. John McNeill suggested a wider approach to Egyptian history, and I am grateful for Richard Stites for the title "The New Mamluks" (it is certainly more interesting than the ten-word title I had in mind). Galal Amin read the first draft of this work; his words of encouragement made the effort that much easier. To John Esposito and John Voll go my appreciations for comments and encouragement, as has always been the case. Thanks to Haiffa' Khalafallah, Carol Graham, and Steve Tamari for our meeting throughout a semester to discuss our various projects. This book has certainly gained from their perceptive remarks. The American Research Center fellowship provided me during 1994–95 was central to finishing this book. The weekly meetings at ARCE to discuss the research of fellows are memorable for the discussion and enthusiasm of a select number of scholars whose interest was focused on Egypt. Here I should mention in particular Lisa Pollard and Mona Russell, the organizers and most stimulating participants at these meetings. It was in Amman much earlier, and later in Cairo for the ARCE fellowship, that I got together with Bob and Elizabeth Warnock Fernea, and we spent long hours talking about culture and the cultural change Egypt was undergoing. Last, no book is possible without an editor, and in that I was blessed with two. Cynthia Maude-Gembler saw the potential for this book, and Mary Selden Evans pulled it through.

A last note about transliteration. I went along with Hans Wehr without using any *shadas* so as to simplify the Arabic words for the reader. The *g* was left as is and not turned into a *j*.

INTRODUCTION

One might see the current revival of Islam as a desire to provide familiar forms for basically non-Islamic ideas and institutions. Many commentators viewed the Islamic movement of the 1970s and 1980s in that way, seeing Islamic activism as primarily nationalist or socialist or economically motivated movements dressed in the garb of religion. . . . An alternative view . . . is that the Islamic community is entering a new phase, not the end, of its history. It is possible to see the current resurgence as a continuation of basic themes, even though those themes may be expressed in new ways.[1]

This study represents an attempt to understand the historical process in modern Egypt and to come to grips with the nature of social transformations there. Islamic revivalism and the radicalism that has become increasingly evident since the early 1980s caught scholars by surprise. They have usually been explained in academic circles as the result of a lack of political participation by Islamic society or a reaction to modernism, to government corruption, and to unequal distribution of wealth. This perception stems partly from the dual interest in Egypt in the West, which is usually studied through its relations with the United States or through the issue of Islamic fundamentalism and terrorism. The general belief is that despite pressure applied by the United States to make Egypt a democracy and the aid that it provides it as an ally, Egypt's uniqueness (shared by the rest of the Islamic world) dooms U.S. efforts to failure. Because of its exceptionalism[2] and difference from the West, Egypt is depicted as being unable to extend true enfranchisement to its masses. Religious revivalism is confined within the parameters of this exceptionalist discourse, whereas similar phenomena taking place throughout the world are not associated with the Egyptian experience. Awareness, for example, that liberation theology in Latin America, Europe, and Africa is closely associated with mass movements from the base has not led to a parallel understanding about revivalism and liberation within the non-Christian world. Rather, for Islam, revivalism is seen through

Gilles Kepel's idea as a "return to God." [3] Understanding society from within its cultural production makes it clear that Kepel is wrong and that among those who believe "Islam is the solution," God never left, but it is the God of the base that is today taking over. Scholars have been so focused on answering the question "Why the return to God?" that they are missing the wider revolution occurring, a revolution involving class struggle with class defined not just politically and economically but particularly culturally.

Although this study involves discussions of power, state-society relations, and class formation as well as power relations, continuity, and change, all of which are the general subject of similar research into the history of Egypt and other countries of the world, there are important differences. Most significantly, it does not present a harmony model through modernization theory. It does not see Egyptian society as unchanging and static, waiting to be moved and transformed by outside influences. Similarly, it does not see Egypt's people as observers of history waiting for elites to decide their fate. Here, perhaps, the most glaring example of the type of paradigm that is taken to task in this study is that presented by one of the most widely used general histories of modern Egypt, Vatikiotis's *History of Modern Egypt from Muhammad 'Ali to Sadat*. It is revealing of the state of the field that that study has gone through four editions and continues to be used in universities throughout the United States, Europe, and even Egypt. In his book Vatikiotis talks about "Egyptianity."

> Conservatism, isolation and a long-established traditional social structure comprise what one might call Egypt's permanent "Egyptianity." The essential feature of this Egyptianity has been that of an overwhelmingly rural nation, whose existence was regulated by the flow of the Nile. Egyptians formed the first unified nation known to history. Their unity and characteristic response to foreign influences at all times have not been the result of any speculative thought on their part. Rather these have been a reflection of their historical conditioning and their style of life: their unity in suffering while clinging to the traditions and beliefs of their society, to their arts and crafts. This constitutes perhaps the essence of the continuity in their history.[4]

The rest of Vatikiotis's introduction details this essentialist picture by pointing out the passivity of the peasantry who constitute the large majority of Egypt's population, the constant invasion of Egypt by outside forces—from Hyksos to Ottomans—and the utter helplessness of Egyptians in any form of decision making. Ruthless military regimes follow one another, including Arab Muslims, *Ayyubids*, mamluks, Ottomans, and Free Officers. All come to rob Egypt and appropriate the land and wealth that belonged to Egypt's peasantry. Changelessness marks the Egyptian scene as the country waits for yet another invader or reforming ruler to bring change, new ideas, or new coercive measures represented by "emblems of authority." In short, the history of Egypt becomes a series of invasions from outside with Egyptians waiting for deliverance from those who oppress them through yet another invasion. They cannot act alone except for sporadic peasant rebellions, irrational destructive actions of ignorant mobs. The people accepted the rule of foreigners with "amazing docility," as Vatikiotis puts it.[5]

In this essentialist picture Egypt is represented as exceptional: its exceptional Nile decides the rhythm of its life, and its exceptional history, the result of its geographical location at the crossroads of empires and trade routes, determines the enslavement of its people by cruel armies of invaders. Strangely enough, this is the picture that continues to be most widely accepted by most people, despite significant scholarly accomplishments to the contrary. Today, people continue to see modern Egypt through the praetorianism of Samuel Huntington[6] or Anouar Abdel-Malek[7] as a residual duality of extreme rich and poor.

In this book I argue that modern Egyptian history conforms to that of other countries in the world in that the last hundred years have included increased integration. This integration is not the same thing as either globalism or cultural homogenization, but a cultural integration that implies several interrelated modalities of life. In this sense this is a revisionist work of historiography that reinforces general ideas of how the modern history of the world has progressed during the last hundred years by showing that Egypt is no exception to the general patterns and should not be perceived as an exception to this pattern of cultural integration.

Although I define culture as the "total of human behavior patterns and technology communicated from generation to generation,"[8] I also see it as an external manifestation of underlying social phenomena. Furthermore, even though culture and cultural production reflect the social forces that produce them, they at the same time play an important role as ingredients in the historical process. Therefore, when examining a particular country's culture, it is imperative to see this culture as in process, that is, constantly changing as it interacts with the transformations taking place around it. If one were to think of culture as cultural production and consider a dominant culture as a reflection of moving forces, then the dominance of Islamic revivalism is evidence that the culture of the base is taking over today and that the sociocultural revolution underway is closing the cultural gap that has marked most of the Islamic world since the beginning of the imperialist experience. Raymond Williams's criticism of the tendency of social theory to conflate society with already completed processes supports my argument that one should not attribute fixed classes, norms, human relations, or social realities to societies. As

Williams argues, these processes "both shape and reflect the quality of social relations."[9]

How does cultural change take place? What direction is this change taking, and what are the sources of the culture that is being revived? These are perhaps the wrong questions, for it is not a particular culture that we can enframe qualitatively or quantitatively that is being revived; rather it is a liberation from imposed cultures even though the culture of the base partly belongs to the cultural heritage superimposed at different times. Here the best way to describe what is taking place is through the idea of cultural diffusion. Cultural integration is in progress, not that the old is giving way to the new to confirm modernization theory. Rather, elements of the old carry on with certain mutations. To understand this one could look at the evolution of archaic words such as *tujjar* (merchants, entrepreneurs, businessmen, or investors) as it is used from one period to the other, for example, moving from thinkers such as ʿAbd al-Rahman al-Jabarti to Taha Hussain, or Sayyid Qutb, and political groups such as the Wafd and Islamic fundamentalist organizations. So one component of this integration is old continuities. This process is different from cultural integration as it is understood by modernization theory, that is, as a hybrid form between the modern and the traditional. Other cultures besides that of Egypt have integrated by using the old more heavily, so they use their old continuities more to move toward modernities. These include such nations as India, Spain, Mexico, and as I show here, Egypt. Although I cannot cover all aspects of cultural integration in this book, my interest is more to show how old relations live in modern times and become a bridge to modernity.

Here the issue of revivalism is crucial. What is being revived is not *turath* (heritage) in the sense of tradition and material culture preceding Westernization. It is also not Islam in a radical form, all-encompassing and demanding an Islamic state. While interest has been focused on Islamic revivalism and radicalism since the Iranian Revolution, it is imperative that one distinguish between Islamic revivalism and religious radicalism and terrorism. The two are linked at some level; after all, both Islamic revivalism and radicalism form part of historical transformations in no way unique to the Islamic world. Rather, they are a natural part of the liberation process that accompanied the struggle against imperialism and neoimperialism. Still one needs to differentiate between the two movements. Whereas revivalism is manifested in society at large, radicalism can be seen as the radical side of this revivalism, the antisystemic antihegemonic arm of this revivalism. Although the two phenomena are taking place at the same time, the two scarcely represent the same ideals, universal concept, or worldview.

"Reacting to modernity" has been used to justify any movements among Muslims that do not conform to Western ways. But such an explanation is too

simplistic and gives the impression that these societies are incapable of changing except when prodded from outside or as a reaction to such prodding.
Rather than the passive society one has become accustomed to seeing in the
Western press, contemporary revivalism is evidence of a vibrant society looking for its own answers. Reacting to outside pressures is one of these answers
but not the essential ingredient. Historical transformations were taking place
and revivalism was part of the process of change rather than a conservative reaction to change or a politically designed movement. Walter Armbrust in-
sightfully explained the complexity of the process of cultural change.
"Egyptian middle-class identity is tied to Egyptian nationalism and rests on an
ideology of transformation from 'traditionalism' to 'modernity.' The process
of transformation is complex, encompassing parallel versions of *asala* (authenticity), one classicist and the other 'folkloric,' which never sit together
comfortably. Heritage is not simply there but must constantly be sifted and
reworked in the cause of progress." [10]

Egypt's elite since the nineteenth century has espoused a strong belief in
material progress, modernity, and industrial development. The ideologies
they adopted were often liberal or Marxist, but they all were based on two opposing concepts of culture. On one hand, culture was an admired positivist
model to be instituted by the government from above. And on the other
hand, it was to be viewed as a heritage of "traditional" arts and crafts that was
to be revered for its own sake and as a resource to attract tourists. But such
heritage is of little significance to modern society, except in as far as it allows
for traditions that support and strengthen the status quo. Thus the intellectual
elite and the government use the word *thaqafa* (high culture, knowledge, intellectualism) for culture, differentiating it from *turath* (heritage), or *'adat*
(customs). For a long time the Egyptian elite have looked at culture as a matter of policy to educate the masses in art and literature, preferably world art
and literature. Under British rule a Western "order" was introduced into what
a foreign or culturally Westernized elite perceived as a backward society because it did not exhibit European culture and values. After 1952 a ministry of
culture was built on socialist models targeted to fulfill the "cultural potential
of nations that previously languished under the yoke of colonialism, and of
their capacity for new cultural and historical creativity." [11] This activity involved an aggressive approach to change; setting up "cultural policy" meant
to achieve "cultural development" aimed at a "cultural revolution." [12]

Thus, the elite approach continued to be directed toward molding society
to fit the needs of material progress and, hence, economic development.
While perceiving and referring to their class as the *khassa* (special class holding
power, molders of law) whose leaders regarded themselves as holding the
wilaya (historically, guardianship of an Islamic ruler over his people), Egypt's

elite saw the people, whom they referred to as the 'amma (general public), as an object to be studied, molded, and changed according to their concept of progress. Issa Boullata described this approach well: "The . . . culture of the marginalized common people . . . is unrecognized by the elite, a culture that is usually considered forbidden—or at best—worthless and irrelevant, though it is that of the majority, whose right it is to determine their own destiny but is ignored by the elite and is often suppressed."[13]

Dealing with *khassa* and 'amma means dealing with state/society power relations. Numerous studies have dealt with the nature of the state, the makeup of its government and institutions, the source of a nation's state power, the nature and composition of ruling classes, the coercive powers at the state's disposal (including police and armed forces), and the hegemonies created by dominant classes to legitimize their rule. On one level this study is a contribution toward understanding state-society relations, for it details the evolution of Egypt's *khassa* since Egypt was part of the Ottoman Empire. That is, however, a starting point. My real focus is on society as it evolved given the growing centralized power of the nation-state. The power of Egypt's *khassa* is closely related to state building, centralization of power, national armies, police forces, managed economies, structured political systems, civil institutions, and just as important, constructed legal systems intended to homogenize and control every aspect of human life from the personal to property to business. Without question, during the modern period the administrative, legal, and coercive power of state centralization increased. This is, perhaps, the basic reason why in most studies of Egyptian society, as in studies of other Third World countries, the model of an absolutist state is so pervasive. In an absolutist state rulers established their power by using coercion, and society was a recipient of change imposed from above, its people acting as observers to historical transformations. I dispute this picture of an absolutist state by discussing different patterns of relations between state and society.

In the seven chapters of this book, I focus on important periods in Egyptian modern history during which state/society relations and cultural diffusion were particularly important. I define these periods by the most important transformations that took place within them. In the first chapter, written in light of the contemporary crisis in Egypt, I indicate the need to rethink what has been understood as the birth of modern Egypt and what modern Egypt was, which leads back before Muhammad 'Ali to the era of the late mamluks. It is a historiographical study of the early modern pre-nineteenth-century period with particular emphasis on the eighteenth. It is a detailed chapter in which I use archival records to build a picture of the social structure before the nation-state project was underway. Eighteenth-century Egyptian society is usually studied as a period of backwardness, of chaos in which mamluks preyed on Egypt's population and in which people were ruled by the whip. The picture given here is different, showing a dynamic society whose members were active in selling, buying, and living. If anything, state-society relations during that period were marked by social maneuverability, and Egypt's population lived in relative security under the rule of law. Understanding the background to the nineteenth century is essential if the significance of nineteenth-century transformations is to be appreciated. It is also important to understand the eighteenth century to know where Egyptian society is going today, toward greater maneuverability and institutions that are linked organically with the base rather than state-constructed and controlled institutions. In this chapter I introduce the hypothesis that the eighteenth century contained legal and social instruments that today have continuing usefulness; state-society relations were marked by the fact that law and order were closely linked with social relations and organically linked with the base. This formula changes during the nineteenth and twentieth centuries with state efforts (only partially successful) in which the state acted as the active creator of law and order through constructed discourses and new legal and administrative structures. Today, a symptom of the crisis facing the state is the moral discourse of the base that is becoming predominant even in the legal and administrative structures that evolved during the last two centuries. Thus, the eighteenth century must be included in this study of Egyptian modern history up to the present crisis.

In chapter 2, "Building the Modern State: Mercantilism in a New Form," I treat the establishment of the centralized mercantilist state under Muhammad 'Ali Pasha and propose that it continued in place until the recent crisis. If the old mercantilist practices were directed toward control of exports and imports by the state as represented by, for example, the early mamluks, this new mercantilism goes beyond control of trade. It takes in production, distribution, and consumption patterns, manipulates the laws to benefit certain classes and groups, and shifts these laws whenever it suits particular members of the *khassa* who are in ascendance. At this time state building becomes a definite pattern in the actions of a central government. These patterns were not new for Egypt, but here one sees an active state with mercantilist intents exercising greater control over production and distribution and taking a direct role in social and cultural construction. In this chapter I also engage in a critical view of the prevailing view of the historiography of Egypt and suggest the need for revision of such long-accepted concepts as hydropolitics and oriental despotism as they apply particularly to the period of Muhammad 'Ali. I further question conventional use of the term *Ottoman* in regard to Egypt before the nineteenth century. Ottomanism was actually part of the social dynamics bridging Egypt into its modern nation-state form, which also included Westernization, modernization, and the immigration of large numbers of people and culture from the Egyptian periphery to the center.

In chapter 3, "Imagining Duality," I discuss the construction of duality from roughly the 1840s to 1952, and in chapter 4, "Foreign Rule and the *Tujjar*," I examine the struggle within the *khassa* as new political formations emerge. In these chapters I treat the European outlook toward Egypt, the hegemonic discourses that were part of imperialism, nationalism, and nation-state building that were to have profound influence on Egypt under colonial rule. I introduce a revisionist historiographical position on the subject of these periods that supposes much modern Western influence is a repetition of older indigenous patterns. I hypothesize that the *khassa* and the Europeans in Europe covered these details by creating orientalist discourses that formed a basis for the future European outlook toward Egypt and Egyptians, an essentialist outlook that emphasized Egypt's backwardness and uniqueness. Because the outlook itself became a blueprint for government policy, colonialism and the accompanying modernism and Ottomanism defined Egypt as a dual structure that, through government policy, became a reality. Foreign rule is defined as an age when merchants, entrepreneurs, and businessmen, generally referred to as *tujjar* in this book, play a major role within the *khassa*. And because the most important *tujjar* under British rule were Europeans, modernity is introduced as a discourse that with economic dependency, social differences, and legal reforms brings about a dual society separated by culture and wealth. At the same time, state control and centralization make this social and cultural gap a reality enforced by the power of the state.

Egypt's independence in 1952 resurrected military power that had remained under *khassa* control since Ahmad 'Urabi's failed revolution of 1882. In chapter 5, "Socialism and Feudalism," I rethink the Nasser era, as do several other writers, from the point of view of today's crisis. The conclusion reached is that the military, representing the national forces of a modern state, once in power practiced prerogatives similar to those enjoyed by the mamluks when they were the ascendant group within Egypt's eighteenth-century *khassa*. State-capitalism is one way of looking at this period, as some scholars have done effectively, as a system connoting government officials' ability to manipulate their senior positions, controlling those who work under them; the ability to receive rent from the power they hold works at one level. But the bureaucratic alliances allowing such actions went beyond one man or group of men manipulating the state to their own ends. Greater complexity is evidenced by the actual participation of *khassa* and *'amma* in raising and receiving rent. Tentacles of patronage—not clientage, which connotes permanency in the system (although that, too, existed, sometimes temporarily, sometimes more permanently in the form of a *tabi'* [crony, familiar, or follower])—extended from one individual and level of the hierarchy across hierarchies. But both the hegemony and the discourses supporting it went further, allowing for legitimacy. Setting up the state as a "grand seigneur," the Nasserist regime incorporated socialism with nationalism to create state-society relations reminiscent of a feudal compact based on reciprocity. The "right" of the state to political allegiance and labor of the people is reciprocated by the state's "duty" to guarantee the security of the nation and provide its people with food, clothing, housing, education, health, and justice. Given the contradictions and efforts and intentions, the discourse scarcely fits actual realities.

As I explain in chapter 6, " The New *Tujjar* and *Infitah*," Egypt's defeat in 1967 and its economic hardships in that period brought about a new orientation toward international capitalism and a new wave of social struggle. In this chapter I pick up on one aspect of this subject that in the long run proved most important, that is, the end of the cultural dualism that had been in place over the past century.

In chapter 7, "An End to Duality?" I explore the end of duality in several areas of Egyptian culture of the contemporary period and theorize about where the historical process is leading today. This examination opens the door to new views of the Islamic trend, the rise of the use of colloquial language, and the major changes in music and theater of the last few years. This chapter is an alternative view to the more common views of writers on this period who see cultural trends as a form of vulgarization and reaction to the West or as some recovery of eternal authenticity (Islamic *turath*).

On the level of methodology the study of modern Egypt is frequently associated with archival research, which has produced a great deal of new thought and information during the last generation. In this work I experiment with using discourse as a window on social history. This line of study has been pursued previously by literary critics; this is an attempt by a historian to use it as a historical source. Scholars will notice that their usage of terms differs from that introduced here, which is popular social usage. My intention is not to introduce a new vocabulary but to employ common usage as a means of understanding actual social reality.

Methodology and Terminology

The terms *khassa* and *'amma* are generally used as dichotomies to describe despotic societies with clearly defined upper-class elites holding absolute power over cowering, helpless peasant or urban lower classes. This is not how the terms are used in this study; rather they are used from within the social outlook to these groups, groups that constitute hegemonic alliances cooperating and conflicting with each other. Their intergroup makeup and relations

shift and power balances alter within the hegemony over time. It is these relations and ongoing counterhegemonic struggles that give rise to the many rich
and changing meanings of terms. For example, *khassa* is usually translated as
"elite." There are two problems here: *khassa* does not mean elite in the English sense ("elite" would be *safwa*), and "elite" itself is a term with little use
for its social analysts because it gives no space for the historical agency of society. For example, "the elite" appears to be one group united by power, privilege, and access to wealth and culture. But that definition does not take into
consideration the diversity of members within the *khassa;* the elite as a distinctive group form only one part of the *khassa*. Other members are different in
function, position, privilege, and wealth. When the words *the elite* are used in
this book, it is to designate a particular group of the *khassa* that is in ascendance at a particular time. This usage is not intended to negate the actual role
played by other groups within the *khassa* or counterhegemonic forces.

There are reasons for using the term *khassa* in preference to a term such as
elite. *Elite* as a term gives the impression of absolutist control. Thus, one does
not speak of an American elite; rather the term is used to indicate absolutist
regimes wielding coercive power. The range of cultural meaning imbedded in
the term *khassa* makes it particularly useful when defining members of ruling
classes. It denotes people who consider themselves the final arbiters of power
and who are perceived by society as playing this specific role. Although the
term *khassa* used earlier by Ibn Khaldun and al-Jabarti is used by Arab scholars to describe their contemporary societies, it is important to understand its
limitations.[14] In this study the *khassa* are not seen as an aristocracy because no
principle of nobility or inheritance is involved here. They also are not seen as
the cream of society in any moral or cultural sense, even though they may consider themselves to be so and may use terms to suggest these attributes. Before
the 1952 revolution, the term *dhawat* (well-born, cultured, elite) was used to
describe certain members of the *khassa* who could be considered elites. During the Sadat period a common word used for members of this stratum was
ahl al-thiqa, "people of confidence." Therefore, *khassa* denotes special groups
holding power who are recognized as such by the people. This power, however, is diffused and differs from situation to situation. Certain groups may appear more often than others within the *khassa* in Egypt's history, for example,
the military, but even the Egyptian military could not be considered part of
Egypt's *khassa* under British rule (1882–1952)—seventy long years of
Egypt's modern history. The military began to regain position in the *khassa* as
the army was expanded after 1936. But the army's traditional role in the
khassa was easily regained given continuities in old cultural perceptions and
changes brought about by the historical process both on the national and international scenes. To talk about the *'amma* as masses—a useful term when

discussing the public in general—gives the impression of an unorganized politically unaware public. That is scarcely the case for Egypt any more than it is
for Europe, Latin America, or Asia. The term *base* gives the same impression
and the idea of helplessness. Helplessness, masses, and base are theoretical
constructs of development and modernization advocates. They do not help
when studying the history of peoples. *'Amma,* as understood by Egyptians
and as used by intellectuals and politicians, recognizes the close relations between the *khassa* and the *'amma,* the relationship and tentacles of patronage
that extend from one to the other. In fact, important sectors of merchants,
government, and military are themselves part of the *'amma.*

Furthermore, describing the *khassa* as upper classes, although useful,
tends to hide the nature of various groups involved in the class and the relationship between them. For example, members of the military who wield
power make up a small segment of the armed forces that during particular periods appropriated arbitrary rights and often enjoyed economic privileges as
businessmen and government beneficiaries. Although they belong to the
khassa, they are not necessarily all from the upper ranks; it is not their rank that
decides the nature and extent of power they wield. Instead, a system of patronage and decentralized forms of personal allegiance, which also exists more
generally in society, enables military *khassa* to win political leverage within and
outside the military. Opposition lies among the groups that are excluded from
this patronage system.

When defining the *khassa,* one must realize that the various allied groups
that form the *khassa* change with time. Thus, the combinations reflect the
gain or loss of power of particular factions. The important thing to note is that
at given points in time different groups in the *khassa* play different roles, but
they all complement each other and are closely allied so as to control the
power within the state. This does not mean that the groups work in harmony;
on the contrary, there is an ongoing struggle between various groups, each
trying to control more power as the road to authority and wealth. The main
interest of the *khassa* taken as a whole lies in controlling the country's direct
and indirect foreign relations and, hence, its trade and its wealth from both
rural and urban areas. Wealth does not mean surplus alone; it goes beyond
that. Thus, in Egypt, while legal and administrative history reveals a complex
attempt at more and more total control, the relationship between members of
the *khassa,* in fact in Egyptian society as a whole, leans toward accommodation
rather than struggle, struggle being itself part of accommodation.

Basically, three groups are commonly part of the *khassa:* the ruling elite, the
military, and the business classes. Various combinations of the three have constituted the *khassa* at different times in Egypt's modern history. Others—most
important being the clergy, professionals, and intellectuals—appear as their in-

fluential allies under certain conditions. These people have provided the *khassa* with their rationale or their culture. Without culture no lord could last. In *Imams and Emirs: State, Religion and Sects in Islam* Fuad Khuri described the *'ulama'*-elite alliance in these terms: "Throughout Islamic history . . . there have always been *fuqaha* (Islamic scholars) and *ahl al-hukm wa al-sultan* (men of government and authority), the first clarifying the religious precepts to be implemented by the second; at times they quarrel, but theirs is a dispute of *takamul* (complementarity) rather than *tanaqud* (contradiction)." [15]

One group in the *khassa* (or as one would say in America, the "establishment") comprised those who ruled, whether Egyptian or foreign (e.g., British, Ottoman, or mamluk). This ruling elite was sometimes mamluks, sometimes *multazims*, and sometimes *tujjar*. For example, the mamluks and Nasserists were military *khassa*, the British were *tujjar*, and the *infitah*ists were *multazims*.

Under the *khassa* was a level of technicians through which the rulers actually ran the state and extracted the wealth. Traditionally, this group comprised largely *multazims*, who had the specific task of collecting taxes from rural areas but who did so for urban centers. *Iltizam* (tax-farm) is usually taken to have applied to agricultural land even though it was also the method by which the Ottoman state raised revenues from urban centers, trade, and ports. There is also disagreement as to when agricultural land became de facto private property: that this only occurred with Sa'id Pasha's (1854–63) land code law of August 5, 1858; that the process really began under Muhammad 'Ali; or that *iltizam*s were turned into *malikan*s (long-term or permanent holdings) before the nineteenth century.[16] Nevertheless, historians agree that *iltizam*s no longer existed and private property became the main form of land-holding in nineteenth-century Egypt. This study proposes that *iltizam* should be considered as more than a system of urban and rural taxation. Rather it should also be seen as a determinant of relations of production, as an economic philosophy underlying the social outlook toward relations of production. As such then, *iltizam* is an important factor in state-society relations. Capitalism has its own economic philosophy and production relations, as does socialism. Each worked out differently wherever it originated or was imported, depending on cumulative historical experience. In Egypt *iltizam* provided a familiar philosophy that guided economic relations whether the system applied was capitalism or socialist, changing in outward shape and nature with changing government and state-society relations, yet playing the same function. The *multazim*'s function and rights were two sides of the same coin, inseparable, and historically appeared in different forms, evolving into the government functionary's prerogatives today. Functionaries include both the government hierarchy and government-owned industries and businesses.

The second usual group constituting part of the *khassa* is the military. The military better than any other group embody the attributes of "neopatriarchy" as described by Hisham Sharabi: "Over the last one hundred years the patriarchal structures of Arab society, far from being displaced or truly modernized, have only been strengthened and maintained in deformed, 'modernized' forms."[17] The function of today's military is to defend the nation, but so did the mamluks. The modern military's concept of power and its relationship with the rest of the population have roots dating back to the mamluks. I show here that in the late nineteenth century, the army that Muhammad ʿAli Pasha built early in the century after his destruction of the mamluks in a massacre in Cairo citadel tried to regain the power role of their forebears only to be stopped once again, this time by the British and their Egyptian allies. Likewise, the Nasser revolution can be seen as a resurrection of traditional military power. Later, under Sadat, through civilianization of the military that began during the Nasser period, the Free Officers changed into a civilian elite and continued as key members of the ruling class.

A third component of the *khassa* is the *tujjar*. With Mubarak the importance of government and business classes meant the reduction of the power of the military. This change was to be expected given historical precedence; expansion of the world market causes greater integration in world power structures. Globalization has meant the ascent of business communities and the integration of armies to serve business interests. But the term *tujjar* does not refer to all merchants, only the long-distance and large-scale traders, groups that control foreign mercantile/business activities and are closely allied with the state. Whereas a *tajir* usually restricted his work to buying and selling on the international market, he often acted as an international banker, became involved in manufacturing and industry, and speculated in stock markets and both national and international real estate. The *tujjar* are responsible for seeing that cash crops are transported abroad and that the country's needs for foreign goods are met. This group is an important part of the *khassa*, whether composed of Egyptian, Syrian, or French merchants or merchants of other nationalities. Rather than merchants one can talk about this group as capitalists, which would be objectionable given the historical context from which they worked and the fact that some rulers actually were also *tujjar*. One example is Muhammad ʿAli Pasha, who took over a large amount of business by establishing himself as chief *tajir*. An interesting combination of the *tajir*'s function and that of a government employee occurs when a public-owned company becomes a "tax-farm" providing benefits to individuals who run it. It is important to understand that the different components making up the *tujjar* cooperate to do business and to hold on to their position within the *khassa;* otherwise they are in constant competition. Robert Vitalis presents a some-

what similar combination, the "business oligarchy" who were the actual pro-
moters of Egyptian industrialization:

> The model of interest aggregation and conflict that I develop centers on rival
> coalitions of local investors, or what are often called business groups. These
> are families or other communally linked investors, typically, with holdings
> that span primary, secondary and tertiary economic sectors—that is, they are
> combination big landlords, bankers and manufacturers. And these groups are
> typically tied by bonds of mutual dependence, consensus and shared advan-
> tage with foreign investors and governing factions. . . . I refer to these
> organized groups collectively as a *business oligarchy*. But it is the conflict
> among oligarchs that is central to understanding Egypt's early industrial
> development.[18]

Vitalis's study, like Armbrust's mentioned earlier, is an important effort to try
to present new ways of looking at Egyptian history and society.

The *'amma* can be divided by occupation as well as by class; for example,
it can include professionals, industrial laborers, *hirafiyyin* (skilled labor, craftsmen), retailers, small-scale importers, or clerical workers in both the public
and private sectors. The rank and file of the armed forces and the police should
be included here as well. Even though the peasantry deserves a treatment of
their own, many writers past and present regard the peasants as an important
sector of the *'amma*. There are great differences in wealth among the *'amma*;
some have managed to manipulate the system to accumulate sizable fortunes.
For example, some *hirafiyyin* have made good use of the rampant inflation
and the scarcity of skilled craftsmen to make fortunes. Others have been attracted by the wealth of the neighboring Arab states and moved there to enrich themselves. Some shopkeepers, such as butchers and greengrocers, have
also been able to take advantage of food shortages and high prices to make
themselves small fortunes. Generally speaking, the *'amma* does not trust the
government, and they have no real access to participation in the formal political process. In addition, they resent the government's interference in their affairs and its efforts to regularize, formalize, and, thus, tax their businesses. A
major part of the activities of the *'amma*, other than those salaried by the formal sector, are part of the informal economy and, thus, remain outside the
sphere of government control. The informal economy thus represents a form
of resistance and competition with the *khassa*.

Experience has taught members of the *'amma* not to trust the *khassa*,
which has the ability to confiscate wealth from the masses, sometimes at will.
Even when wealth among the *'amma* is acquired in accordance with the
state's laws, the laws may be arbitrarily changed to assure that real wealth stays

in the hands of the *khassa*. Therefore, a common problem for members of the *'amma* is how to defend themselves. Historically, the form of their defense has been in the realm of culture and religion.

Dividing society into *khassa* and *'amma* should not lead to the conclusion that coercion is the basis upon which the *khassa* exercise power or that the *'amma* are quite powerless in such a system. For even though class relations in Egypt are traditionally based on relations of power rather than wealth, one finds as elsewhere both consensus and coercion. However absolutist or authoritarian the structure seems on the outside, in fact the interaction between these various groups suggests far more consensus than has generally been realized. Besides, societies like that in Egypt may not have the same patterns as Western democracies simply because they have different experiences in politics. Still, there are analogues, or at least homologues, for municipal government—trade unions, a press, a party, and elective parliamentary system—to mention a few of the characteristics of contemporary civil society.

An important question in understanding any social structure has to do with the relationship of different classes to each other and to the state. Students influenced by Max Weber regard the state as an entity of its own with its own laws and forms of legitimacy. Legitimacy is reflected in its elected representatives, its separation of church and state (the United Kingdom being an exception), and its independent judiciary and legislature. Studies that have concentrated on the nature of the state as an end in itself have come up with some interesting models, such as the "bureaucratic-authoritarian state,"[19] the "authoritarian-modernizing"[20] state, "tributary state,"[21] or the "positive state" versus the "traditional state."[22] Such models seem to call for complementary studies that concentrate on what exists within and beyond the state. In the case of Egypt, if one were to remove the umbrella called "state," one would find a different picture from what is generally assumed. Michel Foucault's idea that the state hides power relations proves useful: "Institutions such as the State and its apparatuses, by acting as intermediaries of power, actually hide it."[23] Because of the state, power is not concentrated as absolute coercion in a visible form but is, in fact, diffused and functions in invisible ways. "To analyze power, one must not link it a priori to repression."[24] Thus, coercive power becomes only one form available to the state. "The traditional notion of a center of irradiation located in the State and its apparatuses is substituted by . . . the idea of a diffuse power, distributed within the body of society, of a plurality of local powers exercised from innumerable points."[25] Foucault's analysis of the state marks a considerable advance over that of Weber, albeit he does not explain how conflict over power takes place.

In an interesting work on the question of power, John Kenneth Galbraith discusses three instruments for wielding and enforcing power: condign, compensatory, and conditioned power. Whereas condign power "wins submission" by the ability to impose "sufficiently unpleasant or painful" alternatives, and compensatory power "wins submission by the offer of affirmative reward—by the giving of something of value to the individual so submitting"—conditioned power is "exercised by changing belief. [It uses] persuasion, education, or the social commitment to what seems natural, proper, or right." Galbraith concludes that conditioned power really is most applicable to the modern world.[26] Conditioned power, which is really in the realm of culture and social relations, is the way in which power relations are exercised. The state itself may be the creature of the *khassa* in general, but power is distributed among the various members of the *khassa* as well as the *'amma*. The *'amma* obeys the system as long as the *khassa* has the power and moral authority to play the leading role. Put differently, the *khassa* wields control through a cultural discourse that allows it to play a hegemonic role.

Opposition to the *khassa* is, thus, usually latent, but sometimes manifest. Successful examples of opposition in Egypt's modern history have presented new discourses, whether national, socialist, Islamic, or liberal, that demand wider participation in the political process and decision making. Furthermore, opposition movements criticize the hypocrisy of *khassa* ideology. During the last hundred years of Egypt's history, the system was supposed to have a distinct shape that was all encompassing, even idealistic and utopian, embodying social equality. Yet in looking into the actual laws, one discovers that they do not reflect these ideals. Thus, laws of the state are, in fact, supplanted and undermined by ministerial-level decisions and executive orders that contradict the spirit and meaning of the laws and are arguably illegal. These contradictions are possible only because of charismatic leadership and patriotic slogans. When such means do not fulfill the purpose, the state begins to change accordingly to create new structures that are appropriate for the existing situation.

The economy evidences a split between the "official" and the "informal" economy. The "official" economy is the realm of the *khassa,* which handles foreign trade, the public and private sectors recognized by the government, and the taxation system, which is designed to ensure the extraction of wealth. An "informal" economy also exists, constituting a hidden sector that includes all economic activities that occur outside of the official sphere: buying and selling; services; and village-to-marketplace trading moving to small workshops and retailers in urban and rural areas. At one time the informal economy was the province of the system's victims, but informality has long been a system used by *khassa* unwilling to submit their profits to state rules or taxation. This was true for both outlying areas and imperial centers. In recent years informality has also become increasingly a province of the *khassa*.

Although Egypt has always had an informal economy, today its significance lies in its continuous growth despite all government efforts to control it. The government's frustration in that effort is an indication that an intricate mercantilist-feudal structure set up by Egypt's rulers to handle the agricultural and manufacturing surplus is finally breaking down.

It is easily observable that the more centralized a state becomes, the more the political system and economic advantages are the prerogative of an elite. That is the case even in free-market economies in which wealth ensures power. It seems logical that central governments create structures ensuring their stability, and that is particularly so when state and ruling class correlate. In early modern Europe, when nation-states were replacing the decentralized feudal system, some new mercantile elites found laissez-faire or free trade most advantageous, so they supported it. But this was the exception; more often, states resorted to internal and external controls of trade to ensure their predominant role in it. Both Holland and Britain, champions of free trade, applied mercantilist policies when it best fit with their interests. In France, mercantilism proved an effective system by which the monarchy and the ancien regime it supported could benefit from the world economy and national markets as well. As Ferdinand Braudel explained, "There was inevitably behind the national market a centralizing political will, fiscal, administrative, military or mercantilist. . . . Mercantilism represents precisely the dawning of awareness of this possibility of maneuvering the entire economy of a country."[27] In Egypt, governments have followed mercantilist policies since the beginning of the nineteenth century and did so during earlier periods.

The classical definition of mercantilism depicts it as an "economic creed that prevailed at the dawn of capitalism, before the industrial revolution"; this creed called for a trade policy designed to generate profit (measured in terms of bullion and tangible wealth) by maximizing exports and reducing imports. To achieve this aim the various forms of industry, agriculture, and manufacturing are geared toward producing items that would be exportable with the widest margin of profit, which is usually accomplished through the center, the plans for production and trade being laid out by a central bureaucracy. Ultimately, such a system by its very nature becomes the prerogative of a small elite, the actual holders of power controlling the production and distribution of goods. To facilitate their job they promulgate laws that ensure trade, at the same time keeping the prerogative of trade in a few hands. These laws change in accordance with new needs. The same can be said of the ideologies, which change in response to new internal and international world conditions. Elite combines themselves change, but that does not necessarily entail a shift in the division of labor or relations of production.

Mercantilism is usually approached in two ways: one treats it in terms of doctrine, the other in terms of policy and "historical process." In the first case mercantilism is seen as a fairly cohesive, "static" set of ideas:

> The doctrinal approach suggests that humans and their ideas may be arranged on a continuum with "mercantile" at one extreme and "liberal" at the other. By contrast, the policy approach spotlights those self-interested forces at work in the economic system bringing about changes in power and wealth. It concentrates on the specific regulations of the mercantile period and how each affected the competing groups of interests held by the monarch, parliament, courts, and producers. It assumes that the driving force of individual behavior in the mercantilist period is the same as the driving force of twentieth-century capitalism, namely, the self-interested pursuit of gain.[28]

According to the policy approach, strategies used in mercantilist systems include detailed regulation of particular sectors of the economy while other sectors are left with little or no regulation. Fiscal policies including currency exchange, inflating or deflating the value of a currency, and controlling currency exchange have proven of particular use. Taxation and subsidies of goods and industries, as well as "legal monopolies in the form of franchises and patents"[29] that allow for exclusive production or trading rights to particular individuals, groups, or institutions have all been methods used to establish mercantilist-style policies even during periods that have been labeled free-market or liberal. Politicians "in *their own interests* . . . will *supply* government monopoly privileges and regulations to individual business people or merchants or to any group whose self-interest leads it to *demand* regulation."[30] It should be noted that deregulation is in itself a form of regulation because it benefited certain groups under particular conditions.[31]

Mercantilism was in evidence in Egypt under the mamluks. Under Muhammad 'Ali Pasha it became an explicit policy. In much the manner of other rulers of his age, Muhammad 'Ali intended to maximize exports, thereby creating larger margins of profit from trade activity. To achieve this aim, the pasha built various forms of industry, agriculture, and manufacturing geared toward producing items that could be exported with the widest profit margins. All trade activities were carried out through a bureaucracy that grew with the growth of mercantilist activities. Laws were set up to ensure that the prerogatives of trade would remain as much as possible in the hands of the state (represented by the pasha).[32]

Foreign capitalists, their local allies after the British invasion in 1882, Nasser's national socialism, Sadat's *infitah* (open-door policy), and Mubarak's development projects all followed mercantilist policies. Generation after generation, the justification offered for such policies was that "economic welfare of the state can only be secured by government regulation of a nationalist character."[33] The laws, structures, and systems introduced to support mercantilist policies, despite declared intentions, worked together to ensure the continuation of a two-class system of *khassa* and *'amma,* the key being control by one class, the *khassa,* of the foreign relations of Egypt. He who controls Egypt's foreign relations and, hence, trade ensures his power base and, therefore, wealth.

To put this more theoretically, one might note that just as capitalism manifests itself in various forms in different areas of the world—depending on the nature of the particular country and the trade zone to which it belongs in a hierarchical world economic system[34]—mercantilism also appears in different forms in different places and in different periods in the same place. Thus, mercantilism has been molded into different forms during various periods of Egypt's modern history. Each age presented its own form of mercantilism, sometimes under the guise of liberalism or socialism, but in spite of the outward differences, mercantilism's purpose remained the same. In fact, molding of the system provides the forms through which an elite can always dominate economic activity.

In Egypt mercantilism meant government interference in economic activities (if not in all other aspects of life as well), which resulted in an overly large bureaucracy and an excessive number of administrative laws, orders, and regulations. Over a long period Egyptian politicians have justified these measures on the basis of "national interest," a higher goal that cannot be questioned. In essence, however, such measures have brought about the regulation of the market and the restriction of licensing and permits in a way that enables privileged members of the elite to, in fact, dominate the process of exchange and thereby not only profit from the country's international trade but control it. The same holds true for internal trading and manufacturing activity.

Mercantilism has had a major influence on the *'amma.* As a class the *'amma* itself has experienced periodic transformation. With the rise of the capitalist world market, mercantilism resulted in a massive bureaucracy to support supervision, taxation, and day-to-day business required by a centralized state: an ever-increasing bureaucracy—not that bureaucracy was new to Egypt—imposed on the backs of the *'amma.* With the coming of the government bureaucrat, a brand new "order" developed with its own hierarchies, a few from the *khassa* and majority from the *'amma.* Laws of all kinds, from religious to administrative and ministerial, appeared daily as a result of the bureaucratic environment. Bureaucracy was a great place to promote slogans such as "the good of the state," "patriotism," "nationalism," "unity," or "Islam," all in effect calling for conformity to a dominant hegemonic discourse. As long as the *'amma* identified with the particular "cause" and as long as the state had the coercive ability to ensure hegemony, the system worked. When either of these was not available, the structure began to disintegrate.[35]

Scholars interested in the question of whether the Middle East has experienced feudalism in the past, and if so, what form of feudalism, should take Egypt's history after the 1952 revolution into account. The survival of feudal habits was noted by Gramsci in reference to twentieth-century Italian agricultural practices: "The institutions and mental habits of feudalism have survived longest in agricultural production (and many still persist). . . . Markets are still restricted, and market transactions have a character which is not very different from primitive bartering."[36] Peter Gran's discussion of precapitalist modes may illustrate this further. "Elements combine and reemerge more than they disappear and become replaced by something else. . . . The modern . . . does not replace the traditional unproblematically as it does in modernization theory; capitalism does not replace pre-capitalism once and for all. . . . Capitalism makes use of precapitalist forms as often in the short run this secures the most docile and least expensive work force."[37] Gran uses this analysis to describe systems that he calls *semifeudal* and *semicapitalist,* terms that are used extensively by social scientists in reference to India and Mexico and that Gran feels are appropriate for understanding the resurgence of city sweatshops, for example in Nasserist Egypt. Gran sees refeudalization as resulting from the "weakening of state capitalism [when] a new system emerges melding together as much as possible feudal or non-capitalist practices with those of the modern sector capitalism."[38] But the tradition was not feudal in Egypt's case; the feudal relationship that existed during the Nasser years did not originate in Egypt's heritage as much as it did in the socialist system that Nasser applied to Egypt. As a system of thought, socialism has roots firmly embedded in the feudal past of Western Europe. If one could separate the theory of feudal relations from the practical application of the term at a given moment, one might see how the theory could be adopted and applied to newer situations even though the characteristics of the superstructure differ from the historical cases with which feudalism is normally associated. This is what gives the term its applicability to Egypt, at least in the form of semifeudalism.

When Nasser talked about *iqta'* (feudalism) he was referring to the ownership of Egypt's agricultural land by a few prominent families, representing members of the *khassa* that his own Free Officers supplanted. He described the system he was introducing as socialism, through which he aimed at achieving social liberation for every individual in society (except members of the previous *khassa* coalition). The results of his system proved different from the intentions. The historical process brought about a continuation and reinforcement of the mercantilist policies already in effect: Nasser used Egypt's army and foreign service in an aggressive way to extend control over agricultural and industrial production, services, and international trade. He introduced a feudal structure (assuming one did not exist already) built on a system of reciprocity to guide the relations between the *khassa* and the *'amma*. Prompted by his need for a political base of support and his genuine belief in social/revolutionary liberation, he extended all sorts of rights to the population. The state itself became a "grand seigneur," offering protection and services in return for political allegiance and labor. Feudalism as practiced by the modern state differs from Western European medieval feudalism, which is concerned primarily with agriculture and whose economic and political base is the ownership or, at least, control of land. This modern feudal order is nationally based and involves a close relationship between high government officials, military officers, international businessmen, and professionals, all of whom are supported by an official clergy that benefits from this relationship and provides it with legitimacy.

Class conflict takes many forms. In contemporary Egypt it is not only peasants and workers but the educated lower-middle and propertied middle classes who are fighting the irrationality of the *khassa*. I hypothesize that today the *'amma* are clearly the moving forces within the society; their culture and worldview are becoming dominant. Marx's analysis of the relations of force could illustrate what is taking place:

> It is the problem of the relations between structure and superstructures which must be accurately posed and resolved if the forces which are active in the history of a particular period are to be correctly analyzed and the relation between them determined. Two principles must orient the discussion: 1. that no society sets itself tasks for whose accomplishment the necessary and sufficient conditions do not either already exist or are not at least beginning to emerge and develop; 2. that no society breaks down and can be replaced until it has developed all the forms of life which are implicit in its internal relations.[39]

In Egypt today there exists nothing short of a revolutionary situation. The power of the *khassa* may be reflected in the distribution of wealth, but those who constitute the moving forces, the *'amma*, are finally bringing about an end to this dual division despite the *khassa*'s efforts to prevent them and to maintain the status quo. In other words, a new historical bloc, long in the making, is finally coming into being, its hegemonic ties being established by the *'amma*. To put it differently, the discourse upon which the hegemony of the *khassa* has been based, a discourse that is usually sponsored and often created and established by elites in modern centralized states, is today being replaced by a new discourse that is organically linked to the base.

The role of intellectuals in this process is an interesting one. Intellectuals, in the sense of those defined according to their credentials, must be included among the *'amma*. This means that even though many prominent intellectuals have been part of the ruling class decision-making process, still the majority may have served the hegemony but were not part of decision making. Here one finds two groups: liberals and leftists. Each was important at one time and conceivably could have played a critical leadership role; neither did so. Their failure can be explained in two ways, at least for the best-studied period, that surrounding the 1952 revolution. First, the 1952 revolution repressed all organized opposition. This repression left only the most dedicated or extreme individuals working consciously for their class, "convinced that it has a historical 'right' at a given moment."[40] Second, their failure can be attributed to their preoccupation with Leninism as represented by the Soviet model, itself a model of oriental despotism. They accepted this model in their approach to understanding Egypt and planning its future. One is reminded more recently of the case of Iran. In discussing the failure of prerevolution Iranian intellectuals to become leaders of the Iranian masses, 'Ali Shari'ati explained:

> Does it suit me, as an intellectual of a different time and place, to mimic the words of the intellectual of Europe in the 19th Century? Are there any points of resemblance between my audience of this society and the working class of Europe in the 19th Century? . . . Any school or ideology that fails to base itself upon the cultural infrastructure of the society from which it stems will not be very different from a book of some popularity kept in a library for public reading. . . . Scholars, students, and other types of readers may read it; or a hundred thousand copies of it may be published. But all this cannot have the least possible effect upon the mass. The mass will remain unchanged. But the intellectual will be estranged from the mass of the society, and this is the greatest danger.[41]

This does not mean that liberal and leftist intellectuals have played roles of little importance. To the contrary, it is, I hypothesize, in their interaction with another group, Islamist intellectuals, that one can indeed see their imprint on the evolution of Egyptian society today. This interaction created a desire to bring Islamic thought together with demands for human and personal freedoms, and this combined with a strong belief in social justice and redistribution of wealth. It is precisely because these thinkers speak in Islamic jargon that they are creating cultural and intellectual change among the masses. They speak in terms that the population at large understands.

In this study I posit a number of theses regarding the social structure of Egypt and the transformation of Egypt's society. First, *khassa* alliances have managed to mold themselves to fit changing world economic and political conditions and to create the instruments of control and ideologies to continue to enjoy their hegemonic role. Second, when Egyptian society is studied on its own terms, it will become clear that today Egypt is undergoing a revolution. Egypt has had its own share of violence in the form of economic hardships and social and cultural alienation. Still, its ongoing revolution cannot be understood in the classical sense of a sudden and violent action by an underclass against its oppressor. What is taking place is a process of self-liberation by which cultural duality is being overthrown. During its modern history Egypt's ruling elite has been "foreign" in culture and ideology. That label applies to mamluks, Muhammad 'Ali's royal dynasty, the British, the socialist Nasserists, and the *infitah* bourgeoisie of Sadat. Except for the first two, these elites adopted Ottomanism, modernity, and Westernization as dominant culture. Today, because elite culture failed to make room for the rising masses, the culture of the masses is becoming the dominant one. What is described today as Islamic revivalism is part of the ongoing process by which Egyptian society is becoming more homogenous, and the cultural gap (which has been one of the great setbacks in Egypt's efforts at development) between the traditional and the Western is being narrowed.

The third thesis presented in this study is that today the forces of change are to be found among the *'amma,* whose social relations and cultural outlook are becoming the norm for the nation as a whole. This is happening because the *'amma* constitute the moving social force today; they are the new effective intellectuals who are writing and reading. Religion is only one of their instruments although, perhaps, it is the most powerful because it is the cultural heritage most familiar to Egyptians. Moreover, because both the socialist and the liberal dialogues were monopolized by the *khassa* and because the *khassa* have stressed the manipulation of Islam as a way of controlling the *'amma,* the turn to religion should not come as a surprise. Not being able to become part of the Westernized elite, the *'amma* are making their own traditions the norm for the country at large. Today the *khassa* combine is itself from the base.

The various aspects of this revolution, that is, the economic-political, the ideological, and the sociocultural, are interconnected; one cannot be understood without the others. Although the ideological provides the vehicle of protest, it is only with the success of the sociocultural that one can expect to see any success in the economic-political; it is only with the closing of the cultural gap that the political gap can begin to be narrowed. Some may look at cultural integration as retrogressive because it connotes an integrated culture dominated by the culture of the base, and perhaps it is, but on the whole it is correcting a big aberration that has made out of Egyptian society a dual entity that supports economic and social structures within the same country.

THE NEW
MAMLUKS

1

THE BACKGROUND

Rewards came as payment for loyalty and not necessarily as a function of the state machinery. The chain of command was diffuse and worked through personal influence, objurgation, and alliances. . . . By the 18th century as a result of increased connections between the mamluks and the *tujjar* for an export oriented collaboration the seeds of a change in approach and in a "philosophy of government" so to speak were sown, and eventually reaped by Muhammad 'Ali and his supporters.[1]

The normative history of eighteenth-century Egypt is the decline of central authority, allowing mamluks to dominate the country's affairs. According to this view, by the last quarter of the eighteenth century, Egypt becomes torn by the incessant quarrels between mamluk factions and between mamluks and Ottoman military units garrisoned in Egypt. Daniel Crecelius gives a typical description of the situation "[These military units] seldom acted in concert during peacetime and were often reluctant to accept the authority of their Pasha. Rather, they frequently quarreled among themselves, competed for control of the more lucrative *iltizams*, and through their general unruliness posed a threat to both the Ottoman governor and to the general populace."[2] Civil strife is also believed to have been caused by the Ottoman policy of playing off the various mamluk factions against each other as one means of continuing Ottoman authority.[3] Altogether Egypt is described as having deteriorated during that time as a result of the breakdown of effective and legitimate authority, competition between mamluk factions and other orders in society, and a general decline in trade and revenue. Decline is said to have also been caused by low Nile water levels in 1783, 1791, and 1792 and plagues that devastated both the human and animal populations in 1785 and 1791, causing famines and economic devastation.[4] These adversities resulted in insecurity and civil disturbances in which mamluk factions battled over political power and, hence, over control of trade routes. The mamluks also used coercion to exact a variety of levies and

1

forced "loans" from the population to maximize the extraction of wealth under different pretexts.[5]

The above picture is shared by Crecelius, Vatikiotis, and P. M. Holt among others. This chapter refutes the principle of decline and chaos. Rather it is an effort to show what the concrete realities of life were by focusing on the life of the people, social relations between society's various components, economic interactions, and legal structures. A review of Egyptian court records covering the last quarter of the eighteenth century does not confirm this picture. Rather buying and selling seemed to continue as usual, and complaints against mamluk exactions were limited. In fact, until the time of the Napoleonic invasion (1798–1801) there does not seem to be a marked difference between registrations during the last decades and earlier decades of the eighteenth century. Not only did registrations in court records continue at a constant rate as before—with people marrying, divorcing, setting up *waqfs*, (religious endowments) disputing rights to particular spots in the marketplace or over property lines—*hujja*s (pleas, documents) from other Ottoman courts such as Tripoli[6] concerning financial dealings were recorded one after the other in Alexandria records. There are notable changes recorded for the period of the French invasion, however. For example, marriage registration seemed to have completely stopped in Alexandria where records show that not one marriage was registered during the period the French occupied the town (1798–1801), whereas demands for divorce by women were constant.[7] Whether this was the result of the population's resistance to paying fees to the French or whether marriages really stopped for those three years is not clear. What is important is that before the arrival of the French no such changes in court records were evident; things seemed to be going on as usual.

These findings are supported by Afaf Marsot, who has shown how simplistic and reductionist a picture of a chaotic eighteenth century is and that conditions were much more complex. While confirming the difficulties faced by Egypt's population owing to mamluk exactions and feuds, she details the life of the people during the eighteenth century as active in trade, social intercourse, exchange, and intellectual pursuits. Her study, *Men and Women in Eighteenth Century Egypt*, also demonstrates a different picture of gender relations than the exotic picture of female seclusion presented by orientalism. Rather, women owned property that they bought, sold, and deeded at will.[8] Peter Gran further illustrates the mistake in accepting the normative view of a society in which violence and civil strife were all-encompassing. He shows that circles of *'ulama'* were intellectually productive during that period, and it is only current dismissal of religious writing as nonintellectual and nonpolitical that makes one miss that picture.[9] Nelly Hanna moves the discussion back to the seventeenth century, showing that Ottoman authority over Egypt had already loosened by then. Rather than a cause for decline, she sees the loosening of Ottoman authority over Egypt as allowing greater trade and manufacturing activity.[10] Egyptian archives dating from the last quarter of the eighteenth century before the French invasion (1798–1801) support Marsot, Gran, and Hanna. Day-to-day transactions—buying, selling, marriage, divorce—were recorded mostly as they had always been. If things had broken down to the point of chaos by the end of the century, surely there would have been significant changes in the recording of such activities, as becomes apparent in Alexandria archives under French occupation.

As more research on the specific history of Egypt under Ottoman suzerainty comes to light, the picture of the pre–nineteenth century is being altered to show a dynamic society involved in the usual activities of populations the world over. Yet, despite the effort of scholars, great-man theory and coming-of-the-West paradigms still continue to hold sway. In his attack on those he describes as "nationalist historians," Khalid Fahmy uses Foucauldian-Derridian techniques of deconstruction popularized by Tim Mitchell[11] to "rethink" the history of Egypt under the rule of Muhammad 'Ali Pasha. While using archival records to enrich our knowledge of the army built by the pasha, Fahmy sees nineteenth-century Egypt as following a period of chaos and considers Muhammad 'Ali's rise to power as almost accidental. There is little appreciation of the existence of power formations, social alliances, and a political process. The complex picture detailed by Afaf Marsot of *'ulama'/tujjar* alliances that brought Muhammad 'Ali to power is an improvement over that presented by Fahmy of a submissive population bending down under the whip of a new Ottoman pasha at the head of fresh military forces sent from Istanbul. That Muhammad 'Ali is best understood as the "last of the great mamluks"[12] gives political continuity in an important province with its own sociopolitical dynamics like those of Egypt its due. As the "last of the great mamluks," Muhammad 'Ali followed in the footsteps of those before him, forming alliances with other social groups, providing expected services and protection for the country. Even while building new institutions, including a strong army as expected from those who ruled and protected Egypt, the pasha was molded by his position as much as by what he brought with him as an Ottoman governor. To see him as another Ottoman pasha who enforced his will upon and molded Egypt by being Egypt's "most brutal of the Ottoman governors"[13] is a return to oriental despotism and great-man theories.

Historical specialization may be at the root of the persistence of this normative view. It is unfortunate that the Napoleonic period continues to constitute a take-off point for the modern history of Egypt. It is just as odd that it constitutes a take-off point for so many other places in the world. But this is part of the wider subjugation of world history to historical events experienced by Europe. Not only have world history and histories of particular peoples been subjugated to Western chronologies that reflect the concrete political and social experiences of the West, but the paradigms formulated by intellectuals to try to map the Western experience have also been used as maps to understand and judge human experience outside the West with little study of the internal dynamics and culture of these areas—hence, the essentialist and orientalist images of decline, passivity, and unchangeability of non-Western societies ruled by despots. Renato Rosaldo warns:

> The translation of cultures requires one to try to understand other forms of life in their own terms. We should not impose our categories on other people's lives because they probably do not apply, at least not without serious revision. We can learn about other cultures only by reading, listening, or being there. Although they often appear outlandish, brutish, or worse to outsiders, the informal practices of everyday life make sense in their own context and on their own terms.[14]

Because the nineteenth century is seen as such an important watershed date, historians have tended to specialize in either the Ottoman or modern period. Therefore, Ottomanists ask questions and pursue research pertaining to a period they see as distinct from what comes before Egypt's Ottoman invasion in 1516 and later under modern nation-states. Although the transition from what is labeled "mamlukid" to what is labeled "Ottoman" in Egypt's history needs further investigation to determine the amount of actual changes that Egypt experienced with the arrival of Ottoman rule, there are indications that the transition was not so dramatic as to warrant consideration as a watershed date. For example, the Ottoman *shari'a* court system had precursors from earlier periods. Marriage contracts dating from the third century Hijra are quite similar in shape and function to the much better-studied contracts dating from the Ottoman period.[15] Recording contracts in courts, usually seen as regulated under the Ottomans, actually existed since Ancient Egyptian times, and were traditional for Islamic Egypt before the arrival of the Ottomans. Thus, papyrus and leather collections include contracts for buying, selling, divorce, marriage, payment of debts, wills, and inheritance.[16] Besides, the first four pages of the first *sijill* (vol. 1) of the Ottoman *shari'a* court archives of the Mediterranean port town of Dumyat, date as far back as 1505, eleven years before the arrival of the Ottomans and twenty-three years before the declaration of *Qanuname* of Egypt in 1528. One of the thirty-seven Ottoman courts listed for Egypt is Ashmunin; it is interesting that the records found at the court of Ashmunin included both pre-Islamic Ancient Egyptian and Islamic records dating from the third- to the sixth-century Hijra.

As for modernists, they focus on the nineteenth or twentieth century, depending on their specific interest, and except for a few, do not see any real reason for going back into the Ottoman period to find continuities between one and the other.

A good question to ask about the Ottoman period in Egypt is why that period is constantly referred to as a mamlukid, hence military, period by modernists when there is evidence that it could just as well be called the merchant's period. Here is where exceptionalism plays an important role in historiographies of non-Western countries. Whereas northern Mediterranean history is acclaimed for the revival of trade experienced in Italian city-states such as Florence and Venice, there is no recognition that such a situation could have existed south of the Mediterranean. Yet, the life of Shahbandar al-Tujjar Isma'il Abu Taqiyya, which Nelly Hanna studied through court records covering forty years of the seventeenth century, shows that grand merchants involved in international trade existed in Egypt, Turkey, and Syria during that period. Accumulation of wealth, borrowing, lending, investment in trade, and manufacturing ventures were all usual activities for Egypt's business classes as evidenced by the registration of partnerships and contracts for buying, selling, and money-lending, all of which were registered meticulously in court records. As Hanna found, court records illustrate the fact that historians have yet to get the full picture of the premodern period. Interestingly, scholars in various parts of the globe whose countries' histories have been studied through imperialist, racist, decline, or exceptionalist paradigms are today undertaking meticulous research and producing a different picture than the one that dismissed "traditional" society as backward, static, and dominant as exemplified by oriental despotism.

Perhaps the most misunderstood issue about the premodern period concerns the general life of the people. In his study of Egypt's Jewish community during the Ottoman period, Mohsen Shouman questions perceptions of Ottoman society that have constituted foundational starting points in the history of the Middle East. While describing the millet system as it existed, with Jews and various Christian denominations constituting recognizable separate patriarchies, Shouman sees that the life of the people in the various cities and towns of Egypt defies the separateness of communities. Although Jews preferred to settle in urban centers in Lower Egypt, especially Cairo, nevertheless, like other Egyptians, they moved naturally between Cairo and Egypt's various other parts and often migrated to take up residence there. Inner-migration was a widespread activity that involved not only natives of Egypt but North

Africans, Syrians, Turks, and Europeans living in Egypt or traveling for business purposes. While Egypt's Jewish community seemed to grow owing to immigration, particularly during the early Ottoman centuries, as Ottoman subjects they lived in relative security. This was particularly so in port towns such as Alexandria, Rashid, Dumyat, and Mansura, where they lived among the wider community and where they held important positions as holders of port *iltizam*s, collecting customs duties on imported and exported goods. In other places Jews had their own quarters, or *hara*s, as in Bilbis, Mahalla al-Kubra, Mit Ghamr, and Cairo. But even where there were Jewish quarters, Jews lived widely among the general population in the various quarters and among various classes. Shouman also shows that non-Jews lived in Jewish quarters that did not seem to function like ghettoes in the European experience. To prove these revisionist findings, Shouman gives the names and locations of those who lived in Jewish quarters during various centuries of Ottoman history and the businesses, addresses, and other important information about Jews in Egyptian towns. His sources are court records that he studied over many years.[17] Although Jews had their own community courts, they very often resorted to *shari'a* courts to solve their disputes and to *shari'a* law to litigate issues not dealt with by religious laws. This was also the case for the Coptic community. Members of that community often resorted to *shari'a* courts to litigate personal or family disputes. This was particularly the case because their own community refused to approve actions such as taking a second wife or divorce.[18]

Jews and Christians were subject to the status of *dhimmis* (protected non-Muslims), a situation that defined them as a minority experiencing some discrimination however subtle. For example, a judge dismissed the case of a woman who demanded that her ex-husband pay her a debt he owed. The reason for dismissal of the case was because the woman's witness was a Christian man, and "the witness of a Christian is not acceptable over that rendered by a Muslim." [19] This case dealt with personal matters involving Muslims, and in such matters the witness of a Muslim always superseded that of a non-Muslim. When, however, a dispute existed between a non-Muslim and a Muslim, the courts treated the litigants as equal. For example, a court case between two Christian men and members of the Mustahfisan troops was won by the Christians because the soldiers could not present sufficient evidence that the Christians had intentionally destroyed the goods that they were transporting for them when they were robbed.[20] This case is interesting because the only detail the two parties differed on was that of intentionality.

The relations between minorities and the state were guided by mutual rights and obligations, with payment of the *jizya* (poll tax) and the state's obligation to protect them and their right to freedom of worship as cornerstones to that relationship. Minorities seemed to have enjoyed the same freedoms and privileges as Muslims; still the distinctions made between them, such as the requirement that Jews wear a blue head-cover, constituted a method of separating communities that hinted at cultural discrimination. Minorities also suffered the same exactions as the rest of the people from mamluk levies and the harm that befalls people during periods of instability.

In a chapter titled "Economic Activities," Shouman details the economic activities of members of the Jewish community. His details are interesting because they tell about the economic life of the *'amma* during the Ottoman period. For as Shouman tells it, the activities in which Jews participated were common activities in which the *'amma* engaged. These activities included their work as treasurers, merchants, tax-farmers, middlemen, brokers, doctors, surgeons, herbalists, interpreters, shopkeepers, and merchants of all classes from the grandees down. They were also craftsmen such as carpenters and weavers belonging to various guilds, were often heads of guilds, and worked as daily wage laborers. Jewish craftsmen worked for Muslim masters and vice versa. Labor was not divided according to ethnic or religious identity. Some Jews belonged to more than one craft and seemed to move from one to the other. Whereas they were interested in agriculture like Muslims and Copts, Jews played an important managerial role and as investors by renting orchards and being involved in growing sugar cane.[21]

The picture of Egyptian society presented by Shouman's important study is one of openness and tolerance, words familiar to chroniclers of the period but rejected by modern scholars. Far from being a society driven by the whip of pasha, mamluk, or janissary, it seemed to function much like other societies around the Mediterranean. Agriculture formed the most important resource upon which the wealth of the country depended, and an active commerce provided for export of such cash agricultural products as wheat and sugar and manufactured goods such as glass and textiles.[22] Jews enjoyed the confidence of society and authority and were very often the chief *multazim*s of important positions such as *saraf bashi* (chief treasurer) of the *diwan* of Alexandria[23] or held important *iltizam*s such as that of Alexandria, which would later be held by Muhammad 'Ali Pasha as an *iltizam* from the sultan. When Christian or Jewish houses of worship were falling apart or needing improvements, they were granted such permission although as with other public buildings the site was inspected first, usually by the *mi'mar basha* (chief architect or engineer), as was usual in big towns or ports.[24]

'Abdel-Rehim 'Abdel-Rahman 'Abdel-Rehim adds a factor of social mobility to this picture. He made extensive use of archival records and concluded that "from reading these documents one can follow closely the patterns of social mixing between the various *fi'at* (groups, classes) of society during the eighteenth century. Marriage was taking place between these *fi'at* at a great rate, and the walls that separated society earlier began to melt so that the children of merchants and other occupations among Egyptians and non-Egyptians turned to marriage with other *fi'at*, military and non-military, as well as other religious groups. Conversions of Christians and Jews increased with the increase in marriages with Muslims."[25]

In her study "Guilds: Between Tradition and Modernity" Pascale Ghazaleh takes issue with Bernard Lewis's description of Ottoman Egypt: that it "did not change from the eighth to the nineteenth century . . . in the Islamic lands, one could find hardly a trace of what might be called a civic spirit or a municipal life. Medieval Islamic cities . . . [present] illusions of prosperity with no basis in solid economics."[26] As an alternative, Ghazaleh proposes that guilds should be looked at as a form of civil society even though they were not entirely autonomous because guilds were expected to enforce state-approved regulations. Guilds were not, however, a creation of the Ottoman state superimposed "on the working classes as a form of organization."[27] As a form of protection and alliance with the *khassa*, "by the late seventeenth century many members of the military corps *(ojaqs)* were involved in commerce and crafts in one way or another."[28]

The relationship between guilds and the state was enforced through the legal system. Although guilds looked into disputes pertaining to their members and generally handled such problems, such disputes were often recorded in court and many cases were taken in front of the *qadi (shari'a* court judge) for arbitration and justice. In fact, disputes brought to court requiring expert witness were referred to the head of the guild and its members to render an opinion. A case concerning property lines from the 1714 Alexandria *shari'a* court provides a good example. A husband and his wife brought suit against their neighbor, who built over the wall delineating their property. and asked that she pay them compensation. She, however, denied the allegation, insisting that she built within her property line. The question, therefore, evolved as to where the property lines stood. So the court assigned the chief engineer of the port, the head of the guild of builders, and a builder to investigate the matter. The three came back with a decision for the litigants.[29] When it came to issues pertaining to the body, the courts sent out a doctor as expert witness or a *daya* (midwife) if it involved a woman.[30] It was the norm to send two experts, one the head of the guild concerned and the other a practitioner within the guild. There also seemed to be awareness about healthy environment, and the people required that such an environment be kept up. A complaint by the inhabitants of Alexandria against the guild of stucco workers was taken in front of the town council *(diwan)* formed of the Hanafi and Shaf'i muftis, the governor of the port, and the Sirdars of the janissaries, Azaban and Odabashi of the Mustahfizan. When preparing the material they used in their business, the stucco workers caused fumes to rise all over the town. Not only were these fumes toxic, they also had a bad smell that offended the inhabitants of the port. The people also complained that the manufacturing of stucco caused water pollution because the workers dumped the residue into the waterways. After ascertaining the veracity of the complaint, the *diwan* ordered that these practices be stopped.[31] In short, there were close connections between society, judiciary, guilds, and members of these guilds, relations of dependency involving security, business, and property.

Using court records for his study, the *Judicial Administration of Ottoman Egypt in the Seventeenth Century,* Galal el-Nahhal dismisses both Ira Lapidus's and Gabriel Baer's discussion of Ottoman guilds. Lapidus's assertion about Cairo, Damascus, and Aleppo markets as being "very imperfectly organized by comparison with the quarters. Professional, merchant, and artisan guilds were virtually nonexistent, and what rudimentary forms did exist were created by the state for its own purposes" is echoed by Baer's assertion that "one of the main characteristics of Egypt's social history is the lack of development of indigenous democratic institutions in that country." Both are reflected in Bernard Lewis's statement quoted by Ghazaleh and discussed earlier.[32]

El-Nahhal correctly criticizes these views as suffering from "lack of information." He also connects this picture to the wider approach to studies of Islamic society with which the present work takes particular issue. "Few literary sources deal with private citizens and the system by which they resisted pressures and expressed their interests, or with government systems for maintaining equilibrium in society. Some of these views also reflect unexamined habits of thought about 'despotic' Middle Eastern governments and 'passive' Middle Eastern societies."[33] As El-Nahhal points out, the picture of guilds, *tawa'if* or *sana'i',* as they appear in court records is very different. His findings are confirmed by other historians who used court records as the main source for their research.[34]

The various quarters of a town were named after guilds or religious and ethnic groups. The head of the quarter was usually also head of the particular guild or group associated with the quarter. It is this leader who represented the quarter in its complaints against those who inhabited the quarters or in regard to conflicts with other neighborhoods. Court records show the multitude of cases that were brought by the head of a quarter to the attention of the courts demanding restitution, compensation, or expulsion of residents.[35] Archival records also show that even though the quarter may have been named for a particular guild or group, in fact, the residents belonged to various religions, ethnicities, and crafts. This diversity is particularly evident in cases brought to court asking for the expulsion of certain individuals, usually for moral or security reasons. The picture described by Shouman in regard to Jewish quarters, the residence of Jews, and who lived in the Jewish quarters applied to other town quarters.

The life of people during the Ottoman period is today a major focus of study among historians of the Middle East. They are helping researchers understand how people lived and interacted together. As would be expected, archival records in the form of court cases are proving to be the most vital source for such research. Although court records differ from one town to the other, they all give an idea of how litigious Ottoman society was. Egyptian court records happen to be particularly useful because there were thirty-seven courts in Egypt at any one time under Ottoman rule. There is also evidence that there were subcourts attached to courts of major towns, whose records were included with the records held by the main court and, hence, their existence was not obvious. Subcourts are the subject of ongoing research by Ramadan al-Khowli.[36] Courts were located with accessibility in mind. People brought their disputes to be arbitrated by the judge or complained of crimes and demanded compensation. Contracts were also registered, and the public seemed to be keen on getting their financial transactions recorded by the courts. Marriages, divorces, and death records were all included in court records. Daily entries recording the sale of property, setting up of *waqf*s (religious endowments), *iltizam,* and sub-*iltizam* agreements, and so on show an active society very involved in financial, personal, and business agreements. Reading the archival record, one is surprised at the continued acceptance of the picture of passiveness and civil strife even in impressive studies such as that of Michael Winter.[37]

Max Weber's description[38] of the legal system in Islamic societies as *"qadi* justice," where the arbitrary decisions of judges were based on their determination of a case as they saw it rather than on any form of cumulative laws and traditions, continues to enjoy great popularity even though the picture presented by actual legal records from the premodern period contrasts significantly with Weber's. Curiously, Weber's interpretation of Islamic law, even though not based on knowledge of the law, on Arabic, or on archival records, continues to constitute truth among scholars. According to that picture, a *qadi* arbitrarily reached decisions about legal problems and disputes taken in front of him. The image is that of a judge sitting under a tree who does not have a real court to function in nor a structure to work through. Al-Hariri's medieval parody[39] satirizing the judicial system continues to formulate a basis for the conceptualization of justice in Islamic lands. In such a system there could be no accumulated laws that formulate legal precedence, so a *qadi*'s decisions were necessarily arbitrary even though he could apply Islamic law as he saw it or traditions of the particular area. All in all, the *qadi* justice paradigm conceptualizes Islamic law as reflecting political conditions of Islamic societies in that it confirms patriarchy, and oriental despotism. In that sense, Islamic law is presented as a very arbitrary and exceptional system because it is not applied rationally based on accumulated laws and intended to benefit the widest margin of society. With that image it is easy to regard state-society relations through despotic modes, with mamluks ravaging populations at will, Ottoman sultans and pashas instituting whatever systems they think best, and a society that cowers and accepts what comes.

A welcome contribution[40] to the history of Islamic law has attacked the Weberian model and showed the fallacy behind *qadi* justice arguments, which, as the author explains, are based more on scholars' predetermined paradigms than on serious research. In his criticism of Lawrence Rosen's[41] application of the *qadi* justice paradigm to the legal system of Morocco, Haim Gerber launched his attack on the applicability of the paradigm to Islamic societies as a whole. He takes particular issue with Weber's view that "Islamic law was judicially primitive and undeveloped" in comparison to its rational archetype in the West. While accepting the principle of *qadi* justice, Rosen does criticize the exotic picture of Muslim judges that is prevalent among Westerners. Still, Rosen continues to describe the legal system in Morocco in Weberian terms as "that form of judicial legitimacy in which judges never refer to a settled group of norms or rules but are simply licensed to decide each case according to what they see as its individual merits."[42]

The Weberian model has proven particularly problematic in regard to gender history, particularly the feminist model applied to Islamic societies that sees Muslim women before the modern period as helpless, veiled, and secluded beings. Having little to do in the public sphere, women in urban centers scarcely left the home except, perhaps, to shop or visit. Everyday life in towns with alleyways, coffeehouses, marketplaces, courthouses, *diwan*s (assemblies) of government, or mosques, was largely the domain of men. Being under the control of the male, be that father, husband, brother, or uncle, was the fate of women who had little to say about the matter and scarcely any maneuverability in using the system. This included all women except, perhaps, the wives of the mamluks who, by virtue of their position within mamluk households and their wealth, could and sometimes did play important political roles and were usually in command of large amounts of funds as evidenced by *waqf* endowments.

There is no question that women lived under a patriarchal order in which a male was expected to be the head of a household. Still, divorced mothers and widows were as likely to set up independent households as they were to move in with their families. So women often lived alone even though there was a general expectation that women not live alone, as was normal for women living elsewhere in the world during that period. The picture of a public/private divide requiring the seclusion of women at home and forbidding any contact with men except members of the family is dismissed through archival records. If coming to court was a possible cause of immorality, as some jurists wrote, then Egyptian society must have been terribly immoral. Women appeared in court routinely, daily. Every second or third entry involved women buying, selling, marrying, divorcing, reporting violence, demanding compensation, seeking custody of their children, and the like. As for veiling, courts required the identification of litigants. Often women brought witnesses with them to identify them, which was usual for tribesmen, and reference to this practice appears in the court record. But more often, the woman identified herself. So women may have been veiled outside court, but it seemed the norm for them to be unveiled in court. We also have cases in which the clerk admired the woman in front of him and, therefore, went on to record what she looked like. An early seventeenth-century clerk described a bride coming to court to contract her marriage as "fair, strong eyebrows, *shawla'* (strong contrast between the whites and blacks of the eyes) in eyes. Arab face with green tattoos, one on her lower lip and the others on her cheeks. Graceful *(malfufat)* in face and tall in body."[43] Here there is no question that the whole face was unveiled and that the woman's body could also be discerned.

There is other evidence against the public/private divide, and here one should look at why women left the home in the first place. One reason was to go shopping, and given the large number of complaints brought to court regarding women going shopping, it is clear that they went out at will and did not worry too much about a husband's approval. Although court cases speak of a woman going to the marketplace as breaking her husband's *ta'a* (obedience), such cases are usually associated with men trying to get their wives back and women refusing to live with husbands who forbade them to go out or would not give them *nafaqa* (financial support). Given the profusion of marital disputes in which husbands explained that the reason they did not pay their wives *nafaqa* was because of their constant shopping, the picture of women's seclusion is put into serious question. If anything, women found it natural to go out and sometimes broke a marriage rather than be forced to stay home.

But did women work? If so, what jobs did they perform? The picture regarding women and work is very interesting. Donald Quartaert argues that Ottoman women played a crucial role in handicrafts, textile, and carpet production during the nineteenth century. By focusing on household economies and small workshops, he challenges the view that manufacturing and its labor force declined during this period.[44] Suraiya Faroqhi also has shown that women were involved and constituted an important part of silk manufacturing and weaving in the Ottoman Empire. According to Faroqhi, women were also organized into pressure groups, showing greater labor awareness. Faroqhi does not describe women outside the all-woman secluded area of labor.[45] Sketches by the savants of the Napoleonic mission, however, left images of women undertaking various steps of spinning and weaving, and William Lane has described the many public jobs undertaken by women at the time he lived in Egypt.

Egyptian archives show that women worked at home and had access to markets to sell their goods. We are also given detailed evidence of the retail part of women's activities. There are many references to women in the marketplace. These references come in various forms. Most important are disputes between women or between women and men. After all, courts were a place to litigate disputes. The most common dispute presented by court records involves physical altercations—two women beating up each other or a number of women ganging up on one. Often a man beat up a woman to usurp her place in the market or because she encroached on his space. Other common cases of women quarreling in the marketplace involved forced abortions. Because a forced abortion brought heavy compensation, this was a financial dispute that appears very often in court records. Very often the claim was that another woman caused the quarrel and caused the abortion. But often a man was pointed to as having caused it by beating up the pregnant woman on purpose, sometimes because his wife instigated a vendetta or because the woman was encroaching on his spot in the marketplace. One cannot claim seclusion of women if strange men could actually beat them and cause them to miscarry.

Women also owned shops and property as Afaf Marsot has shown. They also held *waqf*s and were very often assigned as executors.[46] As executors they were responsible for collection of income, and even when this job was delegated, it still involved contact with strangers, including men. Direct evidence exists that women were themselves running their shops, although they may have delegated this function when the shop was far away. This was the case with Maghribi women living in Alexandria who owned or inherited property in North Africa and delegated the collection of income to others, usually men, probably because they traveled and could carry the money back.[47] It was normal for women to bring goods and sell them in the marketplace, a fact corroborated by travelers to Egypt and other areas of the Islamic world who described the kinds of food sold by vendors, many of whom were women. Certainly women were very involved in what has been described as "petty capitalism."[48] Furthermore, women owned shops and were involved in their day-to-day management. An interesting example is that of a "will" *(wasiya)* registered in court by an *odabashi* (senior officer of a janissary corps) who was sick and expected to die in which he declares his inheritance as being confined to his wife Khadija and to his previous master who manumitted him. As part of the details of the property he owned or held, the *odabashi* declares that his wife owns half the coffeehouse in al-Hussayniyya quarter of Cairo and that he owned no part of it nor had anything to do with it except for a few items like a table and tent. One could assume from this that he ran the coffeehouse on behalf of his wife except that he included his mother-in-law in this affidavit in reference to the coffeehouse, saying that she owed him nothing. One reads this to mean that the coffeehouse was owned by the two women, that he was a partner, and that the mother was the one running it but that all accounts between her and him were cleared.[49]

Women were also quite active in administering their own property and often came to court to press their rights. For example, there was a case from the town of Ballas where a woman sued three brothers who were her neighbors because the house they built encroached onto her property the measure of eighteen *dhira'* (about one foot). The brothers denied the fact in court, but the woman presented her witnesses and the court asked other members of the men's family. The case was finally settled by the brothers offering financial compensation. The woman accepted the amount offered after which she asked the court to dismiss her suit as required by the court to close its investigation.[50] Whereas this Ballasi woman appeared in court and presented her case herself, in a second case from the same town, a son represented his mother in a lawsuit in which she claimed a share of property containing palm trees that were held by others. She also laid claim to her share in the produce of the palm trees.[51] So the picture is a complex one; people had choices and acted accordingly. Strict constructions like public/private are simply not supported by evidence. If anything, there was a substantial degree of legal maneuverability open to Egypt's population. Under Ottoman rule, the Hanafi code was the basis of Ottoman executive *qanun* (executive law), but in *shari'a* courts the Maliki, Shaf'i, and Hanbali *madhahib* (law schools) were practiced as well. In Egypt, where the Maliki *madhhab* was preferred in Upper Egypt and the Shaf'i was the *madhhab* of the majority in Lower Egypt, each courthouse had separate rooms for the various *madhahib*. A person wishing to take his case in front of the Maliki judge went to his courtroom. So although the chief *qadi* of Egypt was a Hanafi assigned from Istanbul, the rest of the court hierarchy was local and served the public according to the public's wishes. This did not mean that those who belonged to one *madhhab* always went to the *qadi* of that *madhhab*; all courtrooms were open to anyone who wished to take his case there whether it was his particular *madhhab* or even whether he were Christian or Jew.[52] The choice was that of the public and was not determined for them by the state. There were certain preferences for a particular *madhhab*, depending on the issue or the group to which the individual belonged. Thus, the Maghariba from North Africa almost always took their cases in front of the Maliki *qadi* because most of them were Malikis. Syrians almost always went in front of the Hanafi *qadi* because that was the school predominant in Syria. In Egypt the Malaki *madhhab* was preferred by women seeking *nafaqa* (financial support) because procedures for receiving *nafaqa* were faster and more woman-friendly than the other three *madhhabs*. At the same time, the Hanbali *qadi* was usually preferred as an arbitrator in regard to rent of *awqaf* land. The Hanbali *madhhab* allowed for the inheritance of rental contracts and refused to increase rent when the contract was renewed. The Hanafi *madhhab*, in contrast, allowed for increasing rent and did not guarantee the inheritance of rental rights to *awqaf* land. In short, one can conclude that courts were organically linked to society and were not, as happened later in the nineteenth century with court reform, an arm and instrument of state control.

One way of estimating state-society relations and the general condition of people's lives is by studying the security that is allowed the general public. Was there security of life and property during the Ottoman period? Did the *khassa* have their own legal procedures? What happened when they had disputes with members of the *'amma*? Could a member of the *'amma* bring legal procedures against those in power, and did he expect justice against them?

A good case comes from early eighteenth-century Dumyat (a port town on the Mediterranean shore of Egypt) that pertains to members of the janissary corps sent from Istanbul to support the Ottoman pasha in Egypt. Here the language used to refer to relationships between the persons involved is significant. Two members of the janissaries quarreled, and one severely wounded the other. In the court document each of the janissaries is referred to as the *tabi'* of a particular head of an *ojaq*. The leader, *sirdar*, of the janissaries in Alexandria sent an emissary to the *majlis shar'* (legal council) of Alexandria, asking the *qadi* to assign court witnesses to investigate and report back to the court for judgment. When the wounded man was questioned, he explained that he had two boxes belonging to him on a ship that had come into port in Alexandria. When he went to retrieve them, the other janissary assaulted him and put his own insignia on the boxes. They fought, and the man was cut by the other's knife. He produced corroborative witnesses to his story, and the case was taken up by the courts.[53] It is significant that the janissaries did not handle their own inner fights but had to take them to the regular *majlis shar'*. It is also significant that the procedure followed to investigate the event did not differ from the usual investigation undertaken by Ottoman courts when the matter had to do with the *'amma*. Honest, upright individuals of the court (*'udul*), were assigned by the judge to report on the events and the damage, and witnesses were required to corroborate the evidence rendered by the injured party. The use of the word *tabi'* is also significant because it has imbedded meanings with social and political significance. A *tabi'* continues to be a person "belonging" to the leader of a group who is recognized for his position of leadership even if the group itself is not officially or legally constituted. *Tabi'* also refers to a person protected by another more powerful person, or at least another person wielding power in a particular situation at a particular point in time and not necessarily because he/she is rich, powerful, or *belonging* to the *khassa*. The reference *dah taba'i* (he is with me) can guarantee safety, confidence, or benefits, depending on the relationship between the group addressed and the person uttering the words. This is part of political culture.

What about a dispute between members of the Ottoman military and common people? Here justice was expected although the results may have depended on the interference of a higher authority. The house of a man referred to as a *hajj* (a man who has undertaken pilgrimage, a respected older person) was broken into and robbed. The court's investigation led to the indictment of two members of the Mustahfizan Ottoman corps. The leader of the corps turned in his two *tabi*'s to the head of the Mustahfizans in Cairo. The latter tried to get a confession out of the two but was not able to do so. The court took them and imprisoned them, but a letter from the "prince sultan," Murad Bey, had them freed and they disappeared. Months later the court was still in search of them, demanding their appearance in front of the court.[54]

In another case from Dumyat, the Agha of Dumyat citadel informed the *qadi* that a man was assaulted by two members of the Mustahfizan who beat and cut him up, leaving him hurt and bleeding. The judge delegated expert witnesses who questioned the injured man. He told them that he had been sitting in a coffeehouse drinking coffee. When he left to go home, six members of the Mustahfizan assaulted him and robbed him of the silver coin he was carrying, clothing, and other items. He named three of them but did not know the other three.[55] In another case a house was broken into by janissaries who were turned over by their leaders, who were responsible for them because they were their *tabi*'s. The janissaries confessed that they had committed the crime together with some of the *'irban* (Arab Bedouins), showing alliances and connections between the two groups. In this case the offenders were allowed to disappear after the court had interviewed them.[56]

What about personal security? Although court records only detail those cases that are investigated by the authorities or brought directly by individuals who were victims of crimes, they still give some idea of legal procedures and questions regarding personal security. A significant number of cases litigated

in court are in the records, which indicates active participation by the authorities in establishing security and a belief by people that they could expect to
find redress. Otherwise, why would they complain in a court of law? Crime
disputes were taken in front of the *qadi* for multitudes of reasons. It could
have been because of theft and armed robbery.[57] If for armed robbery, the
courts were very strict in applying the *hudud* because this was considered by
Islamic law to be a major crime against God. The authorities also acted in answer to public pressure such as when the people of Dumyat appealed to the
sirdariyya (leader of the janissaries) through the *'ulama'* about a thief who
was caught during a theft. Because he was a danger to the townspeople, committing armed robbery against them "by day and by night," they considered
his release a danger to the community. They demanded that he never be re-
leased from prison, and the *hakim* agreed.[58] The usual punishment for robbery was imprisonment.[59] Other punishments included death, flagellation,
and payment of *diya* (blood price), which could also be accompanied by fines
as in rape cases.[60]

Court records also tell us about violence against women, including murder. In one case from Upper Egypt, a husband killed his wife and then came to
court where he confessed, indicating that he "executed God's will" (*"nafadha
fiha amr allah"*), which may be one way of indicating that she had broken
God's commandments, perhaps by committing *zina* (adultery). The court
declared him a murderer for killing his wife, but the records do not indicate
what his punishment was.[61] The records describe family members in court demanding the punishment of a killer of a member of their families and demanding they be paid a *diya* to compensate for their loss. For example, two
women came to court to declare that, besides his brother, they were the only
heirs to the murdered son of the first who was also the husband of the second.
Public morality was also important and was dealt with judiciously.

In front of *mawlana al-sheikh* Nasr al-Din Aly al-Minawi al-Hanafi, appeared
his honor al-Nasiri Muhammad b. Shihab al-Din al-Sakkandari the *tabi'* of
. . . *al-Janab al-'Ali* the Prince Misli Katkhuda . . . Captain of the Port . . .
and informed him that the above-mentioned Katkhuda learned that a strange
woman was *mujtami'a* [meeting together] with a stranger inside a warehouse located in a *khatt* [road] between al-Burjayn in the Port with the intent of committing *al-fahisha* [sin] and he asked that the matter be looked
into. . . . He was given permission to do so and he found in the mentioned
warehouse a man named 'Amir b. Khafaga al-Sharnabawi from the quarter of
Buhairat b. 'Issa who lives in the warehouse and a woman who said that her
name was Fatima daughter of Muhammad al-Mansuri who is unrelated to
the mentioned 'Amir but whom she claimed used to be her fiancee but did

not marry her. . . . They returned with this information to the *qadi* declaring that they deserved the expected *ta'zir* in accordance with the *shari'a*. This was written down to keep a record to be referred to if necessary.[62]

The above account was a case involving mutual consent or prostitution. The courts also looked into complaints of rape, which seemed to be always brought forward by the victims or their guardians. Here it was usually a question of proving the rape and asking for compensation. For example, a seventeenth-century woman from Giza asked for compensation from a man she claimed had raped her and made her into a *malqata* (pick-up, easy woman), thereby causing her great harm. She asked for compensation for his act. The man denied her allegations, but she produced witnesses to his attack on her, upon which the *qadi* ordered the man to pay compensation and had him whipped.[63]

In another seventeenth-century case from Cairo, an accused rapist categorically denied a woman's claim that he threatened to kill her then raped her, and she was unable to present corroborative witnesses to the rape, whereas his witnesses refuted her allegations and testified to the woman's immorality. The court found against her and ordered her expelled from the *hara* (residential quarter) at the request of the man she accused.[64]

As the last case shows, when a woman could not prove her rape allegations to the courts, the court often punished her for bringing an erroneous case to court. For that reason, alleged victims or their *wakils* (deputies, guardians) often withdrew rape complaints from court because they feared the repercussions. In one case a brother who had brought a claim of rape against a man on behalf of his sister returned to court and withdrew his complaint, indicating that his sister had made a mistake.[65]

The way courts handled cases of rape and violence is indicative of the legal system as a whole. The whole system seemed to be built on witnesses. There were court *shuhud* (official court witnesses) whose job was to witness transactions undertaken in court. Expert witnesses, such as the *daya*s and court engineers mentioned above, could be of two types: those attached to the courts and called upon when there was need and those who were brought in for specific cases either by the courts or the parties concerned. Corroborative witnesses provided the basis according to which the *qadi* judged veracity. Then there were character witnesses who were brought in to vouch for the parties involved and even to vouch for the witnesses brought in by them. So in cases when a man accused of rape denied his accuser's allegations and she presented witnesses to corroborate her story, she won her case. The same applied to other forms of crime such as beating, stealing, and *sab 'alani* (public slander), to mention a few. When witnesses were lacking, a victim often asked the court to administer an oath to her alleged rapist. The oath was quite important to the court. It was assumed that an individual would not perjure himself and would tell the truth when asked to take an oath. In crimes it was up to the victim to bring the case to court and to determine restitution from within the boundaries of the *shari'a* and according to local *'urf*. So that even though *zina* is punishable by a hundred lashes reduced for those unmarried according to the Qur'an, courts seemed to settle rape cases differently. For example, in cases of proven rape where an unmarried woman was the victim, it was normal for the court to give her the choice of marriage to her rapist. Quite often the victims and their guardians agreed; in other cases they did not and insisted on the *hudud*. The choice probably depended on the circumstances and on the *kafa'a* (social parity) between them. The rapist was expected to pay her an acceptable *mahr* (advance dowry) and *mu'akhar* (agreed upon delayed dowry paid at time of divorce or husband's death).[66] In this type of situation, when the rapist married his victim, she or her guardian were expected to appear in court and withdraw their complaint, indicating that she "had no claim in regards to the removal of her virginity by . . . who married her and consummated the marriage."[67]

Thus, redress had to be sought by the "property" owner; the rape of a person, or the "robbing" of virginity, was equated with a sense of personal proprietary right. No matter how dishonorable or psychologically harmful rape may have been, the paramount concern in the mind of the court was how the victim was to be compensated for the harm that had befallen her or him. A *diya* had to be paid, as did the *diya* for lost *nafs* (life, soul, living being), loss of a limb, nose, or other parts of the body, or for any other physical harm from, for example, severe wife beating. Determination of *diya* depended on a number of criteria pertaining to the particular case. Important criteria included the religion of the rapist, the age of the victim—whether she was a minor *(qasir)* or an adult woman *(baligh, thayb)*—and whether the victim was a virgin *(bikr)*, married, free, or a slave. The sex of the victim was also important because males were often victims of rape.

Even though courts treated rapists severely and delivered justice to the victims, it was, nevertheless, extremely difficult to prove a case of rape; this was and continues to be the most difficult obstruction to controlling rape. In one case after another women complained to the courts, but the *qadi*s deemed their proof not good enough. Proving the case was particularly difficult when the alleged rapist was of a higher social standing than the victim. Two cases from the seventeenth and nineteenth centuries are typical. In the first, a woman from Suez brought litigation against a sheikh who had earned the title of *hajj* for having performed the pilgrimage. She claimed that he had raped her and made her *muhiba* (awakened her sexual instincts), which brought her to the sorry end of becoming a streetwalker in Bab al-Luq in Cairo. She asked for compensation for the harm that befell her from his act. As would have been expected, the sheikh denied all allegations, and she could not present sufficient proof. The *qadi* found against her and forbade her from pestering the sheikh; he did not, however, have her punished.[68] In the nineteenth century case the alleged victim was a servant in a home and was, thus, legally under the protection of its male head, who was held responsible for her safety. She claimed that one night the man attacked and raped her. Not knowing what else to do, she remained with the family for some time without divulging her secret. When she realized that she was pregnant, she complained to the authorities. The man, however, completely denied her allegations and defended himself as "an honorable man whose house was located near a mosque, where he prayed regularly, and that he would never do such a thing." Because the girl could not present evidence to support her allegations, the court decided that she had no cause against the man and asked her to keep away from him.[69] That the court saw no reason to punish either woman may be an indication of the believability of their stories even though they could not prove them.

There also seems to be a general bias against women in the court's tendency not to believe witnesses presented by a woman as much as they believed witnesses presented by a man. Perhaps this was because the severity of the crime of rape required greater scrutiny. Nevertheless, the bias against women in rape cases was demonstrated in the unwillingness of courts to accept testimony presented solely by women using *shari'a* as basis,[70] even when the witnesses presented by the male adversaries proved unacceptable to the court.[71] However, as explained earlier, expert witness from a *daya* who examined the victim and proved violent rape had taken place was acceptable in court.

The above cases give an idea of people's lives in Ottoman Egypt. Although crimes were a common occurrence, there was relative security of life and people expected to receive justice. Social interaction and economic exchange seemed to go on as normal and the cooperation between guilds, courts, and troops created social alliances, allowing security for life and property. The relationship between the people and the state seemed to be loose, and people had relative maneuverability and choice in making their own decisions about personal and business issues. Institutions of civil society existed: guilds, courts, and *majalis-al-'ulama'* (clergy seminars, meetings, councils) in the Azhar and other important mosques and circles that met in the houses of *'ulama'* and intellectuals. The father of the famous chronicler 'Abd al-Rahman al-Jabarti held a "salon" where intellectuals such as Isma'il al-Khashshab and Hassan al-'Attar met regularly. The people were involved in the politics of their age and voiced their opinions to the *khassa* through the agency of the *'ulama'* and leaders of their guilds, town quarters, or churches. But they also did so directly. Al-Jabarti tells how the public met in Cairo mosques to discuss events of the 1798 French invasion and to discuss Napoleon's message to the Egyptians in which he called their attention to French military power, his demands that they surrender, and his promises that he would deliver Egypt from the tyranny of the mamluks. One also learns from al-Jabarti that Egyptians were armed. When the French occupied Alexandria after fierce resistance by its population, they found bodies of men and women who were killed as they shot at the French from rooftops. The picture of helplessness is, therefore, unwarranted even though whatever firearms the people of Alexandria held scarcely could stop the French invasion of Egypt from Alexandria with a fleet of four hundred ships and thirty-six thousand men.[72]

Merchants constituted one of the most important groups in Egyptian society. They also represented one of the richest groups during the Ottoman period. Egypt was an important trade center through which trade routes to Arabia, East Africa, and India passed via the Red Sea; goods were carried over the Nile to Sudan and Abyssinia; and the Mediterranean saw active trade between Egypt, Syria, Anatolia, and southern Europe. Court records illustrate the importance of Mediterranean trade through Egypt's port cities of Alexandria and Dumyat. In Dumyat a significant Syrian merchant community undertook trade with Egypt while the large Maghribi community in Alexandria and Cairo gave evidence of important and steady exchange with North Africa. Marriage records from the city of Alexandria illustrate the frequency with which Maghribi traders came and settled in Egypt and their trade activities with Syria and Arabia. The argument that east-west trade was once considered irrelevant in comparison to the south-north trade linking North Africa to Europe is discredited by archival details. Alexandria's archives also illustrate the importance of that town as a trade and administrative center long before the nineteenth-century European community made it so. The volume of goods passing through the city, the presence of European consul representatives, and frequent mention of Jewish and other representatives of European trade companies all indicate its importance.

Coffee constituted perhaps the most important item traded. It was brought yearly from Arabia through the port of Suez, whose importance as a trade center has been well-researched by Laila 'Abd al-Latif.[73] Just as important was the trade in textiles and spices from the east. Trade from Nubia and Sudan through Darfur and Sinar was the source for slaves, ivory, ebony, and gum arabic.[74] The Mediterranean trade included silk and cloth from Syria and Istanbul, weapons, furs, wool, paper, metals, glassware, and porcelain. Egypt's chief exports were rice, cotton cloth, henna, wheat, dried vegetables, and the re-export of coffee, ivory, ebony, and gum.[75]

Egypt's merchants belonged to many classes, depending on the geographical range of their trade, their wealth, items they traded in, and alliances they formed with other social groups. The most important merchants were the *tujjar*, who were involved in long-distance trade, who formed significant partnerships, invested in manufacturing, borrowed and lent large quantities of money, and had large capital invested in their trades. The most famous of these was al-Mahruqi, who was one of the chief activists in bringing Muhammad 'Ali to power. But he was clearly not unique as evidenced by archival records. Shahbandar al-Tujjar Isma'il Abu Taqqiya and his partners al-Damiri and al-Ruway'i traded in large quantities of money, formed partnerships, and had their own agents in ports where they traded. Abu Taqqiyya and al-Ruway'i have a street and a quarter, respectively, named after them in Cairo that exist today.[76]

Merchants are traditionally included in the middle classes outside of the power elite. But this exemplar does not fit the *tujjar* during the Ottoman period because of their wealth and connections with other members of the power elite. Therefore, they are easily included in the *khassa* because of the important economic role they played and their wealth. The *khassa* of the eighteenth century constituted a combine formed of mamluks, *tujjar*, and *multazims* with the *'ulama'* constituting part, if a separate part, of the combine. Even though the *tujjar* neither constituted military forces nor wielded military power and were not part of the government hierarchy, they still constituted a necessary part of the *khassa*, ensuring the smooth operation of internal and international trade. Whereas *multazims* extracted the agricultural and manufactured wealth, *tujjar* undertook its sale, both inside and outside the country. *Tujjar* were often involved in the production process itself, providing capital, promoting the cultivation of marketable crops, and investing in land. Therefore, they were allied and interconnected with *multazims* and were often holders of *iltizams*. The state received large revenues from the *tujjar;* mamluks and Ottoman pasha resorted to borrowing from them. The *shahbandar* (head *tajir,* or elected head of the merchants' guild), usually the wealthiest merchant, had links to mamluk beys, sometimes through marriage, but usually through trade or other financial dealings. Al-Jabarti writes that some *tujjar* actually owned mamluks and had them attached to mamluk households to rise in rank to positions of leadership, hence cementing alliances, patronage, and protection. One example is Yusif bey al-Sharaybi, who became one of the "princes" *(umara')* of the mamluks.[77] Therefore, not all of the *tujjar* belonged to the middle classes; depending on their wealth, connections, and nature, volume, origin, and destination of their trade, they constituted an important element within the *khassa.* The long-distance merchant involved directly in foreign trade is described as a *tajir* in this study. Long-distance trade in coffee, spices, and cloth most interested them in the eighteenth century. They lived quite luxuriously, and unlike their small-scale counterparts, they lived far from congested city centers. "They lived in sumptuous palaces . . . which resembled the palaces of the members of the ruling class. . . . They sought to establish their abodes out of the overcrowded and congested center, in quieter areas, where vegetation and water were still plentiful. . . . The wealthy merchants tended to behave like the ruling class to which they were linked by many ties."[78]

These large-scale merchants were closely connected with other levels of the merchant classes. Retail shops were located according to item sold in different marketplaces: paper market, textile market, silk market, jewelry, tobacco, slave market. In large cities such as Cairo, the marketplace was usually covered. This was where retail business took place. *Tajirs* located their business in *wikala*s (*tajir*'s headquarters), which were buildings used by several *tajir*s or for the exclusive use of one *tajir*. There the *tajir*'s inventory was warehoused and facilities for housing traveling merchants and business partners were located. It was here that the *tajir* conducted his business, usually in attached offices or in an attached open courtyard. The lower level of a *wikala* often consisted of small shops rented out to shopkeepers, and the upper levels could consist of apartments rented out to the public.[79]

The tradition of large-scale trade through *tujjar* was nothing new for Egypt. Even under the mamlukid Sultanate before the arrival of the Ottomans, when government monopoly of trade in certain items was a fact of life, wealthy *tujjar* with connections and power were the norm. In other words, government monopolies did not hinder the *tujjar* from amassing immense fortunes. *Karimi* merchants (traded in spices) in particular possessed such wealth and influence that they acted as bankers for foreign rulers. Hanna writes of various cases such as that of the *karimi* merchant Sarag al-Din Ibn Quwaid, who acted as banker and creditor to the West African ruler Mansa Musa during the fourteenth century. "Many of these merchants became notorious for the extent of their wealth."[80] Important foreign merchants traded with Egypt, and some founded large establishments in Cairo. Jacques Coeur, who was the banker of the French kings Charles VII and Louis XI, is a good example.[81]

During the late eighteenth century, Cairo's commercial elite grew smaller and became increasingly composed of members of European-linked minority groups.[82] The mamluk beys borrowed heavily from the *tujjar* because they needed to purchase new mamluks or equip their forces, thus providing one basis for the relationship between the two groups. Foreign merchants, who had access to international contacts, fulfilled this function, which helped establish them in positions of importance. The number of these merchants de-

clined as a result of European competition with Egyptian goods and the decline of the Sudanese trade during the late eighteenth century, which forced
the mamluks to find other ways of gaining immediate access to wealth. One
way consisted of extortion from the *khassa*'s weaker dependents, particularly
merchants, *multazim*s, and crafts manufacturers. Such actions hurt the *tujjar*
particularly because they had invested their profits in both land and workshops.[83] As mamluk extortions increased, the pressure on the *tujjar* caused
foreigners among them to call on their own nations' leaders for assistance.
This phenomenon may have helped launch the Napoleonic invasion of 1798
in answer to requests sent by French merchants to their government demanding that something be done. "France's economic interests in Egypt were rising in the eighteenth century, by the end of which Egypt was France's leading
trading partner, outside of the sugar islands of the Caribbean."[84]

Foreign merchants in Ottoman Egypt enjoyed special protection in the
form of capitulations, which were essentially commercial because foreigners
living in Egypt acted primarily as merchants. These capitulations included the
merchants' right to trade in the empire and special privileges regarding customs dues, taxation, law, and the "inviolability of domicile." Because of the
growing rivalry among foreign communities over Egyptian trade, disputes
among foreigners and between foreigners and Egyptians required regulation.
This matter was resolved in the foreigners' favor. Legal jurisdiction was divided according to whether the two parties to the dispute were of the same nationality, one was foreign and one was native, or both were foreigners of
different nationalities, in which case they fell outside the local courts' capacity.
This system had its roots before the Ottoman invasion. Under the mamluk
Sultan al-Ashraf Qaitbay (1468–95), "disputes between foreigners and natives were tried by the President of the Custom House, with an appeal to the
sovereign himself."[85] The French capitulation of 1535 provided that such disputes would not be heard by ordinary local courts but would be brought before the sultan or his "principal lieutenant." Capitulations did not provide for
the settlement of disputes between foreigners until the eighteenth century
when it was agreed that such disputes would be arbitrated by the consuls of
the parties involved.[86] This capitulation indicates the growing foreign commercial interest in Egypt and the competition between various European
countries over Middle Eastern trade.

The characteristics of the *iltizam* system at the end of the eighteenth century provide a basis for understanding social interaction and society's approach to government business. *Iltizam* has been studied as a system
innovated by the Ottomans in 1658 to replace direct taxation and first applied
by the Ottomans in Egypt.[87] New research based on court records, however,
has shown that *iltizam* began much earlier, evolving from the system of

muqata'at (land grant, tax farm), *amanat* (trusteeship), or *daman* practiced earlier in Egypt, in which an *amin* (a guarantor, superindentent) supervised the land and assessed the taxes on it. The *muqata'a* system had failed because of the difficulties of supervision and the corruption caused by the *amins'* illegal extortions and assigning of others to assume their duties while they became absentee superintendents.[88] According to Mohsen Shouman, *iltizam* was used since the time of Sultan Selim, the first recorded *iltizam* dating from 939/1529. Based on the chronicler al-Qalqashandi, Shouman concludes that *iltizam* may have been introduced so early because

> [*iltizam*] resembled the system of *daman* which was applied during the *Mamluk* sultanate. *Daman* was used as a method of tax-collection for a very long time in Egypt, and it was prevalent in the mamlukid period. The person who had the right to collect the taxes, called the *damin,* paid a certain fixed sum to the treasury and kept some of the revenue for himself. One can therefore observe continuity in practice between the mamlukid and Ottoman periods, in spite of the changes in the political scene and in spite of the different name applied to the system.[89]

Described as a system by which "the land, theoretically owned by the state, was made over to tax farmers for the collection of its revenue,"[90] *iltizam* provided the logical alternative through which the Ottomans used existing social forces to extract wealth and at the same time gain the consensus of those forces by making them partners who benefited from Ottoman rule. Ra'uf Abbas and 'Asim Disuqi detail the historical background to this system. "When the Arabs opened Egypt in 641, they left its [agricultural] land in the hands of its people, and confirmed the land-tenure system in place under the Byzantines. Thus the land belonged to the treasury and the peasants paid the *kharaj* tax. Subsequently, some of the caliphs cut off large estates subject to the *'ushr* tax, which was free property to its owners to be inherited, bought, and sold."[91] As a system, *iltizam* was not designed for a particular class, nor was it meant to create land-tenure policy. Rather, land policy was based on the expediency of tax collection, a system stemming from early Islamic invasions when conquered territory was treated in accordance with the type of tax to be garnered from it, for example, *'ushr* (one tenth, tithe) or *kharaj* (land tax).[92] This meant that *iltizams* were open to any individual who could meet the system's demands. The demands, however, were designed to cement alliances between the powerful classes who could raise the advance money to ensure control over the *iltizam* and who possessed the authority to ensure the production and extraction of agricultural wealth. A system evolved in which various competing groups found that they had to cooperate to make the system work to their greatest advantage. Thus, the groups forming Egypt's *khassa* found a mutual interest in ensuring the most efficient extraction of the country's wealth, which meant competing orders, mamluks, *multazims*, and *tujjar* had to cooperate during the late eighteenth century. By that time *iltizam* had changed, permitting *multazims* to gain control over the land, alienate it, and leave it in inheritance to their heirs.

Thus, a *multazim* was ideally a man with some authority stemming from the command of troops or from a close relationship with those in power. His wealth came primarily from tax collection. His tax farm stipulated that he deliver to the state a defined amount; whatever he extracted over and above that amount, a *fa'iz* (surplus), remained his own. He was also given the right to cultivate certain portions of the land assigned to his *iltizam* and to use peasant labor for this purpose. Thus, farming provided a second source of income for the tax farmer. Some *multazims* entered agricultural production in more direct ways by extending credit to peasants and undertaking the sale of the crops. Profit from the sale of agricultural goods encouraged *multazims* to interfere in village matters and the production process to increase output. *Multazims* came from different groups and classes in Egyptian society. Some were members of janissary corps, some were mamluks, others were *tajirs*, and still others were *"afandiyya* (civil servants) bureaucrats, some women, sheikhs of *sufi tariqahs* (mystical orders), some heads of Bedouin tribes." [93] In this system the peasant was theoretically able to leave the land whenever he wished and could actually sell his right of usage to any other person and could plant whatever crop he chose without interference from the *multazim*. In practice the *multazim* could force him to raise a particular cash crop and the state could punish the peasant or force him back to the land if he abandoned it. [94] Peasants were also free to bring their goods—grains, cattle, vegetables, handicrafts—to towns to sell them, except at times of trouble. [95] In situations where monopolies were set up by grandees of an area, peasants who came to market were forced to pay extra exactions for the right to sell, as is evidenced by local complaints to the authorities.

Multazims had close connections with the *'amma* through the system of sub-*iltizams*. For one thing, the *multazim* was assisted by a multitude of other persons, each of whom profited from the system and constituted a stabilizing factor for it within peasant society. Among these assistants can be included the *"mashshad, al-saraf* (cashier, treasurer), *al-shahid* (the witness), *sheikh al-balad* (village head), *al-kashif* (supervisor, inspector), *al-khowli* (overseer)," [96] each of whom had his own rights and payments due him from the peasants. Sub-*iltizams* also provided tentacles between the *multazim* and the rest of his society. Sub-*iltizams* seemed to be the norm in Ottoman Egypt and were applied to both agricultural and urban *iltizam*s. According to this system, a large *ilitzam* would be granted to the highest bidder, who would then divide it into smaller sections as sub-*iltizam*s to be administered by a larger number of people. The latter, in turn, could divide it into yet smaller parts as sub-*iltizam*s and a wider number would benefit from them. At every level contracts were signed in court and either the *multazim* designated some property as collateral or brought someone who would act as guarantor for him. The person acting as guarantor could be held liable for the assessed tax if the *multazim* did not fulfill the contract. In this way large numbers of the public were actually associated in business deals, each one collecting state revenue at his level while receiving profit that constituted the difference between the assessed tax and the actual tax collected. This meant that some holdings could be acquired for relatively small sums. This, in turn, opened the door to obtaining a holding for numerous civilians. In other words, a person did not have to be very wealthy to become a tax farmer. For a few thousand nisfs, a small holding could be obtained that gave its holder extra income. Broad participation was, therefore, possible, and many more people were involved in the system than is recognized. Thus, sub-*iltizam*s allowed an efficient system of tax and income collection and at the same time allowed tentacles of patronage to form from the *'amma* up to the *khassa* holders of *iltizam*s.[97] A couple of court records explain how this worked. In an 1120/1708 entry in the shari'a court of Dumyat, a man certified that he received what was due him from his *muqata'a* (share) of the *iltizam* held by another man. He also indicated that payment in return for his use of the *muqata'a* was due the *multazim* for three months in full as per their agreement. The record also indicates that the holder of the *iltizam* was a member of the 'Azaban corps and that he was now liable to the Diwan al-'Ali in Cairo for the income from the *iltizam*.[98] The second record is from the shari'a court of Dishna and is dated 1274/1843. "A man by the name of Isma'il Gibril al-Samman from Faww South, attested that he *iltazam* (took the responsibility or monopoly) with the *maqbul* (debt) of butter in Dishna markets for Wednesday and that he will be paying 'Abd al-Rahman Ahmad . . . of Dishna the amount of . . . *jarida* (free of duty). This *iltizam* begins from the month of Rabi' al-Awwal 1273 to Safar 1274.[99] This last contract is important not only because of the details it presents about business agreements and the administration of markets but also because it shows that *iltizam* as a method of business continued to be practiced even after Muhammad 'Ali canceled agricultural *iltizam*s.

Because *multazim*s were expected to make a partial payment in advance at the time their *iltizam*s were awarded, they needed access to capital. For that reason, *multazim*s usually maintained close connections to moneylenders who could advance them credit. The *multazim*s also turned to the *tujjar*, who had wealth and were willing to invest it. The growing practice of awarding *iltizam*s for life consolidated the *khassa* and made it difficult for others to become members of the privileged classes. A *multazim*'s effectiveness and his ability to extract wealth depended on his relationship with the peasantry: he needed to maintain authority to ensure their cooperation, and at the same time he needed to remain on good terms with them. He, therefore, used local agents, who acted as a buffer between him and the peasantry, to undertake his day-to-day business. Depending on the size of the *iltizam*, this process may have entailed various levels of functionaries, with each level answering to the one above it, creating a hierarchy of officials who stood to gain from the operation. They all stood together, defending the *multazim* who provided legitimacy to the profit they earned.

One way that *multazim*s ensured the peasants' acquiescence to this system was through services rendered to the peasantry. Thus, the *multazim* protected the peasantry from exactions of mamluks or other officials and often brought grievance cases before the pasha or to the court on the peasants' behalf. In addition, conditions in the village were highly dependent on the *multazim*, who was supposed to shoulder the government's responsibility in maintaining irrigation work.[100] The hierarchical nature of the *iltizam* system meant that at each level the participants profited and that each level was dependent on the level above it. Most of the functionaries were recruited from among local inhabitants, peasants, or clan leaders, so the hierarchical *iltizam* system permeated the social structure, thus helping continue its activity, however abusive it became.

On another level, the *multazim* had to secure his alliance with other members of society whose cooperation he needed for his operation to function smoothly. For example, he needed close relations with the clergy, and quite often the *multazim* was a member of the clergy. Because the clergy, in their function as *qadi*s (judges), gave legitimacy to the *multazim*'s right to collect taxes, it was important that the clergy favor the system.[101] Conversely, the position of many *multazim*s as members of the clergy helped give a legal basis to the whole operation.

The relationship between *khassa* and the *'amma* during that era is interesting: local merchants and the artisanal elite, who possessed their own capital or instruments and had special skills that the *khassa* demanded, enjoyed a special relationship with the *khassa* built on profit and patronage. After all, it was the mamluks in particular who were the principal purchasers of luxury items imported by merchants or produced by craftsmen. This relationship created solidarity within the ruling class. The *'ulama'* gained influence under the

French, who tried to cultivate their support to use them to obtain the population's acquiescence. Weakened during the nineteenth century, the *'ulama'* reappeared as legitimizers of the state by the end of the nineteenth century.

Before Muhammad 'Ali's bureaucratization of the *'ulama'*, they earned their living in various ways, including serving as administrators of *awqaf* property, which gave them importance because they controlled a large array of assets. The *'ulama'* could have inherited their wealth, been active in trade, or been *multazims*, as has already been indicated. They also received income by teaching private lessons to the wealthy and by serving as scribes to both wealthy people and needy people who were petitioning the government. This created close connections to the mamluks, whom they served as teachers and *multazim* tax collectors. As *'ulama'* they gained in social prestige and also protected their families from arbitrary confiscation of property, a fact that encouraged families to send their sons to become *'ulama'*. Using al-Jabarti's obituaries, Michael Winter shows that most *'ulama'* originated from villages. "It is significant that not one of the *shuyukh* of al-Azhar in the eighteenth century (and also the nineteenth century) was born in Cairo; all were from villages." [102] The infusion of *'ulama'* from the countryside into the intellectual and political centers of al-Azhar and Cairo, which continues today, are an example of the importance of the periphery in shaping the center. Thus, the close association of the *'ulama'* with the ruling *khassa* was essential to both. While receiving protection from the mamluks, the *'ulama'* supported the existing social order from which they benefited, a role they continue to play today. Although the *'ulama'* generally spoke for local interests, they tended to speak more specifically for the more prosperous and influential classes. [103] As junior associates of the *khassa*, they acted as a buffer for and legitimizers of the social hierarchy. Their particular importance increased in times of social dislocation and decreased when stability existed.

The *'ulama'* are usually placed in the middle classes in Egypt's social structure. Because, however, the influence of the role they play, based on their authority as interpreters of religious law, gave them access to power and wealth, their position within the social structure really depended on their usefulness in providing support for the *khassa*. They also could mobilize the public in demonstrations of power. According to one eyewitness report of the period, "They have the ability to assemble in a single day a powerful military regiment of at least seventy or eighty thousand men who are docile and loyal to them, and in this way they can assist the Governor." [104] The *'ulama'* as an order must not be seen as constituting members of one class: some were part of the *khassa*, others were junior partners with the *khassa*, and still others wielded very localized influence that was detached from the centers of power.

As a body they were cemented together by a patronage system not unlike the ones in which the *multazims* or the mamluks participated.

At the end of the eighteenth century the *khassa* combine was headed by the mamluks. They became the dominant order, the elite of the *khassa*, encroaching more and more on the prerogatives of *multazims*, *'ulama'*, and *tujjar*, who shared less in the material benefits of power. The foreign *tujjar*, with their financial interests at stake, found that mamluk incursions did not help their trade function smoothly, in spite of the legal agreements binding the Ottomans that guaranteed certain privileges to these foreigners. When the Ottomans sent an army led by Hassan Pasha Jaza'irli to try to reestablish Ottoman control, he was welcomed by Egypt's social orders, including the *tujjar*, the *'ulama'*, and the *multazims* who hoped to balance mamluk power by allying themselves with the new Ottoman forces. Jaza'irli Pasha discovered, however, that he could do little without the support of the mamluks who dominated the system. Not satisfied with the taxes he levied first on Christians, then on the *tujjar* and the *multazims*, thereby gaining the opposition of the *'ulama'*, Jaza'irli Pasha finally turned to the mamluks, whom he had earlier put down, and recognized the mamlukid leader Isma'il Bey as Sheikh al-Balad. By allying himself with the mamluks—in itself a recognition of their continued importance within the system that Ottoman military power could not simply eliminate—the pasha successfully collected what was owed to the Sultan and departed, leaving the mamluks in an even stronger position than when he had found them monopolizing power with the near-breakup of the power combines that had combined their interests with those of other social forces.[105]

Muhammad 'Ali, later striving for much the same purpose as Jaza'irli Pasha, opted for the destruction of the mamluks. He seemed to have followed an earlier recommendation to the Ottoman Porte regarding regaining control of Egypt that pointed out that "the bulk of Egypt's population would desert its Mamluk tyrants and join the Ottoman army." [106] But Muhammad 'Ali succeeded where Jaza'irli Pasha had failed because he took the time to cultivate consensus among the vital groups constituting active social forces. The support that Muhammad 'Ali received from *'ulama'*, *tujjar*, and *multazims* in his bid for power may be explained by the desire of these groups to restore stability between the various social orders. The deterioration of the *multazims* and the *tujjar*, who had to mete out even larger shares of their profits to the mamluks after the departure of Jara'irli Pasha, and mamluk coercion to extract this wealth had reached a point unacceptable to society at large. Thus, these groups, encouraged by the pasha's promises, expected him to end mamluk abuse and thereby open the way for them to dominate the *khassa* and to regain the power that they had lost because of the mamluks. They assumed that

Muhammad 'Ali would become the pasha, representative of the sultan in Egypt, to whom tribute was to be paid and who would ensure stability and security, and the country's business would revert to the *'ulama'*, *tujjar*, and *multazim*s. The results, however, would prove quite different from their expectations.

2

BUILDING THE MODERN STATE

MERCANTILISM IN A NEW FORM

In any case, we are not looking for a "perfect" national market; none such exists even in our own day. What we are looking for is a system of internal mechanisms and connections with the outside world . . . in other words a large scale economy, covering a wide area, "territorialized" so to speak, and sufficiently coherent for government to be able to shape and maneuver it to some extent. Mercantilism represents precisely the dawning of awareness of this possibility of maneuvering the entire economy of a country; in fact it could be described as the first attempt to create the national market.[1]

Because agriculture constituted the most important industry in Egypt and because Egypt depends on the Nile for survival, hydropolitics has proven popular in descriptions of Egypt's political system.[2] Bureaucratic centralization, introduced by Muhammad 'Ali and continued by his successors, the government bureaucracy's increasing arbitrariness, the government's ability to expropriate wealth, and the integration of the "dominant religion . . . in its power system"[3] have made models of oriental despotism neatly fit the Egyptian case.[4] From ancient Egypt to the modern period, including the reign of 'Ali Bey al-Kabir, Muhammad 'Ali Pasha, and Gamal Abdel Nasser, Egypt's history can be seen as despotic rule based on coercion,[5] or what Karl Wittfogel has described as a form of rule that "connotes an extremely harsh form of absolutist power."[6]

Perhaps the first problem that such a model encounters relates to its division of society into distinct governmental and nongovernmental forces. "The hydraulic state is a genuinely managerial state. . . . [It] prevents the nongovernmental forces of society from crystallizing into independent bodies strong enough to counterbalance and control the political machine."[7] In such a division, government's concern is the protection of the state against external enemies, thus requiring strong military forces, which are equally often used against internal forces of opposition to rulers. The government also constitutes an agromanagerial bureaucracy "whose leaders are the holders of despotic state power and not private owners and entrepreneurs. . . . [A] *bu-reaucratic* landlordism, a *bureaucratic* capitalism, and a *bureaucratic* gentry [exist]."[8]

The nongovernmental forces are described as kin groups, autonomous religious organizations, "independent and semi-independent leaders of military groups (such as tribal bands or armies of feudal lords); and owners of various forms of property (such as money, land, industrial equipment, and capacity for work)."[9] By categorizing society into opposing dichotomies, theories of oriental despotism miss the possibility that governmental and nongovernmental forces could in fact be integrated and that one actually lends support to the other, thereby achieving a consensus. For a ruling class to establish its hegemony over a society, a form of consensus must exist among the population at large and particularly among the various groups making up the ruling classes and their allies; coercion alone never suffices.

If one takes hegemony to mean " 'moral and philosophical leadership,' leadership which is attained in a society,"[10] then the specific groups that form this society and the relations between them should be the focus of study. The absence of models not indigenous to the particular society, although worthy of study because of the questions that such an absence could raise, should not lead to conclusions about the final nature of the state or of the relationship between state and society. Unfortunately, this has been a common theme in studies of the Middle East. The absence of certain models has led to conclusions that may be dismissed when the question is examined from a different perspective. For example, exact replicas of the institutions that ensure civil liberties in Western societies do not occur in the Middle East, leading to the conclusion that no such liberties existed. Perry Anderson contends that "Islamic political traditions possessed no conception of urban liberties. Towns had no corporate or municipal autonomy: indeed, they had no legal existence at all." As with other scholars who accept the *"qadi* justice" paradigm, Anderson argues quoting Bernard Lewis: "Just as there was no state, but only a ruler and his agents, no courts but only a judge and his helpers, so there was no city but only a conglomeration of families, quarters and guilds, each with their own chiefs or leaders."[11] The conclusion reached from this argument is that in Islamic societies coercion is the only means of rule.

If one were to go beyond the state and state bureaucracy and divide the *khassa* into its distinct groups of conflicting orders of mamluks, *tujjar,* and *multazims*; examine the relations between them and the ruler—who usually belonged to one or all of these contending groups—and consider the overlapping functions and interests of these orders, it would become clear that describing modern Egypt as an example of "oriental despotism," however useful, actually molds reality to a model, thereby clouding the reality. A look at the *khassa*, the groups that comprise it, and their relationship with each other and the *'amma* would help illustrate the patterns of rule, relations of power, and consensus that exist in such societies. Egypt's *khassa* and *'amma* cannot be divided into governmental and nongovernmental sectors, which is one important reason for the general stability of the country. *Khassa* alliances combine the official with the unofficial and the formal with the informal; the tentacles of patronage extend from one group to the other, thereby supporting the system as a whole. Cultural continuity in allegiance to family, village, and patriarchal structures and in general social outlook helps to provide consensus among the *'amma* and, therefore, makes physical, administrative, and ideological domination successful.

Moreover, what makes coercion successful in such a system is the fact that it is limited and weighed against the population's consensus. The different economic and political structures imposed from above in modern Egypt represent the methods of various *khassa* coalitions in their efforts to continue ruling under particular national and international conditions, the struggle within the *khassa* over dominant leadership, and the particular relations required by the *'amma*'s evolution. The focus in this chapter is on the early nineteenth century when the roots of Egypt's modern mercantilist structure was laid. Some aspects of this mercantilist structure and the class relationships between various societal groups, particularly within the *khassa*, are discussed. In addition, I examine how cultural patterns and the continuity of historical experience provided a base for political hegemony and legal systems that were molded by the *khassa* to suit the particular needs of this period of transition.

Some of the basic methods used by Muhammad 'Ali Pasha had precedents under the mamluks, but the system set up under his rule was quite comprehensive and outlasted him. His trade, industrial, and agricultural monopolies; the *nizam jadid* (modern Western-style army); modern education and health services; and bureaucratic growth and rationalization fit within the traditions of mercantilism, albeit with necessary adjustments. In early modern Europe mercantilism was usually associated with the rise of a commercial middle class that was allied with the monarchy to protect budding industries and promote mercantile activities. The monopolies established by the pasha were designed to protect Egyptian industries from the growing encroachment of European goods. Although the pasha built most of the protected industries, his policy was aimed at increasing the state's wealth. Even though his policies did provide protection for local *tujjar* and manufacturers, they resulted in the weakening of Egypt's old *khassa*, and the pasha may be described as assuming their role as chief mamluk, *multazim*, and *tajir*, if not being the only mamluk, *multazim* and *tajir*. What the pasha did was to take over monopolies that had been shared by these groups. Thus, he took over the *iltizam* of Alexandria and other ports that he held directly from the Ottoman sultan. As *multazim* of ports he collected customs revenue, paid the sultan his due, and kept the rest. The *iltizam* of the port was nothing new because the port was farmed out throughout the Ottoman period to various persons by the Ottoman treasury. The same thing transpired with his actions as *tajir;* he placed a monopoly on trade in certain items, but he acted through local merchants and not as a merchant himself. So rather than as an oriental despot, one can say that Muhammad 'Ali actually acted much in the tradition of Europe's mercantilist monarchies, protecting Egypt's trade and manufacturing in accordance with the system available to him.

Although the earlier *khassa* coalition was all but destroyed, important sectors of this *khassa* continued to thrive, and other forms of *tujjar,* mamluks, and *multazim*s evolved to become part of a new *khassa* coalition. The same logic that had previously allied the mamluks with each other and with other members of society continued under the pasha. Perhaps the best way to describe Muhammad 'Ali's actions vis-à-vis the *khassa* is that he superimposed himself and a new *khassa* alliance on an already existing system. His destruction of the mamluks and *multazim*s and his weakening of the *'ulama'* and *tujjar* did not mean a complete change in the system; rather, it indicated a change in attitude toward mercantilist practices and necessitated a centralized state and bureaucracy. The various groups that had existed previously would reappear under new conditions and in a shape more appropriate to the changing superstructure.

One of Egyptian society's distinctive characteristics has been the conflict and cooperation between groups making up the *khassa*. When Muhammad 'Ali Pasha arrived in Egypt at the beginning of the nineteenth century, the mamluks who survived the French invasion and regrouped formed the most viable opposition to his rule. Consequently, Muhammad 'Ali had to destroy them, which he accomplished in the famous massacre at Cairo Citadel in 1811. It was by uniting with the *tujjar* and the *'ulama* that he was able to bring about his appointment by the Ottoman sultan to the position of pasha. The pasha had won the confidence of Egypt's *tujjar* and *'ulama',* and they saw in him the answer to their problems with the mamluks. After the Ottoman sultan invested him as pasha, Muhammad 'Ali continued to depend on the two groups, borrowing from the *tujjar* and receiving the support of the people through the *'ulama'*. Ultimately, he turned on them, controlling trade, canceling the *iltizam*s and controlling the *awqaf* that had enriched both the *tujjar* and the *'ulama'*. There is no reason to believe, however, that destruction was Muhammad 'Ali's original intention or that he proposed to rule through his bureaucracy alone. More likely, the pragmatic needs of Egypt's internal conditions and the international situation at the beginning of the nineteenth century prompted his actions vis-à-vis other groups of the *khassa*. Perhaps the *'ulama'*, as a distinct group, endured more change than any other group under the pasha. Such change, however, resulted primarily from the erosion of their financial base through the cancellation of *iltizam* and the introduction of Western education and institutions that seemed to shake the foundations of their authority and cause them to begin carving a new basis for power relations with the nascent mercantilist state.

If one thinks of the pasha as replacing the mamluks in the earlier *khassa* alliance and remembers that he originally was a *tajir* with a commercial outlook toward government business, then it seems logical that he would not use his military power to destroy the channels through which the wealth of the country and its exchange of goods took place. Rather, he used these channels and molded them for his benefit. In short, the pasha chose the route of cooperation rather than destruction. As far as the *multazim*s were concerned, the system had to be changed and titles and rights transformed. Yet the former system's outlook remained very much part of the new system. As is usually the case with a changing of the guard, new faces would mean new patronage relationships.

Muhammad 'Ali's monopolies hurt but did not destroy the *tujjar*. In fact, the pasha worked through them in many cases. The indigenous Egyptian *tujjar* felt the sting of the monopolies, and their number fell during his rule. During the first decades of the nineteenth century growth was obvious in both internal and external trade, but the profits from this commerce went to the pasha's monopolies and to the foreign merchants who acted as intermediaries for all external commercial operations. The number of European *tujjar* actually increased from sixteen in 1822 to seventy-two in 1840, and the port of Alexandria grew in importance as an export center, with forty-four commercial houses. Of these, thirteen were French, seven British, and nine Austrian.[12]

Muhammad 'Ali did not oppose wealth and power wielded by the *multazim*s for political reasons; rather, their demise was closely related to his mercantile policy. Eliminating *multazim*s represented a logical step toward creating government monopolies to circumvent the impact of customs policies that were required of Egypt as part of the Ottoman Empire. The need for resources to aid in the revival of Egypt's economy provided a second reason. As heir to the mamluks, the pasha also inherited the responsibility of providing services and reforming and rebuilding state structures; in these functions, his predecessors included Barsbay, Qalawun, and Qaitbay. As a modern ruler in a capitalistic world and involved in state centralization, the structures he introduced included a positivist materialist outlook toward change. The *tujjar*, in particular, would have expected this attitude from him, both foreign *tujjar* who wanted to be the conduit for the import of industrial equipment and local *tujjar* who desired protection from competition with foreign industrial goods. As a *tajir* Muhammad 'Ali must have wanted to control the market for maximum profit.

The pasha had a complex relationship with the *tujjar*. Foreign merchants constituted one type of *tujjar* that existed in Egypt at the beginning of the nineteenth century. With headquarters in Cairo or the ports, particularly Alexandria, they transacted with foreign sources for the export and import of goods. Many of these *tujjar* were attached to the consulates of foreign countries and, therefore, wielded some power. A second group of *tujjar* consisted of Egyptian merchants whose headquarters were either in Cairo or in other urban centers, such as Assiut. They supplied imports needed locally, bought local products for export purposes, and were involved in the Sudan and Red Sea trade. A third group composed of foreigners and Egyptians really served as middlemen between the other two groups, providing capital to finance transactions. Their headquarters were situated in the main ports and Cairo with branches wherever needed.

Using family archives of nineteenth-century Assiut, Terence Walz has illustrated the interaction between these various *tujjar*. The al-Jawharis seem to represent the local *tujjar*, the 'Ubayds the middlemen, and the Cassavettes the foreign *tujjar*. Walz shows how the al-Jawharis and the 'Ubayds conspired to control the Sudan trade, particularly in ivory. Because they did not have the contacts to market the ivory in Europe, where it was in demand, they turned to the Cassavettes for that stage of the trade.[13] Thus, three groups were involved in the trade: foreign merchants, with knowledge of the European market; the Egyptian merchants, with knowledge of the Sudanese market, the Red Sea market, and the local market in general; and go-betweens, who arranged transactions among the other groups. The trade that Walz describes took place in the 1840s and 1850s, after the dismantling of the pasha's monopolies, but there is no reason to suppose that such transactions did not take place while the monopolies existed. In fact, some leading merchant houses of Assiut continued to act as agents of foreign rulers, for example, the sultan of Darfur, and the government itself was a client of these *tujjar*. "The al-Hilalis had close contacts with the government, acted as *sar-tujjar* and often as the government's bankers in Asyut."[14]

One problem in studying the Egyptian *tujjar*'s fate under Muhammad 'Ali Pasha is the lack of accurate sources and data. Walz said that he could not find detailed records for the Assiut families before the 1840s, and one may logically assume that the pasha's monopolies were a factor creating this phenomenon. Susan Staffa's data regarding the number of merchants before and during Muhammad 'Ali's rule are based on Edward Lane's assessment, and as she points out, the evidence is inconclusive concerning the types of merchants found in Egypt in the 1840s. For the year 1795 she gives the number of import-export merchants at four thousand, petty merchants at five thousand, and artisans at twenty-five thousand. For the year 1839 the total number of merchants is thirty thousand, including petty merchants, shopkeepers, and artisans. Staffa does not provide a separate figure for import-export merchants. "Although the relative size of the general division appears to have remained constant, there is no way of knowing the size of the constituent groups in 1839." She concludes, "It is also probable that the import-export merchants increased substantially by virtue of the influx of foreign population."[15]

Various merchants fared differently under the pasha's rule, but the big losers were probably the middlemen. At the beginning the pasha allied himself with indigenous *tujjar* and used them in his efforts to achieve power. Thus, Muhammad 'Ali allowed them to function freely at first. When he no longer needed them, however, having secured his power, he turned them into "servants of the state" in a system somewhat reminiscent of the monopolies instituted by the mamlukid Sultan al-Ashraf Barsbay (1422–37). In short, the middlemen became "state-merchants" who ran the trade for the pasha while retaining a percentage of the profit. The pasha, like the earlier sultans, must have been "willing to permit this siphoning of funds,"[16] however reluctantly. Various merchants who suffered from competition with the monopolies or with foreign merchandise moved their businesses out of the trade centers and reestablished themselves in smaller, growing towns. *Sufi* activities were widespread throughout Egypt during this period, an indication that public life was quite active and towns were thriving.[17]

One feature of mercantilism is "the transfer of control of economic activity from the local community to the state."[18] To control external trade the pasha needed to control internal trade as well, which he did by building infrastructure, including the digging of canals to transport goods from their point of production to overseas ports. Thus, the city of Alexandria grew from what was described by the French expedition in 1798 as no more than "a little village and a nest of pirates, inhabited by barely eight thousand men,"[19] into an important commercial center. This picture is, of course, based on the condition of Alexandria after it was invaded and destroyed by Napoleon's armies. Earlier the city was an active prosperous center of trade as evidenced by *shari'a* court records. As an imperial port, Alexandria was an active center of commerce with Europe and the Ottoman lands. Control over Alexandria differed at different times. Although trade was generally left free, ships and goods leaving from the port to any other port, at times all ships leaving Alexandria were required to head directly to Istanbul,[20] a practice that probably contributed to the weakness of the port while other ports, for example, Dumyat and Rashid, continued to thrive throughout the Ottoman period.

Muhammad 'Ali Pasha sought to reestablish Alexandria as the imperial port it had been under the Ottomans when trade with the Western Mediterranean was carried out and the representatives of European nations and important mercantile companies resided and did business there. He had the existing port enlarged and built a new one to accommodate large military and commercial vessels.[21] As Alexandria grew in importance, Dumyat, another imperial port, began to lose its position as an important trade center. The main reason for this decline was that its port could not accommodate the larger and deeper commercial vessels that were being built to carry increasing quantities of goods during a period of incredible commercial growth. The people of Dumyat complained of the lack of interest in their port and asked the government in Cairo to undertake such a project, but Alexandria became the favorite residence of foreigners in Egypt and the country's commercial center as well. Cairo had its own port, Bulaq, which was important for internal trade and for the transportation of goods to the north. The pasha enlarged and rebuilt Bulaq, adding a new stone wharf constructed to meet the requirements of new steam navigation.[22] The importance of Alexandria and Bulaq reflected "a shift in emphasis from south to north . . . [resulting from] the change in the Red Sea route."[23] An important repercussion of this new emphasis toward a south to north trade was the exclusion of important manufacturing and trade towns in Upper Egypt, for example, Qus, from the trade. Ultimately, it meant "Upper Egypt was to become more and more isolated from the rest of the country."[24]

Muhammad 'Ali's activities included building a modern army and navy, opening schools, providing services to the population, increasing agricultural production, constructing dams, digging canals, and building factories. These efforts required vast amounts of money, and he directed the country's resources toward financing these plans. He extracted wealth from the same sources that the earlier *khassa* had manipulated—revenue arising from land, whether agricultural production or taxes, and a monopoly on both internal and international trade. To achieve this end, land tenure, taxation, production, and distribution all had to be directed that way.

It should be pointed out that the pasha did not act according to a predetermined plan; rather, Egypt's circumstances dictated many of the policies that he instituted. In 1820, the Ottoman sultan ordered that customs duties should not exceed 3 percent.[25] Low duties favored foreign merchants; because the European consuls in the Ottoman Empire were themselves merchants, they used their influence to bring about favorable trading conditions. In this situation, creating monopolies seemed the only answer to Egypt's predicament of having no control over its customs duties and no protection from European competition. By controlling both production and trade through monopolies, the government provided de facto protection to its industries and native manufacturers.

At first the pasha focused on existing workshops, providing them with raw materials and monopolizing their products. The wish to have a favorable balance of trade and conservation of bullion, however, directed him to enter the manufacturing process. Besides, the pasha was pressured by foreign merchants to buy industrial machinery, and these merchants must have played an important role in convincing him to industrialize. According to Patrick Campbell's 1840 report to the British government, foreign merchants convinced the pasha to buy machinery and to build factories despite the high price of equipment, potential losses, and the fact that importing the same goods could have been much less costly. Campbell blames the European consuls in particular because they were involved with trade and transacted to bring the pasha industrial machines.[26] Foreign *tujjar* in Egypt did not embody one cohesive group; rather, they represented the capitalist and vested interests of different countries.[27] Whereas some merchants may have wished to sell industrial equipment, other merchants were interested in buying cash crops. When the pasha began his industrial programs, Egypt logically represented an excellent market for industrial hardware, but with the expansion of Europe's own industrialization in the 1840s, interest shifted to buying cash crops and exporting finished goods. Thus, the foreign *tujjar* included those who would have supported the pasha's monopolies at first but later worked to undermine him. There is no reason to suppose that that was always the case or that Muhammad 'Ali had a blueprint of industrialization all ready to be executed.

Because cotton was in great demand as a result of the industrial revolution in Britain, a *tajir* such as the pasha typically would be interested in the textile industry, particularly because Egypt had been a great exporter of textiles before it became less competitive with Europe's cheaper and higher-quality machines.[28] By 1828 thirty cotton-spinning and weaving mills had been built in Egypt. Woolen and linen factories were also established. Other industries were developed, including sugar refineries, "glass, paper, tanneries, sulfuric acid and other chemicals." Important industries included weapons manufacturing in an Alexandria arsenal and shipbuilding for the navy and the merchant marine.[29]

It cannot be mere coincidence that the 1820 orders mentioned above were executed just before rural revolts hit Egyptian provinces. The reasons generally given for these revolts include Muhammad 'Ali's coercive measures, the arbitrariness of his bureaucracy in extracting taxes and cash crops, corvée labor required from the male population, and monopolies over agricultural trade that denied the peasantry sufficient food. In his important study of rural revolts that took place in the vicinity of Qina in Upper Egypt in 1820–24, Fred Lawson shows that much deeper reasons existed for these revolts. Distinguishing between peasant outbursts that served as mere expressions of anger and the more organized uprisings of the 1820s, Lawson shows that the latter were "neither directionless jacqueries nor examples of 'archaic' or 'prepolitical' social protest movements."[30] Rather, they constituted "violent political movements by local artisans and pieceworkers in the province's cloth industry."[31] These outbursts were motivated by social and economic dislocations resulting from the destruction of Qina's cloth industry by competition with European machine-produced textiles that "left Sa'idi cottage cloth workers in a desperate economic situation." At the same time, "agricultural production in the province was disrupted by drastic changes in the structure and composition of Egypt's foreign trade."[32] Craftsmen clearly suffered because of the industries that the pasha built, but the trade monopolies could be seen as a form of protection for local industries in general necessitated by "liberal" Ottoman trade policies meant to benefit foreign *tujjar*. Later in the century, with the destruction of the monopolies and the "stability" of a market economy, the foreign *tujjar*'s dominance hurt the local artisans as a viable market-economy competitor. Moreover, during the first half of the century, a number of privately financed modern plants emerged, and Egypt once more began exporting textiles to its neighbors.[33]

In addition to trade monopolies, various methods were used to finance the emerging industries. These methods included a wide array of taxes, such as levies paid in advance on agriculture, arbitrary impositions, and compulsory loans. Fiscal policy provided another means of attaining such income and of controlling economic activity. Muhammad 'Ali's fiscal policy was quite mercantilistic. Bullion was all "the more necessary in that Egypt was not acquainted with other methods of payment, which could reduce the use of coins, such as paper money whose velocity of circulation is higher than that of coins. [Muhammad 'Ali] therefore attempted to retain precious metals in Egypt by prohibiting their exportation."[34] All governments followed fiscal policies that fit with their own forms of mercantilism, thus ensuring that the particular *khassa* combines controlled the nation's wealth. For the pasha this meant a very strict monetary policy designed to guarantee that his government handled all gold and silver. When the treasury needed French currency in 1812, they forced merchants to provide it and to accept Egyptian piasters in its place. In another case the government imprisoned Jews who supplied bullion to the treasury because they had sold specie to the public because of the great demand. Furthermore, port agents searched travelers leaving the country on pilgrimage or for other reasons; the foreign currency they carried was confiscated and exchanged for Egyptian piasters. To ensure compliance with this government policy, the state used spies to mingle among the people and discover those who withheld foreign coins. People caught were punished and forced to surrender whatever foreign currency or bullion they had with them.[35] The state forbade anyone to leave the country without first receiving the government's permission, reducing travel outside of Egypt to the prerogative of only a few.[36]

Fiscal policy also involved setting maximum prices for goods to reduce inflation, thereby preventing the government from having to increase salaries or prices for Egyptian products. The government fixed prices for necessary items, including meat, lard, cheese, and candles. Those who broke the tas'ira, or government-fixed price, faced corporal punishment. As occurred after the pasha's reign later in the nineteenth century, price-fixing caused producers to hold back their goods from the market and to sell them informally, an act declared illegal by Egypt's governments. Prices rose so high in the informal market that such commodities became quite unaffordable for the majority of the population. During Muhammad 'Ali's time, as under later governments, export items became untouchable and even the peasants who produced them could not afford to consume any.[37]

The profits from the trade monopoly and the control of agricultural production and distribution provided the most important sources of revenue for the pasha. These controls allowed the government to buy products at low fixed prices and to sell them for maximum profit. Such methods led the people to complain to the 'ulama' of the Azhar "of stagnation, the reduction of the means of living, the desolation of villages, and the impoverishment of their inhabitants."[38] Although contemporaneous descriptions of the people's low standard of living and misery under the rule of the pasha may be exaggerated, it should be remembered that such exactions and indirect taxes were not new methods and had been resorted to previously by mamluks and multazims. Furthermore, local prices adjusted to international prices during the nineteenth century, largely as a result of the revolution in transportation and the growth of international trade. Local prices that had been protected from outside inflation were catching up with international ones, and food prices rose because the government increased exports of Egyptian grain to benefit from the greater profits available on the world market.[39]

The government became the arbiter of the crops that farmers planted, usually choosing those demanded by foreign nations, including cotton (Jummel type), rice, sugarcane, and poppies. The government found ways to assure the compliance of peasants who refused government orders about what crop to plant. For example, in one case when the peasants refused to plant the same crop for a second year, the government simply doubled the area to be planted with that crop. When the peasants found that they could not succeed in defying the government, they were only too happy to return to the previous year's conditions. In addition, the government specified the amount of crop to be delivered for each acre planted.[40]

The peasant could not sell his produce wherever he desired but was instructed to deliver it to government agents at specified points. The government fixed the price, and the producer had no control over it. Furthermore, because the government lacked money, it did not pay the peasant directly but first deducted the cost of the seeds loaned to him at time of planting and the taxes owed on the land. The remainder was paid in the form of certificates, not in cash; to receive cash, the peasant had to sell the certificate at a discount. Altogether, the pasha received most of the peasant's production. While the pasha received money for food crops exported to foreign shores, Egypt's people often had no food or had to pay inflated prices because of the shortages commonly caused by exports. As al-Jabarti lamented, the country became filled with poor people and beggars as never before.

> The pasha ordered all registrars of Upper Egypt to hold back the grain and allow no one to sell or buy any of it. . . . They asked for all grain belonging to the people, even that which is stored in their homes for food, and they took that too. They stretched this to the point of raiding the houses and taking whatever grain they found, not paying for it, but saying that they would discount its price from the next year's tax. They then loaded the pasha's boats with it . . . and transported it north where it is carried to the boats of foreigners.[41]

In the 1830s, however, the peasants' condition brought about a change in policy, and the government stopped exporting the most vital crops, such as maize and beans.

How could such a system continue? "Most foreign observers agreed that the agricultural population could not have been persuaded to undertake all this extra labor without coercion, and this must have been generally true."[42] Coercion, however, is too simple an explanation. Overuse of coercion brought about the flight of the peasantry, which was counterproductive to the government's purposes. The answer lies in the new land-tenure system and in the peasants' attitude toward the pasha. At the beginning of his reforms, the peasantry actually rejoiced at the pasha's actions, seeing an end to their previous exploiters. The peasantry scorned the *multazims* who had ruled over them, and they were proud to describe the land they cultivated as being the pasha's land.[43] This attitude was reversed by the end of the pasha's life; class antagonism at the beginning of his reign, however, helped establish state control.

The new land-tenure system also created a new class of owners and controllers indigenous to the areas where they lived and worked. This new patronage system, which involved both government employees and nongovernment groups, extended into the rural population, creating its own hierarchical network of alliances whose interests were tied to agricultural production. The new system recalled the alliance structures that had supported the *multazims* before. As explained in the background section, the land-tenure system that existed in Egypt before Muhammad 'Ali was *iltizam*. The Ottoman Empire as a whole had begun to abolish *iltizam* at the beginning of the nineteenth century, so the sultan did not stand against the pasha's actions. By 1814 the pasha had abolished the *iltizam* system and compensated the previous *multazims* with pensions for life. This action was received with anger and rioting, particularly among holders of smaller units of land who became destitute without it. "The people were distressed. . . . [They] met with the *mashayikh* . . . who wrote Katkhuda Bey . . . [protesting] . . . 'How can you deny people their livelihood when there are widows and elderly, each owning one *qirat* or half *qirat*.'"[44]

After the cancellation of *iltizams*, the government through a new class of agents surveyed the land, assessed its size and value, taxed it, depending on its quality, and evaluated which crops best suited it.[45] The land was then "divided into plots varying from 3 to 150 feddans and distributed . . . among the *fallahin* for cultivation."[46] Local sheikhs and dignitaries were granted between 4 and 5 percent of the land to use tax-free in return for distributing the land among the peasants, for representing the government in the localities, and for extending hospitality to travelers and government officials. Thus, the *'umad* and sheikhs became the nucleus of native landownership in the country, gained in power and prestige, and became the main source of the system's support. The system recognized the peasants as having the right of usufruct, with ownership resting ultimately in the hands of the state. As long as the peasantry paid their taxes and followed the government's orders, they retained control of their land. The *'umda* (village chief), although often a source of abuse and arbitrariness, nevertheless had ties to the peasantry through kinship relationships; ultimately, he remained interested in the good of his district.

The new land-tenure system also brought about landownership in various ways. The pasha's policy sought to achieve the greatest productive capacity for the land at the least expense. One way of achieving this was by giving large plots of land that lay fallow to people with capital to invest in making the land productive, arrangements which became the basis for future landownership. The government also allocated plots of land to *'umdas* who were expected to use its income to pay the extra expenses of tax collectors, government accountants, and guards, who routinely checked on crops and collected what was owed to the government. This served as another way to reduce expenses. This land became the property of the people to whom it was assigned.

Ultimately, therefore, the pasha's mercantilist system created its own protégés, beginning with the village *'umda* and including all of the state's functionaries who dealt with the public and who managed by virtue of their roles to exact certain payments from the peasantry. This new body of functionaries replaced the *multazim*s holding similar functions in the larger picture as *multazim*s had before them. As controllers of the land they facilitated the extraction of wealth in the name of the state, claiming a share—a form of *fa'iz*—by virtue of the role they played. "The [peasants] are humiliated and treated arbitrarily by their chiefs, witnesses, and [the] Christian accountant who acts like a *'umda* when it comes to collecting taxes. He wrongs them and denies [what they paid]. . . . He has whomever he wishes imprisoned, or beaten, demanding complete payment . . . then refuses to give a [receipt] closing the account until he has received some payment, a gift, or a bribe." [47]

The pasha also attempted to maximize production by launching massive irrigation works, including the building of dams, the most important being the Nile Barrage at Qanatir al-Khayriyya outside Cairo, which allowed for perennial irrigation, thereby increasing crop levels appreciably. Canals were dug to increase land reclamation and to expand crop production in distant areas. The banks of the Nile were fortified and raised so that the Nile flood would not devastate the areas around it; as a whole, irrigation and drainage were improved. The peasant population must have welcomed the revival and extension of irrigation. Providing corvée labor for such purposes was not new to the peasantry and could not have been viewed as an evil because they benefited from it. The same, however, could not be said for corvée labor for massive projects outside the peasant's own district; against these projects there was peasant opposition, massive desertions, and the heavy use of force. It is estimated that at one point while the Nile Barrage was being built 775 men deserted their work, leaving their instruments behind, and that a few nights later another 500 men deserted.

Historians have documented the use of the *kurbaj* (whip) as a form of coercion. The whip, however, was not used on the peasantry alone but on urbanites and government bureaucrats as well. Al-Mu'alim Ghali's punishment in 1816 for withholding taxes that he had collected for the government illustrates how such coercion worked. [48] Significantly, when al-Mu'alim Ghali was first put in prison, a number of his fellow Christian competitors actually came to the Katkhuda Bey to testify against him. Their reward was to take over his position as tax collector. [49] Thus, intergroup struggle may have allowed such arbitrary action. Furthermore, actions taken against important personages were often not the pasha's prerogative. A great deal of competition existed between the various groups making up the *khassa* as well as within each group, and often the group itself demanded the ouster of one of its members. Al-Mu'alim Ghali represented one of many such cases. Al-Jabarti says that had it not been for the pasha's absence, nothing would have happened to the *mu'alim* (master of a trade). Another case is that of Sheikh al-Dawakhli; the other sheikhs petitioned Muhammad 'Ali to have him replaced as Naqib al-Ashraf (head of the Ashraf descendants of the Prophet Muhammad) by Sheikh al-Bakri, a friend of the pasha's consultant in matters of trade and the Hijaz, al-Sayyid al-Mahruqi.[50]

When *iltizam*s were canceled and *multazim*s were receiving compensation through government pensions, the pasha saw nothing wrong in acknowledging inheritance rights for the servants of mamluk *multazim*s. This phenomenon served to recognize the patronage system that was part of *iltizam*. Patronage connections were one basis of the state's power under the pasha's rule. Members of his family and other state dignitaries wielded much authority that conflicted with the pasha's own interests. For example, his son Ibrahim Pasha created a commercial monopoly over the distribution of Upper Egypt's sugar. By making himself a major supplier of sugar, he forced buyers to pay a premium to purchase it.[51]

The pasha's style in ruling Egypt suited his mercantilist practices well. On one hand, he was quite authoritarian, ruling strictly, watching every little detail, and supervising the execution of his orders. On the other hand, he realized he could not rule alone, but needed personnel and advisors to assist him. Muhammad 'Ali was open to suggestions and was willing to try different methods to solve problems. The pasha used a governing elite consisting largely of Ottomans, Albanians, and Armenians with whom he felt comfortable to rule; most of them had arrived with him or come to Egypt to enter his service. Muhammad 'Ali chose this course because he did not speak Arabic and did not think particularly highly of Egyptians. In fact he was altogether illiterate until the age of forty.[52] The new governing class numbered ten thousand, about the same as the *khassa* they replaced.[53] Like their predecessors, they were culturally alien and lived a life of luxury, consciously separating themselves from those around them. This new foreign governing elite mixed least with other groups and a number of features distinguished them from the rest of the population. They continued to adhere to the Hanafi legal code, and they were nearly the exclusive owners of white male slaves (mamluks). Like their predecessors also, they were rarely seen except at Cairo where they occupied governmental and military positions.[54]

With the ascendance of this new elite to dominate the *khassa*, the cultural makeup of the *khassa* undergoes a transformation with deep impact on Egyptian society as a whole. It is true that mamluks had earlier constituted a foreign elite who usually chose wives from within their own castes, often importing them from the Caucasus and other places for that purpose. But mamluks adhered to the Shaf'i *madhhab* to which belonged the majority of the people of Lower Egypt. And although mamluks may have originated from outside of Egypt, Egypt constituted the only country they had allegiance to, unlike the new elite arrivals whose affiliations and loyalty continued to be in Turkey, Albania, Syria, or Armenia. Whereas the children of mamluks became undifferentiated from Egyptians in general as did the children of most members of the Ottoman Ojaks who remained in Egypt, the new elite continued to have close connections with their Ottoman homes and looked down upon the Egyptians among whom they lived and worked. In other words, the Muhammad 'Ali period ushers in a rate of Ottomanization not experienced before. Ottomanization involved mainly the elite but was soon to spread to other levels of society and culture and law in the form of Hanafism.

The *Qanuname of Egypt* issued in 1528 by the Ottoman Sultan Selim I, who invaded Egypt in 1516, gives a good idea of the shape and rules according to which Egyptians lived at the beginning of Ottoman rule. Immediately after the 1916 invasion, the sultan assigned a *wali* (governor) for Egypt, Khayyir Bey, who remained more than five years at his post, organizing and establishing Ottoman authority. When Khayyir Bey died, he was replaced by Joban Mustafa Pasha, who found himself facing a revolt of the *kashifs* (supervisors, inspectors, provincial governors), contingencies of the Ottoman forces, mamluk *amirs* (those with authority to rule, leaders, princes), Arab tribesmen, and the population at large. As a way of quieting down the revolt, Joban Mustafa negotiated with the mamluks and Arab tribal chiefs, making them allies of Ottoman authority in Egypt. In an effort to stop future revolts, he declared his intent to reduce taxes and to leave Egyptian laws and customs as they were. He then fired the mutinous *kashifs* and went to war against them and the Ottoman military contingents that supported them. Because Joban Mustafa's declarations to the Egyptian people were not followed up by *walis* after him, revolts against Ottoman occupation continued and did not stop until Ibrahim Pasha, chief minister of Sultan Sulaiman *Qanunji* (law-giver) traveled to Egypt to look personally into the revolts. After investigating matters, he concluded that the continuous revolts were caused by the Egyptians' rejection of alien laws and heavy taxes and that the revolts aimed to reestablish Egyptian customary law. So the laws in place since the mamluk Prince Qaitbay were recognized in Egypt. The *Qanuname of Egypt* makes that clear: "Let the '*ada* [usual practice] and law that were *sa'idin* [dominant] at the time of Qait-bey in regards to *kushufiya* [financial supervision] fees, be respected and put in force, and they should not be superseded to begin with." [55]

So the continuities were in practice from the pre-Ottoman into the Ottoman period. The Hanafi *madhhab* that became dominant in other parts of the empire was never enforced in Egypt but became the *madhhab* of Ottoman citizens moving to Egypt from other parts of the empire. While Qadi al-Qudat was always a Maliki, the Sheikh al-Azhar was almost always a Shaf'i with a few exceptions of the choice of Maliki by the sheikhs as their recognized head. Hanafi practices began to grow in usage in certain towns and among certain classes that found it particularly advantageous owing to the *madhhab*'s "friendly" attitude toward capitalism and administrative authority. For example, the town of Dumyat, which was experiencing a remarked commercial growth under Ottoman rule, began to shift slowly in practices from a strict adherence to Shaf'ism toward Hanafism. By the end of the seventeenth century almost half of all registers in court records were undertaken according to the Hanafi *madhhab*. Interestingly, during this period of transition wealthier families would resort to celebrating marriage in front of both the Shaf'i and Hanafi Muftis of the port, showing the continued importance of the Shaf'i tradition even while the Hanafi *madhhab* gained in importance. Other towns, such as Alexandria, did not experience any change in the *madhhab*s being applied during the Ottoman period. In Alexandria the Maliki code continued to predominate followed by the Shaf'i. These different trends were probably the result of the movement of population within and from outside of Egypt. Whereas Dumyat, located to the East, was a trade center for the eastern Mediterranean and experienced a constant movement of people from Syria, Anatolia, and other parts of the Ottoman Empire, Alexandria was a center where North Africans traded and lived. Internally, migration from Southern Egypt, where the Maliki *madhhab* predominated, was part of Alexandria's history; Dumyat attracted Delta migrants more.

Muhammad 'Ali did not change the legal system to any great extent except to create the administrative and legal structures that would allow the state to handle its more independent international and internal role. Thus, the way in which court records were kept did not change much. They continued to be based on Qadi courts on a first-come first-serve basis. It was later in the century that courts were regularized and record keeping systematized. The changes introduced by the pasha included organizing councils to help administer the country, establishing Majalis Ahkam to homogenize laws in various parts of Egypt (a greater application of the Hanafi code) and state centralization as a basic policy. There was also a marked differential treatment for foreigners, which was to be expected given the greater international independence of Egypt, Muhammad ʿAli's ultimate interests as a *tajir*, and increased European pressure and interest in Egyptian affairs exemplified by the Napoleonic expedition.

To help administer the country a variety of committees were organized according to specialization. A council or government branch was set up whenever there was need for one. Thus, in 1837 a new *diwan* (council) similar in function to a ministry of the interior was given the function of setting "basic orders . . . executive actions . . . and a penal code." [56] This represented part of the government's need to ensure compliance with its laws. These *diwan*s reflect very well the needs of a mercantilist state. Headed by a chief *majlis al-aʿla* set up in 1824 intended to bring together representatives of the various productive forces in the country, the executors of the pasha's laws, and the leaders of the people who have leverage over them.[57] Thus, the *diwan*, which consisted of 157 people, according to one count,[58] included members of the clergy, representatives of the country's merchants elected by the *shahbandar al-tujjar*, delegates from the provinces, dignitaries, and accountants and personnel.[59] There was also the *diwan al-iradat* (treasury), whose personnel acted as inspectors responsible for collecting all revenue owed to the pasha. The *diwan al-jihadiyya* bore responsibility for the pasha's new army. A mercantilist state required an aggressive international policy and a strong army to assure access to markets and security of trade routes.

The *diwan al-madaris* was intended to educate Egypt's young men so that they would be capable of running a modern state infrastructure. Beginning in 1926, when forty-five young men were sent to France, the *diwan* sent exceptional young men to Europe where they finished their education and returned as teachers to educate others. The *majlis al-sihha* fulfilled two purposes: first, it provided Egypt with the medical infrastructure that Egypt's *khassa* traditionally sponsored through *awqaf*. Second, it could combat epidemics that periodically devastated the population. Controlling epidemics also assured the smooth operation of Egypt's ports, and, hence, of the transportation of goods into and out of the country. The growth of sea transport was also accompanied by greater fears of the spread of disease. For this reason, the international community took steps to ensure that ships would be warned away from epidemic areas. Consequently, the pasha needed to give Egypt the medical force and facilities to combat such epidemics.[60]

The *diwan al-fabriqat* resembled a ministry of industry. It built new industries intended to make Egypt self-sufficient and to end its dependence on European manufactured goods. Future national governments always set up such a body, and its responsibility remained to create import-substitution industries. The *diwan al-bahr* bore responsibility for building a merchant marine and for transportation and storage of goods. Along with the *diwan al-afranj wa'l-tijara,* the *diwan al-bahr* was central to mercantilism. The need to give specific responsibility to a council reflects the importance of sea transport, and the question of treatment of foreigners and dealing with foreign countries tied in with the importance of trade. It is almost as though Egypt's foreign relations depended primarily on the smoothness of international trade. The pasha and his successors were very sensitive to foreigners' needs in Egypt. In fact, foreigners received privileged status and preferential treatment from Egyptian authorities. The same applies today, proving the importance of foreign relations and, hence, trade. What is known as *'uqdat al-khawaja* (complex of foreigners) is partially based on preferential treatment given to foreigners.

One means of studying this preferential treatment and its long-term impact is through the dual legal system that resulted. For foreigners, the legal system and the execution of laws applied to them by the pasha reflected the power of the states that supported them and their importance as *tujjar* in the international *khassa* alliance and the mercantilist system. The pasha honored capitulatory rights, granted by the Ottoman sultan, and foreign nationals were tried in front of their own courts. These rights provided the basis for consular courts in which the defendant's court handled a suit by someone of a different nationality. The pasha often oversaw disputes involving a foreigner and an Egyptian so as not to anger foreign powers. A multinational committee of judges judged conflicts between different nationalities, the forerunner of the later mixed courts that constituted recognition of foreigners' dominant role in Egypt.[61] Local courts handled only cases in which the defendant was an Egyptian.

The French remained in Egypt only three years (1798–1801), yet the impact of their invasion continues to be a point of great controversy. Perhaps it is in the area of law and after the departure of the French that one sees their greater impact in the shape of application of French codes into the Egyptian legal system. Thus, the pasha followed Napoleon's steps regarding commercial disputes, creating a voluntary commercial court in Cairo in 1826 to handle business disputes among nationals and between nationals and foreigners.[62] The court's members were chosen from among various nationalities. According to Palmerston, "two were Turks, three Egyptians, two Moroccans, two Greek Levantines, two Greek Orthodox, two Armenians and two Jews."[63] Consulate activities in Egypt and their interference in Egyptian affairs increased along with economic relations between Egypt and Europe. Because many European consuls also acted as merchants, it was natural that the relations between their countries and Egypt were linked to trade. As the pasha's monopolies over trade grew, it became more difficult for these men to profit from their positions, a situation that had dire consequences for Egypt.

Muhammad 'Ali also extended security by ending the constant disputes between mamluk factions and by controlling the marauding Bedouins who preyed on travelers.

Religious policy also helped the pasha's mercantilist aims. Ensuring cordial relations with foreign countries included allowing the ringing of church bells and the holding of public mass by heads of Christian denominations, both of which had been previously unknown in Egypt. These feats gave his rule legitimacy and gained for it the consensus of both the local population and foreigners. Security helped the internal productive processes as well as the movement of goods and trade. It also meant that foreigners could safely come to Egypt, and large numbers of them arrived, some as representatives of European governments, others to trade. Often, they combined both purposes. Still others came to invest their capital for profit or to find employment as army officers, industrial engineers, or teachers. It is estimated that nearly five thousand foreigners, mostly Europeans and Levantines, resided in Egypt in 1837.[64]

Furthermore, the pasha required his personnel to give respect and assistance to foreigners to provide them with comfort and security.[65] An interesting story illustrates the care taken with foreigners and their property: "A man was humiliated and made to ride a donkey backwards, clutching his tail . . . with his eyes covered . . . after [they] shaved half his beard and mustaches . . . [because] he forged a deed which concerned the property of a foreign woman and sold some of this property while she was traveling.[66]

Political patronage enjoyed by foreign merchants and dignitaries was evident in the lax controls on export of precious pharaonic artifacts.[67] Even when the pasha responded to pressure to put a stop to such practices and issued orders to that effect, such regulations were badly enforced and smuggling was unofficially sanctioned.[68]

The outlook toward law serves as one way to understand the relationship between state and society in general. To see the connection one must go beyond the outward manifestations of power to discuss the culture and society's view of the ruler's role and the laws he follows. For example, a despotic ruler would be expected to establish new laws suited to his particular needs without respect for already established traditions. This was scarcely the situation in Muhammad 'Ali's case; rather than instituting brand-new laws, he established laws based on established traditions but took necessary changes into consideration. The *qanum al-siyasatname* (legal code) promulgated by Muhammad 'Ali Pasha in 1837 to organize the local government and the different *diwans* of the bureaucracy illustrate this policy. The law created structures through which the country's affairs could be organized: "Each nation of Europe has a set of laws that is suitable to its nature. Since it is clear that the law of one kingdom would not suit another kingdom, it was of course impossible that the law of one could be taken in its entirety *(nasuh wa fasuh)* to suit this country."[69] Thus, there was an awareness that new laws could be workable only to a limited extent; new laws would be tried and the suitable statutes accepted. Preference was for familiar laws, laws familiar to *khassa* and maleable to their hegemony, which was to be the Hanafi code and later Western codes to be practiced in native courts.

So with an administrative and commercial elite, state building, and centralization, Hanafization of Egypt's courts and laws accompanied the Ottomanization of Egypt's bureaucracy and *khassa*. State centralization was extended to law in the form of institutions such as the *majlis al-ahkam* (legal council), which began to homogenize laws and mold them in accordance to the Hanafi school of law wherever a particular situation was brought to its attention. Because Egyptian courts applied various schools of *fiqh* (Muslim jurisprudence) and people had the liberty of going in front of the *qadi (shari'a* court judge) of the school of their choice, this new Ottoman-led *khassa* begins the Ottomanization of the legal system. This may appear contradictory because Muhammad 'Ali did his best to break out of Ottoman authority, but Ottomanization of the *khassa* and the laws of the state did not mean submission to the will of the Ottoman sultan.

Furthermore, it is true that mamluks were of Circassian and Turkish origins, but Turkish and Ottoman are two different things. Mamluks were brought in from Asia; their culture was that of the tribes from which they originated; they were brought up in mamluk households in Egypt and were not molded as Ottomans as were the janissaries brought in from Eastern Europe during the heyday of the empire and molded into servants of the Ottoman sultans. The Ottoman hierarchy in Egypt was represented by a pasha who mostly remained in Cairo Citadel and usually stayed for one year. His main job was as representative of the sultan and to make sure that taxes were collected and sent to Istanbul. The pasha was assisted by janissary and Ojak corps, and these soon became integrated with the people of Egypt, forming part of the *khassa/amma* alliances that would be the prerogative of the police in the modern state. As for legal hierarchy, as the recent study by 'Abdal-Raziq 'Abdal-Raziq has shown, except for the chief *qadi* and the *qadi askar* who handled the affairs of Ottomans in Egypt, the legal hierarchy was formed of Egyptians at every level. It should also be mentioned that although the Ottomans followed the Hanafi code, the mamluks were Shaf'i as were the Ayyubids before them. Hanafization of the legal system, perhaps the most important part of the Ottomanization of Egypt, actually begins in the nineteenth century with Muhammad 'Ali and grows as the *shari'a* law of the modern state during the latter part of the century when homogenization, standardization, and categorization of law took place as part of modern legal reforms.

Ottomanization took place in other ways. Muhammad 'Ali brought troops with him and soon attracted hundreds of Ottoman citizens who entered his bureaucratic hierarchy. He provided employment for those familiar with the Ottoman system, including Armenians, Greeks, Syrians, Bosnians, and other Eastern Europeans, who looked for employment opportunities. The nineteenth century included great commercial activities and the movement of populations globally. The Mediterranean had become more active than ever with the facilities provided by steam engine transportation and the needs of the industrial revolution and the commercial and financial revolutions soon to follow it. Those who came to work for the pasha helped him construct an outlook toward state rule that reflected Ottoman structures. This would, however, take place under international pressures caused by the movement of goods and peoples, the centralization of national and monarchical governments heading nation-states and interested in controlling people within and without their territories. One of the main sources of power of states is its control over its peoples, and that was to be achieved through nationality and citizenship laws that Europe sought to internationalize and enforce globally so as to protect and, hence, control citizens anywhere they might be. It suffices to say here (see chaps. 3 and 4) that the process began under Muhammad 'Ali, and this process meant heavy Ottomanization as legal codes were formulated and enforced by state power from above rather than organically linked to people from the base.

Harsh treatment of offenders by the pasha should not be judged against modern secular laws. Whereas the latter are designed to ensure individual rights (e.g., an individual is innocent until proven guilty), customary law, 'urf, is designed to safeguard communal welfare. The primary concern of modern secular law is to punish a proven offender, and customary law is intended to prevent the offense and thereby safeguard the welfare of the community at large. As one nineteenth-century British lawyer working in Egypt observed of a sheikh's reaction to the civil courts created after the British occupation in 1882: "The Sheikh was more impressed with the number of wrongdoers that would escape punishment than with the occasional, or even frequent conviction, of the wrong man."[70] In this he was only partly correct. Whereas the legal system, with its intricate system of evidence and witnessing, ensured that an offender was first found to be guilty, the punishment itself was usually quite harsh and was intended to prevent similar crimes from taking place.

Not every dispute was taken to *shari'a* court. Until the mid–nineteenth century, guilds took care of their own problems. Each guild's sheikh had the authority to punish those who broke its rules. The head of all the sheikhs of any particular trade could approach the pasha to discuss serious complaints of the guild or guilds he represented. The government also recognized the sheikh's position, often requiring payment of a sum of money in return for his position as *sheikh al-shuyukh*.[71]

The various quarters, *haras,* of towns and the villages generally had their own sheikhs or chosen elders who arbitrated disputes.

> Formally the organization of the quarter was expressed in its officials, provisions for collective responsibility and defense. The *shaykh al-hara,* who derived his authority more from local prestige than governmental appointment, had broad powers. Frequently he seemed to have held a responsible position in a professional corporation or religious order as well, enforcing his rule with multiple sanctions. As an intermediary between the groups of neighbors and the government, he maintained order, settled disputes, and expelled those who disturbed the neighborhood.[72]

As in the eighteenth century, the parties did not always take their disputes to the *qadi* when the problems occurred in the marketplace or between *haras* (town quarter, narrow alley). Often the quarter had its *futuwwat* (vigilantes, thugs) force that took care of the inter-*hara* battles and disputes. In fact, the strength of such "gangs" provided security for the inhabitants of these quarters or villages. Various *haras* were famous for their *futuwwat,* but in Cairo the most famous became that of Husayniyya, established during the mamlukid period. In this case, the butchers, formed into three different corporations with a membership of nearly 2,200, were all-important.[73] Like other professional quarters, the Husayniyya had its own *sufi* order, the Bayumiyya, and participated in its own feasts and rituals. *Haras* continued to be sensitive spots for Egypt's governments into the 1950s. It was during *mawlids* (religious feasts) of patron saints of these quarters or the countrywide celebration of the Prophet's birthday, *al-mawlid al-nabawi,* that the collective strength of town quarters became most obvious. Their solidarity, often cemented by the *sufi* orders, often used those occasions to voice their discontent to the ruling elite. Even after 1952, the government continued to use sheikhs of *haras* to call young men to the draft, to take the census, and to act as government appointees in the quarter.

Muhammad 'Ali Pasha's rule cannot be seen as oriental despotism. The pasha clearly wielded great power and held final authority, but he did not do so by virtue of his own person alone. Rather, he was enabled by the shape and structure of the system and the consensus it received, which were ultimately based on the diffusion of power and on cultural continuity. Continuing the patronage system, honoring local *'urf,* and respecting the role played by traditional institutions such as guilds, *haras,* village leaders, and sufi orders allowed for an acceptance among the masses. This does not mean that Muhammad 'Ali's rule was either benevolent or mass-oriented: he used coercion, but directed it as much toward those classes with money as toward the poorer *'amma.*

The pasha largely dominated the *khassa* although they still enjoyed a great deal of power and ability to enrich themselves as allies and agents of the state. The *khassa* differed from its earlier counterparts in ways that helped increase the pasha's power. Thus, whereas the Ottoman viceroy generally had been contained by "the previous pattern of an alliance between mamluks, *'ulama'* and *tujjar* . . . [who] exploit[ed] the country's resources to their advantage," [74] Muhammad 'Ali Pasha led the new combination, replacing the mamluks as holder of effective power. The *tujjar* continued their vital role in business transactions. Although the Egyptian element weakened to some extent, the foreign elements gained in power and prestige, particularly toward the end of the pasha's reign. When it came to foreign relations and trade—the realm of the *khassa*—the laws instituted were intended to facilitate trade and to ensure cordial relations with foreign powers, to keep trade alive while ensuring Egypt's own integrity. Thus, the duality that later became a permanent feature of the legal system gained firm roots under Muhammad 'Ali.

*Multazim*s were destroyed as a group but reappeared first in the form of landowners whose function was to ensure the production of cotton and its delivery to *tujjar* to be exported. The other characteristic of *multazim*s was to appear in the form of government functionaries who profited from the government bureaucracy and the positions they held. In much the same way as earlier *multazim*s, the new bureaucrats created their own forms of levies and when in positions of revenue raising, they delivered only part of the revenue they collected, keeping part for themselves. The pasha depended on a new class of local elite to replace the *multazim*s. The new group had been emerging since the eighteenth century; they had acted as functionaries to the *multazim*s but were ready to supplant their absentee masters. The *'ulama'* also became servants of the state and became involved in a fight for survival as an influential group demanding its traditional role. By the end of the century, they had managed to retrieve part of what they had lost under the pasha.

3

IMAGINING DUALITY

THE CONSTRUCTION OF CULTURE

The health services . . . did not give a moment's thought to water purification for the twelve million peasant volunteers who serve this country. At the same time Maslahat al-Tanzim is concerned with watering its trees planted alongside its streets and roads. . . . So we see the trees being irrigated by purified water while the peasants are drinking contaminated not-fit-to-drink water mixed with microbes and germs and the ovum of various diseases.[1]

The French army that invaded Egypt in 1798 remained for three years before being forced out by a combined British and Ottoman force and the uncompromising struggle of Egyptians who attacked the French in spite of the heavy toll in lives and property.[2] The invasion itself accomplished few political or economic advantages for France, but the knowledge contributed by its scholars changed the Western view of the Middle East and was the beginning of Egyptology. Traveling all over Egypt, French scientists recorded what they saw and studied. Flora and fauna were described and drawn in detail as were the lives and customs of contemporaneous Egyptians. Towns, villages, roads, houses, mosques, and marketplaces were illustrated. Scientific and medical knowledge was explored and assessed. Most important for the 151 savants—members of the Commission des Sciences et Arts—was the discovery of pharaonic monuments, some already unearthed while parts of others peeked out of desert sands with the promise of hidden splendors.

The *Descriptions de l'Egypte* was the most important work in which these observations, compositions, and drawings were published, becoming a most sought after work by libraries, collectors of rare books, and historians interested in Egypt, the Middle East, and Napoleon. The first volume of the first edition appeared in 1809 at the direction of Napoleon Bonaparte. Eight more volumes appeared by 1822. The second edition was more ambitious and was published in twenty-six volumes between 1821 and 1829. Another eleven volumes were dedicated to the drawings and maps recorded by the mission.

Interestingly, the first edition, dedicated to Napoleon, began with descriptions of the modern conditions of Egypt, but the second, dedicated to Louis XVIII, began with the focus on Ancient Egypt. While Napoleon's interest had been colonizing the Egypt he invaded, the fascination of Europe later focused on Ancient Egypt, a fascination that would later be titled "Egyptomania" in art, architecture, and museum collections.

For the discipline of history, the *Description,* other writings of the savants recorded in French expedition journals such as *la Décade égyptien,* and the observations of Western travelers who were attracted by the mysteries Egyptomania promised, were dramatic. The impressions, hence judgments, they left were of backwardness and Western distress at finding the "origins of Western culture" covered by the "squalor" of Arab natives living in dwellings that the Western eye contrasted negatively to what was European, familiar, and hence superior. "We searched for the Alexandria of Alexander built by the architect Dinocharàs; we searched for that town where was born, where were formed so many great men, that library where the Ptolomies assembled a depository of human knowledge; we searched finally for that commercial town, its active industrious people. We found only ruins, barbarity, degradation, and poverty all over."[3]

The representations left by savants and travelers alike are valuable for understanding Egyptian society at the turn of the nineteenth century as relayed to Europe through the Western eye. But, historical interest was in Ancient Egypt, moving on to the Greeks to make a leap to medieval Europe, hence the incongruous structure of Western history textbooks, which begin with Ancient Egypt and Mesopotamia, then move to the Greeks and Romans, and, except for a short detour on Islamic expansions, turn East only when Napoleon conquered it. The Egyptian had little to offer to the Western eye that observed. The value of the knowledge preserved of the "modern day" Egyptian, as Edward Lane[4] called them—however sympathetic—was still the image of the outsider looking in who judged but did not become involved and, therefore, could not really comprehend the dynamics of what he observed.

The savants recognized that there were glaring differences between Western aesthetic and cultural appreciation and that of Egyptians. "Egyptians . . . do not at all enjoy our music and find theirs to be enchanting; as for us, we enjoy our own and find the music of Egyptians to be detestable: each believes themselves correct."[5] The French musical expert of Napoleon's savants made this perceptive assessment after studying the various types of music found in Egypt. Rather than appreciation of different tastes and perceptions, negative Western impressions built on limited knowledge gained permanency among orientalists and were implicitly accepted by historians and echoed in Western literature. It also became the image accepted by a modernizing *khassa* by the late nineteenth century. Beginning with a description of the *hamam* (Turkish bath), the savant De Chabrol relates: "Diversions of this type [the Turkish bath] may appear to be very trivial to the European, but it is enough to give an atmosphere of luxury to that unconcerned Egyptian who enjoys himself surrounded by perfumes, tobacco fumes and scented mists. . . . The Egyptian shall remain a slave, miserable, apathetic, lazy, tormented by suspicions without concern for the pitiful situation he is in."[6]

A like description with an added level of racism was recorded by Florence Nightingale as she traveled by boat down the Nile in 1849: "A crowd of Arabs, the busiest and the noisiest people in the world, came immediately on board, frantically gesticulating, kicking, and dancing—an intermediate race, they appeared to me, between the monkey and the man, the ugliest, most slavish countenances."[7]

Similar words were attacked by the French doctor Clot Bey, director of the medical school of Qasr al-'Aini opened in 1827 to educate Egyptian doctors. The words belonged to his critics, those who could not conceptualize modern medical science being taught to Egyptians and who criticized and attacked Clot Bey in an effort to belittle his accomplishment. "They [Western critics of the school] claimed that Arabs had neither the intelligence nor the capabilities of other people."[8] This negative impression also forms the basis for the contemporary image of "Egypt's permanent Egyptianity" painted by Vatikiotis.[9]

After invasion by England in 1882, the same outlook guided the policies of colonial administrators vis-à-vis Egypt and its inhabitants: "To hear the Egyptian talk, you would imagine that his one desire was to improve his mind, to raise himself to the equal of highly-educated Europeans. As a matter of fact, the Egyptian has no mind"[10]—not that Egyptian observers found much to admire about the French conquerors. Although the military power and discipline evidenced by Napoleon's army, which easily defeated the mamluks at the celebrated Battle of the Pyramids, and the scientific experiments undertaken by members of the French mission all caught the fancy, admiration, and curiosity of Egyptian observers, Egyptians found little to admire about French civilization or morals. Thus, the chronicler 'Abd al-Rahman al-Jabarti does not mince words in describing what he considered to be uncivilized habits of the French that Egyptians found to be at best distasteful, including not cleaning after going to the toilet, not bathing, sleeping with any woman, and spitting in the streets.

> They follow this rule: great and small, high and low, male and female are all equal. Sometimes they break this rule according to their whims and inclina-

tions or reasoning. Their women do not veil themselves and have no modesty; they do not care whether they uncover their private parts. Whenever a Frenchman has to perform an act of nature he does so wherever he happens to be, even in full view of people, and he goes away as he is, without washing his private parts after defecation. If he is a man of taste and refinement he wipes himself with whatever he finds, even with a paper with writing on it; otherwise he remains as he is. They have intercourse with any woman who pleases them and vice versa. Sometimes one of their women goes into a barber's shop and invites him to shave her pubic hair. If he wishes he can take his fee in kind."[11]

This was how al-Jabarti saw Frenchmen; his judgment continued to be shared by non-Westernized members of Egyptian society, what is referred to as "traditional" sectors of society. So there were glaring differences in the attitude of these two peoples in regard to each other's habits, and Egyptians were not ready to jump on the French bandwagon no matter how superior the French considered themselves to be.

But the picture presented by orientalists was more than simply discourse. The discourse became a blueprint for the hegemonic ambitions of a *khassa* that came to mirror much of the picture presented by the savants of Napoleon, by the Western travelers, painters, and writers who described the "natives." It also guided historians, who structured histories according to Western chronologies. As the discourse became that of a centralizing state, the discourse was translated into an ideology and forged into a reality. New class divisiveness was to be culturally defined as never before. The *khassa,* now summited by culturally "superior" Westerners and a new monarchy aping Western ones—looking for legitimacy from its Western creators—opened the door for upper and lower classes who accepted the new hegemonic paradigm that combined Ottomanism with modernity. As state plans were put into effect through centralization, schools, military and police training and coercion, legal and court reforms, and new media technology, a dual structure was built that was reflected in class, culture, and the political economy. At one end was a hegemonic state with its *khassa* and supporting *'amma* alliances who embraced modernism and Westernism to varying degrees. Although during the next century Egypt experienced a slow growth toward modernity and the integration of the "periphery" into the needs and structures of a hegemonic "center," the process of change proved to be much more complex as the dialectics of history were being played out. For as center and periphery met, ultimately the culture of the periphery transformed the center. Never starry-eyed with modernity, practical in its application rather than romantic in its positivist ideology, as greater numbers of people moved from village to town, their morals and traditions diffused to and helped form the other.

Numbers and steady influx were in favor of the periphery, as contemporary society illustrates.

For the nineteenth century, however, the orientalist picture that dealt
with the modern and the "traditional" as opposite dichotomies defining class
hegemony was expanded and endorsed. This dichotomous discourse was
shared by the Ottoman elite surrounding the Muhammad 'Ali dynasty, who
distinguished their culture and traditions from those of common Egyptians.
It would later be adopted by an Egyptian nationalist elite who embraced
modernity as hegemonic discourse. *Tanwir* ("enlightenment") became a goal
and an ideology of several generations of statesmen, teachers, lawyers, intellectuals, and artists. The socialist and communist movements adopted *tanwir*
as much as did the capitalists and industrialists whom the socialists attacked.
Believers in *tanwir* looked down on "traditional" Egyptians who "kept the
country behind." *Tanwir* ideology has continued to be a central part of intellectual and state cultural discourses. The Hay'a al-'Amma li'l-Kitab, the official book organization of the Egyptian government, which sponsors and
publishes books by Egyptian writers, has a long-standing series with the title
"Al-Tanwir" that specializes in publishing the writings of great Egyptian
thinkers. All those who have been labeled as great Egyptian thinkers and are
included in this series are fairly much part of the *tanwir* project.[12]

During the nineteenth century a new *khassa* emerged headed by Europeans and Ottomans, both of whom saw themselves as superior. But divisions
also appeared within the Ottoman experience in Egypt. Although most Ottomans were Muslim, Syrian and Armenian Ottomans, mostly Christian,
began to move into the European Francophone circle while the Muslim Ottoman, Turkish or otherwise, moved increasingly toward the local Muslim circle. The process was natural, especially because the European saw his
superiority as historically, culturally, and religiously based. But being Christian
was not enough; only by becoming Westernized was a local Christian to become the equal of Westerners. So it was not only the Muslim who became the
subject of conversion efforts, the Christian Copt became much more so. Tens
of missionary groups set up their churches and schools in Egypt against the
opposition of the Coptic Church, which resented the activities of missionaries
and the facilities they received from the government as a result of foreign pressure. Western missionaries posed a threat to the Coptic Church through missionary schools that taught foreign languages and subjects to both Copts and
Muslims and through free medical services provided by missionary societies.

Fifty years ago the Church Missionary Society decided on a forward movement in Egypt. Half a century before the society had opened work in Egypt
with a view to influencing the Coptic Church, and stimulating Coptic Chris-

tians to bring the light of the Gospel to their Muslim Brethren. For some years this object was pursued but difficulties and discouragement led to its abandonment. Twenty years later, however, namely in 1882, the year of the British occupation of Egypt, C. M. S. work was resumed with a change of method and plan. From that time onwards the policy of the Mission was and continues to be that of direct evangelization.[13]

The Coptic newspapers *Jaridat al-Watan* and *Misr,* which began publication in 1877 and 1895, respectively, relate the pressures facing Egypt's Coptic community. Not only was sectarian strife on the rise given the rhetoric of religious and nationalist leaders such as National Party leaders Mustafa Kamel, who favored strengthening Egypt's relations with the Ottoman sultan after his fallout with Khedive 'Abbas II, Sheikh 'Ali Yusif, publisher of *al-Mu'ayyad,* friend of the khedive, and Sheikh Abdul 'Aziz Jawish, who was no friend and a severe critic of the khedive. After the assassination of Butrus Pasha Ghali because of his role in the tribunal following the Dinshwai affair by Ibrahim al-Wardani, whom the authorities described as a religious fanatic, a general Coptic congress was held in Assiut, March 1910 to study the situation of the Copts. Interestingly, not only was the issue of discrimination brought up, but also guarantees were demanded for Coptic equality including making Sunday a public holiday as Friday was for Muslims, stopping discrimination against Copts in government hiring, and allowing Coptic religion to be taught to Copts in schools.[14] But missionary work as well was central to the congress; the government allowing free access to missionaries to work among Copts was a particular sore point. To counter missionary activities that involved giving beautifully bound Bibles, the church called upon its people not to accept such Bibles and began to give out their own.

Still, conversion helped increase social mobility, as Coptic converts to Protestantism, Catholicism, and Anglicanism found. Education and job opportunities became more available. To be socially mobile under colonial rule, Westernization was a must, and knowledge of a Western language was critical for those who aspired to be part of the *khassa.* It is telling that so few of the tens of thousands of foreigners who came to Egypt, many of whom lived, died, and were buried in Egyptian soil, ever spoke Arabic or spoke it in more than the broken accent of the *khawaja* (foreigner). Lord Cromer, who nearly ruled Egypt from 1882 until 1907, never learned to speak Arabic properly. What would have been the point? All the answers were with the foreign community, and the locals had little to offer. It was the local who had to learn a European language to be modern and become part of the civilized world. And so it went, foreign teachers were to teach in foreign languages in Egyptian schools, and foreign judges sat in courts of law, and foreign languages were to be used by judges, district attorneys, and lawyers applying a multitude of European codes next to Islamic ones.

Like language, education was critical in creating the culture gap that defined Egyptian society for the next century, a gap that appeared insurmountable at one time but is today proving to have been transitional and part of the dialectics of history. But the gap was without doubt intentional, based on a discourse of racial and cultural superiority characteristic of modern hegemonic nation-states. British colonial rule seriously undertook the reform of Egyptian education. By reform was meant a reorientation and reorganization to fit the British concept of education that followed Cromer's liberal view that education was a commodity available only to those who could afford to pay for it.[15] Knowledge of European languages was also a requirement for education; modern sciences after all could only be taught in "civilized" languages. In government schools until the 1920s, only grammar, arithmetic, Arabic, and religion were taught in Arabic, whereas "scientific" subjects such as georgraphy, physics, and chemistry were taught in English.[16] At the beginning of the twentieth century, twenty-one of thirty-three hours of school were taught in English at the secondary school level and the Secondary Education Certificate examination, required for admission to specialized schools and government employment, was partially in English.[17]

As students studied Western languages, spoke them, wrote them, and thought in them, they became alienated from their communities and began to identify with Western culture.[18] Most became lost in-between, feeling superior to one and incomplete with the other. This was not a unique policy that colonial powers applied to the 'amma. They applied it to the monarch as well, trying to mold him into their own image so that he would "belong" to Western culture. Thus, the British government insisted that young Prince Faruq (1936–52) be sent to England to be educated in English schools, a precedent that would be repeated by other princes and heirs to the thrones of British colonies in the Arab world and other places.[19]

The difference between knowing and not knowing a European language was the difference between entering a specialized school and becoming a member of a profession and joining the middle classes and remaining without social mobility. Egyptian schools that had earlier been opened for all Egyptians free of charge were now closed except to those who could pay the fees and knew European languages. Article 13 of the 1899 laws for the Khedivial School of Law states that "no students will be admitted to the School of Law who are on scholarship or studying for free."[20] Interestingly, free education or reduced fees were available in the schools of agriculture[21] and arts and crafts,[22] perhaps because of the need for agricultural engineers and skilled labor as agricultural assistants and as superintendents of railroads.[23] Scholarships were also granted to students at Dar al-'Ulum who were to provide future teachers for Egyptian schools. Interestingly, the curriculum of Dar al-'Ulum included, besides Arabic language and literature, mathematics, history, geography, calligraphy, Arabic, French, English, and Turkish languages. It also required the study of Hanafi Fiqh—not Islamic Fiqh, but Hanafi Fiqh.[24]

The requirements made it difficult for any to study engineering, law, or medicine except for those who knew European languages and had money. So language, education, and class were being molded together. Earlier efforts to use Arabic as the medium of instruction, to translate books, and to use Arab-speaking graduates of schools to teach in Arabic were abandoned. Foreign teachers were imported and took over teaching in these specialized schools. The students had to learn the teachers' languages and not vice versa. Even after the opening of Fuad I University (Cairo University today) against British wishes, through Egyptian efforts and money donations, English continued to be important and a main medium of instruction. Donald Malcolm Reid gives an intriguing picture of what was seen as the "battle of the languages" at Cairo University after Egypt's 1922 so-called unilateral independence from Britain. Although French was the preferred language of polite society, English was without doubt the language favored in government schools and administration.[25] As would be expected, English as a medium of instruction had the effect of reducing the number of graduates and of limiting the participation of Egyptians in professions.

A good example is presented by the School of Hakimas, originally opened in 1832 and restructured in 1892 as the Medical School for Girls to produce nurses, midwives, and women doctors. According to the school's rules, only the three top students at the end of the first year of education were to continue on. The rest were to be assigned as assistant nurses in government hospitals for one year after which, if successful, they received a certificate of nursing. Those who continued through the second and third years and successfully passed their exams received certificates as midwives. To go beyond the third year and join the Qasr al-'Aini Medical School to specialize in gynecology, a graduate of the Medical School for Girls had to pass an oral exam and have fluent knowledge of a European language as well.[26] That made it almost impossible for Egyptian women to become doctors, and the numbers of qualified midwives and nurses could not catch up with the growth in population. Not surprisingly, large numbers of nurses and midwives and doctors from Europe and America as well opened their practices in Egypt.

As with women medical practitioners, Egypt's growing needs for professionals were not met with the numbers a tightened school budget could produce, so Egypt's doors were opened to larger numbers of foreigners to come and work there. Some opened private practices as lawyers, doctors, builders, and engineers; others were hired directly by the government. Almost daily, government orders licensed foreigners—mainly Europeans—to work in Egypt. Interestingly, the salaries of foreigners hired by the government were always higher than what Egyptians received for the same jobs. So while schools controlled the numbers that could be graduated from them and tightened the graduates to those who were culturally Europeanized, Egypt like other colonies, became a place for European excess labor, professional and skilled, to become employed under favorable conditions. Craftsmen as well came and set up shop: mechanics, carpenters, jewelers, dressmakers, filmmakers, newspapermen, artists, theater producers, and actors. Greater Syria, in particular, proved an important source for artists and journalists. Egypt's most important and longest-surviving newspaper, *al-Ahram*, was opened in 1875 by two Syrian brothers, Selim and Bishara Takla. Egypt's first and most famous theatrical troupes were also opened by Syrians. These included Ali al-Kassar, George Abyad, and Najib al-Rihani. Egypt's administration, however, remained staffed with Englishmen in favor of other nationalities. As advisors to Egyptian ministries, they enjoyed power, prestige, high standards of living, and lucrative jobs.

Although Egypt's administration and colonial rulers were English, its foreign community was much more diversified, and the profusion of languages and cultures melded into the "European" or *"khawaja."* After 1840, when international treaties made Egypt into an "open free market," the door to Egypt was open wide to those who wished to come, live, invest, or work there, and as the number of foreigners grew, so did their influence multiply. Foreign rule made laws and regulations simpler, easier, and safer for foreigners. In 1907 Europeans reached 150 thousand (sixty-three thousand Greeks, thirty-five thousand Italians, twenty-one thousand Englishmen, fifteen thousand Frenchmen, eight thousand Austrians, two thousand Germans, three thousand Russians, and one million Swiss and Belgians, plus other nationalities such as Americans and Spaniards). By 1936 Egypt's foreign population reached 360,000. Egypt attracted so many foreigners that at one point its government issued orders that boats arriving in Egyptian ports not allow any more foreigners to disembark. Since the end of the nineteenth century, the foreign community preferred to congregate in particular towns, especially in ports such as Alexandria and Port Said[27] because of the cooler weather and business activities there.[28]

By far the largest community of foreigners was the Greeks, who arrived quite early in the century and worked as grocers, moneylenders, and as producers and sellers of alcoholic beverages and soft drinks; the most famous were Zotos, Janaklis, Stella of the famous beer, and Spathis. Greeks preferred to live in Alexandria, which they considered to be the city of Alexander the

Great and, therefore, "theirs." It is estimated that on the eve of the 1952 revolution the Greeks constituted about one-quarter of Alexandria's population of one million. The British community was diverse; ten thousand Englishmen worked as soldiers, administrators, and active wealthy exporters. Another fifty thousand from British colonies with British citizenship included Maltese, Cypriots, and Indians. Italians, too, preferred the city of Alexandria and were mostly professionals, teachers, and artists employed in building and crafts. The French formed an interesting group of Frenchmen, Tunisians, and Maghribis. Many French Jews owned the large department stores, such as Cicurel, Shemla, and Hannaux.

The foreign community in Egypt can be considered within the category of *tujjar*. Except for the professionals—doctors, lawyers, engineers, teachers, and so on—who came to practice their professions there, foreigners were all involved in one type of business or the other, and they controlled both national and international trade, chambers of commerce, retail, and manufacturing. During the "liberal" period of Egypt's history under British rule, foreign *tujjar* constituted the most important element, that is, the elite, in the *khassa*. Their culture formed the state hegemonic discourse. Modernity became a hegemonic instrument of the *khassa*, and Westernization divided Egyptian society. Reform became a goal, touching everything at once, a claim for legitimate rule and an instrument of control. Perhaps nothing exemplifies this more than the changes introduced to the legal system. Part of the power of being a foreigner, for example, was exemption from "personal taxes, taxes paid by craftsmen, taxes on shops and industries (except for import duties)." While making it difficult for Egyptians to compete in business, retail, manufacturing, and even crafts, these privileges allowed foreigners to dominate all aspects of Egypt's economy.

> Foreigners congregated in foreign communities, which under the umbrella of foreign privileges were completely independent of local authorities, constituting a government within a government, each community being under the supervision of the consul general it followed. . . . Europeans succeeded in the businesses they practiced owing to their experience, privileges, and government encouragement and owing to not establishing a fee determining the wages between the worker and the owner, which allowed them to control labor and the country's economy.[29]

Establishing or not establishing fees, or a *tas'ira* (government-fixed price), for services or labor was discriminatory, binding weaker and poorer parts of the population while privileging the richer. Thus, the government did not establish wage scales for business owners, who could determine the pay for those who worked for them. Fees paid by the public to doctors and lawyers were also left to the discretion of the doctor or lawyer. Only where the fee was part of a court settlement did a judge determine the lawyer's fee, but that had little to do with what his client paid him. When it came to domestic workers or servants, an employer's responsibility for his servant's actions was extensively regulated by law.[30] If the servant caused harm to the property or person of another, the employer was prosecutable. Yet the state never attempted to regulate the pay that servants received as wages. This "laissez-faire" policy was also not applied in situations where the public received services from small businessmen, such as those who provided donkey or carriage rides, water carriers, or tourist guides. Fees and pay scales were established by law for such services, and stringent rules and punishments were outlined against those who broke the *tas'ira*. The rules for guides set by law in 1894 and still in service into the second decade of the twentieth century fixed the pay of a guide at eight piasters per hour or twenty piasters per day. The punishment for demanding more than the fixed fee consisted of a fine ranging from fifty to one hundred piasters, the loss of the guide's permit, and an imprisonment of one to three days in cases where someone acted as a guide without a permit.[31] It should be noted that this was so in tourist areas where services were provided to foreigners. In more populous areas of the city, fees for riding donkeys or transport were determined by the market, but other services such as selling water were regulated by the state. "The *saqa*s (water carriers) cannot demand for transporting water to the ground floor and first floor a price higher than two millimes and a half per *girbah* (water container, often made of leather); for upper floors this price can be increased by half a millime."[32] The maximum size of the *girbah* was set at 67 liters, and infractions were punishable by a fine of one hundred piasters. A permit was required.[33]

Although prostitution was nothing new for Egyptian society, the modern state not only recognized it but regularized the way prostitutes practiced their profession. Houses of prostitution could be built only in particular areas of towns, and prostitutes could only walk certain streets. Court records show that cases against "maisons de tolérance," as mixed court records referred to them, were often brought in front of the court and policies regarding their practices set. Mixed court deliberations dating May 23, 1889, regarding regulations of July 15, 1896, concluded:

> 1. They are considered "maison de tolérance," those houses where there are two or more girls together who make a living through prostitution, even if they live in separate rooms, or if they meet together only temporarily.
> 2. Houses of prostitution cannot exist except in the quarters specially designated by the governor or the *mudir* (director). They should have no

more than one entrance nor should they be connecting in any way with other apartments, shops, or establishments. . . .

5. All those who propose to open a house of prostitution have to make a written declaration to the governerate or to the *mudiriyyah* (governerate) at least fifteen days earlier. . . .

8. Forty-eight hours before opening the house, the owner must present to the governorate or the *mudiriyyah,* a list containing the name, first name, age, and nationality of the girls, the servants, and all other persons attached to the house. . . .

14. All girls found inside a house of prostitution have to carry a card that will be given by the police and contains the picture of the girl. The card has to be renewed each year.

15. All girls found in a house of prostitution have to make a weekly visit to the doctor charged by the authorities or, in default, by a doctor specially authorized by the sanitary authorities. The date of the visit and the observations of the doctor will be recorded on the card. The police have the right to examine the girls who, without justification, do not present themselves for inspection and to control the certificates of sicknesses produced as excuses.

16. All girls who contract venereal diseases have to stop living in a house of prostitution and

17. Must be sent to the hospital by the doctor where she will remain until cured.

18. These rules are applicable to the women owners of houses of prostitution. If they have reached the age of fifty, then they are exempted.[34] The laws applied to prostitution also differed when the prostitute and the customer were foreign or local and according to the class the prostitute served and the class to which the customer belonged.

Class differences became part of the wider social discourse and were established in every aspect of public life and services. They were even introduced into religious practices outside of the mosque. According to the 1905 announcements of the cost of accompanying the *mahmal* (the procession carrying the new black, gold-embroidered cloth covering of the Ka‘ba that was sent yearly as a gift from Egypt to the *Hijaz* at the time of pilgrimage) on pilgrimage, the government published the following prices: L.E. 25 for first class, L.E. 23 second class, L.E. 20,500 third class, L.E. 14 per person in third class if two pilgrims travel on the same camel, L.E. 10,500 for children four to ten years old riding the same camel with another child or with a parent. The price of food was not included in these prices.[35]

The system as a whole made beneficiaries of the *khassa* and of the male population. The modern state was also a patriarchal state whose laws differentiated among nationalities, classes, and genders. As was explained in earlier chapters, Egypt's legal system was largely built on *‘urf* (traditional generalized laws) as interpreted through *madhahib*. Whereas the state had its own *qanun* guiding its administration and political agenda, law as practiced in *shariʿa* courts was cumulative, based on the *shariʿa* interpreted through *madhahib* and local *ʿurf* and emanating from those living by it and familiar with it, and, therefore, allowed people a degree of maneuverability. Continuous legal reforms by the government during the modern period codified, standardized, and rationalized the legal and court system to enable the state to extend its control over it. Thus, Egypt's legal system was divided into five categories. The mixed courts, created in 1876, satisfied foreign businesses' need for extraterritorial legal control, and national courts, established in 1883, served Western-oriented propertied classes. The mixed and national courts, at least theoretically, operated largely according to French codes even though Islamic codes were included where it suited.[36] Significantly, national courts handling the affairs of Egyptians used French court cases as precedents in reaching decisions regarding local cases brought to the court by Egyptians. The law of reference was not *ʿurf* but French law and the French legal system. Counselor courts continued the practice of allowing foreign nationals to be tried by representatives from their own countries. Islamic *shariʿa* courts were left to the clergy, whereas *milla* (religious community) courts handled problems of non-Muslim religious groups. Through the *milla* and *shariʿa* courts the state extended its authority over social relations while allowing the clergy a role, a form of partnership that extended the state's hegemony and made religious authorities into spokesmen for the state. Theirs was the realm of personal status, marriage, divorce, custody, and inheritance. Religious courts were "reformed," legal procedures and codes standardized, and personnel arranged in hierarchies.

The architect of mixed courts was Nubar Pasha, an Ottoman Armenian whose uncle, Boghoz Bey Yusufiyan, worked as translator for Muhammad ʿAli. Educated in Switzerland, Nubar entered government service and through family connections and European financial patronage rose high in Egypt's administration finally to become its first "prime minister." Mixed courts were intended to litigate all civil disputes between persons of different nationalities. If a dispute existed between an Egyptian and an Italian, for example, the case had to be brought up in the mixed court and Italian law applied. The same went for a dispute between two Italians, Frenchmen, or an Italian and a Frenchman; cases were taken to mixed courts and applicable codes applied. If the dispute was between two Egyptians, then it was taken to the national courts. The majority of the judges in mixed courts were always foreigners representing the foreign communities in Egypt and European powers such as England and France. Mixed courts of first instance were located in Alexandria, Mansura, and Cairo, and an appeals court was located in

Alexandria, all of which were important centers where foreigners lived and undertook their businesses.[37] It was understood that business litigation was at the heart of these courts even though family and gender disputes constituted a substantial part of their business. The Statute of Judicial Organisation for Mixed Courts in Egypt reads:

> ARTICLE 2. Each of these tribunals shall consist of seven judges, of whom four shall be foreigners and three Egyptians. The judgments of the tribunal shall be pronounced by five judges, of whom three shall be foreigners and two Egyptians. One of the foreign judges shall preside with the title of vice-president, and shall be appointed to that position by an absolute majority of the foreign and Egyptian members of the tribunal. In commercial causes, the tribunal shall be assisted by two merchants, one an Egyptian and the other a foreigner, elected by the tribunal, and having an equal vote with the judges in their deliberations. ARTICLE 3. There shall be at Alexandria a Court of Appeal consisting of eleven judges, of whom four shall be Egyptians and seven foreigners. . . . The decrees of the Court of Appeal shall be pronounced by eight judges, of whom five shall be foreigners and three Egyptians.[38]

The various interests involved in Egypt's legal system are obvious from the very structure of mixed courts. Foreign and commercial interests were the most important. The powers, France in particular, seemed to have provided the largest number of judges. Still, nonpowers with large communities in Egypt, such as Greece, had judges sitting in these courts. The preponderance of French judges was reciprocated by the predominance of French law and the Napoleonic Civil Code seemed to have become something of a *"lingua franca"* in mixed courts, as it had internationally. Standardization played an important role in the diffusion of law. To be able to handle the complexity of relations between nations, citizens, and law, the international community tried to agree on standardized laws. This was not new and was the subject of lengthy debates and international agreements. The French Civil Code proved most useful, already having been implemented in large areas of Europe. The idea applied in Egyptian legal reform was to select laws acceptable to wide areas of Europe.[39] Languages commonly used in mixed courts were French, English, and Italian, not Arabic.

The five-court system suited two classes in particular. One class was made up of foreign (mostly European) investors who wanted to be given legal guarantees regarding the security of their investments in stock-owned companies. Thus, they insisted that all matters regarding property or commerce, even when it had to do with an Egyptian-owned company, would be decided by the mixed courts as long as foreign interests were involved. Conflicts in jurisdiction between these five court systems were not laid to rest until mixed courts were abolished in 1949 and *milla* and *shari'a* courts became part of the national court system in 1956.

The second group that was satisfied with the legal system was the landowners because it guaranteed their ownership of land, extended it, and allowed for inheritance of land by their children. Resentment toward British control was leveraged with the sort of benefits that landowners received through the new legal codes. This was particularly so because landowners managed by decree of the various foreign powers interested in Egypt to make all the laws of the Egyptian government applicable to the native courts. Likewise, through the agreement of foreign powers signatory to the convention setting up the mixed courts, those courts were ordered in 1889 to apply all the laws of the Egyptian government pertaining to lands, embankments, and canals.

Another group that saw advantage in the five-court system was the *'ulama'*, who were involved in setting up the court system and were beneficiaries of the new structures. This may appear surprising because the order of *'ulama'* was in control of the legal system when it was based on the *shari'a*, before the legal reforms. However, given the changed superstructure and the new *khassa* alliance that evolved during the nineteenth and twentieth centuries, the *'ulama'* were ready to seize an opportunity that would ensure them a continued close association with the *khassa*. Before the coming of Muhammad 'Ali, the clergy's power had been great during the eighteenth century and had reached unprecedented levels when they organized and lead the struggle against Napoleon, who recognized them as leaders of the people. But this status was slowly eroded during the nineteenth century, and the *'ulama* found themselves becoming increasingly marginalized as modern schools were established and modern, Westernized, educated judges, teachers, and lawyers took over functions that were once the exclusive domain of the *'ulama'*. This was happening at the same time as their base was shaken with the cancellation of *iltizam*s and the establishment of government control over the *awqaf* (religious endowments), which had been the prerogative of the *'ulama'* and an important income source. Therefore, they had to carve out a new role for themselves; whereas some turned to entrepreneurial and artisan activities to supplement their incomes as religious functionaries, most, particularly the high *'ulama'*, found that they could retrieve some of their power by becoming partners in building a nation-state and becoming junior members to the new elite alliance. Thus Sheikh Muhammad 'Abdu, a reformer of Islamic law who called for the reopening of the door of *ijtihad* (religious interpretation) and tried to find Islamic roots for modern concepts, was very concerned with the position of the *'ulama'* within the social structure.[40] One of the most important accomplishments of the sheikh, who was chosen as *mufti* through the support of Lord Cromer, was to finalize the process, begun in 1876, of organizing a clerical hierarchy within the government. The hierarchy consisted of seven positions, each of which had its own job description, pay scale, and educational requirements. The positions were as follows: *imam-khatib* (preacher), teacher, superintendent of maintenance, *mu'adhdhim* (man who summons Muslims to prayer), Qur'an reciter, servant, and *muqim sha'a'ir* (ritual overseer found only in very large mosques).[41] According to the reforms, employees in these positions became a class of government functionaries.

Before the 1876 reforms, a court *qadi* was theoretically chosen according to his wide knowledge of religious and legal traditions in a particular *madhhab* (see chap. 1). The new laws turned over the responsibility of selecting *qadi*s to a board of notable *'ulama'* selected by the Ministry of the Interior. Formal criteria and procedures were set for employment, promotion, and dismissal. Salary structure and court fees for different cases brought to court were also established.[42] Examination and certification became basic requirements for *qadi*s, who were tested in a specific number of assigned books on Arabic grammar, theology, Qur'anic exegesis, logic, *sunna* (prophetic traditions), rhetoric, jurisprudence, and arithmetic. Books and exams were standardized, and a candidate's extensive knowledge of theology was no longer the priority. In this way the maneuverability of the *'ulama'* in selecting the particular codes to be applied, codes largely based on the *'urf* of the various *madhahib* practiced in Egypt, mainly the Shaf'i and Maliki, were replaced by a legal code based primarily on the Hanafi *madhhab,* which was compiled by state committees and which *qadi*s were required to apply.[43]

The reforms instituted and the extension of state power meant a number of important repercussions for Egyptian society and its relationship with the state. If before the reforms one can talk of the courts as being an indigenous social institution organically linked to the people they served, after the reforms one can see the state giving itself the role of lawgiver as the provider, institutor, and guarantor of law and courts. The *la'iha* (code) of the state became the basis on which the worth of a *qadi* was decided, whether he would be promoted, employed, or dismissed. It was how effective the *qadi* was in instituting the will of the state—justice as interpreted and codified by the state and as determined by legal procedures rather than justice "for itself," and according to acceptable and expected norms—that became the paramount objective of the legal system.[44]

The reorganization of the courts, which involved upgrading recordkeeping and increasing the dependence on supervisors to make sure there was no corruption, resulted in an increase in personnel and types of skills required. These changes, in turn, increased the expenses of going to court and thereby made courts less accessible than they had been earlier. Using the Hanafi code against serious complaints of the *'ulama'*[45] seemed natural for a centralizing, commercial-minded, state-building elite. After all, the Hanafi code was more strict and attuned to capitalism than were other codes and, therefore, it appealed to a new capitalist *khassa*.[46] Furthermore, the new *khassa* that saw its origins with Muhammad 'Ali was Ottoman, whereas the Hanafi code was the preferred code of the Ottomans. It is true that the Hanafi code had become more widely used during the Ottoman period, but Egypt was basically Maliki and Shaf'i. As explained earlier, towns that experienced growth as administrative centers or where there was a marked immigration from other areas of the empire (for example, Syria, where the Hanafi code predominated), began to turn increasingly Hanafi after the Ottoman invasion. Muhammad 'Ali Pasha extended Hanafism further through *majalis al-ahkam* organized in various capital towns of Egypt, which began a process of legal centralization and homogenization that was to continue throughout the nineteenth century. The Majalis almost always preferred the Hanafi code when faced with new problems even though the membership included Maliki and Shaf'i sheikhs. But the Majalis followed the guidance and orders of the Ma'ya, central "secretariate" of the pasha and his heirs. Egypt's royal family was originally Ottoman and Hanafism was natural to them. Furthermore, the Hanafi code emphasized class and patriarchy in various ways, for example, through the strict application of the Islamic concept of *kafa'a* (equity), which, as interpreted by the Hanafi code, gave a father the right to ask for the nullification of a daughter's marriage if he considered the husband not her social equal, even if the girl was adult and the marriage was by her choice.

The connection between new *dhawat* classes, capitalist classes, and the selection of the *talfiq* (patch work) that took place in regard to new personal and family laws cannot be ignored. Since successful hegemony building required acceptance of hegemonic discourses, making family laws tighter and more patriarchal in their emphasis on male authority over wife and children was important in extending support of the state among *khassa* and *'amma*. That was particularly so at a time of dislocations and structural transformations as in the nineteenth and twentieth centuries. This *talfiq* grew through state actions, beginning with the *majalis al-ahkam*, and by the 1920s finally was established through personal status laws. An early case from Hamaqa in Daqahl ya Province, dating from 1856, illustrates this process. In this case sent up by the *majlis* of Zaqaziq to the *majlis qadaya al-ahkam* of Alexandria for consideration, a man seduced a girl into marrying him even though her family had already refused his earlier proposal of marriage. The marriage was contracted in another town where the girl gave a *tawkil* (power of attorney) to a man not related to her to act as her deputy in the marriage. Because she was of age, both her *tawkil* and choice to marry were acceptable to the *qadi* who married them. When the girl's parents found out, they complained to the court of Zaqaziq, and the court put the man in prison and handed the girl to her parents. The court further decided to write to officials and demand that orders be sent to *qadi*s and *nuwwab* (deputies of *qadi*s) of the various *nawahi* (places, quarters) that no marriage of a previously unmarried minor girl was to be contracted except in the presence of a legal *waliy* (guardian), whether the guardian was a man or woman. If the girl claimed that she had no guardian or that her guardian was dead or living somewhere else far away and the judge became suspicious, then he should contact authorities in other areas to assure that she did not have a legal guardian. If that proved to be the case, then the *qadi* should follow the *la'iha* of the *qada'* (judiciary) in such matters. The marriage of a previously married girl who had reached her majority had to be contracted in front of a *waliy 'asib* (a guardian with the right to force her to marry).⁴⁷ The above example combined the Hanafi interpretation of *kafa'a* with the Maliki interpretation of *wilaya* that required the presence of a guardian at any marriage at which a previously married bride, adult or minor, was considered by Maliki and Shaf'i rules as legally incapable of marrying without one. The Shaf'i accepted a woman as guardian; Hanafi *qadi*s in Egyptian Ottoman courts, unlike Ottoman courts elsewhere, granted women guardianship the same as they did men.

As the century progressed, Hanafism continued to gain precedence in family and personal law. It played an important role in class differences. For example, for a wife to sue for divorce, physical abuse had to be severe enough to show bodily harm such as a broken limb. In cases involving wife beating, class formed an important basis for the decisions made by the judge. *Kafa'a* admonishing that a girl be given in marriage to her social equal was used to justify severe beatings of wives by husbands from the lower classes; such treatment was not acceptable for upper-class wives and husbands. *Kafa'a* was used to place abused wives under the physical power of abusive husbands on the pretext that because women of the poorer classes were accustomed to the verbal and physical abuse of their fathers, they would not be obedient unless treated the same way by their husbands.⁴⁸ The fact that wife-beating was by no means exclusive to lower classes nor a practice of most members of the lower classes was not taken into consideration. The elitism of this approach reflected the class elitism of the modern legal system.

This elitism and the power of the patriarchal *khassa* is further evidenced by modern *shari'a* court records. The most celebrated such case was that of Qut al-Qulub al-Dimirdashiya, the daughter of Dimirdash Pasha. In September 1937 she asked the courts to divorce her from her husband on grounds of *darar* (in her case, mistreatment). The court granted her the divorce, and the judge's decision was very indicative: divorce should not be sued for on the basis of *darar* if the [couple] came from a *bi'a* (environment) in which this type of treatment was familiar. Another earlier celebrated case was that of Sheikh 'Ali Yusif, the founder of the journal *al-Mu'ayad,* who married a woman of the elite classes against her family's wishes. Even though the woman was of age, the court divorced her in response to her father's demand. Her father, Hifni Nasif, held the title of bey and sued on the unsuitability of Sheikh 'Ali Yusif because he was not his daughter's social equal. The Hanafi code supported Nasif because it allowed a father to have his daughter divorced if she married someone the father considered not of the same class, that is, without the necessary *kafa'a* (equity), even if the daughter wished to remain married to him. An exception was made only if she was pregnant.

The impact of legal reforms on the "rights" of women was quite dramatic. Before modern legal reforms, women went to court as a matter of course to dispute contracts, property rights, or inheritance, to report rapes and other forms of violence, to ask for financial support from husbands, and to ask the *qadi* to divorce them. The system was direct and sentencing almost immediate once the judge was satisfied with the evidence presented and the worthiness of the witnesses. When a woman asked for divorce, she was almost always granted it. She could claim *darar* out of fear of physical harm, her husband's ill treatment of members of her family, or lack of support for her and her children. She was almost always granted a divorce if her husband traveled to another town and wanted her to go with him, which would take her away from family and familiar surroundings.[49] The new laws made it very difficult for a wife to divorce against her husband's wishes and created a new institution known as the "House of Obedience" *(bayt al-ta'a),* allowing husbands to incarcerate disobedient wives who did not want to live with them.[50] New divorce codes set up specific *shari'a* criteria that governed when a wife could sue for divorce. Male impotence was perhaps the most specific way out *(al-gib, wa'l-'isma, wa'l-khissa,* or "types of male impotence"), but only if it was incurable and the wife had no prior knowledge of it.[51]

The power of the patriarch family was increased at the cost of individual freedoms by raising the age of majority to twenty-one. State modernity, in fact, promoted the nuclear family and the control by father and male relatives. The Napoleonic Civil Code, which became a main source of law and legal procedures in Egyptian national courts, has been described as "especially based on the rights and authority of the husband as chief of the family, and on the respect which has to be paid to him by his wife and children, as the one who is best able to manage the family fortunes, and in that respect and in his capacity as head of the family, the rights given to him sometimes override those of his wife and children."[52] This position was reflected in Egyptian laws of guardianship even though they were the domain of *shari'a* courts presumably applying *shari'a* law. Here European patriarchy and Ottoman Hanafism were in agreement: "A mother has no right to guardianship *(wilaya)* over person or money [meaning property] according to the rule of law. But she could be selected as guardian *(wasiya)* over money by the father or the grandfather."[53] Even though *hadana* (raising or nursing a child) belonged to the women, in fact, as per law 25 of 1929, control of the child remained with the father or male *wasiy* (legal guardian) even while he stayed with the mother. Unlike in Turkey and Syria,[54] in Egypt, before the modern period, courts almost automatically gave guardianship to the mother over her orphan children and their property. As applied in Egypt after the reforms, a male guardian—father, grandfather, brother, uncle—delegated this authority to her. Even then, the male guardian held supreme authority over her actions. The similarity between the Hanafi code and the European outlook toward guardianship of children, exemplified by the Napoleonic Code and applied in mixed courts, made it logical that this was the system to be applied. The philosophy toward gender that established the father as supreme head with absolute physical and material powers over women and children even after they reached *rushd* (rational majority) and *bulugh* (puberty) at about the age of fifteen was new for Egypt. Clearly in favor of a strong patriarchal order, the Hanafi code was used by the state to establish its own hegemonic control over gender and family relations. In 1974 a mother demanded that the Maliki code rather than the Hanafi code be applied to her child custody case because it was more favorable to the rights of mothers and children. In his argumentation, her lawyer focused on the contradictions between law 78 for 1931, which confirmed guardianship on the basis of the Hanafi code, and the Egyptian constitution. According to the constitution, "the *shari'a* was a principle source of law for Egypt" and "family is the basis of society [whose] foundation [*qawamiha*] is religion." Accordingly, for the state to select a particular *madhhab* and indicate it as the only source of law was against the dictates of religion and against the constitution. Furthermore, requiring the courts to apply only one *madhhab* meant closing the door to *ijtihad* (legal interpretation) and the ossification of it.[55] The case came to court in April 1976; the court dismissed the case and ruled for the validity of law 78. When explaining his ruling, the *qadi* said that the choice of a particular *madhhab* was the prerogative of the *mushari'* (lawmaker), and the judiciary were obliged to follow it. After all, it was the right of the *mushari'* to decide what was most appropriate for the conditions of society and to use the power available to him to consolidate the people under one law, thereby putting an end to differences and making it possible for all to understand a uniform law with which all could deal.[56]

The *qadi* added that the Hanafi code was, at any rate, the most appropriate for modern society: although the Maliki *madhhab* allowed a son to stay with his mother until he reached puberty and a daughter until she was married (Abu Hanifa estimated the maximum age of *hadana* at ten for boys and twelve for girls), Malik based his decision on a girl's inexperience and her mother's ability to handle her. Abu Hanifa, in contrast, was concerned with the age a girl reached puberty, or *hadd al-shahwa* (age of carnal awareness, twelve years), when she needed protection from men. Women went out in modern times and so had greater need for protection from evil enticements.[57] Here the *tanwir* discourse is clearly laced with patriarchy. Limited knowledge of "traditional" society and the life of women and an acceptance of the picture of life before modernization is evident in the judge's discussion.

Patriarchy was further extended by the nationality laws of 1869 in the Ottoman Empire. Whereas citizenship and nationality were moot questions for those living in the Ottoman Empire, by the last quarter of the nineteenth century, every person had to be defined by the country to which he or she belonged. Structuring and defining citizenship became an important basis for gender difference and inequality. As nation-states worked out definitions of citizenship and nationality, rather than defining women as individuals holding citizenship on the basis of birth or naturalization, they defined them as holding whatever nationality their husbands held. A woman in Egypt was usually identified as "daughter of so and so" or "mother of so and so" rather than "wife of so and so" and never legally referred to by her husband's name. Defining a woman through her husband was, therefore, an imported idea, part of the diffusion of culture in an increasingly interdependent world. Adopting a husband's name only took hold among Westernized classes through the usage of the title "Madame so and so." Legally, women continued to keep their family names, but their citizenship followed that of their husbands.

Citizenship laws and their adoption in Egypt were part of its Ottomanization and modernization. As part of the Ottoman Empire, Egypt was expected to follow the Ottoman *firman* (edict of the sultan) of 1869 regarding citizenship. The Ottomans' particular concern in passing the *firman* involved their fear that the "empire's subjects who looked for ways by which they could take advantage of capitulatory privileges [reserved for foreigners]" would look at citizenship laws as one method of doing so.[58] Acquiring foreign nationality was one way. Still, the Ottomans did accept the principle—as in Europe and America—that "the wife follows her husband," whereby an Ottoman woman who married a foreigner took his nationality and lost hers, and foreign women who married Ottoman citizens became Ottoman subjects if by virtue of their marriage they lost their own nationality. The two balanced each other.

Egyptian courts hesitated to follow the Ottoman lead. They did not object to giving Egyptian nationality to foreign women who married Egyptians; they questioned the legality of a Muslim Egyptian woman taking the national- ity a non-Muslim foreigner. The compromise is interesting and telling of how laws diffused together to bring about new codes. A court case illustrates this change. In 1909 Saliha Hanim, the widow of Prince Muhammad Ibrahim, was placed under *higr* (guardianship because of incompetency) of her grand- mother by the *majlis hisbi* (guardianship court). She appealed the decision on the basis that Egyptian courts had no jurisdiction over her and that the case had to be judged in front of the mixed courts. Because she had married a Russian citizen after the death of her husband, she had lost her Egyptian na- tionality and gained that of her new husband, that is, she was a Russian citizen and Egyptian courts did not have jurisdiction over her. The court of appeals ruled against her on the basis that she was a Muslim and the widow of a Mus- lim man, and as a Muslim she had to abide by *shari'a* law, which made her marriage to a Lutheran in a Lutheran Church in Russia illegal. In its findings the court differentiated between what it called "political nationality" (*jinsiya siyasiya*) and "sectarian nationality" (*jinsiya ta'ifiya*), or "religious national- ity." The husband and wife could be joined in the first according to the princi- ple "a wife follows her husband's nationality," but this would not be valid if they differed in the second. Marriage was a question of *jinsiya ta'ifiya*, that is, a religious matter and not a secular matter. Establishing *milla* courts and state recognition of the particular religious groups that would have legal rights over their communities in Egypt was a further extension of defining an individual through his religious affiliation rather than as an individual with generally rec- ognized rights. These freedoms would be determined on the basis of sectarian affiliation. Christians, too, were expected to follow the rules of their domina- tions, and the marriage of a Copt to a Catholic or an Italian Catholic to a Cop- tic Catholic, for example, proved to be very problematic because it would not be recognized by both churches. Deepening gender discrimination was one of the results of this changed legal system and the diffusion of law that took place as a result of the multiplicity of codes. For example, the Coptic community, finding no Coptic laws of inheritance to apply to their community, chose to follow the Muslim inheritance laws, which meant that women would inherit one-half of a man's share. They also followed state laws (law number 25 for Dec. 25, 1920, amended in 1929, 1979, and 1985) regarding incarcerating "disobedient" wives in Houses of Obedience by court order, and as happened with *shari'a* courts, found religious justification for the laws. Ordinances 140 to 151 of the personal status laws for Orthodox Copts issued by *majlis al-milli* in 1938 and reconfirmed by *naqd* court in 1973 were enforced by court using scriptural quotes: "obedient to your man as Sarah was obedient to Abraham, whom she called her master." In one court case dating from 1953 the *majlis al-milli* court of Damanhur rendered the following decision: "The obedience of a wife to her husband is a duty according to Church law and according to the traditions of the *majlis al-milli.* [This is because obedience] is the cornerstone of the family no matter the severity involved in the interference of the executive authorities to assure execution by forcible compulsion [*al-quwa al-jibriya*]. Without this the family would be at the mercy of tremendous dangers [*akhtar jasima*]."[59] *Ta'a* laws among both Muslims and Copts justify *ta'a* in similar terms, that is, the reciprocal duties of wives and husbands. Even though the Coptic laws accept marriage as a sacrament and Muslim laws describe it as a contract between two persons, there is agreement as to the reciprocal responsibilities discussed earlier, namely, that the husband provides financial support and the wife renders obedience. The big difference comes in the fact that the new laws gave the husband *absolute obedience* for *ta'a* whereby a woman became required by law to surrender herself or, until 1985, be forced by the police to surrender herself and live with a husband, no matter how abusive. These laws have been a subject of dispute in the last decades[60] and are part of revivalism discussed in chapter 7.

Although discourses of reform present legal modernity as a positive move for all members of a community, the advantages were actually not equally distributed no matter what the discourse or the intent. Modernity, without doubt, raised standards of living and the quality of material existence. It also eventually allowed women greater participation in the political life of the country through greater state mobilization into the national job market. Nevertheless, not only did the multiple court and legal systems differentiate between classes, nationalities, and religious groups, they also created a hierarchy of "guardians" and dependents. Guardians were male and adult; dependents were female and minors. This division was instituted throughout the legal system, the legal code or the particular court implementing the laws notwithstanding. "Personal status laws" confining women to the power of husbands, restricting the rights of wives to travel without a husband's approval, and nationality laws that continue to deny the children of foreign fathers and Egyptian mothers Egyptian nationality rights are a result of legal reforms.

The legal system as a whole became less accessible to the *'amma*. New legal procedures required the presence of lawyers and the presentation of legal briefs. The various levels of appeals meant that victims had to wait longer for justice to be delivered and poor people, therefore, could not afford the price of justice. Previously, *shari'a* courts dealt with all matters, from marriage to buying and selling. The courts were easily accessible, and the public used them frequently. With the introduction of the modern courts, this was no longer the case. For one thing, fees were too high for the poor.[61]

Lawyers who understood the new unfamiliar codes were required. Law became a highly sought profession and education in Western law was considered essential. It should, perhaps, be pointed out that the interpretation of law was often molded to suit the *khassa*. The new Khedivial School of Law set out a syllabus illustrating the centrality of Western law. Obligatory courses consisted of "1. European languages, French or English, history, philosophy, and literature. 2. Translation. 3. Islamic law. 4. Civil law (commentary on indigenous civil law and comparison with mixed civil law and different European codes). 5. Criminal law (commentary on penal code and instruction in indigenous criminal law and comparison with European codes). 6. Civil and commercial procedures (commentary on indigenous code and comparison with mixed codes). 7. Commercial law (commentary on indigenous code and mixed codes). 8. Administrative law. 9. Private international law. 10. General introduction to the study of law. 11. Principles of political economy. 12. Organization of public administrative and judicial powers. 13. Roman law."[62] The student body was divided into two groups according to the European language in which they pursued their degrees, that is, a French section and an English section. Courses, such as Islamic law, that were taught in the Arabic language were attended in common.[63] Graduates of this school were quite Europeanized in their approach to law and court procedures. Court records illustrate the fact that French legal cases were actually taken as precedents to be applied in Egyptian courts. This was not only acceptable but declared as the policy of these courts.

Furthermore, the importance of European law and the education of Egypt's lawyers, judges, and future legislators in European codes was to have an important impact on the political process. After all, lawyers in Egypt, as in other parts of the new modern global order, became the core of a new political class who made a profession out of politics. Mustafa Kamil, Egypt's renowned national hero, explained in an 1891 letter to his brother his choice to study law. "[Law school] is the school of writing, oratory, and the rights of nations and individuals."[64] Mustafa Kamil entered the Khedivial School of Law in Cairo. He soon realized he had to do more to gain credibility among French politicians and French public opinion. The occupation of British troops since 1882 and England's continued evasion of promises to evacuate the country caused nationalists to look to France for leverage against Britain. That was Kamil's plan as he enrolled in the French law school opened in Egypt and then sought a French degree in law from the University of Toulouse.[65]

That law could be manipulated to suit *khassa* needs was no secret. Egypt's *khassa* understood this notion and used it quite effectively. If anything, they wanted to enforce more arbitrary laws, and except for conditions in Egypt after the First World War (the revolution of 1919, the murder of Lee Stack, and the break-up of violence), they probably would have. Thus, at the request of the Egyptian Ministry of Justice, its counselor, Sir William Brunyate, drafted a project of constitutional reform proposing a representative assembly elected among Egyptians that would have consultative prerogatives only and an upper house with legislative powers to be formed of official appointees, including Egyptian ministers, British ministerial counselors, and any other British civil servants of their rank. The upper house would also include fifteen foreign and thirty Egyptian elected representatives but on condition that foreign members would always form a majority of total membership. Furthermore, laws could be passed by the upper house directly without reference to the council of deputies.[66] That same year ten British lawyers wrote a memorandum to the committee formed to look into cancellation of extraterritorial privileges enjoyed by foreigners. They demanded that all new laws promulgated in Egypt be written in English, that legal codes be copied from corresponding British laws, and that lawyers address the court in English. It was suggested that in national courts there always be a European judge next to a national to look into local affairs.[67] Such proposals seemed fair to their authors because they protected the interests of foreign communities in Egypt.[68]

"Security" and executive laws became another instrument of control by the *khassa*. Beginning in 1894, every important position in the police security force was given to an Englishman.[69] A dual security system—one responsible for the security of foreigners and the other for the security of Egyptians[70]—in operation since the time of Khedive Isma'il, became institutionalized in Egypt's police force. New police methods were implemented, such as photographing criminals, fingerprinting, keeping files on suspects, categorizing criminals according to specialization, and shadowing methods, and in 1940 a special secret police force was organized.[71] Shadowing and the secret police were used widely because the Egyptian public did not cooperate with a police force that they recognized was working for foreigners.[72] Crimes were categorized into social crimes (including murder, burglary, and theft) and political crimes. This division gave governments in power the ability to enforce their will against their political opponents. Class duality was institutionalized into the prison system where room and board depended on social position, political connections, and ability to pay. Laws governing the administration of prisons legitimized such differentiation. Those who were "temporarily imprisoned" could be required to sweep and clean their rooms and the prison corridors and halls, but in exchange for money they could be exempted from any work according to their "habits and standard of living." Prisoners could also pay to be allowed to have their private rooms furnished differently from the rest of the prison, including magazines or any other home equipment that would entertain them.[73]

As the role played by the police was strengthened and widened, so were their power, privileges, and ability to extract wealth. A police school was opened in 1896 in Bulaq, then moved to Abbasiyya in 1906. Not only was the secondary school certificate required for admission, but a yearly fee of L.E. 30 was also required, which the large majority of Egyptians could not afford.[74] Corruption was introduced quite early because the rank and file of the police force were recruited from villages and were very poorly paid, and the *ghufara'* in the villages not only were badly paid but were expected to pay fines if any harm befell property while they were on guard duty.[75] One index by which to measure police "collusion" is the percentage of cases filed as unsolved. According to police records, in 1922, 61.3 percent of cases were filed unsolved; in 1926, 61.8 percent; in 1930, 57 percent; in 1934, 49 percent; and in 1936, 47 percent.[76] Police positions became a form of unofficial *iltizam* reminiscent of the old-style janissaries and *'azabs* (auxiliary garrison soldiers), who exacted various forms of *firda* (informal or unofficial exactions) from the populations they were protecting.

In 1923 a law was passed giving police the right to watch and arrest vagrants. "Vagrants" were defined as narcotics dealers, prostitutes, procurers, known felons, gypsies, gamblers, soothsayers, the homeless, anyone found walking at night in the suburbs, villages, or between the *'izab* (landed estates, farms), and all those who had at one time received prison sentences.[77] Such a law was quite new for Egypt but proved an important vehicle for control of the social and political process because it also limited the freedoms and maneuverability of the *'amma* in the name of security. During the nineteenth century, in general, violence of many types increased significantly. Violence was not new in Egyptian society, but the range, seriousness, and constant increase in violence was a notable phenomenon caused by social dislocation and population movements from rural to urban centers. According to the yearly reports of the judicial advisor of the Egyptian government, crimes of all types were increasing from year to year in the various districts *(marakiz)* throughout Egypt. In 1898 *markaz* tribunals oversaw 70,591 criminal cases of various types; by 1908 the number had reached 153,333.[78] Perhaps the most surprising types of crimes were those performed by and against children. Although *shari'a* court archives dating from before the nineteenth century show that there were crimes against children and that it was not unknown for children to be abandoned or to be taken to the *qadi* to be handed over to a foster family to care for them, the numbers involved were miniscule. The methods used to handle and punish "juveniles" were diverse and interesting. Of the 1,836 tried in Cairo in 1912 at the court of juvenile offenders, "there were 247 acquittals; 47 were sentenced to imprisonment, 100 to fines, 1,200 to whipping, 151 to the Reformatory, and 91 were handed over to their parents."[79] So much for Lord Cromer's claims for having abolished the use of the *kurbaj* (whip) in Egypt! Besides "children's courts," state control over children was extended through the State Administration of Public Assistance set up by a 1904 law to handle "found children (lost children or foundlings), abandoned children, poor orphans, mistreated children, discarded or morally abandoned."[80] Abandoned children became an acute problem, and orphanages, nonexistent in Egypt before, were now resorted to as an answer to the problem of unwanted abandoned children.

Archival and police records give a good picture of the general increase in violence throughout various parts of Egypt. This violence was political and social and seemed to encompass society at large. Perhaps the best proof of this prevalence was the growing rate of suicide, which was reported daily during the first part of the twentieth century although such reports were rare earlier. This does not mean that suicide did not exist before because the lack of such reports in *shari'a* court records may be more a matter of how such cases were reported or handled by the *shurta* (police, or peacekeeping forces) rather than by courts. One does not, however, find financial or inheritance disputes arising from the death of individuals by suicide, which would have been recorded by the courts. At any rate, the incredible growth in suicides as reported by the police and the alleged reasons for suicide provide a background to the family dislocations in which children found themselves. It was not uncommon to find districts of Cairo or Alexandria, cities that were constantly growing in size and population, reporting five or six suicides per week during the first decades of the twentieth century.[81] Causes of suicide were diverse, but they ranged from failure at work or to find employment, sickness, family disputes, and gender violence against women,[82] which included[83] marital abuse.[84] This is not to say that marital violence was nonexistent before; court records discussing marital abuse and violence are recorded mostly when they are pertinent to divorce proceedings.[85] Sometimes abuse escalated to a husband murdering his wife, in which case he often surrendered himself to the authorities and confessed.[86] During the modern period juvenile suicides were frequent, for example: the suicide of a ten-year-old barber apprentice because of his father's abuse,[87] the suicide of a sixteen-year-old girl by poison "*takhalusan min al-hayat*" (to be rid of her life),[88] or the suicide of a seventeen-year-old student because his father was harassing him for not studying harder.[89]

Violence against children was of various types, such as child stealing[90] or abandonment.[91] Accidents against children were frequent; sometimes the victim was a child working in a factory or a child who happened to be crossing the street and was hit by a carriage. Parents would come and complain in court, demanding compensation, and most of the time they would return and withdraw their complaint, probably because they settled outside of court.[92] A series of crimes recorded in a single *sijill* dating from 999/1591 illustrates that violence was not anything new. One case involved a claim by parents that they were assaulted by a sheikh, whose actions caused the death of their son. They later returned to court and completely renounced the charge that such an attack had taken place.[93] Another case involved an attack on a woman in the street that caused her bodily harm,[94] suspected infidelity leading to domestic violence,[95] and a man attacked in the street and left for dead.[96] But there are significant differences between modern and premodern crimes; perhaps the most obvious is the proliferation of child infanticide reports during the early twentieth century. Bodies of newborn children were discarded in various places in the city, including bridges,[97] street corners,[98] and even train cars.[99] All newly born, these infants clearly had been left to die; for example, the umbilical cord had not been tied[100] or the babies had asphyxiated.[101] In some case reports men had been caught carrying the bodies of newly born infants to dispose of them.[102] Because there was also a great proliferation in the number of foundlings, one can assume not only that was there a deterioration in morals in general but that there was an increase in gender violence and incest. Although not enough reports of incest exist to make a judgment, the alarming increase in the number of reported rapes against juveniles of both sexes and the longer prison terms determined by newly enacted criminal laws against rape by members and friends of the family points to the realization that incest was a real problem.[103]

Egyptian society was defined further through the division of public space into areas of usage by particular classes. First, second, and third class categories appeared in public transportation, hospitals, and public buildings. Mosques remained an exception to this rule; as egalitarian centers they emphasized classlessness and Islamic egalitarianism. The connection between antihegemonic struggle and the mosque as center would later prove natural. The division of public space according to class was a European import and did not exist in the Islamic world before the modern period. For example, *maristan*s (premodern hospitals) were divided into male and female sections. Modern public hospitals during the period of colonial rule were divided into sections according to class. Qasr al-ʿAini hospital under British administration was divided into five sections, each with its own fee scale to serve a particular class of people. Free medical services were offered only in the fifth class where the destitute were treated. Division of public space—buses, trains, cinema, theater—by class still applies today in Egypt in the form of first, second, and third class categories.

Before 1952, the cultural and social chasm between *khassa* and *'amma* had become plainly manifest. The *khassa*, living within their own physical and mental confines, constituted a separate society from the rest of the population. Foreign communities lived in their own quarters, and foreign quarters were given great care by the government. The cities and towns of Egypt began to reflect the physical duality of colonial cities elsewhere. The "dual city" was divided between the "traditional" city with its alleyways, narrow streets, closely built houses, and small shops, and the other parts with wide streets, pavements, paved tree-lined roads, and large squares decorated with statues of kings and heroes, most of whom were foreign, for example, Soliman Pasha [French Colonel Séve] Square and Simon Bolivar Square. When needed, a street was cut right through a traditional quarter, destroying buildings at random in an effort to widen the city, make shortcuts between its various quarters, and widen roads for increased traffic, first of horse-drawn carriages and later of automobiles. Tim Mitchell points out that cutting roads through quarters gave access to state police forces to penetrate through the traditional mazes, whose inaccessibility had made them ideal for political dissidents, narcotics dealers, and fugitives from justice.[104] As modern buildings dotted modern skylines, minarets continued to dot old town skylines.

Being a member of the middle classes did not necessitate living in a particular part of the city. If class was determined by wealth, then "traditional" middle classes continued to live in popular quarters or new middle-class quarters that appeared in Cairo. Comprising mostly professionals such as doctors, lawyers, army and police officers, and members of the higher bureaucracy, these groups tended to move out of the popular quarters into new middle-class quarters as part of social mobility. As social mobility continued and other newer middle-class quarters began to grow on the periphery of the city, usually closer to the Nile, members of middle classes moved into more modern structures and took over the cultural aspects of Westernization, Western clothes, apartments, and furniture. A successful doctor who moved to Jamaliyya could later move to Garden City or Zamalek to rub shoulders, do business, even intermarry with the *dhawat* (people of culture and class).

A member of the *dhawat* lived in the modern part of the city, was defined by speaking Western languages with the proper accent and inflections, and wore Western clothes. For men that meant suits and ties; women wore shorter dresses and pants. Elite men continued to wear the *tarbush* (red, brimless, high, skull-hugging hat), which was a concession to Turkish high culture. The combination of a thin, transparent, black Turkish veil over Western clothes worn early in the century by women gave way to shorter-skirted Western clothes after the return of the Wafd delegation from the Paris Peace Conference, where the Egyptian delegation under the leadership of Sa'd Pasha Zaghlul failed to receive a hearing for Egyptian independence. Hoda Sha'rawi's gesture in removing her "veil" as she and her colleagues returned from the trip has stood long as a symbol of feminism. Ironically, today Islamist feminists see donning the veil as a sign of freedom from imposed foreign cultures.

But being a member of the *dhawat* also meant different moral habits. If the daughter of Sheikh Sharqawi lost her life after the departure of the French in 1801 for having "shamelessly" consorted with French women followers of the Napoleonic army, going out unveiled, riding horses, and laughing in a loud voice, this did not seem to be a problem for daughters of Egyptian *dhawat* under British rule. They traveled freely, drove motorcars, dressed in sleeveless clothes and high heels, and wore makeup, fancy hairdos, and no veil. They went to clubs where they mingled with young men of their same class. They attended and threw parties in each other's homes where they danced to the sounds of Western music. The *dhawat* at leisure meant horse racing at horse tracks opened in country clubs in Cairo and Alexandria—Gezira sporting and Semuha sporting clubs—playing cards, going to the theater, and drinking alcohol. Being secular, this group did not pray regularly, and most did not fast during Ramadan. Yet in this picture of mixing of the sexes, conservative patriarchy continued to guide family and gender relations. Love marriages were frowned upon, although they did take place through the family's guidance, and dating was considered a dishonor for the girl. As Egyptian movies illustrate, a "fallen" woman invariably paid the price, often with her life. Families held very tight control of their daughters, who were outwardly garbed and cultured as liberated women but who attended foreign schools, often run by nuns, and were raised with a very Victorian outlook toward sex, family, and home. Ultimately, Westernization of women meant educational opportunities and mobilization into the work force, but if anything, gender roles became more clearly defined. The ideal for a woman was to become a mother and wife in a nuclear family established under the bourgeois ideal of "Home Sweet Home." The *tahmish* (peripheralization) of women made them dependents on husbands who were recognized by law as heads of families. Looking at the family as the essential unit of society was in itself a new idea.

Qasim Amin has been hailed as the "emancipator of women," yet the early Amin believed in the seclusion of women "because our religion . . . demands that men gather without the presence of a single woman, and that women gather without the presence of a single man."[105] Later, in *Tahrir al-Mar'a*, Amin did attack the veil as being a tradition and not *shar'* (religious law)[106] but suggested the "legal veil" as dictated by the *shari'a*. His "legal veil" was actually a head cover that women of the Westernizing middle classes were starting to wear at the beginning of the twentieth century in Egypt.

Formed of a transparent silk head cover that came in front around the neck, it was a form of Ottoman harem wear. Such a cover, he argued, allowed women to participate in public life but still keep a symbolic seclusion possible. The family laws he proposed for reforming Islamic society were actually a confirmation of the new state-patriarchal order that granted full rights in regard to marriage and divorce but made the state a participant in these decisions.[107] Amin would probably be surprised at how much Arab society today reflects his ideas.

As the twentieth century grew older, standards of beauty for Westernized women were based on the same standards expected of Western women. Fashion magazines were imported and fashions imitated. Local women's magazines featured articles on diet, clothes, facial and hair care, and other matters of interest to the modern woman. Shops and department stores newly opened in Egyptian towns sold the fashion, jewelry, cosmetics, and perfumes in demand. Coffeehouses and restaurants proved to be very lucrative businesses, catering to the wealthy upper classes. At the same time, coffeehouses for men became possible and later "traditional." There they sat, chatted, and drank coffee. *Al-hawanim al-dhawat* (ladies, an Ottoman appellation) became involved in social and community services, throwing dinners and attending balls held in embassies, the royal palace, and the villas of their peers. The glaring differences between the images presented by the *dhawat* and the *'amma* were satirized by the famous poet Bayram al-Tunsi—born in the popular quarter of Saida Zaynab—who used popular and simple *zajal* forms to contrast the modern with the traditional. In one of his *zajal* collections, al-Tunsi takes over the role of a thirty-five-year-old inexperienced sheikh on his first visit to Cairo. In the modernized centers of the city, he found only *hawanim khawagat* (foreign-looking ladies) from whom he felt alienated. In the popular quarter of al-Ghuriyya near al-Azhar mosque, he found beauty that excited him: haunches of a size "superseding the pyramids," therefore worthy of his following behind; beautiful legs attracting attention with their anklet *(khulkhal)*; large, heavy bosom, towering height, a taut, ripe body, a small waist, fair in color and hair, and a sassy walk *(tata'awad wa tatabakhar)*.[108] Although the traditional woman was exciting covered with a *milaya laff,* a long, silky, black cloth that is wound tightly around the body showing its contours and leaving the arm, neck, and face naked, al-Tunsi found modern women most intriguing dressed in swimsuits on the seashore, lying on the sand sunbathing, and laughing at each other's stories.[109]

The pashas' world with its villages and chauffeur-driven cars contrasted to that of the rest of the *"ru'ah"* is a common theme in Egyptian literature and media.

Forbidden to other than its own people, this world was known as the world of the pashas. . . . Those who lived within this feared world appeared to those outside of it as peacocks: official black suits, elegant with long tails . . . high red *tarbushs* that resembled crowns, an elegant walk, and grandeur in a gala of servants, followers, butlers, eunuchs. . . . Pashas lived in their world far away from the world of the *ru'ah,* they ate the food of pashas . . . drank the water of pashas . . . even spoke a different language.[110]

Modernity had been laid down as the model. To enter the middle classes and hope to rise to a position associated with the *khassa,* an individual had to wear Western clothes, have some knowledge of Western languages, become secular, and look at Islamic culture and heritage as a reason for backwardness. Recovery of Ancient Egypt became central to state modernity; it presented a memory of pre-Islamic times, of greatness in contrast to a black Ottoman period painted by the Muhammad 'Ali dynasty's historians, whose job it was to exaggerate the importance of Muhammad 'Ali, his descendants, and their accomplishments. But if this was the discourse of those who aspired to become part of *khassa* combines and those who were becoming part of the economy, military, and high culture of the modern state, the majority of the population was not sold on the modernity discourse and the *khawaja*s who espoused it. The word *khawaja* itself is a caricature of the *tajir.* Once a respected word meaning a great *tajir,* a *shahbandar tujjar,* the word was diminuted and used to refer to foreigners who could not speak Arabic or who spoke it brokenly. Because foreigners were perceived by the general public as being in Egypt for the purpose of making money, they were simply referred to as *khawaja*s. Interestingly, Egyptians who spoke foreign languages in preference to Arabic or whose accents showed an imperfect Arabic were also referred to the same way. When an Egyptian mimicked foreigners, he could be insulted to the face with "*inta 'amili khawaja*" ("making yourself out to be a *khawaja!*") or referred to as "*'amil ruhu khawaja.*"

The observations about musical tastes made by the French musical savants of Napoleon's army continued to be valid into the twentieth century. But it was not only music as representative of culture that exemplified what separated Egyptians from Europeans. The opera house opened by Khedive Isma'il to celebrate the launching of the Suez Canal, where great Western ballets, operas, and operettas were played, remained outside the interest and experience of 99 percent of Egyptians. Only the "cultured" lamented it when it burned down in the 1990s, and its replacement in Gezira continues to be outside the interest of most Egyptians even though operas have been translated and played in Arabic. This cultural contrast continues to be expressed in literary discourse all the way into the twentieth century. The figure of the *khawaja* wearing a suit and hat becomes something of a fixture in Egyptian cartoons, films, and jokes. Those who imitated the foreigner also became the target of jokes and satire, and those who remained traditional were also the object of jokes. Bayram al-Tunsi's dialogue between a man and his wife on their visit to Paris is enlightening:

> "And so you, man, you remove my *milaya* and my *burqu*'[net veil] and make me walk nude in the street!"
>
> "You want to walk in Paris wearing a *milaya* and *burqu*' and have the people surround [and gape] at us? Better we should have brought a monkey and donkey with us so the show would be complete. This way, naked, you are better—one among four million. No one knows whether you are Egyptian or Cypriot."[111]

4

FOREIGN RULE AND THE *TUJJAR*

Analysis of the actual course of modern Imperialism has laid bare the combination of economic and political forces which fashions it. These forces are
traced to their sources in the selfish interests of certain industrial, financial,
and professional classes, seeking private advantages out of a policy of imperial
expansion, and using this same policy to protect them in their economic, political, and social privileges against the pressure of democracy.[1]

The *tujjar* constitute an essential stra-
tum of the Egyptian *khassa*. In this study they have been identified as those
groups who facilitated and benefited from Egypt's trade with the rest of the
world. Theoretically, such a group is composed of entrepreneurs who possess
the commercial savvy and connections to allow them to reap great profit from
commerce. In Egypt, as in most other countries under colonial rule, however,
the *tujjar* did not always act as independent businessmen who worked best in
a free-market system. Thus, although modern Egypt's history shows that
trade *(tijara)* constituted a vital ingredient in the nation's economy and that
the *tujjar* remained important members of the *khassa* from one age to the
other, the *tujjar* have appeared in different shapes within the social and political order. The *tujjar* also acted as partners in ruling the country, manipulating the laws and shaping internal conditions to ensure their ability to
maximize their income.

The *tujjar* could be regarded as individuals, companies, or groups led by
the ruler himself, as in the case of Muhammad 'Ali Pasha. The state bureaucracy often took over the *tujjar*'s prerogatives or permitted the *tujjar* to function freely only as long as they allowed other members of the *khassa* to profit
along with them, both formally and informally.

Although the *tujjar* quite often were Egyptian nationals, during those periods of Egypt's modern history when the *tujjar* have been the elite group in
ascendance—as opposed to ascendant military forces or *multazims*—actual
control of mercantile activities has rested in the hands of foreigners, residing

either in or out of Egypt. For example, historians of modern Egypt have shown how foreign *tujjar* pressured their governments to end Muhammad 'Ali Pasha's monopolies. They achieved their goal with the passage of the 1838 Treaty of Bulta Liman, which confirmed Egypt as a free zone for Western businessmen. As part of the Ottoman Empire, defeated in battle by 1840, Egypt had to abide by the agreement, dismantle the monopolies, and follow the capitulatory regulations. Thus, the end of the pasha's monopolies marked the beginning of the foreign *tujjar*'s rise as the most important controlling group within the ruling *khassa*.

The foreign *tujjar* continued to dominate during the period of British rule that began in 1876. The actual occupation of Egypt by the British in 1882 marks another phase in this process because they became the wielders of military power. Even after Britain granted unilateral independence to Egypt in 1922 and agreed to the 1936 Anglo-Egyptian Treaty, foreigners remained the dominant element within the *khassa*. In fact, as a semi-independent state, Egypt proved easy to control and manipulate by foreign interests, who established modernity as a dominant discourse and thereby facilitated hegemonic control by a Westernized *khassa* combine. Thus, Egypt's elite, foreign and Egyptian, built up a new order that ultimately suited their own interests.[2] At the summit of this new hegemonic structure stood a new type of Western-style monarchy, which endeavored to build a monarchical structure similar to those extant in Europe.

Another traditional member of the Egyptian *khassa*, the military, had to remain subdued for the *tujjar* to play the leadership role assisted by a new landowning class who facilitated the extraction of wealth, a function that *multazims* had previously performed. Controlling the armed forces began before the British invasion in 1882: the 1840 Treaty of London had tried to limit Egypt's army to eighteen thousand men, and neither 'Abbas Pasha (1849–54) nor Sa'id Pasha (1854–63) showed interest in strengthening the army. Khedive Isma'il's rebuilding of the military schools should be seen as part of his plan to forge a modern European-style monarchy and to create an instrument for expansion into Africa rather than an army that could withstand European pressure. The correspondence between the *khedive,* his minister of war, and the chief of staff of the armed forces, General Stone, are illustrative of this plan: commanding posts in the army were given to Europeans, and recruitment of foreign officers—including Americans[3] and Irishmen[4]—was encouraged. At the same time, selection of Egyptian officers was to be controlled so that only those "suitable" would become officers. To be admitted to the "new" military school, which reopened in 1872, a student had to have knowledge of Arabic, Turkish, English, and either French or German,[5] which assured a preponderance of Turkified Westernized elements among the officer class.

The British followed similar policies. Before 1882, the Egyptian army numbered nearly 250,000 men, and the artillery constituted its strongest segment. After 1882, the British insisted that the Egyptian army cut back in size, eliminate the artillery, and give up its leadership positions to the British. When new headquarters were built for the military school in 'Abbasiya in 1909, yearly fees of L.E. 16 made the school prohibitive for the vast majority of the population.[6] It was not until the treaty of 1936 that the British agreed that the Egyptian army be strengthened to replace British forces that were to be concentrated around the Suez Canal. The lack of effective Egyptian forces and the presence of British military units during the "liberal period" of Egypt's history gave the foreign *tujjar* effective power.

The most important step taken to weaken the military was the defeat of Ahmad 'Urabi Pasha by British forces at Tel al-Kabir in 1882. It effectively stopped an indigenous military force from reviving the role played by their mamluk counterparts before Muhammad 'Ali's arrival. The 'Urabi incident has been aptly described as nationalism; as the desire of the Egyptian officer class for equal treatment with their Turkish counterparts; as Islam against Christianity, exemplified by the sectarian violence in Alexandria; as a bourgeois revolution; and as a demand for parliamentary rule.[7] A number of 'Urabi's contemporaries considered his actions to be focused on the military's vested interests rather than on national concerns. Most Egyptian members of the *khassa* who were at first attracted by his call for constitutional reform later turned against him. "The Egyptian bourgeoisie was not prepared to replace the Palace's autocracy with an army dictatorship."[8] Muhammad 'Abdu supported 'Urabi and went to prison because of this support. Yet he, too, later concluded that the military leader's primary concern had not been government reform but self-interest and hatred toward highly privileged Circassian officers. To the *imam*, the real intention of 'Urabi and his Egyptian colleagues was to enjoy "special privileges [of officers]" to which they felt they had a right.[9] 'Urabi's own explanation is informative:

In 1880 the Egyptian army was composed of twelve infantry regiments. In 1881, during the Ministry of 'Uthman Pasha Rifqi, it was decided to reduce it to only six regiments. The practice in Egypt was to tend to discriminate by race. And so all the promotions, decorations and rewards went to those of the Circassian race, since they were from the Mamluks, the paid retainers of either the Khedivial family, or of the aristocracy who were in turn also Mamluks of the Khedivial family. After this faction came that of the Turks and others who were not Egyptians, along with those of mixed origins. Thereafter came those Egyptian by race; they were neither promoted nor indeed employed except by necessity, only when others were not available. That is why, up to that date, not a single man born and bred Egyptian had attained the ranks of Pasha, or General in the army despite the undeniable suitability and competence of some.[10]

'Urabi was giving a top-down characterization of Egyptian society in which foreign elements stood at the head of the *khassa*. The army was being reduced in size, thus jeopardizing its position as the arbiter of power. Class struggle within the army pitted dispossessed Egyptian officers against culturally alien leaders aligned with the very groups within the *khassa* that did not want to see military power revived and the system dominated by a military force. Because the *khassa* against whom 'Urabi struggled was composed of foreigners and their Egyptian allies, he was recognized as a nationalist hero. The support that the 'Urabists received from the Egyptian peasantry in the form of petitions of support, donations of their meager resources, volunteers to fight in the army, and outright violence all indicated the class struggle extant in Egypt at the time.[11]

Sharing power with a new indigenous military force was as unacceptable to Egypt's Ottoman and indigenous elite as it was to the foreign *tujjar;* after all, the revival of military power would have meant the reintroduction of the most powerful partner in Egypt's traditional *khassa*. Thus, the new landlord class stood against 'Urabi and the revival of military strength. British presence guaranteed the power and wealth of this new and as yet fragile landed and governmental class. During the 1921 Adli-Curzon discussions about granting Egypt a certain degree of independence, 'Adli Yakan Pasha, prime minister of Egypt, showed how dependent his class was on British protection: "Of course, we do not want Britain to evacuate Egypt. Our country continues to be in bad need of your care." [12] Egypt's national hero, 'Aziz al-Misri, criticized Egyptian leaders because of their stand regarding British presence in Egypt. He called them tails who cannot think except with the mentality of the occupiers and who work for his welfare with devotion. "We cannot liberate our lands from the British except if we get them out of our thoughts and minds." [13]

Even the nationalist leader Sa'd Zaghlul, who unquestionably wanted England out of Egypt, had similar feelings about the military. In 1924 when his government's program was attacked in Majlis al-Nuwab (the lower house of the Egyptian parliament) because it did not include plans to strengthen the army, Zaghlul, then prime minister, answered evasively: "A budget proposal will be presented to you; if the wish and good of the country calls for increasing allocations to be used for strengthening the army, there is nothing to stop you from making such demands."[14] In fact, he had no plans regarding the army, which should not come as a surprise, considering the apprehension that members of the elite felt toward the military. They did not wish to resurrect military power. Men such as ʿAdli Yakan, Saʿd Zaghlul, and Muhammad ʿAbdu were nationalists and wanted to see the British depart Egypt, but each in his way cooperated with the British. They represented members of new class alliances carving a new role vis-à-vis foreign, monarchical, and national elites.

The origins of this new Egyptian *khassa* date back to the nineteenth century with the changes in land tenure. Until then, the peasant's right to the soil was based on usufruct,[15] "the right of enjoying all the advantages derivable from the use of something that belongs to another."[16] Theoretically, all land belonged to God and was in the keeping of the state. Various laws enacted throughout the nineteenth century introduced landownership. Each phase of legal reforms constituted an extension of the previous one and fit well with the direction followed by the *khassa*'s pragmatic needs.[17] Muhammad ʿAli began the process by giving *shafalik* (private estates) and *ibʿadiya* (untaxed, usually uncultivated land) to those who could reclaim and cultivate it, aiming to maximize production at the least cost to the government. Saʿid Pasha took the second step in the process when he issued an 1854 land law extending landownership and giving it legitimacy and stability. He recognized *ibʿadiya* land as full property whose owners had the right to sell or mortgage it. The rest of the land was considered *kharajiya* (taxed land) owned by the state. Its holder, defined as anyone who had cultivated it for at least five consecutive years, had rights of usufruct over it. In 1866 *kharajiya* land became transferable through bequest or inheritance.[18] Ismaʿil permitted unrestricted ownership of land even for foreigners.[19]

Even though the laws regarding agricultural land introduced since the time of Saʿid were not intended to differentiate between small and large landholders, conditions made it very difficult for an ordinary peasant to retain his land, and many peasants, therefore, lost their land and became wage laborers. For one thing, the government no longer provided seeds to start planting, as had been the case under Muhammad ʿAli's monopoly system. Others found that they fell into debt quite fast and lost their land in the process. The fluctuating international market, the rising and falling price of cotton, and the borrowing of small holders led to a reduction in the number of landholders and the concentration of land in the hands of the new class of landowners. In 1894, 1.3 percent of the population owned 44 percent of Egypt's agricultural land (5,837,500 feddans) in lots of fifty feddans or more. In 1934, about 0.53 percent owned as much as 93 percent of the land. By 1952, when land reform laws were passed by the Nasserists, 94 percent of Egypt's landowners owned

35 percent of the agricultural land, 6,000 landowners owned 20 percent, and the remaining 45 percent was owned by only 2,136 landowners.[20] The lending policies of credit companies operating in Egypt had helped concentrate land in a few hands. As had other underdeveloped countries, nineteenth-century Egypt proved attractive to investors. Little banking and investment existed in Egypt, and lending mostly took the form of usury at interest rates that reached as high as 12 to 20 percent annually for good risks and 5 to 6 percent per month for high-risk peasants whose crops provided the only guarantee of payment.

The establishment of an open market for European investments and guarantees of extraterritorial privileges to investors made most commercial activities the prerogative of foreigners. Muhammad 'Ali had refused to resort to borrowing, and his monopolies meant that he did not have to. The governments that followed his resorted to various schemes, including borrowing, to keep the state running so that rulers could implement ambitious modernization schemes. Public debt began to accumulate by 1858 and swelled rapidly so that by the time Isma'il came to power, Egypt already owed sixteen million pounds. By the time he was replaced by his son Tawfiq (1879–1892), Egypt's debt had reached ninety-one million pounds.[21]

The government was not the only debtor institution in Egypt.[22] Because cotton was in demand, agriculture constituted an area of great interest to lenders, who were often investors and industrialists as well. Foreign banks and credit houses provided loans for cotton cultivation. Lenders' activities helped to create an economic gap in Egyptian society because such companies as the Credit Foncier Egyptien, founded in 1880 by French financiers, concentrated on large landowners whose land backed such loans and who, in turn, could become shareholders in these companies. Most of its loans were in amounts exceeding L.E. 500, far beyond a peasant's reach or needs.[23] Board members of these companies were usually foreigners, important government officials, or members of the royal family.[24] Newly opened government banks extended loans to small farmers, and the National Bank of Egypt made loans ranging from twenty to fifty pounds, which only benefited small or mid-sized owners who could provide collateral for the loan. Most peasant holders could borrow only from the village moneylenders, usually Europeans charging exorbitant interest.[25] The result of such policies was that the peasantry, constituting the country's majority, held only a tiny share of the land. A peasant either owned his own plot, sharecropped, or paid cash for rent to the *khowli* (overseer) of an absentee landlord. The budget of a peasant family in 1931–33 was no more than two to five piasters a day, or a total of L.E. twenty-four per year. From this the peasant had to pay rent of L.E. five to sixteen per feddan per year. In addition, the price of land was going up all the time because of its excellent investment value, so the possibility of buying land became all but a dream for the peasantry. The peasant and his family had to work in the fields to make ends meet or lose their precarious hold on their land. Still, a peasant with access to land was quite privileged, for the majority of the peasantry became wage labor, agricultural or urban. Within the peasant class structure wage labor was not the most onerous, for below that was the level of *tarahil* (mobile wage labor), those who cannot find jobs in their villages and have to move to other villages or provinces to find work. Here the exploitation was extreme: as Yusif Idris demonstrates in his masterpiece *The Sinners*, it was a struggle to find a place on the trucks taking the *tarahil* (mobile labor) to work, and still another struggle to be hired once the trucks arrived at their destinations, all to make enough to survive.[26]

Lending patterns also helped to ensure that Egypt's economy became dependent on one crop. Peasants planted the crop, foreign companies exported it, and landowners acted as the agency through which it was channeled to those foreigners. "Four foreign houses exported almost half of the cotton crop. . . . All were companies or subsidiaries of companies based outside Egypt."[27] As desired by foreign *tujjar* and Egyptian landowning classes, the area of cotton cultivation was extended from 1 million acres in 1903 to 1.5 million in 1912. Improvements in agriculture and irrigation resulted in an increase in cotton yield from 2.7 to 4.25 qintars per acre during the same period.[28] The British also were interested in building dams, digging canals, and facilitating transportation by building new roads and railway tracks. Reclaiming land and improving and extending the irrigation system constituted the most important British achievements; while service and educational sectors experienced severe budget cuts in the name of repaying the debt, irrigation works and dam building were expanded as never before. Favored industries, such as cotton gins and cotton refineries, that processed primary products, were foreign-owned, and "there were no forward or backward linkages to sectors of the economy other than the production of beverages, cigarettes and houses for the urban rich."[29]

Thus, business interests, foreign lending patterns, and the application of Western legal principles of property to agricultural land had dramatic results for the social structure. The appearance of large landed estates and destitute landless peasantry who formed a new mobile agricultural and urban labor force constitutes the most obvious change.[30] But determining the extent to which these transformations changed the division of labor is not that simple. Changes in the social structure do not necessarily entail a change in the relations of production. As 'Ali Barakat explains, "The peasantry moved from a nonorganized form of exploitation to a systematic and planned form."[31] This process resulted in the introduction of new methods of codifying law, which allowed the *khassa* to amass greater power but deprived the peasantry of much of the maneuverability that had acted as a cushion for them in the past. Landownership became one method of achieving political power and wealth according to Sayyid Mar'i's discussion of the 1920s. Because 75 percent of large landowners were absentee landlords, they used middlemen to collect rents or oversee cultivation of the land. These middlemen received their own form of *fa'iz*, sometimes through cash payments and other times through enlarging their own landholding at the peasants' expense.[32] The middlemen sometimes were private overseers or *khowlis*, but more often they were government-appointed *mashayikh* and *'umad*, who received certain powers over their villages. Thus, they decided which peasants were suitable for the military draft, which land was to be expropriated for service utilities, and which land to consider unproductive and, therefore, exempted from taxes. In addition, they also decided the quality of particular pieces of land and the taxes to be collected on them.

Landowners and village heads maintained close connections, supporting each other. The Egyptian landed element of the *khassa* originated from this class of functionaries, and members of their families often continued to act as village leaders. In fact, the laws and regulations set by the government for choosing *'umad* and *ghufara'* (security guards) for Egypt's villages required that a family relationship exist between the appointees and the dominant or property-owning families of the village in which they were to be assigned. "Each village should be provided with one or two sheikhs or *ghufara'* depending on the size of the village, on condition that the chosen ones be relatives of the *mashayikh* or be from the property-owning notable families, should be of thirty to fifty years of age, healthy, and of good repute."[33] The same requirements were made for the *'umad*.

Thus, the landowners and their attendants performed functions similar to those of the earlier *multazims*. With the cancellation of the *iltizam* system, the village head, instead of representing the *multazim*, became an official government representative[34] and an unofficial representative of landowners. The landowners, acting through the village functionaries, directed the peasants' production to harmonize with the *tujjar*'s interests and channeled the peasants' crops to the *tujjar* for trade. Therefore, under British rule landowners fulfilled the function earlier performed by *multazims* because they ensured the production of agricultural crops, extracted them from the peasantry, and, finally, delivered them to the *tujjar* for export.

It is important to note that the whole concept of *iltizam* was scarcely dead because Egypt was being structured according to modern designs or because it was becoming more involved in world trade and capitalism. The government of Egypt continued to conceptualize its legal and fiscal relationships in traditional terms even during the "liberal" period of Egypt's history. The contracts enacted by the Egyptian government under British rule defining the relationship between it and utility companies are examples. In one such contract, dating from 1928, concerning Sharikat Tawrid al-Kahraba' wa'l-Thalg (company for delivery of electricity and ice) for the city of Ismailia, the government referred to the company as *multazim* and to the utility concession as *iltizam*, which in modern legal terms meant an obligation that must be fulfilled. According to this contract, the government was to receive a yearly *atawa* (tribute) amounting to 12 percent of the total gross amount collected or due from subscribers, if that amount was less than L.E. 40,000, and 14 percent if the total was L.E. 40,000 or greater. At the same time, 1 mills. would be charged as *atawa* for each kilowatt hour dispensed to the ice factory (Art. 4). Various other details are given, but the important terms used here are *multazim, iltizam,* and *atawa,* terms that have specific meanings. It is important to note that *atawa* did not refer to taxes, thus Art. 17 reads: "The *multazim*s are responsible for paying all taxes imposed or to be imposed by the state and all local and general fees as well, including specific taxes pertaining to distribution centers." [35] In short, the government continued to "farm-out" income-producing resources (that it considered as belonging to the state and which that state was unable to exploit directly) in return for a share of the dues collected (rather than the profit). Furthermore, the state continued to pay *fa'iz iltizam* compensation to those holding rights to the original *iltizam*s canceled by Muhammad 'Ali Pasha all the way into the twentieth century.[36] *Iltizam* as a system and a philosophy remain symbolic today of attitudes of state bureaucrats and individuals toward their positions and relations within and without the administration. The term itself changed and the "business" also changed, but the idea of receiving rent for services contracted or unseen remained a basic part of the economy and a main form for redistribution of wealth. So *iltizam* as a system and a philosophy were scarcely dead. The economic philosophy of *iltizam,* allowing for wider distribution of business activities and income-producing services that theoretically belonged to the state, did not die because the outward manifestation of the system changed or ceased to exist in the classical sense of the term. The state facilitated the production process by legitimizing the landowners' efforts to extract wealth from the populace. In turn, the landowners developed a close relationship to the peasantry whereby the peasant worked the land and the landowner shared the land's production. The relations of production between the two did not change appreciably; the owner held the means of production in the form of land, equipment, seeds, and capital, and the peasant had only his labor to sell. Even those peasants who managed to retain their small landholdings found that they could not act independently without the local landed magnate's approval.

Iltizam type holdings, Mafia style and perhaps typical to Mediterranean culture, evidenced themselves in the form of monopolies held by individuals or groups of individuals who created hegemonic alliances to control particularly lucrative positions. As discussed in chapter 3, monopolies were nothing new but had existed since the mamlukid period and probably earlier. The newer forms of monopoly coming with the modern state allowed for expansion of granted powers or the simple creation of power centers, which the central government usually ignored unless they went out of control or were contested by someone with authority. One can talk about these monopolies as forming smaller *khassa* alliances at various locations. Certainly the *'izba* system, allowing for the control of peasant populations by *a'yan*, rural and urban, was such a monopolistic system. A more usual one in regard to commerce and exchange was the usurpation of market places and the establishment of *iltizam*-style monopolies over them by which no one could bring their goods to market without paying a "passage" fee usually estimated on the basis of the profit expected. The right to sell certain goods on certain days was dispensed to the highest bidders.

> We have heard that some merchants have a monopoly over spots on the shore that are labeled "project of so and so" for the marketing of the people's produce and selling goods not available to the people living there. On the outside this looks like a form of *tijara* [commerce], but freedom is forbidden the people because the agents and the *tujjar* located there have arrangements with a number of individuals through whom they could take whatever they wished of the people's produce at less than value and no other merchant could get into the spot appropriated by another so that buying and selling could be according to demand. . . . [It was brought to our attention] that Musa Bey al-'Aqqad is monopolizing four streets, two for a time with a partner named 'Abdal-Sammad and the other two with partnerships with Abu Zayd Agha but which are in his *hiyaza* [control, property] alone, and two other streets [the right to which] he bought from the Khawaja Andrée Robono and the second from Khawaja Fibli, and he has a fifth project as a partnership with a man called Khorshid Agha, and his agent has been given permission to buy the partner's share. . . . According to the information that he [Musa Bey] gave to the finance department [*maliya*] regarding [his wish to] *isqat haqihi* [drop] his *manfa'a* [right of usage] from the five streets mentioned to the government and that he wrote his mentioned agent that he was raising his hand . . . steps must be taken to remove the monopoly [*raf 'yadd*] of these individuals . . . to stop the abuses and allow freedom of trade.[37]

The above communication from the Ma'ya Saniya to the governor of the province of Faiyūm and Beni Suef dating from 1864 is interesting on various levels. The bey concerned was allowed to have his monopolies, and only when he dropped his *manfaʿa* did orders arrive to stop the ongoing abuses. The hegemonic *khassa* alliance worked on the level of state and its *dhawat* at that level. The rights to *manfaʿa* giving control of commerce over whole streets was allocated to various individuals, even foreigners. These rights of usage could be bought and sold, and establishing monopolies seemed to be an acceptable practice even though government policy was freedom of trade. The hegemonic alliance over the marketplaces probably broke up because of disputes among the different partners, and the bey who was the link with the state was probably changing tactics, balancing his power by bringing the power of the state to bear.

In the *ʿizba* (estate) system the landlord's power base in the village was cemented through the protection and services that he offered to his district's population. The *ʿizba* system that rose during the nineteenth century illustrates the importance of these landlords and their patronage relationship with the peasantry. An *ʿizba* was officially characterized as "a group of houses constructed for agricultural laborers . . . which generally take the name of the proprietor [of the land]." [38] Landowners built hospitals and schools for villagers [39] and also provided patronage, which was important when it came to villagers' educational and employment opportunities, military service, criminal problems, and social mobility in general. The landlord helped the peasant's children go to school and to find jobs in town. He gave villagers jobs as "field inspectors, veterinarians, engineers, stable managers, night watchmen, and menials." [40] Ultimately, his wealth and power stemmed from the peasantry, whom he exploited but who supported him as the link between them and the state.

Muhammad Sultan Pasha's rise from *sheikh al-balad* to owner of thirteen thousand acres in the Upper Egyptian town of Minya, presidency of the Consultative Chamber of Delegates in 1881, and the deputy directorship for Upper Egypt in 1885 is illustrative. When the failed ʿUrabi revolution occurred, Sultan first sided with the nationalists against Khedive Tawfiq. Upon realizing which side was stronger and seeing ʿUrabi as more of a threat to his class, he joined Khedive Tawfiq and the British and became active in influencing other landowners to take the *khedive*'s side, an effort for which he was handsomely rewarded. [41] The source of his power lay in land that he inherited, in political positions in the government bureaucracy, and in the patronage he received from Ismaʿil Siddiq (Khedive Ismaʿil's corrupt foster brother) and, later, Khedive Tawfiq. Sultan Pasha's ultimate value to the ruling regime, and his real source of power, lay in the important function he performed as a village leader. His intimate knowledge of village life and management of the peasantry proved invaluable. This was one reason why landowners became involved in provincial administration as governors, judges, and administrators.[42] Similar examples, until 1952 and after, are the Abaza, Badrawi, and Sirag el-Din families from Lower Egypt, the Sha'rawi, Ghali, and Sultan families from Upper Egypt, and later the Mar'i and Fiqi families under Nasser and Sadat.[43]

As part of the *khassa* alliance of that period, and as the instrument through which the cotton crop was produced, landowners benefited from government regulations that assured the *khassa* full control of agricultural production and distribution. These regulations included executive policies that determined the particular agricultural crops to be produced, the amounts, and even the prices. The *khassa* thus obtained the same control over production and distribution enjoyed earlier by Muhammad 'Ali Pasha. The regulations, which served as executive and bureaucratic prototypes for the Nasser regime, were quite normal for Egypt under British tutelage. The government often acted as a buyer of cotton to stabilize its price and interfered with the production process to assure the quality, quantity, and prices of the cotton to be produced in any particular year. Beginning with 1926, a year in which cotton prices fell sharply, executive orders determined where cotton would be planted, who would be licensed to plant the crop, who would be licensed to sell cotton seed, and what type of seed would be planted.[44] As a form of protectionism, the export of certain plants was forbidden; for example, a 1928 decree prohibited the export of palm trees. Compulsory prices were set for particular products of strategic importance, for example, chemical fertilizers.[45] The government required farmers to plant certain areas with wheat and barley and then confiscated a ratio of the product of both crops. To be exempted the landowner presented a petition explaining the reasons. Needless to say, patronage was essential to receive such exemptions. The following description of Mexico at the turn of the twentieth century applies to Egypt during the same period:

> Any position of authority implied an opportunity for self-improvement. . . . Government, in particular, was a prize to be exploited. . . . It was not thought of as corruption: it was the way things had always been done. The system that emerged in the twentieth century merely institutionalized this praxis: the government exercised power with authoritarianism and rewarded loyalty with patronage.[46]

Coercion, whether of the peasantry by the landlords or of the landlords by the state, was, therefore, limited but effective. Two cases of coercion enacted by British authorities and by Egyptian authorities illustrates the use of coercion, the type of intimidation used to frighten the population into submitting to the will of the state, and the alliances between otherwise competing *khassa* groups when it came to acts that represented antihegemonic threats. Such threats did not need to be directly political; defiance of British absolute superiority of government personnel sufficed.

The first incident occurred in 1906 in the small village of Dinshwai and was so serious that it resulted in the assassination of Egypt's Coptic prime minister, Butros Pasha Ghali, with sectarian repercussions, and the firing of Lord Cromer by his government. At Dinshwai, at Lord Cromer's orders, a military tribunal, on which sat Butrus Pasha Ghali and Sa'd Zaghlul's brother, Fathy Zaghloul, sentenced villagers to various prison terms and handed down death sentences because the villagers had chased away and beaten British officers who had decided to hunt village pigeons on village grounds without prior permission. They caused fire damage and wounded one peasant woman. As they ran in the summer sun, one of the British officers suffered a sunstroke from which he later died. Cromer decided to make this episode a lesson by setting up a summary court and building a gallows to hang those involved and to whip others even before the court had sat in session. The sentences were carried out in front of the villagers with the families of the victims watching helplessly. The executions themselves were stretched out—one victim was brought out at a time, one hanging was followed by one whipping while other victims watched and waited their turns like animals waiting to be slaughtered.

In the second event, the celebrated one of Badari, the result also was the firing of the prime minister, Isma'il Pasha Sidqi, by his government. The case of Badari exemplifies the diffusion of power and patronage that tied together the various levels of those benefiting from the *khassa*. Badari is located forty kilometers from Assiut. Three Badari families struggled over power and the position of *'umda*. The two smaller families decided to ally themselves against the much larger 'Abd al-Haq clan known for its strong *'izwa* (dignity, power). The two families also allied with local government officials, particularly the police officers of the district. The latter systematically persecuted members of the 'Abd al-Haq clan. When the *ma'mur* (police lieutenant) was found murdered, two young male members of the clan became the primary suspects and were imprisoned and tortured to force them to confess. When such a confession was not forthcoming, the chief of police of the town of Assiut sent the *hajana* (camel-mounted soldiers) into Badari where they forced family members, men and women, out of their homes. The mothers of the two suspects were then stripped naked, and the soldiers heaped white paint on their faces. When the youths still refused to confess, the police began to strip the clothes off the other 'Abd al-Haq women, an act which would have entailed loss of face for the clan forever. That could not be countenanced by the clan, and a confession was finally coerced from the two suspects. During their trial,

which took place in Assiut, witnesses described how this confession was coerced from the two men. Rather than take the witnesses' word, however, the
court actually sentenced the witnesses to one-year prison terms for rendering
false witness. Government-assigned *ghufara'* (security guards) who had the
courage to testify about what happened were sentenced to five years in prison.
When the matter was brought to the attention of then Prime Minister Isma'il
Sidqi Pasha (1930–33), he supported the position of "his men." The public
outcry through the press brought about another trial in Cairo and forced
Sidqi Pasha's government to resign. Badari was but one incident of "administrative persecution" in which the police and local officials allied with local
groups in "revenge" to teach the population a lesson after ensuring patronage
for themselves from a government that ordered such persecution when it
suited it to do so. The Badari incident illustrates the workings of alliance and
patronage from the local level to the top of the government hierarchy.[47]

From 1882 to the 1930s, government policy under British occupation facilitated foreign interest in buying cotton, manufacturing it in Europe, and
re-exporting it at great profit. At the same time, the British did not favor the
establishment of Egyptian industries and Egyptian textile firms, whether
owned by Egyptians or foreigners, failed because of government policy. For
example, the Egyptian Cotton Mills Company, founded in 1901 and owned
entirely by English investors, was required to pay an 8 percent tariff, the same
as if its products had been imported from abroad. Exceptions based on patronage were made to this trade policy. For example, the Anglo-Egyptian
Spinning and Weaving Company was exempted from paying all duties for the
first five years of its existence. The company owners included members of
Egypt's royal family, and the company was headed by Sir Elwin Palmer, an advisor to the Egyptian government who was also a personal friend of Cromer.[48]

Banks operating in Egypt—including the National Bank of Egypt—were
controlled by foreigners, as were both capital and management, and profits
were usually channeled overseas rather than reinvested in Egypt. As a first step
in fighting for Egyptian economic independence, Muhammad Tal'at Harb
founded Bank Misr in May 1920 in the midst of the boom that immediately
followed World War I. To ensure that Bank Misr would remain Egyptian,
ownership of its shares was restricted to Egyptians. Bank Misr's goal was to
give Egypt "a say in its economic affairs and defend her interests as other
banks defend their countries' interests . . . to encourage the various economic
enterprises . . . and assist in the establishment of financial, commercial, industrial, agricultural, transport and insurance companies."[49] Bank Misr and the
other activities of the Misr Group were financed with the surplus money accumulated by large landowners and Egyptian merchants who had especially
profited from the war years.

The government's policies changed in the 1930s; protectionist measures were enacted to help promote Egyptian industrialization. But these new regulations conformed to the interests of the *khassa* combine of the thirties and forties, which had extended their activities into the industrial spheres, particularly after the economic shifts taking place during the two world wars. Still, even though industry experienced significant growth during the 1930s and 1940s, its contribution to the Egyptian economy continued to be minor and remained concentrated in a few hands, the majority of which were foreigners. This was mainly the result of the nature of foreign capital investments. Before the 1930s most foreign capital was invested in mortgage lending and land reclamation, but in the 1930s a shift took place and investments were directed toward industry and trade. In 1933 the share of industry in foreign capital investments was 17,062,000 pounds, constituting about 16.5 percent of total foreign capital. In 1945–46 new industrial investments suddenly jumped to 24 percent of new capital invested. The large share of these investments went into joint textile-manufacturing projects. Commercial activities also experienced a surge of interest with the building of insurance companies, services, banking, transportation networks, and utilities. Investments in retail increased from 10 percent of total foreign investment in 1922 to 33.5 percent in 1933.[50]

"Egyptianization" of capital during the 1940s took place for many reasons, including changes in the world economy resulting from the Second World War that assisted indigenous development of industry. The 1937 Treaty of Montreaux, ending the capitulations and decreeing the cancellation of the mixed courts, was one important reason for the reduction in foreign capital in investments in Egypt. The delay in executing the cancellation of the mixed courts until 1947 allowed foreign *tujjar* to restructure their interests according to the new conditions. In 1947 a law was passed requiring that foreign capital invested in any new company opened in Egypt not exceed 49 percent of its total capital. Thus, the Egyptian share in commerce and industry grew while foreign interests in Egypt looked for new methods to benefit from the changing system. Some interesting projects resulted: The Egyptian Textile Manufacturing Co., established in 1934 by joint Anglo-Egyptian capital, included only two Egyptian partners, who had in reality put up no more than L.E. 1,000 each out of a total capital outlay of L.E. 80,000. In 1940 three Swiss, three Belgians, and two Egyptians founded another textile factory with a capital investment of L.E. 40,000; again, the real share of the two Egyptians was minor, no more than L.E. 800 each. These two were typical examples; foreigners remained dominant in all aspects of industry not only in investments but also in the technical, professional, administrative, and managerial sides of industry. They also resorted to placing influential members of the

Egyptian *khassa* on their boards or paid their share in the capital of new industries so as to have them as a *wasta* (go-between) to get through the regime.
The famous Egyptian writer Fikri Abaza has often told the story of how he was
invited to attend the organizational meeting of a proposed joint foreign-
Egyptian company. On his way into the meeting, a number of company shares
were put in his pocket as an incentive to speak on behalf of the project and
thereby persuade others to join. Because Abaza did not, the shares were removed from his pocket on the way out of the meeting.

The introduction of what has been termed a "free-market system" after
1840 is often used as proof of a liberal phase in Egypt's history. But as described in this chapter, government policies regarding agriculture, industry,
and trade scarcely supported such a system. Liberal policies allowing for uncontrolled export-import activities and investments were clearly of use to a
khassa combine that could control production and distribution. A true market-economy entails an uncontrolled economy at all levels and presumes that
class differences do not impede universal benefits. In his discussion of similar
types of situations worldwide, the political economist Ralf Dahrendorf explains that "versions of capitalism may have been the driving force of economic and social development in some countries, but actual modes of
development were almost invariably mixtures of forces. . . . For capitalist
methods to work, certain social preconditions must be given. One is contract
rather than status as the basis of labor relations. Opportunities of market participation are not a matter of course, nor is the 'spirit' which enables people to
put growth first and consumption second."[51]

Theoretically, a free market may have been established in Egypt, but the
peasant had no control over the distribution of his product: he was still directed by the country's laws to produce goods needed by the *tujjar*. Capital
growth in this instance was predicated on precapitalist modes, that is, the market remained "mercantilist" in nature, suiting *khassa* needs. "The mercantilist
state . . . reserved to itself the right to single out and promote whichever economic activities it considered desirable and to prohibit or discourage those
which it considered inappropriate. To achieve its objectives, the mercantilist
state granted privileges to favored producers and consumers by means of regulations, subsidies, taxes and license."[52]

This period's political situation is interesting when seen from the point of
view of the *tajir* and landowner. If one regards the alliance of foreigners and
landowners in these terms—foreigners controlling the surplus produced by
landowners—other events in Egypt's history become clear. The relationship
between the British embassy and the Egyptian throne was scarcely cordial because the British were interested in maintaining the *tujjar*'s supremacy over
both the monarchy and the Egyptian elite. Although the British guaranteed

the throne's existence, the monarch was no more than a figurehead: when a king or *khedive* squirmed, he was removed or had his feathers trimmed. 'Abbas II's (1892–1914) recollections of Cromer are instructive of the relationship between the monarchy and the British representative: "He was constantly searching for ways to humiliate and belittle me . . . [and he] tried to hurt me by pretending that the Egyptian people would have revolted against the dynasty but that the British had come to protect it and to reestablish order. 'Don't forget,' he told me, 'that the Urabist movement still exists and that, if I raise my little finger, it can make a reappearance and throw the dynasty outside the country.'"[53]

Cromer also shared the uncompromising British position regarding any question of their final authority within the country:

> It soon became apparent that it would be necessary to revert to the system of vigilant and active British supervision, and more direct interference on the part of the representative of the British government. . . . Lord Kitchener speedily gained the confidence of all sections of the Egyptian public, but it is especially worthy of note that he did so, not by allowing the Egyptians to govern themselves, but by exercising a stringent control over the proceedings of the Khedive, and by himself governing the Egyptian.[54]

Even before the actual occupation of Egypt, Egyptian rulers could not act independently of foreign control. Khedive Isma'il's lack of effective command over Egypt and his lack of military power reduced his power and helped lead to Egypt's indebtedness. To increase his income he resorted to entrepreneurial projects, trying his hand at being both a *tajir* and a *multazim*. He bought the land that had belonged to princes 'Abd al-Halim and Mustafa Fadil in 1865 and 1867, respectively. This land was located in Upper Egypt and was well suited for growing sugarcane, which Isma'il planned to plant, process in his own factories, and sell on the international market.[55] He also tried to increase Egypt's agricultural productivity, spending a great deal of money digging canals, extending railway lines, constructing bridges, and rebuilding the port of Alexandria. He also tried to establish a new form of legitimacy by building an image befitting European royalty. In addition to creating a new elite with a hierarchy of titles, honors, and rituals, Isma'il was particularly interested in building palaces like the ones that European monarchs lived in. He paid personal attention to the details involved, whether it was a staircase, a window, or the quality of marble to be used,[56] and seemed to favor Italian architects and Carrara marble.[57] Isma'il also undertook to modernize the center of Cairo (adding a new opera house), to beautify Alexandria, and to build the garden city of Isma'ilia. These activities helped to bankrupt him and to force him to sell his shares in the Suez Canal to England in 1875. They also induced him to pass the disastrous Muqabala Law in 1873 through which he hoped to raise badly needed funds. The Muqabala Law constituted a form of *iltizam* because it asked landowners to deliver taxes for a number of years in advance. In return, landowners' taxes would be commuted after that date. Cromer records thirty-seven other "petty taxes" raised by Isma'il.[58]

King Fuad (1921–36) gave his rule the veneer of a constitutional monarchy like those of bourgeois Europe. Fuad spent his early youth and career in Italy, so it was there that he looked for inspiration when creating court formalities, medals, and titles that would cement monarchical hegemony over the *khassa* alliance. One name that could be given to the period of his rule is the "age of the pashas." Egypt's earliest pashas had been delegated from Istanbul to serve as functionaries of the Ottoman Empire in governing Egypt. With the rule of Sa'id Pasha, pasha and the lesser designation of *bey* became coveted titles designating those closest to the ruler. A title was also attached to ownership of land, high rank in the army, and to important administrative responsibilities. Because both land ownership and administrative positions were the prerogative of the ruler, pashas became committed to him personally and were popularly known as "palace pashas." For these men a title meant power and patronage and was, thus, highly sought. Power was a means to wealth, beginning with a land donation that came with a title, which often amounted to one hundred acres. Titles became more diffused in the twentieth century and could be obtained in various ways, such as recommendation by the British envoy, payment of a huge bribe, service to the ruler, or inheritance. One way was becoming a minister, which often meant compromising political ideals in return for social power.

Titles, medals, and court pageantry were symbols of allegiance to the *khassa*. The importance attached to them under the Egyptian monarchy was meant to build up a hegemonic relationship supporting the monarchical structure. The system followed Ottoman precedents that began early in the nineteenth century as modernizing monarchs, for example, Mahmud II, began building new Western-style court "aristocracies." The rivalry over such honors kept the members of the *khassa* competitive, each striving to please the monarch, the embassy, and the prime minister, who had nominating powers. Thus, a code for civil titles was initiated in April 1915 and greatly elaborated by royal decrees in 1923, 1926, and 1939. Five civilian ranks were established to be granted according to services rendered or governmental positions held. "Presidency" was to be granted solely to prime ministers of Egypt; "excellency" to ministers or those in similar positions as long as no more than eight men held the rank at the same time; "pasha" to high government officials receiving more than L.E. 1,800 per year, to important *a'yan*, and in exceptional cases to provincial governors and administrators; and "bey" of first and second class to government administrators according to salary received (more than L.E. 1,200 for the first and L.E. 800 for the second). Each rank had its own form of address, for example, *sahib al-dawla*[59] for "presidency," *sahib al-sa'ada* for a "pasha," and *sahib al-'izza* for a "bey." Each had its own insignia and the right to wear it at public functions.[60]

An intricate system of medals *(nishan)* and badges *(wishah)* was also set up. Each category of medal had various levels of distinction based on continued service to the monarch. The medals themselves were elaborate; for example, the King Fuad Military Star was a five-pronged, white-enameled star, edged with gold, its center covered with red and blue enamel. The Egyptian royal family's emblem, a golden wreath over a royal crown inside which were two crossed swords, comprised the center of the star.[61] The inspiration and design of the medals were European, as was the whole concept of public exhibition of such "honors." The three most prestigious medals were for exceptional service to the state: the Muhammad 'Ali Medal, the Nile Medal in five levels, and the [Khedive] Isma'il Medal in four levels. Junior allies of the *khassa,* particularly professionals, police, and bureaucracy, were also eligible for honors. Thus, a number of other medals were targeted to particular groups, including the King Fuad Military Star; Medal of Agriculture *(filaha)*; Medal of Perfection *(al-kamal)* to be granted to women only; Badge of Excellence *(al-gadara)* for long, excellent, or special service to the government or social organization; Badge of Duty to be granted to members of the police and security, including *'umad, mashayikh,* and *ghufara';* Badge of Commendation *(rida),* of three levels (gold, silver, and bronze), for service to the royal family of at least thirty-five years; Medal of Knowledge *(ma'arif)* in three categories, for excellence in the arts and sciences; and a Medal of Industry and Trade, in three classes.[62]

At the same time, as mentioned in chapter 3, the British tried to mold the monarch into their own image so that he would become familiar with Western culture. The British government's insistence that the young Prince Faruq (1936–52) be sent to England to be educated in English schools provides a good example of this policy.[63] Prince Faruq benefited from the *khassa* power alliance but could not control it. Unlike his father, Fuad I, who played the game of political manipulation well, Faruq did not take advantage of the fact that the British needed the Egyptian ruler as a legitimate buffer through whom they could establish their hegemony by giving the Egyptian people a symbol of national pride. The situation after the treaty of 1936 and the withdrawal of the British army to the Canal Zone differed little from circumstances under Khedive Tawfiq. The ultimate power remained in the hands of the "British Embassy with, of course, the weight of British forces in Egypt and of

the British Empire behind it. In the final analysis British might was decisive." [64] The presence of British troops in the Qasr el Nil Barracks in the center
of Cairo and the frequent visits of the British Mediterranean fleet from its base
in Malta made this quite clear.[65]

To become and remain a pasha was no easy matter; it took constant struggle and cooperation among *khassa* members to hold onto power. For a pasha
to continue to be part of the *khassa,* he needed a position in the government,
and the struggle for such positions was incessant, causing real harm to the political system. Being part of a ministry or its head had its own significance.
Power was a road to wealth for the individual, his family, friends, and *mahasib*
(protégés). Whereas the leading characters of their wealth could be described
as men who did not enrich themselves through holding office, certainly each
had an entourage that gained or lost depending on the leader's own position.
The tentacles of patronage and social connections were a primary characteristic of the political process in Egypt. No wonder the struggle for political office
was quite accute; as described by a contemporary witness: "I saw—then I was
no older than twenty years old—many struggling over the presidency and bat-
tling over the ministry, almost losing their self-respect and national pride to
become heads of ministeries." [66]

Manipulation of the political process and control of opposition through
arbitrary "legal" methods became a norm. When Zaghlul (January 28–November 24, 1924) headed the short-lived *wizarat al-sha'b* ("people's ministry"), he used his popularity to agitate against the king, opposition parties,
and the opposition press. He was also known to switch employees often and
to assign his own friends and relatives to important posts.[67] The king and the
embassy often manipulated elections to stop their opposition and often encouraged various ministries to do so. Perhaps the most infamous of all ministries for such actions were those of Ahmad Ziwar, Muhammad Mahmud,
and Isma'il Sidqi. The 1930 elections that brought Sidqi's specially created
al-Sha'b Party to power were named "the most corrupt elections in Egypt's
history" and were boycotted by the *'amma*. A popular joke told about the
election of Mahmud Fahmi al-Nuqrashi in 1946 illustrates the *'amma*'s perception of the political system. The joke went that whenever a villager came to
the election booth, he was asked, "*Bitigra?*" (colloquial for "Do you read?");
because the usual answer was "*Mnigrashi*" ("We don't read"), it was noted
down as a vote for Nuqrashi, the *q* being normally pronounced as a *g* in the
rural areas.

Changes in elective laws, arbitrary executive rules, and police authority
proved to be effective "legitimate" instruments for ensuring results of elections and other political goals. Hence, men such as Sidqi and Zaghlul insisted
that they hold the portfolio for the Ministry of the Interior at the same time

each was prime minister. In a 1952 election (nine different ministries took office in 1952 before the Nasserist revolution), Ziwar's government not only influenced the elections to keep the Wafd Party out of power but fired those *ʿumad* and *mashayikh* who refused to cooperate. Village heads who resigned in a show of solidarity with their peers were tried in court according to a law that regarded any three officials who resigned at the same time as conspiring against the state.[68] Winning elections did not insure results. The 1925 elections resulted in a Wafd victory, but the king, who hated Zaghlul, disbanded parliament on the same day that it first met and introduced new indirect election laws to replace existing direct ones. A crisis ensued in which political parties refused to recognize the new laws, and the British high commissioner, fearing the outbreak of violence, convinced the king to reinstate the old elective laws. The new elections again resulted in an overwhelming victory for the Wafd, and Zaghlul insisted that he be the one to form the new ministry. But neither the king nor the British would agree to this demand, and to ensure that Britain's word carried the day, Lloyd George, then British high commissioner in Egypt, had his government dispatch a British gunship to Alexandria in a demonstration of power. Zaghlul was forced to agree to refrain from pressing the issue.[69]

The king played an important role in this political intrigue, maneuvering ministers against each other and, when it suited him, having the 1923 constitution abrogated and replaced with the more dictatorial one of 1930. Ministries that presented problems were changed, which happened quite often: thus, there were, altogether, sixty-seven ministries during the British occupation (1882–1952). Because ministerial positions were a route to wealth, there were always takers to form a new ministry. Given the standard of living pashas were expected to attain, which emulated a standard set up by foreign residents and the royal family with its court, pashas were in constant need of money and were easily turned into protégés toward that end. *Yigaru al-mazahir* (keeping up pretenses) was a way of life for the Egyptian *dhawat;* "out of sight" was "out of power," which meant out of funds. To remain "in sight" meant the culture established from above had to be emulated at all costs.

The history of Mustafa Nahhas Pasha tells the story of the struggle and alliances within the *khassa*. Born in 1876, Nahhas came up the political ladder through the legal profession, first as a lawyer, then as a judge, a common route for Egypt's political culture. He became associated with the Wafd from the very beginning in 1919 and was considered the most faithful follower of Zaghlul: he joined him in exile to the Seychelles in 1921, was minister of transportation in Zaghlul's government in 1924, and became Zaghlul's heir to the leadership of the Wafd after the leader's death in 1927. As leader of Egypt's most popular party, Nahhas knew a popularity experienced by no other leader of Egypt except Zaghlul before him and Nasser after him. His funeral in 1965, even after he had been out of the political scene since 1952, was attended by millions.

Altogether, Nahhas headed seven ministries from 1928 to 1951. Each was different, with its own circumstances and problems, and involved a different *khassa* alliance. His first ministry was a coalition with the pro-king Liberal Constitutionalist Party, at the insistence of both the king and the British embassy, even though the Wafd was the clear victor of the people given the massive public demonstrations demanding the return of the party to power. The ministry, which lasted for only three months, clashed constantly over the powers of Britain in Egypt. When it seemed as if Nahhas was ready to push through a proposed law legalizing public assembly and demonstration, the British, who feared that such a law would weaken their power, actually threatened Nahhas if his government did not cease discussing the project within seventy-two hours.[70] To get rid of Nahhas, not only did the king have four Liberal Constitutional ministers resign so as to raise a question of confidence in Nahhas, but a fictitious charge of corruption was brought against Nahhas, which not only caused his resignation but brought him to trial in December 1928. At the trial the witnesses to the alleged corruption confessed to having been hired to present false documents.[71]

But Nahhas had learned his lesson, and in the next government he headed (1936–37), he signed the unpopular treaty of 1936 with the British. This treaty suited the *khassa*'s different needs, guaranteeing British financial interests and their geopolitical position at a time of war while granting the Egyptian *khassa* the freedom to expand their financial base into the industrial and trade areas by giving them greater control over internal affairs. After 1936 Nahhas became more open to patronage, giving jobs to friends and associates and promoting allies; conversely, officials standing against the government were fired from their positions. His nepotic actions, usually blamed on his wife, Zainab al-Wakil, extended to medals, titles, and government concessions.

The February 4, 1942, affair is of great significance in understanding the interconnections and struggles between members of the *khassa* coalition of that period. On February 2 demonstrations took place in Cairo in support of Romel's victory over the British in the Western desert. The British suspected that King Faruq was behind these well-organized demonstrations to exert pressure on the British. After 1936 England was not supposed to interfere in the choice of new governments, but that was not to be, perhaps because of the coming of the Second World War. After the demonstrations of February 2, the pro-palace ministry of Hussain Siri resigned, and the British demanded that a popular government be invited so as to satisfy the people, even though that meant inviting Nahhas, whom the British earlier opposed, to form the new government. The king, who hated Nahhas and the Wafd's popularity, would not agree except to a coalition government. This Nahhas refused. In the ensuing debacle, a clash took place in which the British threatened not only to depose King Faruq but to cancel the monarchy altogether. The British sent a written ultimatum to the king, indicating that if he did not ask Nahhas to form a new government before six o'clock that evening, then he would be held responsible for the results. In answer the king invited all Egyptian party leaders, including Nahhas, to meet with him, and in a show of solidarity they turned down the British ultimatum. The British reacted by deploying forces, attacking and surrounding the palace with tanks while the British ambassador went to the king's bedroom and gave him two alternatives, either to accept the threat or to abdicate. King Faruq called party leaders and ordered Nahhas to form a new ministry immediately. The ministry that followed was a very active one, pursuing the direction of "Egyptianization." But it was also one in which Wafdists used their position to great advantage, becoming enriched through *mahsubiyya* (clientage).[72]

The new *khassa* combine cooperated together, yet their relationship was one of competition and struggle. Egyptian members of the *khassa* never really accepted British rule, even though they managed to become partners with the British and to benefit from the situation. Still, they understood well that however important their role, however wealthy they became, they were still no more than the tools of foreign elites who dominated Egypt for the purpose of financial gain and personal interest. Egyptians were needed to ensure the extraction of wealth and to facilitate British sanction of their imperial interests, the titles and positions granted them, and the modern education and law they came to believe in; the constitution and even monarchy they upheld were all meant to ensure that one end.

When Egyptian *khassa* members protested, or showed they had minds of their own, they were disposed of. Thus, in 1919 when national leaders wished to present the case for Egypt's independence to the Peace Conference, they were exiled to Malta and not allowed to return or to travel to Paris except after Britain was assured it would be granted Egypt as a protectorate.[73] The treatment of Muhammad Farid, Mustafa Kamil's heir to leadership of the Watani Party (National Party), is also illustrative. Because Farid wrote the forward to a book of poetry that attacked members of the *khassa* for ingratiating themselves with the British and the ruling family, he was tried and sentenced to six months hard labor. Each time Farid agitated or lectured against the regime, he was returned to prison.[74] It is interesting to note that because of their fear of angering the embassy or the palace, nationalist leaders who considered themselves Farid's companions in the national struggle never lifted a finger to help him even after his death in 1919 while in exile in Europe. No one but a small merchant from Zagazig, Hajj Khalil 'Afifi, came forward to pay for the expenses of transporting Farid's body for burial in Cairo.[75]

Furthermore, a clash existed between Egyptian government officials and the British employees who were assigned to supervise them. This clash in official decision making extended to all levels of the government and provincial administration and intensified at the higher levels of the hierarchy. Foreign officials hired to work in Egypt's administration must be seen as having a vested interest that they closely safeguarded by holding onto and increasing their powers over this administration countrywide. It was also natural that Egyptians who worked with such officials became obsessed with the idea of independence. Thus, 'Abd al-Rahman Fahmi's hatred for the British began with the direct confrontation he had with Ireland, the inspector of irrigation of Giza Province in 1911, which ended with Fahmi losing his job as governor of Giza. The clash concerned the governor's ability to make decisions without the control of the British supervisor.[76] Even "good friends" of the British chafed under their rule. Thus Isma'il Pasha Sidqi, a confidante of the palace and personal friend of the high commissioner Sir Percy Lorraine, did not mince words regarding the interference of the British in every bit of administration and business.[77] One particular incident stood out in his memory in 1945 as he wrote his memoirs forty years after the fact. As general secretary of the Ministry of the Interior, a position created for him by Minister Muhammad Sa'id Pasha (Ministry of Butros Ghali), he became the administrative superior of the British directors of Egyptian prisons, health services, and municipalities. When Sidqi called his first staff meeting, the British directors refused to attend and sent delegates instead. Sidqi was outraged by this calculated snub, but with his well-known political acumen, he postponed the meeting and made an administrative crisis out of the situation, thereby forcing the British counselor of the Ministry of Interior to make sure that this slight was never repeated.[78]

Another source of anger was the unequal treatment, pay, and benefits that Egyptian employees received as compared to foreign employees hired to do the same job. Egyptians were particularly resentful of the large numbers of foreigners who were employed by the British-run Egyptian government. Not only were Englishmen given the highest positions, but sensitive positions were given to non-Egyptians, mainly Syrians and Armenians (who constituted more than one-third of high government positions in 1922). Furthermore, persons chosen for employment were not necessarily better qualified than their Egyptian counterparts; in fact, most were not. Still, they received very high salaries and "benefits" packages. With the exception of a category of English officials in Egypt brought in to extend and improve Egypt's irrigation

system—for example, Sir William Willcocks—whose contributions were recognized by their Egyptian contemporaries, there was general disdain for the
majority of Englishmen hired to work in Egypt. Their employment was
viewed as based on patronage and family connections. The same was true for
foreign-owned private companies in Egypt, who scarcely employed Egyptians
but preferred any other nationality.

One illustrative example is that of the chief of police of Alexandria,
Alexander Gordon Ingram, who died in 1929, leaving a wife and two sons.
The benefits paid his wife included a pension of L.E. 39 per month and com-
pensation of L.E. 6,048. Because Ingram wished his sons to be educated at
Woolish Military School and Dartmouth Naval School in England, the government decided to grant the sons L.E. 2,000 extra to pay for their education.
Another L.E. 1,000 bonus was given to Ingram's wife, and an L.E. 486 debt
owed by Ingram to the government was canceled. Compare this to the pension received by the wife of Sheikh Muhammad 'Abdu, the *mufti* of Egypt.
Her pension was one Egyptian pound and 583 mills at the time of his death in
1905. In 1929, in answer to a petition, this pension was raised to L.E. 15 by
the Muhammad Mahmud government (1928–29), which insisted that the
amount was the best it could allot. Interestingly, this was the same government that had awarded the extra benefits to Ingram's wife and sons.[79] Osten-
sibly, the benefits allowed Ingram's family were explained as being in return
for the hardship that colonial personnel had to suffer away from the comforts
of home, even though Ingram was actually an employee of the Egyptian government. But colonial officers were generally depicted as disinterested persons
in the service of their kings and countries at personal cost and hardship. Khedive 'Abbas II, who experienced British colonialism at its highest level under
the leadership of Lord Cromer, gives a different picture, one shared by Egyptian nationalists and causing them greater anger at the presence of British colonial personnel at every level of the state. As 'Abbas II describes the actions and
benefits of colonial personnel, the picture lends direct evidence to J. A.
Hobson's thesis, *Imperialism: A Study,* that imperialism was stimulated by
vested interests,[80] in this case it is the interest of colonial personnel who benefited from the positions they held. As 'Abbas II illustrated, colonial personnel
were in Egypt to help their careers and to take advantage of opportunities that
they would not have at home. The British colonial administration was, thus,
seen as a meritocracy of its own, with its own laws, personnel, and privileges.
The experience of an officer in one colony was taken with him to another; the
differences between the colonies were unimportant because it was the interests of the British and their colonial officers that counted. Whether in India or
Egypt, the British assumed an attitude of racial superiority. The personality of
the colonial officer was very important; personal ambitions, friendships, com-

mon interests, and individual animosity played a prominent role in the running of colonies and in political events.

Sa'd Zaghlul's memoirs reveal more of the constant day-to-day friction between foreign and Egyptian civil servants. As minister of education, Zaghlul had well-known conflicts with John Dunlop, the counselor of the ministry whom he nicknamed "the assassin of education in Egypt"[81] and who used to be the tennis partner of Lord Cromer, according to 'Abbas II. Having been a small country teacher in England, Dunlop was hired to direct the Egyptian educational system, a job for which 'Abbas II and Zaghlul felt he was ill-equipped. Still, Lord Cromer supported him against severe complaints. Zaghlul wanted to increase the number of Egyptian teachers in public schools, expand the curriculum taught in the Arabic language, and pay attention to Egyptian culture in school curricula. Such plans, however, stood in direct conflict with the government's foreign officials, who were pressuring the government to hire more foreigners as educators, judges, and administrators at every level of the civil hierarchy.[82]

What frustrated the Egyptian *khassa* most was their inability to control the distribution and, hence, their share of the profit they received from the cotton they produced. The lack of control was illustrated during World War I when the Egyptian government profited from forcing landowners to sell their cotton at fixed prices to government and British exporters. Numerous attempts were made by the Egyptian *khassa* to control the situation. The General Agricultural Syndicate was established in 1921 to protect markets for Egyptian crops during times of crisis and to allow growers of agricultural products to negotiate directly with industrialists and thereby deny the middlemen their profit. Because, however, most middlemen and industrialists were foreigners, and one was quite often the same as the other, the syndicate did not succeed. Thus, when the syndicate approached cotton spinners in Britain with their proposals, showing the possible advantages to both groups, the spinners refused to do business with any other than foreign merchants in Egypt. The syndicate appealed to French and German industrialists but received the same answers.[83] The syndicate tried to set itself up as a middleman by buying all the crop and then controlling its sale. Even though they found a bank, American Express, that was willing to advance the money for the purpose, their efforts failed because strong connections existed between European manufacturers and merchant firms.[84]

Thus we find that however different Egyptian national leaders were in personal and intellectual outlook, they all wanted independence. Meanwhile, they cooperated with their "enemy" to ensure their position within the *khassa* alliance. The meaning of independence, however, was different for each person, depending on his ideology, wealth, social connections, and cultural background. Even though most were joined by their support of the 1919 revolution, they scarcely represented a homogenous group but were rather continually struggling over political power. Their memoirs reveal deep dislike for one another; they were divided by self-interest, intellectual outlook, education, and group alliances. These differences help explain their inability to take an effective stand vis-à-vis the British. Instead, as individuals they became quite successful in becoming wealthy and powerful, largely through cooperation with their declared enemies, that is, the British, the foreign middleman, and the crown.

Friends such as 'Abd al-Khaliq Tharwat Pasha, 'Adli Yakan Pasha, and Isma'il Sidqi Pasha were no newcomers to wealth, luxury, power, and court intrigue. They counted among their close companions other members of the power elite, including King Fuad, whom Sidqi considered "an exemplary king" who was intolerant in his devotion to his country.[85] Tharwat, Sidqi, and Yakan belonged to the *dhawat* and, like other members of their class, were more facile with French than with Arabic.[86] Their comfort with Western culture stemmed from the fact that they were not the first in their families to have traveled to Europe to live or study. Tharwat and Sidqi, like their fathers before them, had been sent to France to study. They had been buddies since childhood and remained intimate friends until Tharwat's death. They understood the value of patronage and how to practice it quite early.[87]

Sa'd Zaghlul did not get along with Sidqi, Yakan, Muhammad Mahmud, or 'Ali Sha'rawi, who were born into the *dhawat*, which was not surprising given his background. Unlike the others, he was of peasant origin, the first generation away from the countryside. His father, a *'umda* of some wealth, was able to send his sons to Cairo for education, and Zaghlul was first educated at al-Azhar in a religious atmosphere, wearing the normal garb of an Azhary, the *'iba* (cloak) and *quftan* (caftan). There he met Sheikh Muhammad 'Abdu and became his disciple for a while, joining 'Abdu's other colleagues, Afghani and 'Abdallah al-Nadim, in their support for 'Urabi[88] and their demand for independence from British influence and the autocracy of the *khedive*. His earliest political activities were at the Azhar where he organized a student committee with the purpose of drawing up a plan for the reform of the Azhar.[89] Activism was central to his character. His actions as 'Abdu's secret emissary to 'Urabi would later be reflected in his secret activities in such organizations as the Wafd's Gihaz al-Sirri, formed by Zaghlul and 'Abd al-Rahman Fahmi to agitate against Wafd enemies. Earlier in his life, owing to the lack of evidence, he had been cleared of the charge of forming a secret organization by the name of Gam'iyat al-Intiqam whose goals were similar to the later Gihaz.[90] In his struggles he stood against not only the British, but the *khedive* and the Egyptian *dhawat*, a member of whom he later became. He was ambitious, knew well how to advance himself, and learned early on to handle his enemies. The fact that he practiced law before studying law is important to understanding Zhaglul's actions. At that time a law degree was not necessary for legal practice in Egypt. Such practice meant that Zaghlul was already involved with the legal process; studying Western legal doctrine gave him an instrument to deal with foreigners and foreign laws rather than providing him with a philosophical outlook toward law and legal "order" as a basis for his legal and political thinking.

In short, Zaghlul was not born into an elite environment nor to luxury as were Sidqi and others of his peers, such as Yakan, Muhammad Mahmud, 'Abd al-'Aziz Fahmi, or 'Ali Sha'rawi. It was only at a later stage in his life, and as a means of bettering his social status, that he studied law and traveled to France. Zaghlul did not find patronage at his fingertips, and later he found that he had to compromise with his "national" enemies to climb the political ladder. Lord Cromer helped him at the beginning of his career when he most needed it, as did Princess Nazli Fazil, whose salon was open to those who would join her in intriguing against Khedive Tawfiq, her cousin, whose politics she did not like. It was through her and her friend Cromer that Zaghlul first rubbed elbows with the *dhawat*, including the future King Fuad, whom Zaghlul met for the first time across a card table, the two being gambling adversaries. Zaghlul, a man who early in his career wore clerical clothes, could not have felt at ease in a society to which he was a latecomer and that only through marrying into the Turkish elite and associating with the very groups he sought to banish from Egypt.

The natural constituency of Zaghlul was among the Egyptian masses. The history of the Gihaz al-Sirri shows the various social classes that were involved in supporting terrorist acts designed by Zaghlul, Fahmi, Nuqrashi, and others who led them. These included students, many of them Azharis from Dar al-'Ulum,[91] a cobbler,[92] custodians,[93] tailors,[94] as well as university professors, government employees, and lawyers.[95] Such individuals (women also were members of the Gihaz al-Sirri) belonged to classes of the *'amma* who were not part of the power elite and worked for its downfall. They identified their enemies as, first, the foreign occupiers, and, second, their Egyptian supporters. Their methods were to force the issue. Sidqi, no less interested in Egypt's independence and reform, belonged to the *khassa* and saw change as coming through that class, through accommodation backed by an iron-hand, as was traditional for Egyptian society, rather than class struggle as practiced by Zaghlul.

Because of this natural constituency, Zaghlul became more dogmatic in his ideas toward other members of the Wafd. His righteousness only emphasized his tendencies toward autocracy. He did not believe in party politics and did not consider the Wafd as a political party as much as a representative of the nation. Nasser would be heir to this tradition, and it is no wonder that the name of Zaghlul would be among those honored by the 1952 revolution. If Zaghlul considered himself a great nationalist, however, others considered him an autocrat who cared more for his own power than for the good of Egypt, and that nationalist or not, Zaghlul was willing to compromise on vital issues when it came to promoting his own power.[96] He was always suspicious of those who originated from the elite, doubting their motives and fearful of their encroachment on the position that he had carved out for himself. Jealous of Yakan's power, he was in constant conflict with him, refusing to support his various endeavors to reach a compromise and to negotiate with the British. His inability or unwillingness to compromise with what he considered to be Egypt's independence was in the same vein as that of 'Urabi and Afghani, who were righteous in their approach, paternalistic in their politics.

Muhammad 'Alluba Pasha, like Zaghlul, did not belong to the old elite. They were both one generation away from a provincial origin, but whereas Zaghlul was a *fallah,* 'Alluba was raised in the Si'id in the town of Assiut where his father had immigrated from his original home in the Hijaz. This meant that whereas Zaghlul still retained the craftiness of the *fallah,* 'Alluba, like other Si'idis, for example, 'Ali Sha'rawi, was much more vocal and straightforward in his approach. 'Alluba and Sha'rawi were also quite conservative in their methods and did not understand the radicalism that Zaghlul displayed when it suited his purpose. 'Alluba was also separated from other members of the *khassa* because of his moral values. Whereas Sidqi had to resign from the first post he held as minister because of the suicide of a woman with whom he was having an affair, who also happened to be the wife of a fellow minister and the daughter of the prime minister, in his memoirs 'Alluba is proud to admit that he never saw the wife his father chose for him until their wedding night.[97]

Other differences within the *khassa* could be described as philosophical and epistemological. If one compares Zaghlul to a man such as Ahmad Lutfi al-Sayyid, one can find a thinker of world capacity among this revolutionary generation. Al-Sayyid stood for an idea that involved human rights and individual freedom. The roots of his thought were a combination of the ideas of the Enlightenment with their emphasis on liberalism, constitutionalism, and parliamentarianism. But these ideas had an important epistemological side that may be his true legacy, which is that ultimately it is only through self-liberation that true independence can be achieved. But self-liberation was the path whose stepping stones were nationalism, political independence, and constitutionalism. Needless to say, such ideas were scarcely within Sidqi's pragmatic or Zaghlul's authoritarian vocabulary.

Zaghlul was a great orator. With his narrowly nationalist outlook, he considered himself a representative of the nation, an Egyptian nation: he was to be its "'umda." His concept of change did not really go beyond the need to achieve independence and bring about educational and other reforms. He did not have a particular belief in human rights, nor did he respect the ability of Egyptians to rule themselves or to participate directly in running their own country. Had he succeeded, he would have been a replacement for the power of the king, and, in fact, he claimed that the throne had been offered him by the British but that he had turned it down.[98]

In this chapter the interaction between the *khassa* under British occupation has been discussed with particular interest in the roles played by the new Egyptian nationals who became part of the *khassa* during this period. Considering this role and the place that this new leadership played as part of the historical process in modern Egypt, I propose that the picture presented by Zaghlul, his heirs, and his opposition is one of a new historical bloc in the making. Antonio Gramsci's description of revolutions as being either "organic" or "conjunctural" may be of use here. One can say that the generation of national leaders who had cooperated in 1919 were instigators of a revolution that was "organic" on one level and "conjunctural" on another.[99] For, on the one hand, the 1919 revolution represented a crisis in the making for decades whereby Egyptians were developing a nationalist ideology that became a legitimate basis for a new hegemony, for "wider social groupings"— beyond the people with immediate responsibilities and beyond the ruling personnel.[100] In the process this potential new historical bloc met with definitive structural contradictions and conservative political forces defending the existing structure and exerting efforts to reform them and thereby conserve them. The early members of the Wafd exemplified these contradictions, agreeing on little else besides the issue of independence; the revolution they brought about was conjunctural, representing one step toward the creation of a new historical bloc. In this sense the struggles between Zaghlul and his associates in the Wafd, as well as the Wafd's struggles with the British and the palace, were really resolved with the 1952 revolution when "the germs"[101] of 1919 were finally historically exhausted. For it was then that the Egyptian element, represented by the rising sons of Egyptian townsmen and peasants, defeated the representatives, Egyptian or otherwise, of the old society, and nationalism became the basis for a new historical bloc.

This type of approach considers class formation as something that is continuous, for even while the Nasserist revolution may be viewed as bringing about the leadership of new social and political forces, the 1952 revolution was really another conjunctural revolution, another step toward the building of a veritable historical bloc. Thus, on the cultural and epistemological levels, without which a new historical bloc is incomplete, a new hegemony was being formed in opposition to the paternalism that has characterized Egyptian history until today and which characterized the practices of different governments ruling Egypt during the modern period. This paternalism is identified by the creation of culture from above, by the institution of systems that are culturally and epistemologically different from indigenous ones, hegemonies that represent the ideals and outlook of the elite rather than society at large, as part of "constructing duality" as the last chapter illustrated. For that reason, however enthusiastic the *'amma* was in their support for Zaghlul, 1919, and the Wafd, the Egyptian *khassa* members were never able to mobilize the masses to bring about independence. In fact, such leaders were interested in using the masses rather than in including them in the political process they were trying to dominate. Hence, the *'amma* had their own forms of struggle against the *khassa* as a whole, including Egyptians and foreigners, and the struggle had its own *'amma* leaders who were more organically linked to the masses than were the Westernizing elite. The Muslim Brotherhood would be one of the first to mobilize the *'amma* using culture and religion.

Thus, if one were to describe the struggle against British rule, one would have to indicate that it took various forms, and each stratum of society seemed to have its own form of struggle. As a whole, however, all strata had one focus—to eliminate British imperialism. The movement evolved through various stages before and after World War I, but the aim remained the same.[102] Before the war, the Egyptian upper classes dominated the movement, although they seemed divided into groups—those who demanded full independence, represented by the 'Urabists, and the supporters of the *khedive*s, such as the National Party of Mustafa Kamel. The second group comprised primarily landowners and is generally referred to as the *a'yan* (rural gentry, big landowners, mostly pashas and beys). This class of people had begun as those who received usage rights to land at the time of Muhammad 'Ali; this right of exploitation, *milkiyyat al-intifa'*, was changed into complete ownership, *mikiyya kamila* or *milkiyyat 'ayn*, in other words, *a'yan*. Most of this group were non-Egyptians at the beginning. Soon Egyptians joined them and, with time, began to control larger areas of land. 'Ali Mubarak, Muhammad Sultan, and Ahmad 'Urabi were among them. Egyptians also received land through what is known as *masmuh al-masatib* (tax-free land of village sheikhs), which constituted about 5 percent of the area of the village. They received this land as compensation for administrative functions they performed and for hosting government workers (*istidafat*) and those in need (*'abiri al-sabil*).[103] This group also supported independence, but they did not want to break the alliance with the British precipitously because they benefited from it. They supported the evolution of this relationship to allow them more power but not the abrupt departure of the British, which would put full power directly into the hands of a monarch who had the authority and legitimacy to rule. Various groups agreed with this position, including high-level *'ulama'*, such as Sheikh Muhammad 'Abdu, who desired eventual independence but who could see some use for the British presence.[104]

The Egyptian members of the *khassa* became transformed during World War I. Before the war, most industrial or manufactured goods were imported from Europe. Control of the political system allowed the British to protect their own profits in this context by using laws facilitating imports and hindering industrialization. During the war years, however, imports fell because transportation became precarious and European factories were redirected toward the war effort. This gave Egyptian investors the chance to begin building factories to produce goods to which the public had become accustomed but which no longer found their way to Egypt. The landowners constituted the one group with the finances to create such businesses, and they began to invest their money in industrial ventures, banking, and building, previously the prerogative of foreigners. Once the war ended and Europe was ready to regain its control of the Egyptian market, the new Egyptian entrepreneurial class, industrialist landlords, naturally opposed European reentry because they stood to lose the most. Professionals and intellectuals also faced the same situation: having replaced foreigners in positions in the Egyptian bureaucracy and service sectors, Egyptians found that they, in turn, lost their jobs as the foreigners returned to Egypt at the end of the war. Thus, the call for independence led by the Wafd Party found an echo throughout the country.

The call for total independence won during the national movement's second stage when various social forces joined together to demand the departure of the British after World War I. These forces included intellectuals, peasants, shopkeepers, laborers, craftsmen, and upper classes who had earlier supported limited independence.[105] Even though all these groups called for the departure of the British, each had particular reasons for supporting this position. The *'amma*'s reasons are easiest to understand because they had opposed British imperialism from the beginning. They also saw foreign rule as a challenge to their traditions and as a reason for the deterioration of their economic welfare: local industries were unable to compete with cheaper machine-produced goods dumped into Egyptian markets by foreign industries. Mustafa Kamel's words on this matter are instructive: "Once commerce is freed from this paralysis caused by the British occupation, then shall the golden horizons open for us and for you, and once industries have gotten rid of the obstructions created by the British, then national industry will improve and the benefits from its advancement will fall upon the people of Egypt."[106] Intellectuals had been excluded from the political system, seen positions of leadership in the bureaucracy usurped by less-qualified foreigners, and found that their dreams of social and economic improvement, which they had hoped to achieve through education, remain unfulfilled.

The *'amma* directed their call for independence at the *khassa*, both the British and the oppressive Egyptian classes. When the Nasserists came to power, they found little in the preceding regime to hold on to. This stance represented the *'amma*'s outlook as illustrated by mass parties during the interwar period. The *khassa*-led Wafd, the leftist-then-Islamic Misr al-Fatat (Young Egypt), and the Muslim Brotherhood all had mass appeal and were able to mobilize the masses in populist movements that called for independence and social reform, each with its own ideology and program. The Wafd and the Brotherhood constituted mass parties; the latter was said to have had more than two thousand branches throughout the country and more than five hundred thousand members.[107] All three movements showed a keen awareness of cultural and national pride in rebelling against a culturally alien class of rulers. The *'amma*'s fight was clearly cultural, for even in the political and economic realms the divisions were according to cultural lines. The Nasserists would bring into power the first ethnically Egyptian rulers since Pharaonic times, but even they maintained a foreign cultural outlook, looking for "order" in other than indigenous terms.

5

SOCIALISM AND FEUDALISM

THE NEW MAMLUKS

The supremacy of a class of specialized warriors; ties of obedience and protection which bind man to man and, within the warrior class, assume the distinctive form called vassalage; fragmentation of authority—leading inevitably to disorder; and, in the midst of all this, the survival of other forms of association, family and State.[1]

The approach to feudalism presented in this chapter differs from Ibrahim Amer's use of the term in his theory of "oriental feudalism." His assertion that "the political aspects of a feudal regime are based on the relationship between the rulers and the ruled, the relationship being that of master to slave rather than that of state to citizen"[2] would seem applicable to the Nasser period except for one missing ingredient—reciprocity. The feudal relationship between master/lord and slave/serf is one of reciprocity guaranteed by law in which the slave has certain rights translated as the master's obligations to him. If one keeps the system of reciprocity in mind, mamlukid Egypt cannot be considered to have had a feudal system although the military nature of the regime would qualify it as one.[3] Similarly, the period of British rule before the 1952 revolution does not fit the feudal pattern even though the economy depended largely on land and the upper classes owned large estates.

The Nasserist regime's feudalism was not based on its military nature alone because it really constituted a combination of feudalism and *iltizam* characterized by a system of reciprocity based on a legal document, *Al-Mithaq al-Watani* (National Charter). Egypt's foreign policy and economy continued to be based on mercantilism, and feudal relations were created between the state and the *'amma* to enable the mercantilist system to continue functioning. Thus, mercantilism and feudalism were systematically integrated into the formal economy; together, they molded the state and its laws to ensure the power and wealth of a new *khassa* headed by the military as the power elite.

122

The need to build a new power base meant offering social rights, which as executed turned out to be similar to a feudal compact in which society shaped the concept of protection or services into a form of traditional *iltizam* with an added feudal element. "In a mercantilist economy access to the market is restricted. Special licenses or permits are required for virtually everything, creating a constant need for assistance from a privileged private group or from the authorities who guard the administrative gates."[4]

This is not to say that the Free Officers consciously pursued the aim of creating a feudal society. Far from it; the reasons for the transformations experienced by Egyptian society under Nasserist rule, which are the subject of this chapter, may first be seen in the lack of direction in the Nasserist regime when it came to the question of how to rule the country. Second, Nasser adopted socialism as a basis for the economy; as the product of European developments, socialism has feudalism as part of its organic makeup. Other countries adopting socialism have had similar experiences. Mikhail Gorbachev's description of the system that theoretically evolved in Russia as a result of seventy years of socialism, illustrates this point:

> Socialism has a different criterion for distributing social benefits: "From each according to his ability, to each according to his work." There is no exploitation of man by man, no division into rich and poor, into millionaires and paupers; all nations are equal among equals; all people are guaranteed jobs; we have free secondary and higher education and free medical services; citizens are well provided for in old age. This is the embodiment of social justice under socialism.[5]

The third reason for Egypt's transformation lies in the nature of traditional Egyptian class relations, including the principles of *iltizam* and patronage alliances. Fourth, the international situation during the 1950s, that is, the cold war and Egypt's desire for "total independence" from any form of Western domination, also provides a partial explanation. Finally, one must include Nasser himself, his obsession with independence, his class hatred for the pre-1952 *khassa* alliance, and his belief in his own manifest destiny, which led him to justify all his regime's actions in the name of higher causes. However arbitrary and corrupt the actions of the *khassa* built around the Free Officers became, it was of no consequence to Nasser as long as the "revolution" was served. Contradictions between vowed ideals and actual results marked the Nasser period from the very beginning of the Free Officers' ascent to power as a politically inexperienced military group.

In *Philosophy of the Revolution* Gamal Abdal Nasser expressed his surprise and disappointment at the lack of enthusiasm with which the Egyptian people greeted the 1952 revolution. Like other nationalist groups in Egypt at the time—the Ikhwan, the Wafd, the liberals, and the independents—the small group of army officers who started the revolution possessed great nationalist fervor and anger at what they saw as political corruption and social inequalities. In his book Nasser discussed the need for two revolutions: a political revolution to readjust Egypt's political role in the international scene and a social revolution to bring a sense of pride and equality to Egypt's people. As Nasser wrote,

> Every nation on earth undergoes two revolutions: One is political, in which it recovers its right for self-government from an imposed despot, or an aggressive army occupying its territory without its consent. The second revolution is social, in which the classes of society would struggle against each other until justice for all countrymen has been gained and conditions have become stable. . . . In the case of our nation, it is going through the two revolutions together and at the same time, a great experiment putting us to the test.[6]

This call for independence echoed a similar call from the time of 'Urabi.

The people's lack of enthusiasm was not the only surprise that faced Nasser. Having gained power, the Free Officers felt unsure about what to do next. They were not part of the *khassa* that existed at the time of the revolution, nor did they agree with the most important opposition of the time, the Muslim Brotherhood. The program they finally hit upon was determined by the class struggle between the *khassa* and the *'amma,* particularly the army's outlook and grievances vis-à-vis their struggle with the king and the British. Despite the fact that the army was part of the *'amma* in 1952 and that the revolution addressed the political, economic, and social inequalities of the time, Egypt's society would be shuffled and remolded to fit within the traditional division of society into two classes. Because this *khassa* was militaristic, the division between the *khassa* and the *'amma* would become patterned according to coercive power more than at any time in Egypt's modern history except, perhaps, during the three-year rule of the French. Again, this may not have been intentional, but may have been a result of the contradictions between the ideals and realities that are inherent to socialism. If the ideal is that "socialism is not an a priori theoretical scheme, in keeping with which society is divided into two groups: those who give instructions and those who follow them,[7] the reality has proven otherwise. So far, in different countries of the world where it has become the dominant system, socialism has divided societies into "those who give instructions and those who follow them."[8]

Nasser strongly believed in certain theoretical ideals such as liberty and freedom. By liberty, he meant the right to participate in decision making and in building a liberal political system. Although scholars usually translate *zubat al-ahrar* as Free Officers, Liberal Officers is as appropriate.[9]

For Nasser, the national revolution constituted part of an international revolt involving man's struggle for freedom: "The ideal example of national freedom . . . is the contemporary continuation of the striving of free men throughout history—for a better life, free from the chains of exploitation and backwardness in all their material and moral representations."[10] Nasser directed his calls for independence, equality, and nationalism against the West and its exploitation not only of Egypt and its people but of the Third World as a whole. To Nasser, the West meant Britain, not the United States, at least not until 1956 and his clash with John Foster Dulles, the U.S. secretary of state; imperialism was a function of foreign interests and their wealthy indigenous allies. Thus, Nasser defined the Egyptian people's enemies as: foreign conquerors with military bases used to subjugate Egypt; an alien royal family who ruled according to impulse and fancy; the *iqta'* that owned the agricultural land and monopolized the labor of millions of peasants; and capitalists who manipulated the political system to extract the country's wealth. He saw all of these groups as allied against the people's good.[11] Nasser faced the task of eliminating all of these groups and establishing social justice as the basis of his rule.

As for the people, "*'ammat al-sha'b,*" Nasser defined them as members of the middle classes, peasants, and workers.[12] The Free Officers strove to establish a strong military force to secure the country's independence and its control of its own fate.[13] Nasser understood the value of power, without which he could achieve little. "I really believed . . . that Imperialism is playing a one-card game in order to threaten only. If ever it knew that there were Egyptians ready to shed their blood and to meet force by force it would withdraw and recoil like a harlot. This, of course, is the state or habit of Imperialism everywhere."[14]

But Nasser also strongly believed in a social role for the army. Perhaps because he had obtained his own professional experience in the army, he saw the military as the only force capable of leading a revolution. The nation meant everything to Nasser; the 1950s were the age of national independence, and nationalism was the ideology that moved the people of other former European colonies. Nasser saw the nation as an entity with its own identity and purpose, a cause for which to live and die. Because the nation also represented a geographical area in need of protection, discipline, and order, its best leaders would be the military. In fact, Nasser believed that the army did not choose to play this leadership role but that such a role was forced upon it. "Why then did this duty fall upon the army? . . . If the army does not move, . . .who else will?"[15] According to Nasser, every revolution needed a vanguard to lead it, and in Egypt the army would serve as that vanguard.

> One of Nasser's important contributions lay in his strong belief in dignity. He saw as enemies those who denied the dignity of the Egyptian people and favored foreign ways over those of Egypt. In a sense, he understood that the liberation of the people lay in their acceptance of and pride in being Egyptian. This idea represented the legacy of earlier Egyptians, like the nationalist Mustafa Kamel, who said at the beginning of the century, "If I were not an Egyptian, then I would have wanted to be an Egyptian."[16]

Nasser's slogans originated from Egyptian sources: he changed Sheikh Muhammad 'Abdu's (1849–1905) idea of "Unity, Discipline, Justice" around to read, "Unity, Discipline, Work"[17] and used it as the basis for Egypt's "regeneration." His feelings toward the *khassa* of the previous period represented the *'amma*'s general class hatred:

> Often, when I go back to turning the pages of our history, I feel sorrow tearing my soul as I consider the period when a tyrannical feudalism was formed, a feudalism which had no other object save sucking the blood of life out of our veins and sapping from these veins the remnants of any feeling of power and of dignity. It left in the depth of our souls an effect that we have to struggle long to overcome.[18]

Nasser's success and his rise to power constitute an important step in the direction of today's cultural revolution. He represented pride in being Egyptian, and his anti-Western stance emphasized the desire to liberate the country from feelings of inadequacy in the face of Western claims to cultural superiority. Nasser also stood against the Circassian and Turkish ethnic superiority of the landed classes and the royal family. Egypt's government before 1952 was in some instances Egyptian and nationalist—certainly leaders of parties such as the Wafd, Liberal Constitutionalists, or the al-Sa'diyun, were Egyptian. But these leaders spoke French as well as Arabic, vacationed in Europe, and sent their children to foreign schools.[19] The Nasserists were culturally proud of their Egyptianness, and they even flaunted it, thus providing part of the reason for their enduring influence. Perhaps the army's failure to play an important role in the *khassa* before 1952 allowed it to play one after that date. Having escaped the stigma of cooperation with the king and the imperialists gave it legitimacy in its claim to make a new start for national pride and independence; it fit better with the changing superstructure. Nasser's adoption of imported ideologies, such as socialism or Arab nationalism, should not obscure his impact on the process of revolutionary self-liberation. The ideals that constitute Nasser's legacy, as embodied in the famous slogan, "Raise up your head, Brother, the days of enslavement are past," best describe the 1952 revolution's legacy.

Moving from the *'amma* to the *khassa* constituted a big step for the Free Officers, which may explain their lack of direction after they seized power. The army officers represented different social classes, from landowners to poor peasants. They shared secular attitudes, despite the fact that several members, such as Hussain Shaf'i, Kamal al-Din Hussain, and Anwar Sadat, had belonged to the Muslim Brotherhood. This association, however, did not remain uppermost in their minds when they first took power although their Islamic ideology certainly affected their later political actions. The differences between the various members became evident later on, as usually happens with revolutions.

The Free Officers as a group represented a philosophy that suited the newly urbanized classes that had been evolving since the nineteenth century. Composed of professionals, members of the bureaucracy, professors, students, and army officers, the new dynamic and mobile classes were ready to play a role in the nation's business. A description of professional classes in the United States applies equally well to Egyptian professionals and shows how universal these modern, positivist, professional middle classes became: "[They] can be defined, somewhat abstractly, as all those people whose economic and social status is based on education, rather than on the ownership of capital or property."[20] Raymond Hinnebusch explained this phenomenon as a "product of a challenge by a rising salaried middle class to traditional upper class dominance."[21] As part of these classes, nationalism and a strong belief in material progress moved the Free Officers. Their nationalism resulted in a strong belief that destiny dictated the 1952 revolution. It had its own "revolutionary legitimacy"; any action committed in the name of the revolution could not be questioned because the revolution constituted the ultimate salvation of the people. That final goal and dream justified mistakes or arbitrary actions. Such logic proved devastating to the country and to the revolution itself.

Nasser's background played a role in his ruling style and explains his success with the *'amma*. Nasser's family came from the south of Egypt, an area that retained its ethnicity longer than other areas of the country. As explained earlier, Egypt's governments have consistently encountered difficulty in bringing the South under central rule. The clannishness of the South resulted in *'asabiya* (ethnic or clan pride). In spite of northerners' jokes about southerners, southerners considered themselves more honorable and looked down on the docility of the Delta peasantry. Nasser brought these characteristics with him to the presidency, and his call for national pride, independence of action, and cultural ethnicity reflect these values. Even his hard-headedness and unwillingness to compromise when survival clashed with matters of principal contrasts greatly with his successor, Sadat, who epitomized the Delta peasant—crafty, shrewd, and willing to compromise for any gain. This attitude reflected the peasant tradition in fighting tax collectors or landowners at the survival game.

Democracy and socialism provided the basis for the new state: "Democracy is the placing of rule in the hands of the people . . . and dedicating it to achieving its goals. . . . And socialis[m] is the correct translation for the revolution as a progressive movement. For socialism is the building of a society of 'justice and sufficiency,' a society of work and equal opportunity, a society that is productive and a society of services." [22] Nasser equated social freedom with justice: "Social justice means [economic] sufficiency and justice (*kifaya* and *'adl*). Sufficiency involves production, and justice involves distribution." [23] In short, he saw equality in terms of economic justice, but this equality took other forms as well. "The freedom of the individual is tied to his needs for survival; by freeing himself from poverty and need, he would have economic sufficiency. He must be free from ignorance because knowledge is one of the conditions for enjoying freedom. And he has to be free of fear so that he would be secure in his present and future life." [24]

Because they had a power base consisting of new classes, different roots in Egyptian society, and an unwillingness to compromise, the Free Officers established a new *khassa* combine to rule Egypt, rather than trying to work from within the old one. [25] Their appointment of 'Ali Maher as prime minister for a time after the revolution and their "policy of creating conditions favorable to private enterprise," [26] indicates only that the new *khassa* was still taking shape. Because the army had not constituted part of the old alliance, the old structure became quite invalid as a ruling partner. Nasser intended to eliminate *iqta' wa ra's al-mal* (feudalism and capitalism) and replace it with a new alliance of the "working classes." By *iqta'* he meant the old regime, with its class structure, unequal distribution of wealth, and imitation of Western traditions, and the schools, missions, and banking systems that supported it as well. The following quotation describes the feelings of the Nasserists and other nationalist forces in the country toward foreign capitalist domination:

This foreign oppression of Egypt's national classes, national heritage, national language and values was the basis for the economic subjugation of the nation. As a result of foreign political and ideological hegemony, total foreign domination was facilitated; the laboring masses received much lower wages than foreigners, and the Egyptian intellectuals became culturally disoriented by Western values and, consequently, isolated from the laboring masses.[27]

The Free Officers embarked on creating a new structure that would unite peasants, laborers, professionals, and white-collar workers. Nationalism provided the cementing discourse, and Al-Mithaq provided the legal basis for this new order. The High Dam provided a national project on which the nation's hopes could focus and for which it would sacrifice. To ensure the necessary support, the Free Officers slowly turned Egypt into a "socialist" welfare system. As one of their first steps, they eliminated the old *khassa* combine and placed control of all means of production in the hands of the government.[28] Nasser's concept of a total revolution then became a series of revolutions encompassing all aspects of life, claiming to work for the benefit of the nation's rightful owners, the masses whom he referred to as *'ammat al-sha'b* (general populace).[29] Egypt's foreign relations became oriented toward expanding this total revolution to include the Arab world, Asia, and Africa. As Ghana's President Kwami Nkruma said of his cooperation with Nasser, "We realized after the Suez War that the small countries had the ability to raise their voices and say . . . no."[30]

Nasser, however, actually created a feudal relationship, bringing together an alliance of the working people and giving the system legitimacy. His nationalist socialist discourse was successful in creating a tight hegemonic structure. Theoretically, no real separation existed between the state and the society—one constituted the extension of the other, and its enemies were weeded out. No reason exists to suppose that the Free Officers did not believe in or desire this end, even though the results proved different: The *sha'b* became synonymous with an impotent *'amma*, and the Free Officers became the new mamluks dominating the system. They functioned as guardians and guarantors of the "gains of the revolution," like righteous heroes whose intentions could not be questioned. This feudal compact worked as follows: the state ruled for the good of the people, the revolution became all-encompassing, and the army had only the nation's good in mind. The government provided services in all forms: jobs, education, health services, social institutions, entertainment, agricultural subsidies, and so on. Socialist laws, which introduced state planning into every sector of society, furthered this feudal relationship. The state guaranteed each person an educational opportunity and every graduate a job; the state promised low-cost housing and commodities. It nationalized privately owned industries and opened new national ones. In addition, the state took the large estates of rich landowners and distributed them among the poor peasantry. It guaranteed seeds, fertilizers, and even mechanization of agriculture wherever feasible.

One result of this policy was an emphasis on the ideals of social and psychological equality among the masses. Class consciousness grew with the Nasser regime's admonitions, and class conflict centered on the demands of the poorer working classes for a greater share of the wealth vis-à-vis the better-off classes, particularly the white-collar and professional groups. Both the wealth and social standing of the latter deteriorated. Since the nineteenth century, modern professions had become established as the bulwark of the new middle class. Educated and modernized, this group formed the professional segment of the bureaucratic and service sectors without whom a modern state could not function. Therefore, they wielded some authority by virtue of their specialized knowledge, which the rest of the population did not possess. Although the officers recognized the importance of such professionals, and the revolutionary government expanded and financed education, particularly on the university level,[31] no appreciation existed of the political role that professionals could play. For example, the government gave doctors the task of running health services, but it did not listen to their opinions in setting the country's health policies. Nasser gave army doctors preference over civilians for high executive positions, including ministerial slots. At the same time, the army became attractive for professionals like doctors and engineers because the army paid more and gave higher benefits.

The educational policy stressed the sciences but assigned no real value to the arts. Thus, only weak students with low high school averages tried to get into colleges teaching literature or law. In 1955–56, 44.1 percent of all students graduated from colleges of applied sciences, but by 1972–73 the number had risen to 66.8 percent.[32] The reasons for this shift included the government's own development plans. Like Muhammad 'Ali Pasha and later, the British, the revolutionary government intended the educational system to graduate personnel who would fit into the *khassa*'s needs. Muhammad 'Ali needed to provide customary services to the people and to build a modern centralized bureaucracy under conditions of growing international interdependency. The British needed clerks to act as assistants to the foreign regime of *tujjar*, professionals, and bureaucrats that they were setting up. The Nasser *khassa* needed a work force to build an industrial infrastructure, run the state machinery, perform the mechanical functions of production and distribution set up by the *khassa*, and at the same time refrain from questioning the *khassa*'s policies or decisions. What need would exist for lawyers in a state where arbitrary power decided most problems and where patronage was the basis of social interaction? As the number of graduates grew, there was a corresponding increase in the number of professionals who became government employees with no real independence of action: they were part of a plan to build the country and industrialize it as fast as possible.

Political equality meant little to the new *khassa*, who represented themselves as members of the *'amma*, as embodying the general will. The officer class generally gained in power, prestige, and wealth, but the families and acquaintances of officers gained even more. A chasm developed between the *'amma* and the *khassa* that felt as large as the gap that had existed between the royal family and the rest of society before the revolution. The *khassa*, however, were not the royal family, and the *'amma* felt little love for the Free Officers, except for Nasser, whose charismatic appeal, personality, and genuine Egyptianness made him loved by the majority of the population, who seemed to forgive his penchant for power and obstinance. The populace associated the oppressive and corrupt policies of his regime with those who ruled with him rather than with him directly.

The evolution of the Egyptian people's political awareness, particularly among the professional middle classes, meant that anger and repression would erupt once the system manifested itself. The same middle classes that originally constituted the base for the revolutionary government were repressed, and they had to contain their anger because ultimately they lacked power. Professionals either became functionaries of the state or were totally alienated from it. The army possessed military power, and the regime had the massive support of peasants and workers. Humbling the bureaucratic and intellectual middle classes became public policy. This strategy involved no freedom of expression, no respect for life or property, and no concept of law above the needs of the state; a state emerged that represented only one order comprising mainly armed officers and their allies.

In fact, one can describe the Nasserist *khassa* as being essentially anti-intellectual. This may appear contradictory because in the post-Nasserist period the flag of Nasserism has been carried by intellectual groups. These groups, however, are remnants of the socialist elements who saw in Nasser a leader who would set the country on the road to socialism. Intellectuals during the Nasser period can be divided into two groups: those who were closely allied to the *khassa* and could be seen as coming into existence or reaching fame together with the Nasserists, and those who opposed them. According to Gramsci, "Every social group, coming into existence on the original terrain of an essential function in the world of economic production, creates together with itself, organically, one or more strata of intellectuals which give it homogeneity and an awareness of its own function not only in the economic but also in the social and political fields."[33] The progressive organization of the Arab Socialist Union (ASU) was supposed to train and indoctrinate young men and women so that they could play the role of socialist vanguard in Egyptian society. The organization had about one hundred thousand members, but only those who proved absolutely loyal to the regime were actually kept while those who did not follow the official doctrinaire line of the ASU were let go.[34] Famous intellectual and literary figures were also either kept close to the *khassa* and presented the regime with the work of their pens or else they were discarded. The most famous among the first group were Tawfiq al-Hakim, Lotfi al-Khuli, and Nagib Mahfuz.

Two journalists, the brothers 'Ali and Mustafa Amin, who founded the newspaper *Akhbar al-Yom*, would not toe the official line so they were made an example to others. One managed to flee into exile while his brother languished in prison. When intellectual supporters of the regime actually posed an obstacle to the interest of certain members of the *khassa*, they were dealt with as though they were enemies. The Kamshish incident, which is the Badari tale of the Nasser regime, was such a case. Salah Hussein fought in the Palestinian war and considered himself a member of the Free Officers, but his allegiance to the government did not help him when he came up against the well-connected Fiqi family, which had accumulated large agricultural holdings despite the land reform laws that limited such ownership. When Hussein became active and vocal against the Fiqi's abuse of the peasantry of Kamshish, he was murdered by an "unknown individual." When his wife, a labor activist in her own right, took the matter to the courts, the village was given government compensation, but the Fiqis were left to do what they liked.[35]

Other intellectuals were even more directly destroyed by the government. Ahmad Hussein, the leader of Misr al-Fatat (Young Egypt), recollected that when he discussed with Nasser the torture and then execution of 'Abd al-Qadir 'Uda, a leader of the Muslim Brotherhood, Nasser explained that "we did not look at the matter from its legal aspects, but rather from its political [ones]."[36] Of all the cases of torture of intellectuals, that which led to the death of Shuhdi 'Atiya at the Abu Za'bal political prison is, perhaps, the most gruesome. He was singled out for special "treatment" by his torturers from tens of other political prisoners on their arrival at the prison. The fact that he was a graduate of Cambridge University, was an English language school inspector, and owned his own publishing house played a particular role in his fate.[37]

The Nasserist *khassa* consisted basically of the Free Officers as well as their relatives, acquaintances, servants, and *tabi*'s. Attachment to ascendant groups became the ideal way up the social ladder, replacing education as the key to social mobility or power. Education could help social mobility within the *'amma*, but not out of it, which became one main reason that Egypt's educational system deteriorated. Although schools were added daily, they graduated only docile state servants, not people who could use their education to promote themselves in any dynamic way. Hanging-on and subservience became the norm. The country was divided between people who managed to find a way "in" and those who did not. Social entry was from various directions. Becoming a minister by the nomination and support of someone close to the president or Free Officers could provide entry as could spying on fellow classmates or workers and reporting them to the authorities if they questioned or joked about the regime's legitimacy. Because this proved a good means of achieving recognition, zealots exaggerated stories, sending friends and relatives to prisons and torture' chambers under the guise of nationalism.

One of the most interesting means of access to power became the government secret service, *mukhabarat,* which was originally organized for national security purposes to weed out foreign spies and enemies of the revolution. Membership in this service, however, gave people access to knowledge and funds that allowed them to wield great power over others and to control extensive resources as well. It is not an exaggeration to say that many of those who managed to win the most sought-after positions in the export and import organizations and in the foreign service during both the Nasser and Sadat regimes belonged to Egypt's *mukhabarat.* Members stood together and assisted each other to create "truths" that would allow them to benefit by virtue of their role. Eye-witness reports testify to the extent such positions and the patronage system were abused.[38] Although both Sadat and, particularly, Mubarak put controls on the *mukhabarat,* they did not end the organization's power. Rather, the characters changed, some becoming independent entrepreneurs or holders of nonsecurity jobs, and they still wielded power by virtue of the connections and knowledge gained during the Nasser period.

Having eliminated the combination of landowning and foreign *khassa* that made up the previous regime, the new *khassa* assumed functions under the umbrella of a socialist state. Nationalized industrial complexes became chips to be handed out to the regime's supporters. Such chips resembled feudal benefits "granted in exchange for service" and, in particular, vassal service,[39] which continued to belong to the state but were given to the vassal for his use. "The estates regularly distributed by the lord to his followers were much more pay than reward, [and] it was essential that they should revert to him without difficulty as soon as the service ceased to be rendered."[40] Such a system allowed the *khassa* control over its various members and "vassals," who remained loyal to continue their enjoyment of such benefits. They maintained a "patron-client relationship . . . [that] involved the maintenance of the client by the master."[41]

A scramble took place over the chips—a struggle over who got which company, position, or title. Competition also occurred over the property of the previous royal family, the *khassa,* and people who were declared enemies of the state. Their houses, jewelry, furniture, cars, and other possessions became booty for the new *khassa* and their hangers-on. Outwardly, the benefits remained government property, and members of the *khassa* became the heads and chairmen of company boards. Their actual positions in these companies, however, proved better than if they owned the firms, particularly because the government covered all losses. The companies were meant to meet the country's needs for food, clothing, goods, and services. Self-sufficiency was to be the basis of the economy; hard currency would not be spent on consumer needs. Consequently, these companies had a captive market: They could sell anything, despite the deteriorating quality of their products and services. In addition to establishing prices and being responsible for all imports and exports, the government also set salaries and rent on land and housing. One can say that the system was turned into a form of barter economy rather than a market economy.

Furthermore, because no differentiation was made between the budgets of public sector companies and the government, the government absorbed all losses. Thus, an interesting situation developed in which companies would produce low-quality goods in insufficient numbers to satisfy the market and would show clear losses at the end of the fiscal years, yet the leadership remained unchanged. The wealth exhibited by the holders of major positions in these public sector companies provided sufficient proof of the informal *fa'iz* that they received. Clearly this constituted a new form of *iltizam*, the right to extract wealth in the state's name and at its expense. Laws and the police force were used to serve the stability of the system.

Because Egypt experienced only partial socialism, managers of these companies accumulated massive amounts of wealth, which they managed to smuggle into bank accounts abroad while they lived in great luxury. In response to complaints the government passed a law known as "How did you come to own this?" The system, however, managed to divert the law away from those to whom it should have been applied, for they were actually asked to execute it, and they used the law to put fear of the state into the hearts of lesser government employees and possible enemies of the state who presented a potential threat to expose the system. The requirement that all government officials fill out a yearly form listing all their possessions provided one such means of control. This system continues today, even though few cases have ever been brought to court under this law. The Office of Socialist Prosecutor was created for the same purpose, that is, to prosecute the enemies of the people. In fact, it has been an instrument used to assert the *khassa*'s policies and, hence, powers.

The government also took over the overwhelming majority of international trade activities. The small number of private sector companies that remained capable of exporting could only function through official authorizations and had to submit foreign currencies earned to the government in exchange for Egyptian pounds. This meant that the *tujjar*'s functions belonged exclusively to the ruling regime, which controlled foreign exchange on every level to the point of severely limiting foreign travel. The activities of the private sector were further controlled through travel restrictions: Egyptian citizens were required to obtain an exit visa, and they were limited with regard to travel on Egyptian carriers, the countries they could visit, and the amount of foreign currency they could take along (a mere twenty dollars).

The policy of limiting travel may be explained by the desire to avoid contamination by foreign influence, which is a characteristic of other socialist states. Contamination, however, is only one reason for such actions; in Egypt's case forbidding travel constituted one method of controlling foreign currency. As explained earlier, small numbers of people were allowed to travel abroad after receiving the government's permission as long as they did not take any money with them. The government allowed Egyptians to migrate to Canada, Australia, and the United States. The state organized educational missions for which it paid and through which it hoped to introduce Western technology into Egypt's universities. Thus, exposure to intellectual contamination could not have been the major issue.

To control foreign exchange, the government created a general monetary authority. The leaders of this organization, primarily army officers or officials of the *mukhabarat,* were well integrated into the *khassa,* and they became quite rich after they took their posts. Government trading companies were opened and received exclusive rights to trade Egypt's cash crops.[42] These companies opened foreign accounts, and audits of them were not permitted for what were described as national security reasons. The explanation that the companies, the most famous being the Nasr Export and Import Company, financed spy networks to counteract foreign spying became a farce after the 1967 war. Members of the secret service had earned promotions and their colleagues' fear; it became clear that the *mukhabarat* was meant not to hunt down the enemy but to weed out dissidents.

The rest of the *khassa*'s relationship with the president resembled a vassalage in which the subject pledged a unilateral fealty without "corresponding oath on the part of the lord."[43] Such an oath may not have been ceremonial, but it was repeated over and over again in every word, gesture, and act of submission that the *khassa* extended toward a lord. To do otherwise meant expulsion. A well-known example of the consequences of questioning authority is the case of a minister of health, Dr. 'Abd al-Mon'im Wahbi, whom Nasser dismissed soon after his appointment because he dared to question the health statistics that were presented to the Council of Ministers.[44] In the feudal sys-

tem "the subordinate was often simply called the 'man' of his lord; or sometimes, more precisely, his 'man of mouth and hands.' But more specialized
words were also employed, such as 'vassal' or . . . 'commanded man.'"[45] Corresponding terms such as *rayyis* (boss) for Nasser, *'abd al-ma'mur* (slave of
God's slave), *aldush* (appendage), *mahsub* (protégés), or *ana bita'ak* (I am
your man) in his relationship to the lord can show the determinative nature of
such a relationship. The very basis of feudalism, "to be the 'man' of another
man"[46] expressed the relationship between each member of the *khassa* and the
leadership tier above it. Social climbers searched for a *wasta* (intermediary,
go-between), or what Yusuf Idris has described with accuracy and humor as a
farfur (leech); the goal of such people was to become the *farfur* of another
farfur in a steady climb toward association with power centers.[47]

The *khassa*'s relationship with the *'amma* became one of reciprocity. To
achieve popular support the new *khassa* went to the peasantry and the working classes and gave them a semblance of partnership in the system.

> After the 1952 revolution, the new government became more systematically
> concerned with the well-being of the rural population. . . . Particularly dur-
> ing the 1960's, the government of Gamal Abdel Nasser made a major effort
> to equip the villages with schools, clinics, cooperatives, and other govern-
> ment institutions and programs.[48]

The National Assembly established a 50 percent representation for peasants
and labor in the Assembly. The slogans rang with promises; the sons of the
peasantry and laborers could expect as prosperous a future as the sons of engineers. Five acres for each family, a job for each graduate, free education, security, freedom, and prosperity to all. As long as the peasants worked in the fields
producing the necessary cash crops and delivering them to the government in
exchange for local currency so that the government could then sell them
abroad for hard currency, the state would guarantee them protection, a livelihood, and social mobility. Thus in reality, opportunity and even the social mobility that came with it remained confined to the *khassa*. Egypt appeared to be
one large feudal estate; its citizens were modern serfs in the form of civil servants, peasants, carpenters, or shopkeepers.

Al-Mithaq outlined the rights of all citizens: the right to health services,
regardless of cost; the right to education in accordance with the individual's
abilities and talents; the right to a job fitting his abilities, training, and education; the right to a minimum wage sanctioned by law; the right to social security against age and sickness; and the responsibility of future generations to
children's rights. In addition, *Al-Mithaq* guaranteed freedom of religion and
faith to all as a basis for personal freedom, and it proclaimed the equality of

women with men, decreeing the destruction of all chains that prevented
equality so that women could join men in fighting and producing for the
country's future.[49] Men were also guaranteed due process and independence
of the courts and legal system. In *Al-Mithaq* ideas were expressed by the saying "We must realize that law in free societies is a servant of freedom and is not
a sword threatening it." [50]

What was the individual to give in return? First, his labor, through government plans. For the purposes set out by the revolution and for the good of
the country, every individual had to work to the best of his abilities. The following typified the slogans used: "Work is an honor. Work is a right. Work is a
duty. Work is life." [51] But work could not be pursued according to whim or in-
clination; it had to fit within the needs of the state and in accordance with state
planning.[52] "Each individual must be aware of his particular duties in the
overall plan, and he has to be aware of his guaranteed rights in its [the plan's]
success." [53]

The people would get even more in return, including the ideal that no
difference existed between classes. A potent ideology, the end of class differences became the basis for the Nasserist regime. As indicated above, peasants
and workers were promised half the seats in the representative assemblies. It
should be noted, however, that in practice the term *peasant* did not necessarily refer to all peasants but to special groups of farmers brought into the system by the *khassa*. Furthermore, the term *worker* did not refer to all
individuals who worked with their hands. Could the independent *hirafiyyin*,
those who had their own shops and crafts, expect to play any role among the
"workers" to be included in the National Assembly? Could the owner of a
small workshop, an electrician, or a plumber realistically afford the expenses of
an election campaign, especially when his opponent would have the support
of the government machinery? Clearly, those workers guaranteed 25 percent
of the seats in Egypt's National Assembly represented the government-
organized and -controlled labor and trade unions. The large majority of
Egypt's working class did not participate in the official industrial hierarchy
and, therefore, did not belong to the labor unions, nor did they trust such
unions. Thus, most actual workers stayed outside the political and legal system and did not actually participate. The picture of who was to be considered
a farmer or worker was not clear to Nasser. In 1966, during a question-and-
answer session with the "progressive forces" of the Arab Socialist Union, he
explained that he left it to the union to identify which peasants and workers
would be eligible for representation in the Majlis: "I have formed a design
stemming from experience and produced a picture of hope, [in the shape of] a
plan for development. But you are responsible for the details." [54]

The story of the Arab Socialist Union (ASU) provides a good example of the contradictions of the Nasserist regime. Touted as the true representative of the people and the only party allowed by the Nasserist regime, the ASU was supposed to be open to anyone who wanted to run for election. In fact, the union welcomed only those who would "fit in" and become amenable instruments for the state.[55] The ASU used camps, classes, trips to socialist countries, and various other methods to inculcate socialism in the members' minds, particularly those members willing to play a leadership role. Their rewards took the form of the material advantages that they gained from rising within the system and remaining loyal to the government and the ruling elite. Although in theory the union led the nation toward a true socialist society, it became no more than an instrument for the regime, a civilian army acting out the *khassa*'s orders. The result was reinforcement of the *khassa*/ '*amma* structure rather than a classless society in accordance with Nasser's declared purpose for the ASU, *tadhwib al-fawariq* (melting class differences) and ending *al-tatalu'at al-tabaqiya* (social climbing).[56]

Within the union no equality existed. The party created an intricate network of concentric circles, sometimes secret, to execute the *khassa*'s real wishes.[57] Intended to discuss national policy and provide guidance for setting up the socialist state, these circles became centers of power that turned the union into an instrument of the ruling *khassa*. The ASU, although supposed to represent the alliance of the working forces, only included the officially recognized working forces—those that the regime could control and co-opt. The professional committees and worker associations built on a socialist model and meant to provide the structure through which the socialist indoctrination could take place lacked notable success because they did not represent the actual groups in the population. The labor, professional, and trade unions that the party organized included unions for industrial workers, service associations, and farmers. But these large associations did not represent the reality of Egypt's society. The majority of the population did not belong to these associations, nor did they relate to the issues the unions raised. As devised, the ASU created these associations in the formal sectors for workers involved in the government's production plans. The system did not include workers outside of the government's formal structure.

The ASU's contradictions exemplified those in the country as a whole as theory and practice diverged. "There was nothing wrong with the Arab Socialist Union structurally speaking, but it was like an abandoned castle, denied power or effectiveness; its members were like employees in a ministry attached to an intangible power divided among various people, each with his own ideas."[58] It remains unclear whether Nasser actually was in control of the union, for he seemed to find great fault with it: "The organization of the Arab Socialist Union until now, 1964, is no more than an organization on paper."[59]

But he headed the political organ within the union responsible for its actions and direction. The *khassa* surrounding Nasser included such men as Sha'rawi Gum'a and Amin Huwaydi, who acted as the connection between the president and the union and seemed actually to control the organization.

The Nasserist *khassa* was quite hierarchical; its members by no means stood on equal ground or held equivalent powers. If any member of the structure fell out of favor with the president, that person lost his position and was shunned and disowned by all.[60] The president had his own friends, family members, servants, and political advisors. Each of these, in turn, had his own group. Primary associations were very important to the Nasserist *khassa* as Robert Springborg's study of Sayyid Mar'i has illustrated. Springborg demonstrated the importance of the *shilal* (groups of friends) surrounding Nasser, the network of family, clan, and friends who had the ability to form and to maintain their connection to power.[61] An army officer most probably served as the nucleus of a *shilla,* but that was not always necessary, as in the cases of Mar'i, who became minister of agriculture under Nasser; Muhammad Hassanein Heikal, Nasser's powerful friend and editor of *al-Ahram;* and Hatem Sadeq, Nasser's son-in-law, who had barely graduated from college before he became director of the Ahram Center for Political and Strategic Studies in March 1972.[62] All three men had close connections—Heikal with Mar'i and Heikal with Sadeq through *al-Ahram.* "This *shilla* was more than a tactical political coalition, as the fact that its members socialized regularly over the years suggests. . . . Marei arranged . . . [supervision] of Heykal's two farms in Mansouriya. . . . With unrivaled access to Nasser, Heykal provided his *shilla* partners with inside information and advice." [63]

Sons and daughters of the president and prominent Free Officers such as Minister of Defense 'Abd al-Hakim 'Amir, their sons- and daughters-in-law and their families, leading civilian members of the cabinet, and famous and popular singers and actors all benefited from this system, wielding great power through their own cliques. The whole system stood together or fell together. From bankers to small clerks, workers did their utmost to achieve power over coworkers or customers. Power and its abuse invariably led to some form of extortion, however small, to permit performance of a particular task. Bureaucrats, in general, cooperated in this practice, and they began to institute systems that gave precedence to bureaucratic power over efficiency. The more power the bureaucracy had over the system through executive laws and simple regulations, the bigger the payments that could be extorted. In short, each job became a right to be used for maximum exploitation.

Thus, a system analogous to *iltizam* became instituted on every level of the bureaucracy. A person paid his dues before getting a job, and even a university education was seen in these terms. Supporting the system meant good jobs for persons or their children. Working within the hierarchy also meant having the right to use one's position for personal benefit despite the illegality of particular actions undertaken. The extremely few cases of discipline applied to governmental and public-sector employees indicates how widespread and acceptable the system was.

The relationship between the various groups comprising the *khassa* was mixed; on one hand, they all stood together, reflecting their common interests within the system. But that did not mean that there was no struggle between them; on the contrary, the period of Nasser is best understood in terms of the struggles within the *khassa*. Problems began among Free Officers from the very beginning, for the March 1954 crisis had a crucial role in deciding the shape of the future *khassa*. General Muhammad Naguib had been chosen as president of the Revolutionary Command Council to ensure respect for the revolution because the other leaders consisted of younger unknown officers with little exposure and no popularity. The Free Officers's interest in retaining control of the Sudan and the fact that Naguib's mother was Sudanese helped to make him their choice. But it was clear that Naguib and Nasser would clash. The issue that would separate them was whether the army would rule or Egypt would be a democratic republic with the general participation of civilian leadership. In addition, Nasser suspected Naguib of siding with the Ikhwan.[64] The army clearly saw the revolution in military terms and had no real concept of sharing power with civilians or political parties of the old regime.

It remains unclear whether Naguib saw only a limited role for the army or whether he turned to the civilian political leadership after realizing that Nasser had become a contender for power and that the army fully backed him. Nasser's success in the confrontation with Naguib, which led to the latter's resignation in February 1954, evidently made the army the dominant force within the country. Army leaders continued to pay lip service to democratic ideas and insisted that army rule would be limited to only a few years during which time the stability of the state would be assured.

As the fighting among various members of the Revolutionary Council continued, Nasser increased his power bit by bit. He eliminated the leaders of other parties from the political picture by depriving them of political rights.[65] In 1956 a constitution was promulgated and the Revolutionary Council was disbanded. The contradictions between statements and actions became clear from the very beginning; the constitution provided guaranteed freedoms, but the government's actions worked against them.

The laws governing elections may have been the very first example of this process. The constitution required free and open elections for a national assembly. The 1956 Suez War had broken out between the first declaration of the elections and the actual elections, and the war had made Nasser a hero because the tripartite aggression by Britain, France, and Israel had not achieved its declared aims. A large number of people nominated themselves for elections in their residential areas, and general enthusiasm about the potential of these elections abounded. Suddenly, Nasser declared that certain elective districts would have only one candidate, the nominee of the authorities, meaning that the president would, in reality, appoint certain members of the assembly. Thus, the authorities determined the first elections, a pattern that continued into the future. The authorities had already agreed on 'Abd al-Latif al-Baghdadi, one of the Free Officers, as the head of the assembly, which simply followed the president's orders.[66]

The other Free Officers did not know that Nasser's bent was toward one-man rule, but perhaps his arbitrariness increased because of the nature of his position. As the acknowledged leader, he made decisions and controlled the other Free Officers. Nasser's popularity with the Egyptian people gave him the legitimacy to act, and through him the whole revolution gained legitimacy. Still, the other Free Officers seemed surprised at Nasser's actions as he quarreled with one after another of them and alienated them from leadership. As the Free Officers' memoirs published after Nasser's death illustrate, the members of the Revolutionary Council found themselves eliminated because they disagreed with Nasser's policies.[67] Despite the fact that these men tried to whitewash their own records and give themselves a larger degree of credit for revolutionary accomplishments, the picture is one of deep differences among the council's members over power, privilege, and benefits.

'Abd al-Hakim 'Amir, head of the armed forces, was one of the last to be eliminated, and the circumstances of his death are cloudy. Whether he died of natural causes, suicide, or murder remains open to question.[68] Perhaps even Nasser did not have the answer because the diffusion of power and its delegation to a "man's man" had become so widespread. Of course, by the time 'Amir was eliminated after Israel's 1967 defeat of the Egyptian army, the *khassa* had become divided into two parts: those who supported Nasser, and those who favored 'Amir. Nasser's supporters consisted of former army officers who had become involved in trade and the bureaucracy, benefiting from both. Men who remained in the army and found that the benefits were bypassing them in favor of an older generation of army officers looked to 'Amir for new leadership that would give them access to the benefits. Nasser recognized this in 1967 when he said, "I have not supervised the army since 1962 and thus no longer know exactly what goes on in it. My aim in so doing was to reassure 'Abd al-Hakim 'Amir of my confidence, but I now consider this to have been a mistake on my part."[69] 'Ali Sabri, the head of the ASU, confirmed this change during a 1987 interview in which he described the "military establishment" as being both separate from and even stronger than Nasser.[70] The 1967 war brought the struggle to a head, but the clash between Nasser and 'Amir was brewing and could have erupted at any time. As Hussain Mu'nis observed:

> The struggle between them was long and bitter, each entrenched behind his own fortifications and castles, which proved to be no more than spiders' webs. And within this power struggle, real power became the prerogative of a strange class of the rats of politics. With shrewdness, slyness, ignorance, and insatiability they controlled the fates of people, and behind the curtain of protecting the regime [nizam], they committed extreme villainous crimes against the people, their wealth, ethics, and moral integrity.[71]

The hierarchical nature of Nasser's regime, the khassa's feudal dependencies, and the army's domination of all aspects of business are best exemplified by the Tahrir project and its ensuing crisis. This incident happened very early in Nasser's career and is, therefore, significant in understanding the nature of the emerging khassa before historical events changed that elite's direction. In 1957 the financial condition of the Tahrir Project became an issue of public concern, and the People's Assembly assigned three members to investigate the matter. The director of the project, Ahmad Hassanain, a protégé of Nasser, tried to bribe the investigators by appointing them to lucrative consulting positions with the project. Nasser protected Hassanain and tried to put an end to an issue that could only undermine the system. 'Abd al-Latif al-Baghdadi, the speaker of the National Assembly, was becoming dissatisfied with Nasser's growing autocracy and refused to accept Nasser's handling of the matter. The Free Officers no longer presented a unified front; younger military officers who wanted a piece of the pie made inroads into the khassa as protégés of Nasser and 'Amir, thereby creating a gap between themselves and the other Free Officers. Al-Baghdadi insisted on pursuing the investigation and on having Hassanain fired.

The ensuing events illustrated that members of the executive branch would ensure that its desires became law even if they needed to manipulate the judiciary. Seeing that the Assembly would investigate and fire Hassanain, Nasser had no choice but to act to protect his protégé as his supporters would have expected by virtue of their compact. Nasser resorted to the High Constitutional Court, which declared that the National Assembly could find no wrong in any of Hassanain's actions because the Tahrir Project Association constituted an "individual entity whose funds were private. The fact that its capital was provided from the public budget [i.e., government] does not mean that its wealth is public. [Therefore,] the funds that were allocated to it became its trust and are considered privately owned according to the law of corporations."[72] To bring about such a decision, Nasser's niece's husband, who also served as the president's legal counsel, put great pressure on the court's members.[73]

Such an action had quite serious results. Nasser had already distorted the election laws to ensure that his protégés would enter the People's Assembly. Manipulating the nation's courts undermined the legal system and opened the door to using the law as nothing more than an instrument of exploitation. Because the Tahrir Project crisis involved corruption, graft, and the disappearance of public funds, this incident also meant that as long as the law was outwardly satisfied, it could be manipulated with the executive power's agreement. Power ensured wealth, and legality became no more than a matter of formality.

Under Nasser's rule, members of the ruling *khassa* acted "above the law" so often that when confronted with suggestions of illegal activity, they simply declared the law to be "on vacation," as Cairo's Governor Sa'd Zayid reportedly stated. Such arrogance and assurance were usual among the *khassa*. Actions of the sort included confining the judiciary's independence by excluding certain judges considered to be opposed to the regime. Approximately two hundred members of the Judges' Club who had refused to recognize government choices as members of their board were disqualified. The club itself was dismantled and a new administration created for it. Most importantly, however, Nasser became the arbiter of promotions, transfers, and hiring in the judiciary.

On another level, the beating of Egypt's great modern legal figure, Dr. 'Abd al-Razzaq al-Sanhuri, exemplified government arbitrary action and lack of respect for law. Al-Sanhuri received this punishment for taking Naguib's side in the 1954 crisis by calling on the Majlis al-Dawla, the country's highest court (of which he was president), to decide in favor of the sanctity of parliament.[74] If such treatment could befall the dean of law, it could happen to anyone.

The Nasserist regime declared freedom from fear and the sanctity of law as the right of each and every individual, in theory. The constitution provided for the separation of the judiciary from the executive and the legislative branches, according to the principle that the law and the courts should be above politics. Such ideas, however, proved highly inconsistent with the dictates of the type of regime that Nasser had created, and the process jeopardized the courts' freedom. Moreover, positions in the legal system were arbitrarily given to the regime's supporters in a form of *iltizam* that led to the corruption of the courts. "The rigid hierarchical structure of feudal society commanded and distributed goods and services not in response to price but in response to law, custom and the fear of condign and markedly painful punishments."[75]

The issue of fear as a form of repression must be emphasized. Based on more than simply prisons filled with the *khassa*'s enemies (particularly the Muslim Brotherhood and the Communists), it was an instrument to eliminate opposition to the regime. The parameters had been established: the revolution's legitimacy could not be questioned, and anyone who did would be punished. Although the full extent to which the enemies of the revolution endured torture did not become known until after the deaths of Nasser and even Sadat, the people were aware that such agonies were occurring.

The regime also used the law to ensure that foreign trade would remain in the *khassa*'s hands. *Al-Mithaq* makes no qualms about it: "Foreign trade must be under the full *ishraf* [supervision, control] of the people, and in this area all import trade has to be in the hands of the public sector even though it is the duty of private capital to participate in the export trade. In this area the public sector must have the major role in the export trade so that there would not be any corruption *(tala'ub)*."[76] In this system, because the public sector represents the people, its authority and integrity cannot be questioned. The public sector and the government had to watch for any corruption in the private sector: because it sought private gain, the private sector provided a source of suspicion. This suspicious attitude permeated the legal system, and it served the *khassa*'s needs to perfection. The public sector remained in the *khassa*'s hands, and they could use it arbitrarily to achieve any form of wealth. Their actions, undertaken in the name of the people, could not be questioned.

The *khassa* arbitrarily used the law and judiciary to permit any actions that the government deemed necessary. Sometimes the law in question was constitutional, but often it was a simple presidential decree. In addition, ministerial and administrative laws were used to arrive at any goal the government desired. For example, *Al-Mithaq's* provision allowing the confiscation of wealth was meant to apply to foreign wealth in Egypt. But the rationale for confiscation had become established and was used against Egyptians. Because *Al-Mithaq* mentioned foreign wealth rather than Egyptian wealth, it may have diverted attention from the fact that this provision contradicted the guarantee of security of life and property. Once the confiscation of wealth became acceptable as a basis for *Al-Mithaq*, which was to guide the future of the state, in the name of the revolution, the state or its representatives (its protectors, i.e., the army) could confiscate anything.[77] "Nationalization is no more than the transfer of a means of production from private to the public ownership of the people. . . . The transfer of any means of production from private to public ownership is larger and more important than the meaning of the punishment involved."[78] Thus, the moveable and nonmoveable wealth of the pre-Nasserist elite passed to the Nasserist *khassa*.

The public sector had a role in matters pertaining to internal trade as well. *Al-Mithaq* defined this role as control over at least one-quarter of all internal trade in the eight years after *Al-Mithaq* was written.[79] Interestingly, this proviso leaves the internal market to the *'amma* as long as they do not make any exorbitant profits from such trade. Foreign trade, however—imports in particular, but exports of cash crops as well—remained the prerogative of the *khassa*-controlled state. Private producers retained control of craft or luxury-item exports because such markets were too specialized and, perhaps, not as lucrative as the cash crop markets. Crafts and luxuries included bazaar specialties, tourist items, flowers, and perfume products.

Freedom of the press, speech, unionization, politics, and elections had legal guarantees as the prerogative of the people; in fact, these freedoms became the prerogative of no one. The government used revolutionary legitimacy as a justification for stopping any action that might be construed as being against the higher good. The regime set itself up as the guarantor of this higher good, so their rule could not be questioned.

The Egyptian people understood the system fairly well and were not fooled by *Al-Mithaq* or any other transparent ruses. The regime succeeded anyway for a number of reasons. First, changes were not instituted all at once; the revolution touched only one class at a time and left the other classes untouched until it was time to deal with them. Thus, most of the middle classes were not really affected until the nationalist laws of the 1960s; the earlier confiscations only touched the *khassa* of the pre-Nasserist era. The first steps taken to change the social structure and to build the socialist edifice occurred during the very early months after the revolution on July 23, 1952. On September 9 the first land-reform law was issued, limiting landownership to two hundred feddans. Another law provided the basis of the rental contract between the landlord and the tenant, giving security of tenure to the peasantry and thereby gaining their support. Between 1956 and 1960 other steps transferred private industries and business to state ownership. This process began with foreign companies and properties, moved to the property of the rich "capitalist" classes of Egyptians, then slowly moved down the ladder to Egyptian-owned factories, companies, and real estate. Not until Nasser's death did the laws he instituted lead to the confiscation of any wealth from the peasantry or really interfere with the informal economy; consequently, a large part of the *'amma*'s activities remained untouched. In fact, the Nasserists encouraged foreign craftsmen to leave the country, which in itself opened up business for Egyptian craftsmen, who took over restaurants, auto-mechanic shops, dressmaking establishments, department stores, and jewelry shops that had been monopolized by Armenians, Jews, Greeks, and Italians. As a result, Nasser remained popular with most of the *'amma* until his death in 1970. The 1967 defeat by Israel certainly constituted a setback, but the middle classes resented it more than the lower classes because the losses were felt in a more concentrated way in the cities. Furthermore, reducing the armed forces' arrogance appealed to the general populace, who felt constant pressure to provide unpaid services to members of the forces who arbitrarily demanded favorable treatment.

Religion was used to give legitimacy to various ideas introduced by Nasserism. Islamic belief provided a basis for the economic system and the rights and duties outlined by the feudal compact. A great deal of innovation took place, but that phenomenon in itself indicates how religion was used to fit the ruling regime's demands. In addition, some clergy willingly went along with the system and in the process became the voice of the government. The Nasser regime did not question the clergy's authority on religious matters but simply used them to fulfill the needs of the structure they were building. This policy held true not only for the Muslim clergy but for the Coptic Church, which was given a new role in the international community. In fact, the government supported the Coptic Church to encourage it to promote Egypt's international role.

The *'ulama'* found a new role to play in the new socialist, nationalist, and expansionist state that was being constructed. Their power was guaranteed but only if they served as members of the team. In this Nasser followed in the footsteps of King Fuad, who had manipulated the clergy to his own end and effectively had driven out all opposition in his failed attempt to have himself declared the next Islamic caliph after the cancellation of the Turkish caliphate by Mustafa Kamal Ataturk in 1922. As a result of the king's actions, the al-Azhar's authority was undermined, dissident *'ulama'* were purged, and demonstrations by that order were crushed. Thus, Sheikh 'Ali 'Abd al-Raziq was put on trial for having published his historic work, *Al-Islam wa usul al-hukm,* in 1927, in which he questioned the authenticity of the caliphate as an Islamic institution but saw it as having political and historical roots rather than religious ones.[80] Such ideas were clearly unappealing to a monarch who was creating a new patriarchal discourse in which he figured as the leader of all Muslims. 'Abd al-Raziq's expulsion from the al-Azhar was an event to be repeated quite often regarding others who dared question the authority of rulers who determined the al-Azhar *'ulama'*s interpretation of Islam. King Fuad's autocratic actions had led to the 1935 uprising of the Azharis led by Sheikh Ahmad Hassan al-Baquri,[81] Sheikh Muhammad Shaltut, and Sheikh

Muhammad Mustafa al-Maraghi, whom the King was forced to reassign as Sheikh al-Azhar to pacify the Azharis.[82]

Maraghi and Shaltut were two of Muhammad 'Abdu's disciples and were imbued with his ideals of Islamic reform. They wanted to resurrect the role of the Azhar, which had deteriorated to the point that it had little to say in national affairs, and turn it once again into an active institution that would participate in the nation's history, watch over its *nahda* (renaissance), and lead its people and Muslims at large. Following in 'Abdu's footsteps, in 1930 Maraghi[83] led his disciples in calling for the reopening of the door of *ijtihad* (interpretation); in emphasizing the need for the unity of Islamic *madhahib* as a basis for unifying and strengthening the *umma* (Islamic nation), he canceled the School of Shari'a Qadis and even suggested closing Dar al-Ulum and introducing modern subjects into the Azhar. The king, however, rejected the project even though the government approved it, and that same year seventy-two Azhari sheikhs who had been involved in the insurrection were dismissed under financial pretexts. The Azhar was then turned over to Sheikh Muhammad al-Ahmadi al-Zawahri (1929–1935), who proceded to implement a reform program that was intended to make the Azhar into a center through which Egypt was to play a central role in the Islamic world. A great deal of building and rebuilding of Azhari structures took place, which not only improved the physical appearance of the Azhar but also provided housing for both Egyptian and foreign students. An active missionary program was established to send trained Muslim *da'is* to different countries to teach.[84] Zawahri clearly had different ideas of reform from 'Abdu, Maraghi, and Shaltut, and the chance to push through the type of reforms the latter advocated only came with the Nasserist regime and its plans to make use of the Azhar in creating a hegemonic nationalist discourse. To achieve this an "alliance" was made with the *'ulama'*, though at the further cost of Azhari independence.

The first actual legal change of the Azhar to occur after the revolution took place in February 1959, when the authority over religious affairs was split with the creation of a minister of Azhar and religious affairs. In 1961, the reorganizing of the Azhar was decreed by law no. 103, which was passed by an extremely reluctant Majlis al-Umma (National Assembly) during a meeting in which nearly 49 percent of its members absented themselves, and in which Anwar Sadat, then the head of the Majlis, used all sorts of pressure to ensure the passing of the law.[85] Sheikh Mahmud Shaltut was the sheikh of the Azhar at that time, a position he held from 1958 to 1963. Even though he was part architect of the law, he was not too happy with it because it meant the integration of the Azhar within the state structure. But the law was clearly a compromise for him because it partially realized the dreams of the Azhar's earlier religious reformers: the law gave a new definition to the Azhar as a supreme institution of Islamic sciences with the responsibility for protecting the scientific and intellectual knowledge of the Islamic nation and with the goal of showing the influence of the Muslims on the evolution of humanity. Expenses and facilities were to be provided as part of the reforms to enable the Azhar to fulfill its wider national and international role.[86]

The reformed Azhar was to graduate *'ulama'* with an all-around education. Thus, to the university's traditional program for religious education were added modern faculties for graduating doctors, engineers, and scientists. A separate college for women was established as well. A new division, Idarat al-Thaqafa wa'l-Bu'uth al-Islamiya (Department of Culture and Islamic Missions), delegated Azhar graduates to teach and preach in Islamic countries and at the same time supervised foreign students studying at the Azhar. Cairo's Madinat al-Bu'uth al-Islamiya (city of Islamic missions) enabled thousands of students from all over the Islamic world to come and study at the Azhar. Primary and secondary Ma'ahid Azhariya (Islamic institutions) became active in graduating *da'is* to be sent out to do missionary work inside Egypt and the rest of the Arab and Islamic worlds. Even women graduates of the Islamic institutions and the Azhar's Kuliyat al-Banat could act as future *da'is* among Egyptian and Arab women.[87] Another institution related to the Azhar, al-Majlis al-A'la li'l-Shu'un al-Islamiya (High Council for Islamic Affairs), brought together for the first time representatives of eight Islamic sects (Hanafi, Maliki, Shaf'i, Hanbali, Ja'fari, Zaidi, 'Abadi, Zahiri) to meet in Cairo in 1962 for theological discussions. The meeting resulted in plans for the publication of the first encyclopedia of its type, *Mawsu'at Nasser li'l-Fiqh al-Islami,* which would cover the similarities and differences in the interpretation of *mu'amalat* (religious term for social relations) according to the eight sects.

Thus, the alliance forged between the Nasser regime and the *'ulama'* turned the Azhar into an educational center that would graduate doctors, chemists, teachers, and engineers who would also be advocates of the centrality of Islam in society. They would also carry with them the message of socialism so that Nasserist Egypt would spread its hegemonic discourse throughout the Islamic world. The inauguration of a special station that broadcasted worldwide Qur'anic recitation twenty-four hours a day was another step in that direction. The laws that Nasser introduced to reorganize the Azhar, although meant to further his political ends, must also be considered a success in reviving the Azhar and in assuring its *'ulama'* of an important position within the elite combine.

The discourse by which religion was molded to suit a socialist state has become legend, and all graduates of Egyptian schools during Nasser's rule learned about "Islamic socialism." This ideology declared that several of the prophet's early companions were socialist, including the caliphs Abu Bakr, who used his money to free slaves, and 'Umar, who was found sleeping on the ground to the surprise of visiting emissaries. Abu Zhar al-Ghaffari, sometimes known as the first *sufi* in Islam, was made out to be the first Islamic socialist thinker. The Qur'an was probed for lines that would support socialism, such as, "So that you would not have a nation of rich people among you." Other socialist principles were also found in the Qur'an, for example, the Marxist motto, "From each according to his ability, to each according to his needs," was reflected in such Qur'anic statements as "And to all are (assigned) degrees according to the deeds that they (have done) and in order that [God] may recompense their deeds, and no injustice done to them."[88] This line was used to show that the Qur'an did not approve of the existence of various classes but, in fact, differentiated between individuals in accordance with their deeds.[89] The line "But it will be no more than retribution for the [evil] that you have wrought"[90] was used to argue for social justice and against all forms of exploitation. In another quote, "Thus have We made of you an *umma* justly balanced that you might be witnesses over the nations and the Apostle a witness over yourselves,"[91] the phrase "*umma* justly balanced" is described as a nation without rich and poor.[92] The Bible also was quoted: "Jesus, peace be with him, has said in certain of his preaching, 'no one can serve two masters; he either loves one and hates the other, or sticks to one and scorns the other. You cannot serve both God and money.'"[93]

In discussing the nature of modern Egypt's transition from feudalism to capitalism, Anouar Abdel-Malek raised the question, "How could a society so tightly integrated into the world market since the 1860s present such a vast panoply of 'relics of feudalism' in the mid-twentieth century?"[94] As an answer, he points to the "persistence of ideological factors (the 'infrastructure')."[95] As shown in this chapter, feudalism was a logical outcome of Nasser's socialist system, especially when socialism was introduced into a society that was already divided into political, cultural, and economic dualities, and in which a military order played the ruling role. Religion, molded by the system to provide legitimacy, became a *khassa* instrument rather than the originator of such a system.

The complexity of the "socialist"-feudal system, which is only seemingly contradictory, has been caught in a tableau by 'Abd al-Hadi al-Gazzar, perhaps Egypt's greatest modern artist. The large (183 x 132 cm.) oil painting, which was painted in 1962 and today hangs in the Museum of Modern Art in Cairo, is appropriately titled "The Charter." One's first impression is of socialist-political art. At the center of the picture is a peasant woman, painted green to imply Egypt's agricultural wealth, carrying a white book titled *Al-Mithaq* in her left hand while her right hand is raised to swear an oath of allegiance. In front of her kneel a worker and a peasant, and behind her is a great lake representing Lake Nasser. The High Dam stands to the right together with Egypt's industrial infrastructure, and to the left are depicted weapons representing Egypt's army and navy.

But the picture is very disturbing, and only after one studies it a second and third time does another picture appear, contradictory in one sense yet really meant to be integral. The most disturbing aspect of the picture is that the green skin color gives the impression of sickness, and the toes, which are gray, give the impression of death. Closer scrutiny convinces one that the artist was trying to convey a sense of lingering death: dead branches are sprouting from the woman's head, and the viewer suddenly realizes that the woman is really the root of the tree. The dead branches and the green face under them are a depiction of Medusa, and the chain hanging around the neck presents pagan inscriptions symbolizing what appears to be a snake. In the center of the head between the tree branches is the *nisr* (eagle) symbol of the Nasser regime, but it appears too much like the symbol of Roman legions. Most telling is the peasant at the feet of the central figure; his head is bent as he looks at a scant quantity of cotton and wheat, disillusionment on his face. Next to him is a "peasant's friend," an egret, standing on the peasant's neglected land deed, the document representing his "gains" from the 1952 revolution.

6

THE NEW *TUJJAR* AND *INFITAH*

What can I do when I am but a weak man without your power? . . . I am forbidden from addressing [you] and I do not have a [mass] media apparatus or a newspaper in which I could write what I wish. No one stands by me except for God. I became angry with the eminent Sheikh al-Sha'rawi the Minister of Awqaf and Azhar Affairs . . . the day he stood here [in the People's Assembly] and made out of Anwar Sadat a God together with Allah.[1]

In early 1969 United Nations special emissary Gunnar Jarring's efforts to promote an Israeli-Arab agreement based on U.N. Security Council Resolution 242 reached an impasse, and the Middle East situation deteriorated as the war of attrition continued. The United States, realizing that a stalemate situation worked against its interests in the Middle East, decided to review its political and military policies in the area. The review resulted in a major peace initiative through which the United States hoped to "encourage the parties to stop shooting and start talking."[2]

Throughout 1969 the United States held bilateral talks with the Soviet Union and multilateral talks with Britain and France, and discussions with Israel, Egypt, and Jordan in an unsuccessful effort to create guidelines for Jarring's work.[3] All of the countries concerned had approved the peace offensive called the Rogers Peace Plan[4] after U.S. Secretary of State William Rogers, and the United States had even declared the possibility that, together with the other three powers, it could guarantee a treaty and ensure that all sides fulfilled their commitments.[5] This initiative, however, only resulted in the ending of the war of attrition and a cease-fire that continued until the 1973 Arab-Israeli war.[6]

Many reasons have been given for the failure of this American initiative after it seemed to be working successfully. Some scholars blamed Israel's reluctance to surrender any territory captured in the 1967 war, and others faulted the Arabs' reluctance to recognize Israel. Still other scholars criticized the Soviets' role in keeping the situation stalemated. Although the United

States had begun the initiative, it did not follow through on its efforts even though Nasser called on the United States to resume negotiations in a May 1970 speech and, despite opposition from other Arab leaders, declared himself fully behind the U.S. peace effort at the Rabat Arab Summit later that year—a statement that the United States considered a positive sign from Egypt.[7] On the surface U.S. actions appeared strange, for rather than pressure Israel to agree to the plan, the United States instead took a hard line with the Arabs, primarily Egypt,[8] and supplied Israel with more military aid than it had received from all U.S. presidents before Nixon combined.[9]

The puzzling attitude of the United States may be explained by the strength of the Israeli lobby in Congress. But there is more to it that was of importance to Sadat's future policies. When Rogers met with Nasser, the two men discussed other issues besides peace: the United States wanted to impress on Nasser that it constituted the only party capable of delivering such a peace and that no solution could be attained with Soviet assistance alone. For the United States to act at that time, however, Egypt would have had to expel its Russian advisors, reorient its political system and economy toward free market enterprise, and begin to play its traditional role as a leader of the Islamic, Arab, and Third World to return to the free market those areas in which socialism had made inroads.[10] The United States was prepared to have Israeli forces withdraw to pre-1967 lines (except for minor changes that would not mean any real gains in territory)[11] and try to solve the Palestinian refugee problem;[12] as a bonus, the United States promised to help rebuild the economies wrecked during the war.[13] The United States outlined this blueprint to Nasser and, later, to Sadat. To retrieve Sinai, rebuild its economy, and achieve peace, Egypt would have to reorient its ideology and economy toward the West.

Two other points must be explained to understand Sadat's subsequent actions. First, a change in the U.S. stand occurred when Henry Kissinger replaced William Rogers. Kissinger was not willing to compromise on any issues regarding peace, and he clearly directed his policy toward exchanging peace for Arab recognition of Israel. Kissinger also considered territory occupied by Israel as the spoils of war and repeatedly declared that the Arabs would have to accept the loss of territory to achieve any form of peace. Nixon's weakness because of Watergate made Kissinger and the Israeli lobby all the more important, and Sadat found that fulfilling the demands set by the Rogers Peace Plan no longer would suffice to make the United States support a fair solution in the Middle East. This point provides an important element in understanding Sadat's decision to go to war: he needed to convince the United States that Egypt would not accept the status quo as Kissinger expected despite Israel's support from the United States. Second, the student movement that reemerged on Egyptian university campuses in 1972 in the form of massive demonstrations calling for an end to the Israeli occupation of the Sinai convinced Sadat that he could not leave the question lingering.[14]

Another reason to go to war was the 1967 defeat, which had undermined the army's legitimacy. The army's performance had caused the people to lose their respect for the army. Respect is essential for claims to power, and without it, the *khassa*'s legitimacy came into question. The army later justified its defeat by raising the question of whether it actually fought in 1967 or was defeated on the home front. But Sadat faced the difficulty of regaining for the army the prestige that would allow it to continue as the bulwark of his power. When Nasser died in 1970 and Sadat came to power, Sadat feared that the state could fall into the hands of a power center led by 'Ali Sabri, the head of the Arab Socialist Union (ASU), who also served as the choice of the Soviet Union to succeed Nasser, and Sami Sharaf, the powerful chief of the presidential offices. Sadat found his greatest support in the army, who backed him as the legitimate president because the success of the 'Ali Sabri–Sami Sharaf clique[15] could have meant the domination of the *khassa* by the Soviet-supported ASU.

General disillusionment with the 1952 revolution also existed among the *'amma*. The 1967 defeat was only the tip of the iceberg. The government's arbitrariness and the lack of freedom stifled the people and caused great turmoil. The student movement was symptomatic of social malaise:

> The uprising of February 1968 marked the students' initial reaction to the defeat and the beginning of their confrontation with the regime. It reflected the failure of the official youth organizations, indeed of the whole range of official political organizations, to contain their movement. Its intensity was attributable to the scale of the military defeat itself as much as to the constraints on self-expression among students and intellectuals long before the defeat.[16]

Sadat knew that he would have to introduce changes to ensure the continuance in power of the *khassa* created by the 1952 revolution. Whether Sadat favored a social revolution, his own career seemed to show that he was a political activist who believed more in independence than anything else. His *khassa*, however, which represented very much the same groups as those who ruled with Nasser, needed to look at the economic and political system anew and mold it to fit a new international situation and changes in Egypt's superstructure, including the growing politicization of the *'amma*, the growth of vocal opposition, and the challenge to the regime that exhibited the beginning of the end of fear as a method of control.

Thus, the new *infitah* (open door policy) liberalization policies came in response to both national and international pressures. The name *infitah* given to the new policy gave an impression of opening up to the world, establishment of a market economy, liberalization of the political system, and removal of restrictions on the growth of the private sector. "Under *infitah* the new policy changes are gradually transforming the centralized state capitalist economy of the past into a liberalized one enhancing free enterprise. The position of the private sector generally is to be strengthened with special attention being given to foreign investors, joint ventures and commercial agents operating in a liberalized foreign trading system." [17]

However positive the *'amma*'s outlook toward *infitah*, it soon proved unequal to expectations, largely as a result of the *khassa*'s reluctance to allow full equality between the various sectors of society. Rather, the *khassa* continued to uphold class difference, and the new policy did not eliminate the mercantilist policies of previous regimes. Sadat's reign represented the rule of a *khassa* that still enjoyed much the same powers and privileges as under Nasser. Comprising the military, although less the arbitrary mamluks of the Nasser regime, the *khassa* was dominated by a new class of *tujjar* who manipulated the laws and pushed new statutes through, thereby enjoying the power of privilege and the wealth that could accrue from it. Finally, the government *multazim*s of the Sadat period continued the same groups as under Nasser and enjoyed their positions and the *fa'iz* that they could make from holding public office, determining executive and administrative laws, controlling most of the country's production and distribution, and importing and exporting goods and services. They performed all of these activities for their own benefit and that of the *khassa* as a whole. With few changes, the *khassa* continued to exhibit the same characteristics in the early years of Mubarak's presidency. In the 1990s, however, a changing Egypt would finally begin to fulfill the promises of peace and *Infitah*.

How does this pattern differ from that of earlier periods? On one hand, the situation differed little: the *khassa* cooperated to ensure their power and wealth. Although the Nasserist elite continued to play a role under Sadat, they became transformed into members of the newly created Nationalist Party. New slogans, institutions, and laws were introduced to keep them in power. Thus, people who had espoused socialism now favored *infitah*, liberalism, Westernism, or even Islamic fundamentalism. Ideologies mattered not—pragmatism was more important, part of the process of self-liberation and revivalism. People who opposed the system generally were expelled from it. The groups composing this *khassa* did not necessarily maintain friendly relations; on the contrary, they competed and struggled over who received which benefits, but they also realized that they stood together or fell together, so they were willing to collaborate as long as they benefited from the system. Thus, if

one considers the conspiracy charges brought against those who tried to over-
throw the Sadat regime and establish Sabri as the head of the state, the sentences meted out and the lax enforcement of the penalties seem surprising.[18]
These phenomena, however, should be seen as part of a system by which the
khassa disciplined members of its own groups. After all, because they shared a
common fate, no one could be overly punished.

Sadat's rise to power produced a marked change in the military's status.
As demonstrated in chapter 5, the military under Nasser enjoyed what
amounted to mamluk powers. As such, military factions represented competing parties, each vying for more power and benefits. Nasser's personality, his
charisma, and the fact that he provided the basis of the regime's legitimacy
meant that he had the final word in the system. That did not mean, however,
that no factions existed. Those who found their way to the top levels of power
became civilian members of the *khassa,* and the lower echelons of the army
tried to gain power through the failed attempt by 'Amir to wrest power after
the 1967 defeat. In his fight for power against the Sabri clique, Sadat used the
same sympathies that had supported 'Amir to gain army support and eliminate the leftist elements headed by the minister of war, Muhammad Fawzi.
Furthermore, the lack of Soviet help in the 1967 war, besides the frictions that
had characterized the relationship between the Soviet experts and the Egyptian officers they trained, played an important role in the army's distaste for the
Left and the army's unwillingness to see leftists become stronger.

As was explained in chapter 5, the Free Officers' power had diminished
before Sadat came to power. Those who disagreed with Nasser had been side-
lined, and others who had opposed Nasser actually ended up in prison. A
number of officers who had affiliations too close with the Muslim Brotherhood were imprisoned and tortured; their membership in the Free Officer
movement or active leadership roles in the 1952 Revolution did not save
them.[19] Under Sadat, the Free Officers, particularly those marginalized by
Nasser, such as Kamal al-Din Hussain or 'Abd al-Latif al-Baghdadi, experienced a symbolic revival. They, however, were marginalized once they proved
unwilling to tag along with Sadat. Sadat's quarrel with Hussain in particular
received a lot of publicity in the Egyptian press and ended with Hussain's expulsion from the People's Assembly to which he had been elected as an independent.[20]

The *'ubur* (the army's successful crossing of the Suez and Barlef line) of
the 1973 war regained legitimacy for the armed forces, but its role would be
different. The top leadership of the country would still come from the armed
forces; Sadat and Mubarak both were military men. Former military men continued to head public companies and to hold important jobs as ministers and
ambassadors, but to a much lesser extent than earlier. One study has shown

how the participation of military men in the Egyptian cabinet decreased significantly toward the end of Nasser's rule.[21] Two different instances of demilitarization were noted: one in 1968 after the 1967 defeat when Egyptian public opinion demanded it, and later in May 1971 during what Sadat called the "corrective revolution" by which his opposition under Sabri, Sharaf, and Fawzi was crushed.[22] The power of the army under Sadat became vested in it as a separate body and not as a body incorporated into the actual governmental machinery. Particularly after 'Abd al-Halim Abu Ghazala became *mushir* (top rank in the army) and minister of defense, the army became a power of its own, a state within a state. It became a separate member of the *khassa*, guaranteeing the country's stability and thereby ensuring the *khassa*'s rule. Thus, whereas military men under Nasser had formed the *khassa*, under Sadat they became only part of the *khassa* and had to make room for new elements of *tujjar* and for sharing power with the government hierarchy. The police also became all-powerful and -important under Sadat, constituting the regime's coercive hand against growing opposition. The selection of Mamduh Salim, first as minister of the interior and then premier, indicates the importance of the police in Sadat's rule.

In addition to the importance of the army and police in providing the regime's security and stability, two important trends emerged during the 1970s. First, the *'amma* exhibited a growing aggressiveness and lack of fear of the state's power of intimidation, a fact of life for Egyptians since the British established the instruments of intimidation eighty years earlier. Second, a change occurred within the *khassa*, which experienced a growing diffusion of power that allowed a greater sharing of wealth by a larger base. These changes did not mean an end to authority from above; it simply meant that what had appeared as absolutist presidential authority based on military power was to become more obviously a form of *khassa* authority. It also meant a shift in the relationship between a changing *khassa* and a freer, more vocal *'amma*.

Interestingly, the opposite process occurred in other countries that had much the same economic problems as Egypt during the 1970s. For example, in one study it is argued that in Mexico during that decade "with the growth of presidential authority . . . power came increasingly from above rather than below and, consequently, the fruits of corruption began to move upward rather than downward."[23] Perhaps if one examines the question of authority in Mexico in a more diffuse way, in Mexico as in Egypt more sharing of benefits took place, even if most of them remained the prerogative of a *khassa* combine. Before this time, *infitah* power and the benefits accompanying it were to a large extent concentrated according to position in the bureaucratic structure, with an elite enjoying great power on top. As John Waterbury described:

At least four administrative strata [exist] within the personnel of the civil service and the public sector with fairly distinct interests and career perspectives. There is a managerial elite of a few thousand, made up of ministers, deputy ministers, division heads, presidents and members of the boards of directors of companies and agencies, and provincial governors. . . . Few of the [other members of the bureaucracy amounting to] nearly three million employees can hope to ascend very far within the bureaucratic hierarchy.[24]

After the introduction of *infitah,* membership in the upper bureaucratic hierarchy did not necessarily provide access to either power or wealth, although for government employees to belong to the *khassa,* they had to be part of that upper stratum. The issue did not involve which role or position was held, rather, the alliances that individuals had made with other members of that stratum and with the lower stratum of the particular agency in which they worked. Connections and patronage underlined the whole structure. Furthermore, depending on the particular position held in the civil service, the nature of the job, and the geographical location of the job, individuals or groups of employees belonging to the lower stratum of the bureaucracy could wield great power and have access to informal sources of wealth, even though this power was not linked with coercion. Thus, lowly sixth-level employees could and did wield incredible powers, even if their fate ultimately remained in the *khassa*'s hands. The position of tax agents provides a good example. Through administrative and executive laws, some agents managed to enjoy intricate forms of power vis-à-vis various societal strata. This process also held true for customs officers, police, and *tamwin* (supply) agents, among others.

The extension of power to new groups created new classes and expanded power to other levels of the government bureaucracy, who consequently had a vested interest in supporting authoritarian regimes. But such a description must be qualified because the makeup and nature of these groups did not remain constant and because although these groups fit the definition of class as "any group within society sharing the same relationship to the means of production and the same level of material well-being, privileges, and power,"[25] they did not have the same economic policies nor did they wield power homogeneously. Thus, Milovan Djilas's description of the New Class in Yugoslavia is appropriate to describe Egypt's post-1952 *khassa*: "The emergence of the new class has been concealed under socialist phraseology and, more important, under the new collective forms of property ownership. The so-called socialist ownership is a disguise for the real ownership by the political bureaucracy."[26] As indicated in this study, these groups did not necessarily constitute new entities but in reality represented more of a reconfiguration of old components of the *khassa*. Arguing that "the Egyptian state has become a social entity in itself"[27] does not eliminate the continuity of the relationship between *khassa* and *'amma,* except, perhaps, in illuminating the new patterns that defined this relationship and guaranteed *khassa* control. Other qualifications to the idea of a New Class include the fact that the Egyptian *khassa* did not comprise only a bureaucracy. Under Sadat and, later, Mubarak, private entrepreneurs of all kinds constituted important segments of the *khassa*. These groups could not be described as living "parasitically on state business,"[28] for they were very much at the heart of the *khassa,* and the state, which had constituted an umbrella molded according to the *khassa*'s needs, began to become less so. These *tujjar* entrepreneurs did not support socialist ownership; rather, they, like the New Class in the United States, took a liberal stand regarding the political system and the economy, which benefited their own interests. Here can be included intellectuals, professionals (e.g., artists, doctors, and engineers), and politicians, most of whom had become businessmen in one way or another, resulting in business conservatism to go along with their liberal consciousness and rhetoric. "Liberalism represents the interests of an elite as opposed to the needs of 'ordinary,' 'mainstream' people. Or to state this proposition in its full Orwellian glory: Liberal notions of economic justice and equality are only a camouflage for the ambitions of a narrow and selfish social elite."[29] Therefore, in the 1970s, what was called the Egyptian "state" really constituted the domain of a bureaucratic *multazim* class with a socialist rhetoric and an entrepreneurial professional *tujjar* class with a liberal rhetoric.

Who were the entrepreneurial *tujjar*? Some *tujjar* were involved in import and export, and others were private businessmen and manufacturers, investors in joint ventures with foreign companies, and commercial agents. Their common role involved them in foreign trade and services. They did not constitute the sole group involved because government companies continued to play the primary role in producing and distributing Egyptian goods inside Egypt and exporting them to foreign countries besides importing most necessities. But the *tujjar* became partners with government organizations, and their role grew perceptibly with increasing foreign influence in commercial activities. None of these groups is really new, except for the commercial agents, whose novelty as a group and growth in numbers elicited scholarly interest. Maalak Zaalouk has correctly identified the role of this group:

> Commercial agents representing foreign companies have on numerous occasions, whether in alliance with foreign capital or singly, exerted pressure on the government and have succeeded in influencing the outcome of decision making both regarding legislation and government resource allocation. The access of this group to state power is an important element in the enhance-

ment of foreign Western capitalist interests, both as exporters of commodities and future investors.[30]

A large percentage of these businessmen and businesswomen[31] whom Zaalouk calls the new bourgeoisie did not constitute new faces, even if their role
was somewhat unfamiliar. Among them and among other members of the *tujjar* were former officers, ministers, heads of public sector companies, members of the *mukhabarat,* and those allied to them through marriage or
patronage, as well as their wives and children.[32]

Important differences between the old *khassa* and the new situation must
be pointed out, including the changed nature of leadership, the circumstances
in which this leadership found itself, the sources of wealth to be tapped, and
the methods of control. Anwar Sadat was a different man than Nasser. When
Nasser referred to patriotism, socialism, and other higher causes, the people
idolized him. When Sadat used the same vocabulary, the people were less
convinced. Perhaps this phenomenon resulted partially from the "political *infitah*" maturing of the *'amma,* but even after Nasser's death and the publication of his regime's arbitrariness and cruelties, most people continued see him
as the *rayyis,* Egypt's national hero. His simplicity of life and stubborn stand
against imperialism and oppression had built an aura around him as a revolutionary and a fighter for freedom. People forgive arbitrary actions of charismatic individuals, as they did with Nasser, who is today remembered for
calling on the dispossessed people of the third world to "raise up their heads in
pride." The incredible grief and anger in the hearts of Egyptians for having
lost a chunk of Egyptian territory—Sinai—owing to Nasser's actions is dealt
with separately from his stand as a hero. Sadat's methods of rule and lifestyle
and that of the *khassa* that surrounded him worked against his image among
the *'amma;* his incredible accomplishments in the 1973 war and *infitah* were
acclaimed, yet his effort at presenting himself as a peasant from Mitt Abul-
Kom (his village in the Menoufiya Province) was in clear conflict with a love
of show and grandeur shared by his *khassa.* The social gap between the rich
and the poor became flagrant under Sadat; although it had existed under
Nasser, it had not been flaunted, and the inflation that came with *infitah*
meant that many who had been protected under the protectionism of
Nasser were now unable to make a go of it financially. The Sadat *khassa*
seemed to live in a fantasy land without true realization of the conditions
around them. In the hearings held in the People's Assembly to debate the
expulsion of Sheikh 'Ashur Muhammad Nasr, whose words are quoted at
the beginning of this chapter, from the Assembly, his defense focused on the
lack of concern for the suffering of the common man by various government
bodies, particularly the People's Assembly. The condescending treatment that

the sheikh himself received at the hands of the Assembly's leadership in itself proved that they considered him and his constituency less than cultural and social equals.[33]

The sources of wealth to be controlled took not only the form of what Egypt itself produced, but also foreign assistance that it received, particularly from the United States and oil-rich Arab countries. Sadat was careful to mention the assistance received by Egypt from such countries. Thus, in his "October Paper" setting out future policies for Egypt, Sadat referred to the importance of aid: "As to foreign capital . . . we accept aid and loans, provided no strings are attached to them."[34] He mentioned countries and amounts of aid received as well: "Last year, Saudi Arabia sent to us 600 million dollars, and Kuwait 500 million, and we were able to overcome the difficulties of 1975."[35]

Scholars have written much about the groups that emerged and benefited from *infitah* and the foreign aid received from other Arab countries and the United States to give stability to Egypt. The growing social gap caused by *infitah* ultimately was blamed on Egypt's reintegration into the world capitalist system and the downgrading of the public sector through the undermining of socialist laws.[36] For example, Raymond Hinnebusch argued that even though "Sadat insisted that the new policy intended no retreat from 'socialism,' but an adaptation to new conditions . . . in practice, however *infitah* spelled a major reversal of Nasirist economics through an unrestricted opening of the economy to foreign imports and investment, a recession of etatist and populist intervention in it and a downgrading of the public sector, Egypt was gradually reintegrated into the world capitalist system."[37]

Egypt chose a new economic direction because of the stagnation of its economy, as growth fell to about 1 percent by 1974 and the foreign debt rose to a staggering four to twenty billion dollars.[38] The elite also saw that great opportunities could come their way and pushed for extension of *infitah* policies.[39]

Although these conclusions regarding *infitah* are logical given its reasons and results, a need exists for some qualification. No reason exists to suppose that instituting a "liberal" policy necessitates the end of socialism. Sadat probably was correct on that point: *infitah* was not intended to undermine the socialist structure instituted by Nasser. In fact, from the *khassa*'s perspective, the two systems could be seen as separate from each other, fitting the duality that permeated the superstructure. *Infitah* involved the relationship between the *khassa* and the outside world; it was the realm of the official, with legal codes and military power. *Infitah* was intended to create fiscal and commercial instruments and political and judicial institutions to facilitate the *khassa*'s trade monopoly with the outside world and to maximize profit from commercial activities. In addition, *infitah* took advantage of Egypt's strategic position and the important role it could play within the Arab world.

The shape that socialism had taken in Egypt actually brought about new patterns of dependent relations between *khassa* and *'amma*. The state theoretically became the owner of the major means of production; in fact, the state constituted nothing more than the institution through which the *khassa* could control national production in all its forms: agriculture, manufacturing, industry, and services. By making socialism into a system of benefits for all, based on a compact of reciprocal rights and duties, by which the *'amma* were given all sorts of material "rights" even as their human freedoms were undermined, socialism became more of a system of feudalism. In his speeches Sadat spoke of socialism's benefits to the people, "The necessity of the socialist solution, namely the achievements of workers and peasants, free education and the equality of opportunities; in other words, whoever has a good average can get into [our universities], while the others will remain behind. The criterion is talent. This is an achievement of socialism."[40]

Sadat often repeated the same ideas of socialist gains and "achievements of our workers and peasants."[41] In short, Sadat's thesis that *infitah* would not undermine socialism meant that socialism became the basis of the relationship between the *khassa* and the *'amma*. Because the *'amma*'s rights would continue and they would also receive the material benefits of their allegiance to the system, *infitah* did not make much difference in this relationship. This point is important because of the light it throws on the duality in the economic system; this duality was consciously pursued by Egypt's leadership.

The approach to the question of *infitah* can be compared to that of glasnost introduced later by Mikhail Gorbachev. As in the latter case, *infitah* was intended to put new energy into the productive process, to introduce the idea of incentive that had been lacking under communism. There was no intention of introducing full "openness," only a limited one in which those in power would continue to hold onto its reins. Gorbachev's words, "This society is ripe for change. It has long been yearning for it,"[42] are fitting for Egypt by the end of Nasser's life. People wished to move freely and work independently; the state's control of the economy had brought about a lack of initiative and a slowdown in economic growth. Because pay and top jobs were not based on performance, but on political allegiance, productivity was sacrificed. The answer that presented itself to the leadership was "restructuring," renewal, and regaining of momentum. Perhaps defeat in war helped bring about the changes in the two countries, the 1967 defeat for Egypt and the defeat and withdrawal from Afghanistan for Russia, both of which undermined self-confidence and brought about moral crisis, if in different ways.

One other interesting similarity between *infitah* and glasnost is the elitist approach of the two, which is perhaps also the cause for their limited success. Sadat's approach emphasized development and pressed Western-style progress. No matter how pious he presented himself, nor his continued reference to his peasant roots and village ties, his whole approach was quite elitist, as his clothes, food, houses, and friends illustrated. To Sadat, Egypt was a country to be changed despite what he constantly referred to as the high morals of its people and its admirable culture, to both of which he paid lip service. Similarly, Gorbachev viewed the growth of mass culture in the Soviet Union with deep anxiety as an aberrant result of seventy years of communist rule. "Decay began in public morals . . . the penetration of the stereotypes of mass culture alien to us, which bred vulgarity and low tastes and brought about ideological barrenness, increased. . . . An atmosphere emerged of 'everything goes,' and fewer and fewer demands were made on discipline and responsibility." [43]

The elitist outlook toward society was similar in both cases; for Sadat the people continued to be the *sha'b* (populace, masses) who should welcome and participate in *infitah*. Gorbachev saw perestroika as "simultaneously a revolution 'from above' and 'from below.' This is one of the most reliable guarantees of its success and irreversibility. We will persistently seek to ensure that the masses, the 'people below,' attain all their democratic rights and learn to use them in a habitual, competent and responsible manner." [44] For both leaders of ruling classes, the Communist Party in one case and the National Democratic Party in the other, the question was the creation of new hegemonies to support their regimes while giving new motivation to economic and social development.

There was a great deal of enthusiasm in Egypt and the Western world regarding the policy of *infitah,* and as Gorbachev and other Eastern European leaders moving away from communism would later experience, for a while it seemed that Sadat could do no wrong. Businessmen hurried to Egypt in search of business opportunities, joint ventures began to mushroom, and hotel building and the tourist industry boomed, ending the lag in visitors after the 1967 war. Foreign banks opened branches in Egypt, and the United States extended credit and aid to the Egyptian government. As Sadat expelled Soviet advisors from Egypt, the United States was enthusiastically to see the first country perceived as a Soviet ally turn away from socialism and reorient itself toward capitalism.

It soon became clear that no economic or political miracle would take place. On one hand, the open-door policy soon only benefited industrial, financial, and merchant sectors of the economy, and even those areas prospered only in a limited way. The open-door policy did not apply to the agricultural sector, and both the peasants' production and distribution remained in the

government's hands. As was instituted under Nasser as part of half-way methods of agricultural mobilization, the government determined what the peasant planted and the amounts to be delivered of a particular crop. Government
decided such quotas according to international market prices to obtain the
highest foreign currency return. The government bought the crops at fixed
prices, which remained low to ensure it maximum profit. "There is considerable government intervention. . . . The price is fixed by the government each
year. It is considerably less than the world market price. This is a sore point
with farmers who are well aware of this disparity."[45] Only after delivery of the
quota could peasants sell the remainder of their products in the open market
at a fair price. The Sadat government changed its relationship with the peasantry mostly by increasing the price at which it bought the various cash crops,
including cotton, wheat, sesame seeds, lentils, rice, beans, and sugarcane.[46]
The open-door principle simply did not apply to the agricultural base; rather,
as occurred since Muhammad 'Ali Pasha's reign, the surplus value of peasant
labor became the wealth for redistribution to cover government obligations,
which consisted primarily of foreign loans, interest on loans, and expenses of
upholding the feudal relationship with the *'amma,* such as salaries and services. Some of these obligations took the form of government subsidies to reduce the prices of essential foods to make them affordable for the people.
Subsidies on bread, sugar, tea, electricity, and water were the most important.
Therefore, the subsidies constituted part of the excess *fa'iz* that the government made from one sector of the population.

This policy also resulted in the peasantry's standard of living remaining
low, and they did not constitute a real buying power for the industrial output
of the country. Although the peasants had more money than in earlier times,
it mostly came from their sons, who worked in other Arab states and transferred their money back to Egypt. Men working abroad numbered approximately four million in 1981.[47] Furthermore, rather than introducing an
open-market economy, the state continued the two-market economic system,
one open and the other controlled, that has been the source of much abuse
and corruption. Thus, the governmental hierarchy continued to extract
wealth from the countryside, using it primarily to pay the salaries of its over-
stuffed bureaucracy and the inefficient public sector, which refused to die.

Why did the public sector continue to exist? The explanations usually include the masses' potential anger at liquidating what is termed the "socialist
gains" of the 1952 revolution. This reasoning is valid but not the only one.
When Sadat and his minister of economics, 'Abd al-Razzaq 'Abd al-Magid,
tried to separate the budget of the government from that of the public sector,
a great outcry rose among National Party members and delegates of the
People's Assembly, which the party dominated. The minister's intention was

to impress upon foreign creditors such as foreign banks and the International Monetary Fund that Egypt was solvent and had a budgetary surplus and, therefore, did not pose a risk for further loans. To do so, 'Abd al-Magid proposed to manipulate Egypt's budget and to separate the government's obligations in the form of services and salaries, which it covered primarily through taxes, foreign aid, Suez Canal revenue, and petroleum, from the budgets of money-losing public-sector companies in industry, trade, and services. Still, his efforts exposed the public sector's condition and showed what a losing enterprise it was. The call that each company should stand on its own and not depend on the government to cover its losses was attacked by the press and defeated by the People's Assembly, dominated by the National Party. It is also interesting that many of the exposed cases of corruption might not have occurred had not both a public and a private sector existed, both of which worked together on the same projects, thereby allowing for gaps through which corruption could take place.

Many reasons were given for retaining the public sector, not the least of which was the fact that many public-sector companies provided consumer products—mainly food, textiles, and medicines—at very low prices that the people could afford,[48] a point stressed by Sadat in his 1974 October Paper: "The public sector has paid the full amount of its transactions and contributed to the stabilization of the prices of goods."[49] Rather than limit subsidies, the president actually emphasized them: "The state spends 150 million E.L. [yearly] to make sure that a loaf of bread does not exceed 5 cents, despite the fact that its real price is 22 cents. The state spends 7 million E.L. to stabilize bus fares, although the price of one bus has shot from 5,000 to 20,000 E.L."[50] The government had to sustain these losses because the people expected subsidies and because elimination of the public sector would have caused widespread unemployment. Another way of looking at this would be that, given the government's feudal obligations to the people, such subsidies could not be cut back without putting into question the whole relationship between *khassa* and *'amma*. The relationship of the government to labor reflected this issue. Because the public sector lost, rather than earned, money, it could not afford to pay out the profit and bonuses (calculated by Sadat at 800 million pounds each year) owed to workers according to the law. Nonetheless, workers continued to receive such benefits, which they expected and badly needed. In 1973 Sadat willingly extended benefits such as raising the minimum wage from 9 to 12 pounds per month, raising the ceiling on pension payments by 67 percent, reaffirming that 50 percent of public-sector profits would be distributed among the workers, and permitting a moratorium on payment of all workers' bank debts.[51]

The issue of labor went beyond the workers' desire to retain ownership of the means of production. The workers recognized as mere rhetoric *Al-Mithaq*'s myths that "workers are no longer a commodity in the production process, but the working force has become an owner of the production process itself, a partner in running it, a partner in its profits with the best salaries and conditions."[52] Continued labor unrest certainly constituted proof of the workers' dissatisfaction with the system as did their demand for more benefits. Workers viewed such bonuses and profit sharing as a "right," according to the basis set out by *Al-Mithaq*. In theory, only profitable businesses paid out bonuses and profit sharing, but in practice even losing companies had to pay them; for example, one month's salary bonuses were almost always paid out to workers at feast time by public sector companies that were losing money. Such a right became as much the government's burden as the right to a job or to education; the government could afford such rights only with great difficulty yet could not stop providing these services without jeopardizing the system.

Most public-owned companies did not produce up to their potential not only because they had too many employees assigned to them but also because the individuals who had the authority to run them often considered their positions as *iltizams*—providing large salaries and fringe benefits in the form of extra cash, travel, car, driver, housing, loans, and so on. It followed that the workers in these companies would demand their own shares of this *iltizam*. This attitude resulted from the diffusion of power and, hence, benefits that took place under Sadat. The public sector's budget remained part of the state budget so that the government would continue to cover the public sector's deficit. Had the *khassa* not accepted this policy, when the corruption became public knowledge, drastic measures would have been taken; in fact, only cosmetic reforms were introduced.

The same voices heard against the privatization of the public sector also opposed the proposal that the pound be freed through a process in which Suez Canal dues, tourism, and other services upon which Egypt's economy was strongly dependent would be paid for in Egyptian pounds, rather than in foreign currency. This change would have bolstered the pound and allowed it to achieve a fair international value. The fight against such proposals, whatever the actual merits of the particular plans, raised the issue of fiscal control by the *khassa*. As was shown in earlier chapters, controlling foreign currency and, consequently, the existence of fiscal duality constituted a source of wealth and power for the *khassa*. By controlling the exchange of money, the *khassa*, therefore, could control foreign trade. Internationalizing the pound would only work against them. Therefore, although Egypt's governments all took steps to try to stabilize the pound, these measures were quite limited and were not intended to make the pound a convertible currency. This should have been expected given the mercantilist nature of the regimes. As mentioned in earlier chapters, mercantilism required control of currency, either in the form of bullion or foreign currency. The important thing was to control the channel through which mercantile activities took place, thereby allowing such activity to remain the prerogative of a few. This matter belied governmental claims of liberalization or efforts to create a market economy because both reforms would work against the *khassa*. It did not matter that the *khassa* became closely allied with the capitalist world and its demands for an open-market economy because the opening would occur in one part of the economy and not extend to others. Furthermore, no reason exists to suppose that foreign interests did not actually prefer this type of duality benefiting a class with which they were closely allied.

Thus, *infitah* brought about no particular liberalization of the system. It did restructure the system to fit within the new *khassa*'s needs and international conditions. In Mario Vargas Llosa's introduction to Hernando De Soto's work on Peru, in which De Soto explains that it is a fallacy to think that Peru ever had a market economy, Vargas takes up the connection between liberal constitutions, imperialism, and dependency:

> One of the most widely accepted myths about Latin America is that its backwardness results from the erroneous philosophy of economic liberalism adopted in almost all our constitutions when we achieved independence from Spain and Portugal. This opening of our economies to the forces of the market made us easy prey for voracious imperialists and brought about internal inequities between rich and poor. Our societies became economically dependent (and unjust) because we chose the economic principle of laissez-faire.[53]

He then points to De Soto's conclusion that Peru never had a market economy "and that it is only now, because of the black market, beginning to get one—a savage market economy, but a market economy nevertheless."[54] Like Peru, Egypt never had a real market economy; rather, its economy has constantly been the realm of a particular *khassa,* which manipulated the economy for its own benefit. The economy under British rule or *infitah* under Sadat is more fittingly described as "mercantilist" than as "free-market." Similarly, De Soto described Peru's economic system as "masquerading as a market economy for generations,"[55] explaining that the state never has constituted the "expression of the people," and that it is really "whatever government happens to be in power—liberal or conservative, democratic or tyrannical—and the government usually acts in accordance with the mercantilist model. That is, it enacts laws that favor small special-interest groups . . . and discriminates against the interests of the majority."[56] To De Soto, mercantilism describes a "bureaucratized and law-ridden state that regards the redistribution of national wealth as more important than the production of wealth. And 'redistribution,' as used here, means the concession of monopolies or favored status to a small elite that depends on the state and on which the state is itself dependent."[57]

The *khassa* under Sadat became a "redistributive combine," to use De Soto's description for Peru's elite. The state machinery redivided the wealth produced and the aid received in a number of directions. The *khassa* received the larger share as benefits of their role, including members of the *multazim* bureaucracy who retired and received selective pensions by virtue of membership in the *khassa*. When the individual died, his family would receive this special treatment. Thus, the *khassa* and their families secured a prosperous existence, even after retirement or death. The *'amma* received socialist, or "feudal," obligations, such services as free education and health, social security, agricultural subsidies, and, most important, jobs. With population growth, poor industrial production, and a static foreign aid package, the government faced severe problems in its efforts to continue satisfying these obligations. The difficulties began under Sadat and caused one of the most critical crises of his rule, the bread riots that erupted in Cairo in 1981 as a result of a reduction in bread subsidies. To end three days of rioting, Sadat used the police and the army, resulting in 77 deaths in Cairo and a total of 150 people killed throughout the country.[58] The rioters' slogans, "They eat meat, we eat bread"[59] showed the people's awareness of the duality of their society: "they" and "we" did not require further identification.

The possibility of another such crisis made Sadat—and later Mubarak—very cautious about how to handle the matter of benefits. It should be pointed out, however, that subsidies were not actually assistance by the government; that was only a matter of appearances. Because the government controlled production and distribution of the most important commodities and, therefore, made the largest ratio of profit on these goods, subsidies became no more than redistributing back to the people a small portion of what the government originally took from them. The whole government structure may actually be seen as a recipient of part of the redistributed output of society's productive forces, rather than seeing them as burdens on the government and recipients of benefits.

Meanwhile, attracting foreign investments became another *khassa* big business. "Every investment law has basically two objectives: to attract foreign investment and to control its activities and effects within the host country."[60] In Egypt's case, Jeswald Salacuse concluded that attracting foreign investments became much more important than ensuring the country's control over those

investments, which seems to fit well with the *khassa*'s intention from *infitah*—
to maximize immediate profit. To attract foreign investments, various concessions gave foreign projects privileges that extended beyond anything afforded
to local businesses. By law 43 of 1974, Egypt extended special exemptions:

> Including those from income and commercial taxes, foreign exchange regu-
> lations, customs duties, certain rules of corporation law, and selected labor
> law provisions. It allowed investment disputes to be settled by international
> arbitration, thus exempting investors to a limited extent from the jurisdiction
> of the Egyptian courts, and it established "free zones," special areas which
> had even greater freedom from taxes, foreign exchange rules, and customs
> laws.[61]

To critics the law amounted to a new form of capitulations similar to those instituted under Ottoman rule.[62]

Development provided justification for the privileges extended to foreign
business and investments.[63] Building an industrial Egypt was not a new idea; it
had been around since Muhammad 'Ali's time. Treating foreigners better
than locals could be explained by the policy of developing the country at all
costs; such treatment served as the policy from the pasha's time onward. The
general population of Egypt, however, had become more politically alert.
Awareness of and pride in indigenousness had spread, along with urbanization, population growth, education, and nationalist ideals. The 1967 war and
the people's disillusionment with the army, for which the people sacrificed,
provided an important factor in the people's cultural revival and their bid for
cultural authenticity. The more alien Sadat's *khassa* became and the more arbitrary their actions and abuse of wealth and power, the more alienated and
angry the *'amma* became. Unlike the Nasser *khassa*, the elite under Sadat took
on the outer appearances of Egypt's old royalty, seeming more similar to
Westerners than to Egyptians. Reading Jehan Sadat's memoirs shows the orientation of this *khassa* to the West, the importance of Western opinion, and
the strength of this elite's desire to appear as part of the West. Throughout the
book, Sadat describes herself as different from other Egyptians: her origins
and relations were British, her best friends were foreigners,[64] the food her
family ate was unlike that eaten by Egyptians,[65] and the role she claims to have
played within her family was that of a liberated Western woman.[66] Anwar
Sadat may not have tried to show such similarities with the West, but throughout his life he was conscious of fashion, mass media, and luxury, and he gave a
general impression of personal and political arbitrariness. He often talked of
himself in comparison to royalty: "In the British Constitution, which is the
oldest democracy, the prerogative to dissolve Parliament is in the hands of the

Queen, as requested by the Prime Minister. . . . I have abrogated this right. . . . I have abrogated it."[67]

The message was lost on no one and was further emphasized by Sadat's habit of using King Faruq's palaces for his own needs. The contradictions of his actions led one Egyptian writer to describe his regime as "democratoriya," meaning a fake democracy *(dimocratiya)* that really constituted a dictatorship *(dictatoriya)*.[68] Another Egyptian writer, discussing the issue of democracy under Sadat, said, "Sadat was a dictator not only in the last month prior to his execution, but throughout his reign. . . . The series of statutes issued from 1971 to 1981 under such innocuous titles as 'national unity and social peace,' 'shame,' and 'the suspicion,' were radical intrusions on the essentials of democracy."[69]

Nasser thought of himself as a revolutionary, a hero who finally rid Egypt of Western imperialism and gained for it independence. Sadat took part in the 1952 revolution, as he constantly reminded Egyptians, but he thought of his position in paternal terms: "I am anxious to provide milk to my sons, the school children, in order to ensure their good health."[70] He viewed himself as the guiding father of the country and a hero in his own right with the successful crossing of the Suez Canal, which began the 1973 war, his political success at Camp David, and the return of the Sinai. Anouar Abdel-Malik expressed the enthusiasm for the success of the 1973 war: "We moved, and the enemy moved. We advanced, crossed [the canal], and raised the flags of honor on important sectors of the Arab World, over Sinai and al-Qunaitera. . . . The motto 'raise your head, my brother' was fulfilled."[71]

Internally, Sadat exulted in the "opening up" of Egypt, putting an end to power centers and the much-hated Arab Socialist Union. His success with the West and the support he received from the United States and Western European powers gained him respect and, thereby, legitimacy. Most important, Sadat put an end to the fear that had provided the basis of the Nasserist *khassa* and brought about, if unintentionally, a democratic opening of the people's own perception of their roles and rights because they lost their fear of the government's arbitrariness and paternalism. The Sadat *khassa* resorted to putting emphasis on the issue of paternalism as a means of continuing their control. Paternalism came naturally to Sadat, who made morals an issue, thus the unprecedented *qanun al-'ayb* (law of shame) passed under him as a moral code against which the actions of Egyptians would be judged. Sadat also constantly provided reminders of the importance of traditions: "I have repeatedly urged the return to countryside traditions and values."[72] Not a new law for Egypt, the first such law was passed in 1855 by Sa'id Pasha, making it illegal to insult the khedive. This law was followed by another forbidding criticizing the khedive in writing. Following Ottoman laws, anyone who insulted "the sovereign was to be imprisoned from three months to six years or pay a heavy fine. As long as Egypt was a monarchy, these laws or similar ones were enforced."[73] The acts of paternalism included Sadat's declaration that those who opposed him would be "hacked" by his own hands[74] and that he would fire any governor who did not follow his orders even though the law allowed for provincial independence.[75] Sadat and his wife gave themselves the right to grant medals, pensions, and positions and presented foreign friends and dignitaries with artifacts from Egypt's pharaonic heritage, literally squandering Egypt's history; items missing or in the Sadats' "custody" have been well recorded.[76] Salaries, bonuses, and pensions were called gifts or grants from the president in agreement with the general approach of the *khassa,* who did not differentiate between personal and public wealth in their own minds.

People who benefited from his rule encouraged Sadat in his actions. Rather than take a stand regarding such important national issues, the *multazims* in the government and the People's Assembly answered as a humble chorus, giving the president the right to forgive those who insulted him,[77] or, better still, demanding the expulsion of anyone who dared to oppose the president in the National Assembly or the press. As long as the general policy fit with the wishes of the new entrepreneurial *tujjar* and the government *multazims,* Sadat was given submissive "adulation" by those surrounding him. New press laws allowed nongovernment groups to publish their own newspapers and journals, and Egypt witnessed an exciting rebirth of a limited freedom of the press similar to what existed before the 1952 Revolution. But freedom of the press did not allow for attacks on the president. At the same time, government-owned mass media, including the press, television, and radio, produced headlines and programs glorifying the president's accomplishments and were characterized by the individuals who ran them as "agencies of falsehood."[78]

Sadat's deep disappointment after the moment of euphoria produced by his expulsion of Russian advisors, the peace initiative, and the Western reorientation of the economy largely resulted from what he considered the lack of appreciation for his accomplishments. He was unaware that, despite these achievements, the Egyptian people could clearly see that little had changed in regard to social relations. The slogans changed, but the *khassa*'s perceptions of *khassa/'amma* relations remained the same. The most vocal opposition to the system under Sadat came in the form of young university students and graduates who saw bleak futures with no real hope of change in it. Disillusionment with rising expectations produced by the 1973 war and the Camp David peace treaty added force to the people's disappointment.

Student involvement in political protest was nothing new; Mustafa Kamel's Hizb al-Watani (National Party) had organized student demonstrations at the beginning of the century. Demonstrations by the Wafd and by Misr al-Fatat (Young Egypt) also used students.[79] Under Sadat, the student movement actually represented a continuation of the student movement which began under Nasser that demanded an investigation of the 1967 defeat. The two regimes' repressive measures to crush the opposition were quite similar in scope and nature. Sadat, however, met with a later stage of the youth movement, with greater anger, more disillusionment, and, because of the government's desire to provide a semblance of democracy, better ability to organize and receive moral and financial assistance from abroad. These students did not constitute part of any organized political group that moved or organized them, as was the case under the Wafd and the Hizb al-Watani, or Misr al-Fatat; they first formed quite spontaneously, often around a nucleus of college student unions. Thus, neither the government nor any other party participating in the official political system controlled them.

Another form of opposition, closely related to the student movement in its stand against Sadat, appeared in the form of radical Islamic groups. The 1979 Iranian revolution provided these movements with moral, psychological, and financial help. This revolution's impact should not be underestimated because it created a state that actively exported its own radical ideology and pushed for radical revolutions against existing regimes. This new opposition had basically the same demands as the earlier opposition—Egypt's independence from foreign control and a social revolution to end existing social inequalities. When the Islamic opposition talked about social justice, they meant a sharing of political power and wealth, but the first rather than the latter. Islamic radicals did not advocate a socialist form for the state but were instead involved with the concept of power and how Islam interpreted it.[80] The dialogue of these fundamentalists regarding Islamic economics, Islamic government, and the role of women in society concerned the hierarchy of power that this opposition advocated, which would allow them to rise to the position enjoyed by the *khassa*. Sadat treated these groups with violence[81] despite the fact that he himself at one time belonged to the Muslim Brotherhood and that at the beginning of his rule he had used Islamic groups on university campuses and elsewhere to combat the influence of other power centers. In addition, Sadat himself introduced the statute that made the *shari'a* "the source" of Egyptian law.[82]

The correct picture for the political system was one in which Sadat created legal opposition for his regime not only to give the semblance of democracy but also to keep out any genuine opposition that could potentially undermine him. Historical facts substantiate this hypothesis. Sadat promised democratic elections from the very beginning of his rule. In November 1971 parliamentary elections were held and "the new MP's emphasized the fact that they were directly and 'popularly' elected to their seats, whereas often the ASU members were indirectly elected or appointed."[83] The first step toward introducing a party system was to create *manabir* (platforms) within the Arab Socialist Union, representing the Left, the Right, and the Center, which contained the president's party, Hizb Misr (Egypt's Party). Hizb Misr was the clear winner in the ensuing elections, winning 280 of 352 seats. Despite enthusiasm for the elections, there was marked voter apathy, with less than 30 percent of the voters showing up at the polls, an indication that most of the population was not really involved in the formal political system.

Secure with his party's win, Sadat allowed the political system to develop further, and in 1977 political parties were allowed to organize and run in the elections. At that time a number of groups with very clear-cut ideologies existed: a reconstituted Wafd, representing pre-1952 nationalism, secularism, and a liberal economic policy; the Muslim Brotherhood, who were as yet undecided about whether to become an official party; the Communists, who knew that they could only play a small role in any political forum in Egypt; and the Nasserists, who were only too ready to make a new bid for power. Because of the popularity of the Wafd, Hizb Misr stood to lose in the coming elections. At that time, people in Egypt were discussing who would be the next president, not only which would be the next party in power. Sadat seemed to have accomplished the impossible—but retreat would follow.

In 1978, a new party was organized to replace Hizb Misr, whose operation appeared tainted with its actions against the opposition. Thus, the National Democratic Party (NDP) came into existence and continues to dominate Egyptian politics today. It described itself as a progressive nationalist party and tried to piece together familiar slogans and ideals, but it was somehow nondescript. Because it did not constitute a real party, but a party of conflicting interests, one could not expect any clear program and found instead one that provided some justification for the rule of these interests. Its slogans included belief in principles of Arab unity, in national unity, in Islam as a source of law, and in both collective and individual interests. It promised bureaucratic rationalization, an end to corruption, and upholding the revolution's socialist gains while allowing the private sector to grow unhindered. It continued its promises of free education, jobs, food, security, and housing, among others.

The government encouraged certain individuals considered acceptable to the ruling party but with varying ideological tendencies to form opposition parties on the Left and Right. As a result, the Socialist Labor Party was formed, headed by a previous minister of agriculture, Ibrahim Shukri.[84] Parties that followed uncompromising positions, such as the Muslim Brotherhood and the Nasserists, were forbidden to run in the election. Of course, both groups remained quite active outside the official political structure.

Some scholars have blamed the food riots of 1977 for the derailment of the opening up of the political system and for the restrictions on the establishment of political parties.[85] Without questioning the validity of this point, a further question must be asked about whether the new political system could be considered real liberalization and democratization or whether the spirit of the law itself was not liberal and democractic in its real intent. In answering this question, the riots served to point out that the *khassa* needed to ensure the continuity of their control. Such actions included prohibiting any parties based on class or religion or any parties formed by different state institutions and functionaries, such as the military, police, or judiciary, who could form centers of power. Most important, the government required that any new party receive authorization from a special government committee. That committee also had the right to dissolve any party that it considered in conflict with national unity or social peace.

The contradictions between religion and politics were symptomatic of the regime. Because religious law continued to be the basis for personal law, the two religious communities—Islamic and Coptic—were kept separate without a "personal" unified legal system. So legal duality was upheld by insisting upon the principle of secularism in the political system, that is, no political parties were allowed whose ideologies were religiously based. Add to this the fact that it was Sadat, in defiance toward Pope Shenouda, who made the Islamic *shari'a* the source of legislation for the country, and the contradictions become apparent. To deny the validity of parties based on class or class-oriented ideology was an admission that the political system (including legalized parties on the Left and Right) was designed to represent the *khassa,* with each party meant to fulfil a particular role within the political scheme.

One thing that the *khassa* had not expected was to see the reappearance of an old *khassa* demanding a new role for itself; however, the Wafd Party reappeared in 1977. This group caused a real stir among the *'amma,* who had begun to look back to the period before 1952 with nostalgia. Time obliterated the anger toward the old *khassa* and the heroes of the past; Sa'd Zaghlul and Mustafa Nahhas were remembered with affection. Sadat and his party became alarmed by the specter, and that in itself showed how limited their access was to various classes of the population. The NDP contained elements of the Arab Socialist Union, which was finally disbanded in 1977. The NDP was in touch mainly with its own functionaries, mostly urban and Westernized. But it was among these middle-class, Westernized groups particularly that the Wafd was strongest. Therefore, the NDP logically felt threatened by the Wafd because its popularity lay among the NDP's basic constituency. Interestingly, the

Wafd did not make any real gains among the lower levels of society, who viewed the party as a continuation of the *iqta'*, as the NDP disparaged them. Lacking contact with the poorer members of the *'amma,* however, and wanting to ensure that the party's power would remain unquestioned, meant NDP's manipulation of the political system.

As generally happens in such cases, the fear of losing power or even of having NDP power questioned became more important to Sadat and his *khassa* than the institution of democracy; consequently, manipulation of the political process became more vocal, direct, and official, rather than unofficial and subtle. Harassment of the opposition took various forms, including the expulsion of members from the People's Assembly for having criticized Sadat, as in the cases of Sheikh 'Ashur and Kamal al-Din Hussain. The target of a May 1978 referendum denying political rights to all those who served in pre-1952 governments was Fu'ad Sirag al-Din, founder of the New Wafd, whom the government wished to eliminate from the political picture. This measure also was used to expel a highly respected Wafdist delegate, 'Abd al-Fattah Hassan, from the National Assembly.

Thus, laws were manipulated to ensure the power of the National Party, which consisted of a hodgepodge of people who are best described as hangers-on and who are recognized as such. Some of the people had changed groups, entered elections, and gained positions with whichever regime was in power. The NDP wanted to create an opposition that would have no chance of actually becoming viable competition and would recognize the ruling regime as its reason for existence. The creation of the Ummah Party (Nation's Party) with its Islamic platform constitutes such a case; in fact, the money needed to set it up was provided by the NDP. The NDP hoped that between the Ummah and the Ahrar Party (Liberals), whose leadership was hand-picked, the voice of Muslim fundamentalists would be quieted.

Sadat's paternalism provided an instrument used to pass laws to support his position as a "divine rights" ruler, who would rule for life after laws were changed to give him the right to seek reelection as many times as he wanted. No one dared to insult him or "touch" his person. He rebuked and reprimanded critics of the government and made his rule appear to be one of honor and chivalry. The *Qanun al-'ayb,* which dealt with those who acted dishonorably toward the state, constituted the crowning touch to his approach, for it equated the president's honor with that of the state. To give his rule credence and respect he began to assign university professors to ministerial and high-ranking jobs within the government, thereby hiding his increasing use of nondemocratic methods and creating the appearance of an intellectual presidency. Jehan Sadat may have had a hand in this process; the steps she took to earn a master's degree and a doctorate were a matter of public show. When confronted with adversaries, Sadat acted like a sore loser, which explains his answer to Coptic demands for equal rights. The lack of equal rights exposed his claims of democratization for what they were. In an act of spite he made the *shari'a* the primary source of Egypt's legislation. Needless to say, this law provided a source of debate that moved the religious question to the forefront of Egypt's class conflict. Throughout the 1970s emergency laws remained in effect; Sadat suspended them briefly in 1980 only to have them reestablished after his assassination.

Even though under Sadat outward manifestations of autocratic rule were obliterated, the *khassa*'s actual controls were extended in subtle ways more appropriate for the country's conditions and the evolution of the superstructure into one that demanded more say for the *'amma* in the country's political problems. Sadat also continued to be wary of the army and its possible role in politics; 'Amir's failed coup after the 1967 war and Muhammad Fawzi's revolt must have shown him the potential. Consequently, Sadat worked to keep the army happy while distancing it from politics. Under him, the police grew in power and new forms of security forces were introduced, such as *quwat al-amn al-markazi* (central security forces) and *umana' al-shurta* (police). Although these various police forces fell under the leadership of the minister of the interior and were meant to cooperate to keep peace, they often clashed over the scope of their rights and duties.

Thus, Sadat created an official political system with parties and opposition. As in Nasser's age, the system continued to use slogans that differed greatly from reality. The major difference between Nasser and Sadat's regimes is that under Nasser the *khassa* ruled explicitly, without obfuscation, whereas under Sadat it ruled through indirect, unofficial means, the most important of which was executive laws. Thus, although freedom of the press was guaranteed by law, in practicality the organization of the press became in itself a method of controlling the kind of press that could appear in Egypt. A Supreme Press Council was constituted in May 1975 that became the final arbiter of newspapers published in the country. Because the council constituted the government's instrument, and the government itself constituted the ruling party's instrument, no real contradiction existed, and, consequently, no real threat existed from the press. The Egyptian press was allowed to attack and even insult the government but was not allowed to discuss the president, who constituted the final guarantor of the government and the ruling party. The president was treated as though he could do no wrong and as a benefactor whose generosity was to be appreciated. As expressed by one member of the People's Assembly in support of a constitutional amendment that would make it possible to expel from the Assembly anyone who attacked Sadat: "[Sadat was] the democratic president who gave Egypt back its freedom, democracy, dignity, and national pride."[86] As a result, the press's impact as true opposition dissipated, and it became part of the official structure, discussing permissible or nonpermissible issues according to the situation's needs. Because the opposition needed the approval of the ruling party to survive, parties of the opposition found a vested interest in the system as it stood; without the system, such parties would have ceased to exist and more popular ones would have formed.

The Camp David peace treaty, the crowning touch of Sadat and the basis of the *khassa* relationship with the United States, could not be attacked by anyone either, including members of the People's Assembly.[87] The situation was helped by the ineffectiveness of the opposition parties. For example, the concern of the New Wafd's leadership seemed to be the past. They continued to fight the ghost of Nasser and to resurrect the memory of Wafdist leaders such as Sa'd Zaghlul and Mustafa Nahhas and used the people's respect for them to gain popularity and a following. But their ideas fit the past and spoke to the nationalists of the 1930s and 1940s rather than to the poor masses of the 1970s and 1980s.[88] Rather than adopt a program that would incorporate the dramatic changes experienced by Egypt since the time of Nasser, the Wafd tried to show that any gains of the revolution had already been part of the Wafd platform before 1952. This is exemplified by Fu'ad Sirag al-Din's words, "The first law that recognized the existence of labor and allowed them to unionize for the first time in the history of Egypt, it was I who decreed it. . . . It was I who decreed the governmental law of 1943 to fight illiteracy . . . nationalizing the National Bank . . . [providing] free high school education."[89]

The opposition created by laws and executive actions could, therefore, be labeled "legal opposition" meant to keep alternative parties to the NDP out of the political system. The electoral law was itself to blame, but it was written by the same people who sat in power as members of the NDP and who abused even their own law when it suited their needs. Thus, Sadat continued the Nasserist tradition in which slogans and intentions contradicted actual actions and results. This policy was almost required by the incongruity of a dual system that was both mercantilist and feudal. The multiparty political system instituted by Sadat as a basis for democracy was anything but a free system, yet it had dramatic results. Although the opposition parties were "official," their very existence and that of opposition newspapers provided a forum for the expression of grievances and encouraged the people to become more politically involved. More important, the inconsistencies demonstrated the uselessness of the whole "liberal" experiment. The *khassa* continued to have all the privileges, and the *'amma* continued to have little power to be heard or to control its own fate. The government's party, the opposition parties, the People's Assembly, and other government-created and -controlled mobilizing agencies such as professional and labor unions all constituted part of the official structure, the edifice supporting the *khassa,* and the instrument through which they manipulated the country's laws.

7

AN END TO DUALITY?

The supreme problem of culture is that of gaining possession of one's transcendental self, of being at one and the same time the self of oneself. . . . [Culture] is organization, discipline of one's inner self, a coming to terms with one's own personality; it is the attainment of a higher awareness, with the aid of which one succeeds in understanding one's own historical value, one's own function in life, one's own rights and obligations.[1]

The term *culture* is generally used to describe the accumulated habits, beliefs, and traditions pertaining to religion, language, moral code, and relations that tie social groups together. Culture is also cultural production in the form of the sciences, arts, literature, and law. As such, culture is a mirror of a society during particular stages in its evolution. In the contemporary Middle East phenomenon of religious revivalism, despite the belief in the "authenticity" of the culture being "awakened," what is being revived today is actually the people's perception of what their authentic culture is. Today's Islamic movement may see the cause as a return to true and pure Islam, or what Muhammed Arkoun described as the "imaginaire" by which Islam "is assumed to be a specific, essential, unchangeable system of thought, beliefs, and non-beliefs."[2] Yet the call for Islam is really a search for solutions to contemporary social problems, and the models presented as answers are in themselves a reflection of the social forces at work within this society. Eric Hobsbawm noted that traditions may appear to be continuous but could in fact be "responses to novel situations which take the form of reference to old situations, or which establish their own past by quasi-obligatory repetition."[3] This is not to say that the traditions being revived are entirely new ones, for "where the old ways are alive, traditions need be neither revived nor invented."[4] Whereas certain traditions, including political institutions such as nation-states or ideologies of nationalism, liberalism, and socialism, are relatively new traditions for the Middle East, the usage of old devices, such as symbolic language, give what is new the authenticity of tradition.

178

Even though the debate regarding the phenomenon of religious fundamentalism has concentrated on how authentically Islamic the phenomenon is,
the real importance of revivalism is in the revival of *an* "authentic" system
rather than *the* "authentic" system. The significance lies in the perception of
the people in their acceptance of "authenticity." In other words, even though
Islam seems to be the center around which revivalism is taking place today in
Egypt, it is really what is perceived as a synthesis of Egyptian cultural
"essence" that is being revived as the basis of social interaction. Put differently, the significance of cultural revivalism lies in the choice of indigenous
cultural traditions as models of greater significance. It points to an acceptance
of self, of liberation from the psychological feelings of inequality, backwardness, weakness, and, hence, continued dependency on alien cultures. With
cultural liberation the whole question of catching up with technologically advanced countries and their own forms of progress becomes moot, not a priority. It is not part of people's everyday discourse, a point of reference in daily
relations. The priorities of society are dictated by the social forces of which the
culture is a mirror, whereas the methods are those actually set up by the cultural framework as evidenced in social relations of the particular phase in this
culture's evolution.

What is generally regarded as culture, such as in Islamic usages—including the use of "traditional" terminology—is more like symptoms, that is, external manifestations of underlying social phenomena. The real meaning of
culture cannot be taken from the surface, from what it purports to say and do,
but is reflexive and reflective of inner social forces. Accordingly, contemporary
revivalism in Egypt would be a reflection of the prevailing class struggle and
would point to the success of social forces espousing this revivalism in establishing their own forms of culture as dominant forms in society as a whole.
Translated into class struggle, this would mean that the culture of the *'amma*
is now becoming dominant, that the *khassa* is submerging into a process of
culture building that the whole country is experiencing, and with it one sees
the closing of the dual social structure and the movement of Egyptian society
toward greater cultural homogeneity.

This process, particularly the diminishing gap dividing Egypt's dual society, is the focus of this study. The gap has been diminishing for two basic reasons: first, the *khassa*'s inability to handle their side of the feudal compact
owing to insurmountable economic and social problems; and, second, cultural revivalism, which is the result of long-term social forces that have been
transforming Egyptian society. The discussion begins with the situation inherited from socialism and *infitah* and the problems faced by Egyptian society as
the result of a new national and international situation. The evolution of society and the answers it reached for to face these new challenges are today bring-

ing Egypt into a new phase of its history detailed here. New cultural patterns and social integration are an important part of the process of change that is culminating in a new historical bloc in the sense of bringing about a more culturally and linguistically homogenized Egypt. Even while the disparities of wealth and power appear to be as great as ever, these gaps are also becoming narrower, at an ever-increasing rate.

The problems faced by Egypt during the eighties and nineties, many of which were inherited from previous governments, meant the government was unable to fulfill the "feudal" benefits instituted in Nasser's time as a means of mobilizing the masses. The state first tried to limit the benefits it could no longer afford. Like other countries, however, that underwent socialist transformations and ended up with huge bureaucracies and a burden of obligatory services, these benefits had become an ingrained part of the system, part of the balance and hegemonic discourse that kept the *khassa* in power. Bureaucracies and obligations toward populations could not simply be dismantled. Since the 1970s Egypt has been trying to introduce democratization in answer to popular demand, to invigorate its economy by liberalizing it, and to limit "feudal" services. These efforts met with only limited success at the beginning owing mainly to the *'amma*'s resistance to losing "socialist gains" and to the *khassa* vested interests that necessitated holding on to mercantilist prerogatives. Although during recent years amazing leaps have occurred in Egypt's economy and infrastructure, the macro situation of the economy appears to be in much better shape than the micro, mainly because of the continued bureaucratic and mercantilist controls over the economy. Egypt's 1999 per capita income of $1,300 per year means that Egypt no longer qualifies for loans from the World Bank, yet the wealth gap between rich and poor has never been wider nor more critical. Culturally, Egypt has not been as socially homogeneous since the early nineteenth century.

Revivalism, and the social homogeneity it entails, should be seen as of revolutionary dimensions even if it has been taking place in an evolutionary way. Homogeneity, which grows with cultural diffusion, breeds a sense of equality, an unwillingness to use power, and at the same time a lack of fear from arbitrary state power. With it comes a change in perception of roles by which the function of the ruling classes undergoes a transformation in people's minds. That *khassa* and *'amma* use the same colloquialisms to communicate, listen to the same songs, enjoy the same literature, follow the same moral codes, and often find no problem with intermarrying illustrates the ongoing rapprochement between the two and helps extend it. The political system cannot but evolve to accommodate these transformations. Equality must first come from within the individual before the potential for political and social equality can be realized. Therefore, cultural revivalism should not be condemned off-hand because it is antimodern; it should be seen as an essential phase of coming to terms with modernity. "It should not surprise us that there is an absence of feeling of complete understanding of others. Lacking a perfect comprehension of ourselves, we can never really hope to know others."[5]

One important reason for the *khassa*'s immersion into cultural revivalism is the changed nature of the contemporary *khassa*. If once the *khassa* consisted of foreign or indigenous Westernized elements, today most members of the *khassa*, whether military, government *multazims*, or *tujjar*, originate from popular sectors of society. Their background and upbringing were quite "traditional"; however, through education, social mobility, and patronage they managed to rise within the class structure and even arrive at positions of power. Some *tujjar* contractors, such as 'Uthman Ahmad 'Uthman, accumulated fortunes in Arab oil-rich states; their experience there made them all the more conservative. To such groups, the threat posed to their power by Islamic radicalism nothwithstanding, cultural revivalism is in the natural order of things.

Furthermore, the conditions under which the contemporary *khassa* came to power pushed the state to play a role in promoting revivalism. When Mubarak first became president, he set out to demonstrate to Egypt how different he was from his predecessor. At the same time, however, he had to confirm to the international community that his regime was a continuation of Sadat's. Sadat was acclaimed at home as a hero for the success of the *'ubur,* for returning Sinai to Egyptian sovereignty, for showing that Israel was not invincible as Egyptians had come to believe, and for bringing Egypt badly needed peace without which democracy, development, and national pride would not have been possible. Sadat was admired abroad and was a friend of the United States, and the *khassa* were in need of these warm relations that worked to their benefit. But because the benefits were shared by a minority of the country, Sadat was assassinated in clear public view. The impact of the act and the way it was undertaken were at once shocking and mesmerizing for the whole country.

That situation explains Mubarak's initial caution and his unwillingness to take any sharp turns away from the policies of his various predecessors. The system worked well for the *khassa;* the question was how to make it acceptable to the *'amma*. This dilemma led to a continuation of contradictions in declared intentions and actual actions as with earlier regimes. The state had to handle immediate challenges, including radicalism, terrorism, sectarianism, hooliganism, and unemployment. Thus, while declaring political reforms, emergency laws remained in effect. While withstanding attacks by critics in and outside Egypt, the threat from Islamic radicalism was systematically subdued. At the same time democratization was declared as the government's objective, and perhaps this was a sincere wish, but it was impossible to fulfill immediately. In the 1984 elections, once confronted with the possibility of losing, the ruling NDP introduced last-minute manipulative changes to the election laws so that only those parties who managed to win more than 8 percent of the votes would be allowed to sit in the People's Assembly. The seats won by parties that received less than 8 percent would go to the majority party. This placed "veto" power over the Assembly's decisions in the hands of the NDP, the majority party. Thus, both the executive and legislative bodies were controlled by the same party. Moreover, because the Assembly nominated the candidates for president, this guaranteed that Mubarak would be the only nominee for the position, further cementing the relationship between him and the *khassa*.

With the contradictions in the *khassa*'s actions and the unwillingness to allow only supporters and allies of the *'amma* political participation, incidents of political violence increased in the following years. The affluence evident in the country's infrastructure and commercial activity are linked to this relative peace. In contrast, 1988 was described by one study as a year of "constant confrontation between security forces and Islamic *jama'at*."[6] In 1992 the specter of whole towns in Upper Egypt being closed to Egyptian security forces, who were unable to breach the hold of radical groups, both Muslim and Coptic, without causing massive bloodshed, caused real concern. The government's experience showed that the use of force by security forces to exterminate religious radicalism only caused further violence and animosity toward the state, at least until citizens became direct victims of terrorism, as in the case of the Luxor bus that contained a majority of French tourists slaughtered at the hands of terrorists. The violence and unnecessary deaths of French tourists and Egyptians when terrorists slaughtered passengers on the Luxor bus and bystanders and the butchery with which the attack was undertaken caused a severe reaction among the Egyptian *'amma*. They who could have been supporters of an Islamic opposition now saw such groups as something to be feared. It was not until 1999 that the threat from Islamic terrorists subsided.

Since Sadat's time, the state had resorted to tactics to support its coercive measures. Coercion was, therefore, balanced through "official Islam" by which the state tried to co-opt Islamic radicalism and revivalism. As part of combating political violence, the state's tactical use of Islam, despite how different the discourse was from that of the radicals, contributed directly toward extending revivalism. Government-owned press, radio, and television were the main vehicles used to spread religious ideas. Popular sheikhs, such as Metwalli al-Sha'rawi and 'Abd al-Hamid Kishk, were given weighty coverage by the media, as were prayers and Qur'an recitation. Television personnel de-ferred to the use of fundamentalist vocabulary, and clothes deemed Islamic became a norm among broadcasters and actors in daily series. Well-publicized debates were held between clergy and radical youth to discuss "true Islam."[7] Massive efforts were exerted by the Azhar to graduate *daʿis* (missionaries) in substantial numbers even at the cost of undermining the quality of education in its university and academic institutions. *Daʿis* were sent out all over the country as guides, particularly to youth and women. Their teaching inevitably concentrated on proper attire and respect for patriarchal authority through blind obedience to the male head of a family, whether father, husband, or president of the Republic. Islam was used as the ultimate arbiter of all moral issues; what was proper was described as Islamic and what was improper as non-Islamic. Where once Islam was taught as a religion of *ʿibadat* (worship, veneration) and *muʿamalat* (social intercourse, mutual relations), today the emphasis is on *ʿibadat* with *muʿamalat*, once handled as a separate category, brought increasingly under the rubric of *ʿibadat,* that is, determined by God's laws and given essentialist authoritarianism. Because these *daʿis* and a large percentage of the clergy are mostly new immigrants or one generation away from rural areas, their concept of morality is really the *ʿurf* (customary law) of the countryside, even though they present it as Islamic. The origin of the teachers and the mass of rural immigrants to urban centers is important in determining the type of culture being diffused or what is referred to as "revived." Here, too, the impact of the periphery is decisive in the cultural direction taken by the center.

The Islamic discourse was helped in particular with the continued outlook toward gender that has upheld the supremacy of the male patriarch, a system based on *shariʿa* law but a *shariʿa* law constructed through government committees dating from the nineteenth century. Not only was patriarchy upheld, but the contemporary period is seeing serious efforts to reverse legal rights won by women during preceding generations. Even though the multiple court system created through nineteenth century legal reforms was unified in the 1950s, the duality of the laws themselves continue. This has meant unequal rights for women—rights guaranteed by the constitution that gave women equal access to education and work and regarded them as equal to men in front of the law. At the same time, a woman's civil rights have been limited under the pretext of personal status laws, which though constituting *muʿamalat* relations between individuals, have been made part of the religious discourse by the clergy and educational systems, both of which are part of state responsibility. Thus, a woman could aspire to become a member of parliament or hold a ministerial position in the government, yet she could not leave the country without a long and costly struggle if she did not have her husband's agreement. In short, her *ahliyya* (legal competence) is not complete. Rather than end the duality of the legal structure and thereby end the contradictions presented by two different legal codes with different philosophical bases—if handled by one court system since the 1950s—the state emphasized a patriarchal interpretation of *shari'a* in deciding gender issues. Laws passed during Sadat's time to better the condition of women in regard to divorce, child custody, and a divorced couple's house, took a step back at the beginning of Mubarak's presidency.[8] Feminist activists did not stop thier bid for change, but the opposition was overwhelming and the *khassa* found itself torn on these issues.

On the one hand, liberal Westernized members of the *khassa* supported by progressive social forces were all for changing personal status laws at least within reason. But conservative commercially minded members of the *khassa* opposed any change and were supported by the large majority of Egyptian men and Islamic fundamentalist groups—the radical and government religious hierarchy. So, gender issues became a focus of intense struggle and incessant activism on the part of new women's groups composed of lawyers, university professors, businesswomen, and international activists. Activism makes for strange bedfellows, as was the case in Egypt. From radical thinkers like Nawal al-Sa'dawi to Islamic Sisterood leader Zainab al-Ghazali, they all called for the right of women to determine their own fate and to have the right to divorce. The film *Four Women of Egypt*,[9] directed by Tahani Rached for Canadian television in 1997, illustrated the activism of four diverse characters, women of different backgrounds and orientation, whose friendship was cemented by love and hope for Egypt. Safinaz Kazem is an Islamicist who sees Egypt's future as an Islamic state; Amina Rashid, granddaughter of Isma'il Pasha Sidqi and a renowned socialist thinker; Widad Mitri, an activist Copt who demonstrated against British occupation; and Shahinda Maqlad, the wife of the victim of Kamshish and its al-Fiqi's landlords, who continued her husband's work among the peasants of Kamshish and surrounding villages.

If it took the work of an Egyptian woman director to bring the stories of these women to the public eye, the activities of others were more obvious and brought about important results for women, although every step seemed to be followed by a step backward. Persistent grievances faced by women since the reform of courts and law in the nineteenth century included polygamy and a wife's inability to get out of such a marriage without her husband's approval and at great expense (see chap. 3). Personal status laws of 1920 did consider a husband's taking of a second wife to be a "special harm," giving her the right to divorce. The wife, however, had to prove that her husband's taking a second wife actually harmed her. That made it very hard to sue successfully for divorce because *darar* was interpreted very narrowly by the courts: as long as he supported her financially, there was no *darar*. In 1979, following intensive feminist activities sponsored by Jehan Sadat—hence the nickname of the law as Jehan's law—Law 44 for 1979 determined that the very act of taking a second wife was *in itself* a *darar* giving the first wife the right to divorce. The passing of this law exemplifying the hopes of the new class of *infitahists* was widely claimed throughout the world. However, it caused a great deal of anger among conservative Egyptians, and in 1980 Egypt's National Assembly reversed the law, declaring that taking a second wife could never constitute a *darar* in itself because polygamy was ordained by God, and God could never ordain a rule that would be harmful to humanity.

Denial of divorce except for specific reasons; a husband's right to take four wives; his right to call her to a house of obedience and, until 1985, have the police drag her there by force; and his right to force her not to work were at the center of the struggle that was becoming even more serious with the growth of Islamic fundamentalism and cultural diffusion from conservative oil-rich Arab states where millions of Egyptian workers and professionals lived and worked long years. In a 1998 court battle, another issue made it clear that women stood to lose whatever freedoms they had achieved through the *Al-Mithaq* and Egyptian constitution. The battle was no longer to acquire more rights and freedoms, but more important, to hold on to already existing ones.

The issue in question was the legal requrement that a wife receive her husband's permission to travel abroad. During August 1998 the administrative court of Majlis al-Dawla, the highest judicial authority in Egypt, reviewed a woman's appeal of an Interior Ministry decision forbidding her from traveling outside Egypt because her husband refused to let her go. The woman was a stewardess by profession and was also a graduate student at a university in London, so the decision was tantamount to denying her access both to her job and to her school. Because the Egyptian constitution guaranteed women the right to work and study, the woman expected to win. The court, however, decided against her by giving precedence to a husband's *ta'a* rights over the wife's constitutional rights. The judge hearing the case went further than the case required by using it as an opportunity to establish precedents for greater patriarchal control. His finding was that not only did the Islamic *shari'a* require a husband's permission for a wife to travel in all circumstances, but it also required that she be accompanied either by her husband or by a *mihrim*, a male to whom she is not sexually eligible because of consanguinity.[10] This finding had no precedent in Egyptian law. Early in the century, efforts were made to establish the need for a *mihrim* to accompany a wife on pilgrimage, but they were never put into practice. Today, Egyptians are familiar with the term *mihrim* in connection with pilgrimages and *ihram*, purification and being in a state of purity to undertake a pilgrimage to Mecca. The word *mihrim* also appears in reference to the requirement of the Saudi Arabian government that any Muslim woman who enters or leaves Saudi Arabia for a pilgrimage or for other reasons must be accompanied by a male relative, who can be a husband, son, father, brother, or uncle, that is, someone who is legally ineligible to be her husband. The extension and definition of personal status laws undertaken by the judge in the above case was a direct derivative of Saudi laws and the result of the experience of Egyptians who worked in or went on pigrimages to Saudi Arabia.

The new millennium saw the culmination of long years of efforts exerted by women's groups to find a way for women to get out of unwanted marriages. This they achieved against incredible odds, and the repercussions are yet to be seen. During January 2000 the National Assembly was faced with a new law defined and justified as aiming to "facilitate litigation and procedures pertaining to marriage and divorce disputes."[11] Three particular issues were in question: the right of spouses in *'urfi* (unofficial) marriages to divorce, the right for a wife to travel without her husband's approval, and the right for a woman to divorce her husband through *khul'* by which she gives up all financial rights due her from him. The first passed without controversy, the third passed with great difficulty and threats from the opposition that it would be challenged and reversed in court—eighty amendments were suggested for the law—and the second was derailed and withdrawn by the government.[12] The new laws regarding *'urfi* marriage made "secret marriages between students legitimate," lamented fundamentalist journalists.[13] Their shock and anger at the new *khul'* law, which they called the "destroyer of families," reflected the general shock of conservative elements. But the government of Hosni Mubarak and its officials—Faruq Sayf al-Nasr, the minister of justice; Fathi Nagib, who headed the committee that wrote the proposed legislation; Fathi Surur, the Speaker of the National Assembly; and Kamal al-Shazli, the majority leader—pushed the law through the National Assembly, and the long years spent by women activists such as Mona Zulficar—the Hoda Sha'rawi of her generation—had succeeded. For the first time since the nineteenth century, women could divorce their husbands at will. According to the new laws, a woman who sues for *khul'* had to wait a three-month period, or six if there were children. She was also required to submit to reconciliation efforts by two arbitrators from her family and her husband's family. If reconciliation failed, and she gave up the dowry her husband paid her and the financial compensation due her at the time of the divorce, the decree was automatically granted. Divorce for harm, by which the wife kept her financial rights, continued as before.

The methods used to change personal status laws are very telling of the cultural revivalism going on in Egypt today. For a long time, women activists used human rights and Western feminist arguments to achieve gender equality without success. The new women's leadership, however, was part of the wider revival of culture taking place in Egypt that this book has been tracing. To them, the source for change could only be from within what is familiar, traditional, and indigenous. It was not a rejection of modernity; rather, it was a natural approach for a new generation of very modern, professional, and liberated women. The source and discourse would be Islam, and for the first time in the modern period women entered into serious debates in Islamic *fiqh* history, and *tafsir* (Qur'anic interpretation).[14] Lawyers and women professors like Zeinab Radwan, dean of Dar Al-Ulum (the Faculty of Arabic and Islamic Studies) at Cairo University, Fayoum branch, proved critical in the process. Nongovernmental organizations like the Centre for Egyptian Women's Legal Assistance, headed by Azza Soliman, specialized in women's issues. Women's intellectual groups like Al-Mar'a wal-Dhakira (Women and Memory), headed by Huda al-Sadda, held yearly conferences to celebrate important female historical figures such as nineteenth-century feminist authors 'Aisha Taymur and Malak Hifni Nassef and remind the public of their accomplishment. Research into the past by scholars like Afaf Lutfi al-Sayyid, Nelly Hanna, and others including myself illustrated how the lives of women were different before the introduction of modern personal status laws, and how many of these laws were not based on the *shari'a* as is assumed but were the result of modern nation-state efforts to modernize and Westernize Egypt's legal codes.[15] Even the Grand Imam of Al-Azhar, Sheikh Mohamed Tantawi, supported the new laws on religious and common-sense grounds. Answering members of parliament who attacked the law in the National Assembly, Sheikh Tantawi said: "Men are not made of gold and women of silver. We are all equal before God."[16]

Thus there has been great effort directed toward improving the lives of women. The new laws are a great accomplishment for democracy and equality, marking the evolution and maturity of the Mubarak presidency. The establishment of a Higher National Council for Women for the first time in Egypt points to greater activism in the future.[17] Headed by Suzanne Mubarak, the new organization is evidence of the state's strong stand behind women's rights, but it is also probably an effort to co-opt what so far has been the activity of a strong civil society. This remains to be seen. There is still much to accomplish: the law regarding the travel of wives is of immediate importance and will prove to be a test for a state that claims to liberalize and promote business ventures for all members of its society. How a husband's travel affects his financial and personal obligations to his wife and family are also of immediate importance given the millions of Egyptians working abroad. Women have already brought cases in front of Egyptian courts demanding equality of hire with men based on constitutional guarantees. Cases brought by women demanding equal rights to become judges or district attorneys have been delayed by Egyptian courts. Most interesting is the case brought by Soad Ibrahim Saleh, head of the *fiqh* department of the women's college in Al-Azhar University, demanding a position in Dar al-Iftaa' (high council for *fatwas*), which would be unprecedented for women all over the Islamic world. The government has pulled back on all these issues. It is curious and telling of the contradictions of Egyptian laws that women have to fight for a role in the legal system and yet have been able to rise to high levels of the government hierarchy as ministers, undersecretaries of state, and ambassadors to important capitals of the world. In 1999 seventeen Egyptian women ambassadors held the top positions in Egyptian embassies and consulates in such places as New York, South Africa, Australia, San Francisco, Frankfurt, and Paris. The Egyptian foreign service has altogether 812 women working in the diplomatic service constituting 16.5 percent; twenty-four of these women hold the position of minister plenipotentiary and twenty-four hold the title of ambassador.[18] This of course speaks for the standards observed by Egypt's minister of foreign affairs, Amr Musa, who has been a force to reckon with in Egypt's active international role during the last decade.

As the battle over new personal status laws illustrates, the Islamic discourse is dominant in Egypt today. As explained earlier this is to an important extent a result of the government's own efforts to combat Islamic fundamentalism while at the same time using Islam to fulfill particular needs of the *khassa*. For example, a *diya* law was passed through the National Assembly in 1999 that allowed financial compensation to be paid by a guilty party to the family of the person he/she hurt or killed, as long as it was a case of wrongful death and the victim's family accepted. Everyone was aware that the law was specifically crafted to benefit a famous businessman whose underage son killed a medical student as he drove his speedboat in a swimming area off the Northern shore. It also helped a famous actor's son who ran over a Bedouin woman and killed her. The law was described as tribal and Islamic and therefore further opened the door to Islamic groups to demand the application of Islamic law according to their interpretations.

As the Nasr Hamid Abu Zayd case shows, the *shari'a* could become an impediment to personal and social freedoms depending on its interpretation. Given the freedom enjoyed by Egypt's courts and court judges, that could prove to be a route through which many legal gains could be undermined. Hence the threat by the conservative opposition in the National Assembly that the new *khul'* laws would be overturned in court. They have reason to expect this to happen because of the changes in the type of judges that sit on the bench, particularly in the lower courts. Thus, using the fact that Islamic law was made the source of Egypt's laws, lower courts have questioned the "Is-lamicness" of cases brought in front of them. Islamic activists then referred these cases to the High Constitutional Court to determine if conditions regarding the application of the *shari'a* were being met. The High Constitutional Court is always careful not to question the issue of the *shari'a* as the main source of law for the state. To get around its actual application the court insists that the amendment to the constitution regarding the *shari'a* is relevant only to new legislation and not to already standing legal codes.[19] So far the decisions of higher courts, whose judges tend to be more liberal and Westernized,[20] have been able to circumvent successfully the application of *shari'a*. Once fundamentalist judges reached higher courts, however, the legal system became an instrument of radical Islam as the 1999 wife's travel case mentioned earlier shows. In the Nasr Hamid Abu Zayd case the philosophy professor was divorced from his wife by a judge's application of *hisba* laws, declaring him an apostate because of his writings. Because his wife never asked to be divorced and the state did not try to stop the court decision even though it did not conform with state laws that required a wife's petition to divorce her from a husband who was an apostate, Abu Zayd became an exile in Holland.

While the state moved to stop the application of *hisba* laws in the future, it did little to help Abu Zayd, probably in order not to anger the religious right. Furthermore, in every arena the state laws emphasized how Islamic its actions were. There was a constant emphasis on describing opposition to the government as a sin.[21] Religious conferences, such as the one held in Iraq in 1989 to discuss peace in Islam, were held by Arab regimes and emphasized by the local press. Discussing issues of peace was an answer to young Arab radicals who took a stand in support of the Palestinian *intifadah* (Palestinian revolt against Israeli occupation of West Bank and Ghaza).[22] An Islamic *jama'at*'s organized conference in support of the *intifadah* at the end of December 1988 was disbanded by Egypt's security police because it attacked peace and was turning into a disruptive demonstration.[23] After labor strikes at the Hilwan ironworks in summer 1989, government-owned religious newspapers were filled with articles on the importance of peaceful relations in the working place and how Islam demands that workers fulfill their duties so that both workers and the state would benefit.[24] A typical article had the title: "Work Is a Trust, and Obstructing Production is Faithlessness to God and His Prophet."[25] Another great effort in this direction was to touch on the sciences and to show how Islamic sciences were being revived and becoming part of the school curriculum.[26] Medicine and health, in particular, were the focus of various conferences held in Egypt during the 1990s; medical doctors, scientists, and clergymen from all over the Islamic world were invited. There the issues of abortion, surrogate motherhood, cloning, and what Islam has to say

)out questions pertaining to "life" were discussed. This was important for Islamic countries facing uncontrollable rates of population growth.

At the same time Mubarak's style of leadership evidenced sensitivity to the rising importance of the 'amma. He appealed first to populist sentiments as "president of the people" through well-publicized inspections of public sector companies and factories. There he was filmed live for television, talking to workers, office staff, common soldiers, and schoolchildren. His chosen *kinaya*s (nicknames) emphasized his populism and showed the importance of Islamic revivalism. His most widely used *kinaya*, al-Za'im al-Mu'min (the believing leader), later in his third term became "holder of the *wilaya*"[27]—ringing names with traditional connotations of leadership. The same strategy was used by other Muslim leaders like King Hassan of Morocco and King Fahd of Saudi Arabia, whose title emphasizes his attributes as the Keeper of the Haramayn, Mecca, and Medina, rather than as king.

The transformations evident in Egypt today, including the cultural transformation of the *khassa*, are the result of the impact of social forces that have been transforming Egyptian society since the beginning of the nineteenth century and, particularly, since the 1952 revolution. Included are social mobility, urbanization, population growth, expansion of free education, and increasing poverty.

> Over the last 40 years there has been an unprecedented rise in the role of social mobility in Egypt, pushing up the social ladder a large segment of the population which traditionally belongs to the lowest levels of society. . . . [Important factors included] the land reform laws of 1952 and 1961, the nationalization and sequestration measures of the early 1960's, the raising of income taxes . . . [and the] expansion of the role of army and government in the economic, social and political life of the country.[28]

The growth in population and increased urbanization meant a larger middle class, the base from which the *khassa* originates, and the constant infusion into that class from the more conservative tiers below it in the social ladder. The "villagization" of Egyptian society can be observed in the dialects spoken, the clothes worn, and the mores and habits of the population, as well as the very aesthetics of Egypt's towns, which were being transformed with the appearance of new social elements. Village practices brought into the city included some unique habits like the tradition of beating drums to wake up people and inform them of a person's death and the place of prayers for his soul. Other traditions included women removing their shoes as they entered to pay condolences to the family of the deceased or women taking turns reciting Qur'anic verses to complete the Qur'an as a form of condolence. Society was also being transformed through the cultural traits acquired by the alleged 4–5 million Egyptians living and working in conservative oil-rich Arab countries.[29]

John Esposito has put his finger on the nature of the transformations experienced by Egyptian society in the modern period:

> Egypt . . . [is] among the most modern of Muslim countries, it has experienced the full array of Islamic revivalist activities. Once a barometer for a modernization that was predominantly Western and somewhat secular in orientation, today it provides a full-blown example of the more complex, and at times volatile, experience of many Muslim societies attempting in a variety of ways to integrate their Islamic heritage and values with their sociopolitical development.[30]

The changes experienced by the city of Cairo, the nation's capital and business center, mirror the changes that have taken place in the country as a whole. Cairo's population rose from about 223,000 inhabitants at the end of the eighteenth century to more than one million in 1927.[31] Today Cairo is estimated to have fourteen million inhabitants, but the figures could be much higher given the existence of informal communities[32] and day labor coming in from the surrounding areas.[33] In the 1930s Cairo was described as a dual city: one part traditional with its *suq*s (marketplaces), alleys, and mosques, and the other modern with large avenues, multistoried buildings with elevators and balconies, squares from which roads radiated and where statues of the famous stood, department stores owned by foreigners and catering to the rich, banks, cinemas, motorcars, and restaurants. In *Midaq Alley,* Nagib Mahfuz showed how separate these two worlds were. Inhabitants of the alley spent their whole lives in it; outside was an alien world, glamorous and seductive.[34] Although this total separateness is at best fictional, the duality is still evident in the physical makeup of the city with its traditional poor, middle-class, and upper-class quarters, and their contrast with the modern middle-class and upper-class quarters.

Cairo at the turn of the twenty-first century is very much like other overcrowded Third World capitals whose services suited much smaller populations. Elizabeth and Robert Fernea saw tangible evidence from the changes that Cairo had undergone since 1959 when they lived there. "My reaction to Cairo revisited: a series of contradictory and debilitating moods: despair, euphoria, distaste, amusement. . . . There's more, more of everything, people, cars, problems. . . . The city is bursting."[35] In 1990 the differences between its quarters are reflected more in land value, location, and recollections than in the actual buildings or condition of the quarters. Previously exclusive quarters

such as Garden City or Zamalek still evidence something of the old grandeur
in the architecture, stretches of green, and the few trees left standing. But they
are no more than shadows of their former selves, and newcomers may have
difficulty determining which quarters used to be exclusive and which were
not. The city itself has grown in size, stretching beyond the Muqattam hill—
the city's usual boundary—from Qatamiya to Sixth of October city beyond
the Pyramids—another old boundary—and from the Qanatir to Hilwan,
making out of these previous suburbs an extension of the city. Cairo's beltway
is nearly complete with flying bridges leading into and flying over the city facilitating traffic but contributing to making Cairo a bizarre, crowded town
whose loss of beauty is lamented by its inhabitants. Today efforts and laws are
being exerted to keep the *dhawat* quarters of Zamalek and Garden City from
being further destroyed and their villas and art-deco buildings pulled down
and replaced by high-rises.

Alexandria provides another example: "[It] arose from almost nothing; in
Napoleon's day it was a poor, decaying place with a mere ten thousand inhabitants." [36] By 1927 the population had reached 57,300[37] and today it is about
four million. Once the preferred location for foreigners, particularly Greeks
and Italians, Alexandria long stood as the Westernized outpost of the country,
with its corniche stretching along Mediterranean beaches where the elite of
the country headed during summer. Families kept summerhouses and small
cabins on the beaches where first the upper, followed by the middle classes,
played at being Westernized. The "racy" novels of Ihsan 'Abd al-Quddus, perhaps the most popular novelist among Egypt's middle classes, are excellent
sources for understanding social relations and psychological pressures of the
modernizing generations of the fifties and sixties trying to break out of social
controls while holding onto the moral code and traditions of an older generation. Girls and boys meeting clandestinely and flirting during the summer vacation were basic themes of these novels. They were a reflection of gender
during the Nasserist period. Today evidence of the dominance of the culture
of the *'amma* is tangible on Alexandria's packed beaches. Where once only
cabin owners were permitted to enter, today the masses spread their food and
umbrellas on the sand and women swim covered in ankle-length *jalabiya*s
(woman's garment covering the whole body from neck to ankle). Where once
the view of the beach from the Corniche was blocked with cabins for the entertainment of the middle classes, army and police officers, press corps, and
other professions, today nothing hinders that view. In a gutsy move, Alexandria's governerate had all the cabins, casinos, and other obstructions removed
and opened the city to the enjoyment of its people and visitors. Only *khassa*
beaches like Montazah, once the king's palace, continue to have their cabins.
The same effort to beautify Cairo and remove the impediments that block al-

most all the Nile banks has been promised by the governor of Cairo. So far the power of the *khassa* who own the casinos and clubs occupying public-owned land, often without permit, has made it impossible to do so. Rather, in an unbelievably destructive move, Cairo's governor moved to fill in part of the Nile at Qasr al-Nil, its most beautiful point, to create a place for people to enjoy the river. The hegemonic power of the *khassa* is best exemplified by this situation, which continues illegal practices against the wishes and needs of the community at large.

Cultural diffusion can be seen in other ways. The cities of Upper Egypt, once inhabited by large numbers of Copts who formed the core of the urban classes in such cities as Luxor, are now exhibiting religious ratios similar to those in other areas in the country. This shift is mainly the result of civil servants moving to work in governmental offices and movement from surrounding villages to towns. For a long time the outward parameters of Luxor were limited; during the last decade the southern urban line has extended almost to the village of 'Udaisat, which is about thirty minutes away by car.

Villages everywhere are experiencing tremendous growth and dynamic transformations. Material changes are evident in the phenomenon of television antennas on rooftops of village houses and the existence of video clubs in remote towns of Upper Egypt. Television antennas on house roofs throughout the Egyptian countryside bear witness to the importance of mass communication in the transformation of the country. Houses increasingly are being constructed from concrete and brick. New houses are still being built of bricks manufactured by traditional methods; topsoil bricks are placed around a kiln and baked. Erosion of topsoil has now pushed the government to forbid this method and to encourage brick making with sand and clay. Peasants, however, continue to use the old methods rather than purchase sand bricks from the factories.

The relative wealth that the villagers are experiencing, which is converted into the limited comforts that the villages exhibit, is to a large extent the result of the transfers of its young men who are working in the Arab countries and send their money home. Capital earned in Arab oil-producing countries by Egyptian workers has also been used to extend capitalist enterprises of various kinds among the peasantry. The best known include agricultural machinery, particularly tractors, which are bought by peasant entrepreneurs and rented out for a fee. Limited land and high land value has meant that the demand for housing is much higher than the supply available, even in villages. Government restrictions against turning agricultural land into housing has further restricted availability of houses. Enterprising individuals are investing capital earned abroad in erecting small apartment buildings. Others construct not only apartments but also shops, which are in great demand because of the increased consumerism in these villages. These enterprises are part of the informal economic sector because most remain unreported.

> It would thus be more appropriate to characterize rural Egypt as being caught up in a perpetual whirl of change than to postulate its unchanging nature. . . . Among the major aspects of this transformation are commoditization, the penetration of capital, irrigation, transportation, mechanization, education, migration, the growth of cities, government policy towards agriculture and rural development. None of these is necessarily consistent with another, although they combine to produce the "change" we perceive.[38]

Egypt's economic and social problems have been an important ingredient in determining the social relations outlined above. The sheer dimensions of Egypt's problems are best measured by a population growing by one million every nine months and expected to reach seventy million in the early decades of the twenty-first century. Expressing his frustration with this high birth rate, which hampers development efforts, Mubarak exclaimed in a speech, "*bitzidu ummam*" ("you increase by nations"). Besides, of Egypt's sixty-three million people in 1999, 40 percent are under the age of fifteen. Population growth is exacerbated by reduced dependency on local food production and by depreciation in the quality of food being consumed, particularly by the poor.[39] "In 1977–78, about 50 percent of all lower income families suffered from slight to moderate malnutrition and 20 percent from anemia, as well as 20 percent from chronic undernutrition."[40] The per capita consumption of bread increased from 75 kilos per person per year in the 1960s to 210 kilos in the 1980s.[41] Despite the government complaint that bread is wasted and fed to farm animals,[42] the real cause for the growth in bread consumption has to do with the inflation in the price of food. The government subsidizes the price of bread to keep its price down, so more bread is eaten because that is all that large sectors of the population can afford.

Egyptians' per capita consumption of bread is one of the highest in the world, causing Egypt to become the world's third largest importer of wheat. The demand for food and lowered productivity have made Egypt dependent on imports of all sorts. The journalist 'Izzat al-Sa'dani lamented these conditions:

> The Egyptians reached an age . . . when they ate what they did not cultivate . . . and filled their stomachs with what they did not produce. . . . Even their piece of bread was no longer Egyptian. . . . Ships now carry to Egypt's shores . . . all that they eat, drink, or wear . . . wheat, meats, fish, chicken, butter, oil, and sugar . . . and machines on wheels . . . and wheels moved by machines . . . what decorates the houses and what beautifies the women.[43]

Pollution is another problem suffered by Egyptians on a daily basis. But the picture is changing. In 1988 Yusuf Idris described it: "You see the citizen walking in the streets of Cairo panting from lack of oxygen. He looks lost, unable to focus, because of the din of noises and microphones. He becomes listless and weary quickly, running out of patience, is inflicted with . . . 'distractions,' making him indifferent to his work. . . . He lives in a hell full of pollution, smoke, dust, and incredible deafening noise."[44]

In the area of pollution, the government has exerted great efforts and is on its way to combating pollution of different types. Cement factories in the suburb of Hilwan were throwing toxins over the city of Cairo and the surrounding areas, so the government shut the factories, which it owned. Because gasoline was one of the main causes of fumes and pollution throughout Egypt, with the help of American aid, a massive project to replace leaded with unleaded gasoline was launched. At the same time people were encouraged to use natural gas, which Egypt has in substantial quantities, through price and tax exemptions and free or reduced cost incentives to equip cars to use natural gas. Plans were set to monitor the quality of the air and announcements are made regularly regarding these conditions.

Nadia Makram Ebeid, Minister for Environmental Affairs, is a hands-on executive with weighty responsibilities. Heading a new ministry staffed with environmentalists and biologists, she challenges any threat to the environment.[45] Yet the last months of 1999 witnessed an unprecedented phenomenon: a thick black toxic fog covered Cairo and would not move away. It caused respiratory problems for tens of thousands—often severe and long-lasting (as in my case). The explanations given for the fog were diverse but seemed to focus on burning of waste in areas surrounding Cairo. Defending her efforts, Ebeid pointed to the responsibility of provincial authorities.[46] The existence of the smog and the difficulty in handling it are symptomatic of what ails Egypt environmentally and administratively.

At one point, the Nile, Egypt's main source of water, was heavily polluted. Low Nile levels had revealed glaring water mismanagement. The High Dam had proven to be Egypt's salvation, but once the level of water in Lake Nasser reached a dangerously low level in July 1988[47] and plant growth began to cover the Nile, there was general alarm. The causes of the pollution had been studied since the 1970s and included the dumping of industrial refuse into the Nile and the lack of sufficient sewage facilities. In 1982 a law was enacted to protect the Nile and other waterways from pollution.[48] A 1988 national conference to discuss problems of water and drainage suggested conserving water by using drainage water, developing underground wells, changing industrial plans, and turning Egypt's northern lakes into reservoirs.[49] For a long time the 1982 law and the conference suggestions seemed to be no more than ink on paper, and the water crisis symbolized the extent of the deterioration the country had suffered. Reminders of Sadat's offer to give Israel part of Egypt's Nile quota as a gesture of friendship appeared to be a horrific example of how Egypt is ruled.[50] But it is in Nile pollution control that the government has achieved perhaps its greatest success, itself a symptom of the positive changes that Egypt is experiencing at the turn of the century. The government of Prime Minister al-Ganzuri has shown real aptitude in dealing with the technological and infrastructural needs of the country. Today, people are talking of a realistic take-off for Egypt given its improved balance, budget, economy, infrastructure, and intellectual openness. The results are becoming evident.

Overcrowding has had repercussions on every aspect of life in Egypt. Sectarian strife provides an example. The growth of the Coptic population necessitated building more churches to serve the spiritual needs of the community. Egyptian laws regarding religious minorities date from Ottoman times and allow only limited building of churches. Under Nasser, Copts could build twenty-five churches a year, and Sadat increased that number to fifty. Still, Sadat let stand the laws requiring that no church be built near a mosque. Because no limit was put on building mosques, church building has been paralyzed by Muslim bureaucrats who stall building permits until a mosque is constructed close to the land designated for building the church in the "building permit request." The Coptic community, which has been experiencing a revivalist movement under the direction of Pope Shenouda, resorted to building churches in secret and without government permission. Urban land, however, is at a premium, and people vie over the usage of limited land resources, a basic factor underlying the violent outbreak of sectarian strife at Zawya al-Hamra in Cairo during June 1981.

Sectarian strife has been an important political instrument since early in the twentieth century. As Yunan Labib Rizk points out, the British used an express policy of "divide and conquer" to undermine Egyptian national unity and strike at nationalist opposition to Britain's occupation of Egypt. One important act culminating Britain's efforts since 1882 is a reservation made to Britain's "notorious" unilateral declaration of February 28, 1922, conceding normal independence to Egypt. These reservations concerned the "defense of foreign interests in Egypt" and the "protection of minorities." Egyptians, Copts and Muslims alike, condemned this policy, realizing it aimed at the Coptic community, defining it as a minority needing protection within its own country.[51] Defining Copts as a minority began a novel discourse that has remained a method of interfering in Egyptian affairs by outside forces as evidenced by the pressure of particular Coptic immigrant groups in the United States that brought about a congressional hearing in what was claimed as "discrimination against Egyptian Copts."[52] When an event of sectarian strife took place, it became widely publicized in the United States, with exaggerations made from one side and denials from the other. Meanwhile, Coptic feasts are celebrated for the first time publicly and on television, and Egyptian Copts resent being called a minority within their own country. At the same time, Copts are demanding equality in jobs and church building.

While Rizk sees the British occupation as having planted the seeds of sectarian strife, both the Islamic and Coptic communities have been subject to fundamentalist movements in the twentieth century as a result of modernity, foreign occupation, and political and class inequalities.[53] Today the Coptic Church is asking for a cancellation of the *khat al-humayyun* (rule made by the Ottoman Sultan) in effect since the Ottoman period, which was actually canceled over 120 years ago but continues in practice. This would put an end to government controls over building churches and renovating old ones. The government has in fact cooperated in giving permits for building churches and for church renovations, but more needs to be done, according to the yearly Arab Strategic Report issued by the Al-Ahram Centre for Political and Strategic Studies in January 1999. "The report notes that Copts often complain about their limited participation in high office and about restrictions of the building of new churches. It recommends a just distribution of important posts to ensure that the most able people, whether Muslim or Coptic, get the opportunities they deserve. At present, appointments to senior positions are usually influenced by personal considerations that have nothing to do with religious affiliation."[54]

Social transformations have left their impact on the *khassa,* the makeup of the groups of which the *khassa* is formed, and the relationship among these groups and between them and the *'amma.* The struggle for power among the various groups of *khassa* became quite pronounced in the 1990s. The results seem to be, first, the peripheralization if not the weakening of military influence and, second, a new power balance, sometimes alliance other times struggle, between the *tujjar* and the government *multazim* bureacracy who continue to be the ascendant group of the *khassa* today. Part of the reason for this is the spread of *multazim* prerogatives and benefits toward the base, allowing wider sectors of the bureaucracy and, hence, of society to enjoy such benefits.

Until his ouster in 1989, the military was headed by the powerful personality of 'Abd al-Halim Abu Ghazzala, a hero of the 1973 war who was supported by the United States. Through him the military had become a chief industrial producer and exporter of military hardware (ranging from guns to missiles) and of machinery for local consumption, including bicycles and kitchen appliances. The military was at one point also involved in constructing roads, houses, and bridges, as well as land reclamation in Egypt. Today military industries aimed at self-sufficiency for military forces and families, are involved in food security, planting crops, raising farm animals, and running chicken farms. It could do all this cheaply because the work was performed by army draftees, including graduates of science and engineering colleges.

However much the public and private sectors resented the advantages enjoyed by as powerful a business competitor as the military, continuing the Nasserist tradition, military affairs were considered a matter of national security and not to be questioned. Even the military budget was not open to the People's Assembly; neither were its business dealings, profits, or military ports and warehouses. Officers received special salaries, retirement, housing, transportation, vacation, and services. Soldiers received few of the benefits of the officers, and most were poorly paid recruits. The military continues to receive exceptional benefits, but its power is shrinking and its mamluk-style prerogatives, which were taken for granted earlier, are no longer as glaringly acceptable.

Still the military continues to be an essential ingredient of the *khassa*. A large percentage of the holders of government and business leadership positions were former members of the military and their power stemmed from that relationship. Besides, for the *khassa* to be able to benefit from their governmental prerogatives, the military and police were necessary to ensure stability and to control the opposition, not just radical Islamicists or industrial labor alone, but all associations. For example, the headquarters of the prestigious Lawyers' Syndicate were surrounded by police forces in 1989 and their elections were canceled because those elected had extreme Islamic leanings.[55]

It is said that those involved in various forms of police work and security belonging to the Ministry of the Interior in Egypt were close to one-half million men, nearly 1 percent of the population in 1989. This is an exaggeration but illustrates perceptions of police power. When riots or demonstrations broke out against government policy, the police were brought in, as happened when labor struck at the ironworks at Hilwan in August 1989 over the question of labor benefits. The chairman of the board, a protégé of the National Party, found the style of the two elected workers on the board insulting to his person, so he simply dismissed them from the board. During the strike that answered this arbitrary action, the workers demanded an investigation of the company's budget, expenditure, and profits. Panicking at the situation, the chairman of the board called in the security forces of the Ministry of the Interior supplemented by army soldiers, who put down the strike.[56] If the police rioted, then the army could be counted upon. In February 1986 recruits of the security forces stationed in Giza rioted in protest over the very poor salaries, long years of service, hard work, and poor treatment that they received from police officers. That event became more ominous because of the burning, rioting, lives lost, and the spread of violence to other security contingents located in Sohag, Assiut, and Ismailiya.[57]

Controls were introduced to the economic system by the government to prevent large-scale scandals. The Sadat government's endorsement of a project to sell ten thousand acres on the pyramid plateau, in an area known to contain unexplored sites, to be subsequently developed by a jointly owned foreign-Egyptian Hong Kong–registered company exemplified the power of the *infitahist tujjar* to make a profit even at the cost of the country's heritage.[58] The company paid $266.10 an acre, or 6.3 cents a meter, then immediately began reselling the land to private owners for seventy-five times that price, or $4.60 per meter. The massive tourist projects outlined by the company's plans never materialized and only two million of the company's projected one billion dollar working capital were deposited in the company's bank accounts.[59] It took the concerted effort of "university professors, cultural organizations, judges, lawyers, and the international press," to stop the project. It was terminated on May 28, 1978, by a presidential decree, the same way it had been instituted.[60] Such scandals involving Egypt's national heritage did not reappear; government and civil society both had been made aware of the destructiveness of speculation and get-rich-fast schemes, notwithstanding their speculative potential to Egypt's development.

Emergency laws in effect since Sadat's rule increased the power of security forces and *multazim* bureaucrats extensively. Besides giving the security forces unlimited coercive powers to hunt down Islamic radicals and other "enemies of the state," the new controls and emergency laws formed the basis of various executive laws allowing ministerial and bureaucratic regulations. Executive laws, in turn, supplied government employees with the authority to extract benefits from private citizens. Because breaking the emergency laws for any purpose constituted a crime, simple mistakes entailed prison sentences. Theoretically, ministerial decrees are supposed to facilitate transactions between members of the public and between the public and the government, but in Egypt, as in other countries with bureaucratic labyrinths, such decrees became in many cases an instrument of control of financial and commercial transactions by the state bureaucracy. The benefactors of these laws included the middle and lower echelons of the bureaucracy, who were sometimes the initiators of such decrees.

The victims of these complex conditions belonged to the private sector, and here, even though one could differentiate between an official and an unofficial economy, businesses found themselves having to resort to unofficial practices to grow. The *tujjar* members of the private sector, involved in export-import or in manufacturing, can be divided into two groups. The first, entrepreneurs closely connected to foreign concerns, are few in number, firmly allied within the *khassa,* and have a say in determining laws. The second group of *tujjar* can be considered a new element that began to grow under Sadat and is escalating in importance under Mubarak by gaining an increasing share of the economy. It is made up of the owners of small factories, *wirash* (workshops), shops, services, and trading companies not in direct association with the *khassa* and, hence, with little actual power to determine laws. Pressure is put on this second group of *tujjar* by government bureaucrats who wish to extract informal *iltizam*-type benefits. Executive decrees from the local office level up to the ministerial are used to ensure benefits for many small bureaucrats (smaller *multazims*). Thus, the nature of the *multazims* themselves has changed with the continued expansion of their power and benefits downward and outward in the government hierarchy.

The fact that these new businesses are not directly related to members of the *khassa* is very important. Even though they find themselves having to contend with the abuses and exactions of the state, they are beginning to present a real opposition to the *khassa*. They may not believe in the political structure as it stands and are not involved in the political process, but they understand the laws and have learned both how to manipulate the law and how to go outside it, finding refuge in informal methods of doing business. It should also be noted that this is clearly a middle class, standing between the *khassa* and the popular sectors of the *'amma*. They do not have the power to stop the exactions of the *khassa,* but their wealth is giving them the leverage to rise beyond the *'amma*. Because the *khassa* needs them for the jobs they provide, the import-substitution products they produce, and the taxes they pay, they have considerable leverage. Furthermore, most have some relationship to the *khassa* that they can call upon in time of need, and their wealth gives them passage through the avenues of the lower echelons of the government structure.

The new *tujjar* amassed great wealth, but that was scarcely the case with other members of the middle classes. Government employees, professionals, and middle levels of the military forces lived in constant fear of falling into the abyss of the lower classes. The seventies, in particular, were difficult owing to static wages and inflation rates estimated at 25–30 percent.[61] The economist Galal Amin considers inflation to have been crucial for social transformation, particularly for the middle classes. Inflation enriched "craftsmen, construction workers and agricultural laborers," who benefited from the shortage in skilled labor caused by the emigration of large numbers of workers to Arab countries. At the same time inflation "lowered the real income of government officials and professionals," whose salaries increased very little.[62] Furthermore, not all members of a class experienced the same changes; vertical differentiation within classes meant that certain strata of a class were enriched while others became impoverished:

> Construction workers and workers related to small private businesses, mechanics, plumbers, furniture workers, etc.; big, medium and even petty traders who, by their extreme reliance on external trade especially in imported consumer goods, have made fortunes in short periods of time. A new class of land and real-estate speculators amassed fortunes; private industrialists, builders and export-import agents; medium and large land-owners; and finally some professionals, mainly doctors, pharmacists, accountants and lawyers.[63]

Class lines were no longer defined according to education, sophistication, or where someone lived as had once been the case. Money was replacing such factors as birth, education, or prestige as the most important criterion in determining social position. Such conditions were under attack by those who did not benefit financially from these conditions and who found their social position deteriorating. Mubarak expressed the frustration of the middle class with these conditions when he pointed out in one of his speeches that it is not government employees who are riding Mercedes cars, an often-used expression of frustration voiced by members of the impoverished educated classes.

Today there are efforts by rich classes to entrench themselves into a new *dhawat* using old elite culture including foreign languages, Western dress, and personal habits. Nightclubs do very good business among these groups who have money to spend, as do health clubs, gyms, and beauty salons. New magazines are published in foreign languages that focus on the rich and provide them with glossy pictures of new fashions for men and women, fashion shows, stories about "society couples," beautiful homes, and advertising for expensive cars and imported consumer items. Weddings of the wealthy are also setting new standards for the *khassa;* families compete to make the weddings of their sons and daughters ostentatious. A new language of snobbism is also appearing, showing disdain toward those who do not belong. A good example is the word *bi'a,* which has replaced the word *baladi* to refer to someone who is vulgar. Because *bi'a* means environment, its usage is interesting: the rich use the term to refer to those who pollute what could be a great social existence. The word *baladi* has too many meanings and has nationalist connotations, so *bi'a* is becoming more widely used especially among the younger generation. At the same time, the word is also used by middle-class educated people who believe themselves to have modern tastes to refer to rich people who have no taste, the idea being that "money does not a civilized person make." Other words—such as *mozza,* meaning the most succulent part of meat but used to refer to a beautiful, desirable woman—used by the sons of these rich classes actually intimate that the origins of these classes are themselves what they refer to as *bi'a.*

It should come as no surprise then that it is among the middle classes that revivalism is spreading. The deteriorating conditions of certain sectors of the middle classes have caused them to turn toward a more family-oriented existence; families with shrinking resources in income, housing, and material conditions need each other to survive. The importance of students in radical revivalism has been the focus of a number of studies that see the prominence of students as proof of middle-class rebellion against frustrated hopes. Gilles Kepel has documented the prominence of students among radicals, particularly Military Academy and Jihad groups. He found that the majority of students originated from science colleges and military schools that have been long considered a route for social mobility. Other groups included professionals, engineers, state employees, and teachers, besides artisans and merchants.[64] A similar observation was made by Nemat Guenena in her study of Jihad groups whose occupational distribution was about 45 percent students, 25 percent professionals.[65]

For political and economic reasons, violence was not limited to radical religious groups. Thus, labor strife was continuous, if not as widely known. Strikes were widespread during the eighties; for example, eight labor strikes occurred in 1988, five of them in major government factories, including the Mahalah Weaving and Textile, and among public transportation workers. The workers in the ironworks at Hilwan, which in 1990 had the largest body of labor in Egypt (about twenty-seven thousand), went on a limited strike in 1987, and a major one in summer 1989 (see above). Workers' demands were somewhat different from those of students even though both complained of the economic situation, inflation, and the arbitrariness of the government. But workers tended to demand better benefits, working conditions, and salaries,[66] whereas students were more interested in the political system, political participation, social mobility, and human rights issues. There was, therefore, little actual political cooperation between labor and students. Violence is a symptom of social dislocation. There are a sense of loss of values and general feelings of insecurity that are evidenced in various ways and evoke inconsistent reactions. The *Al-Ahram Strategic Report for 1998* pointed to another form of social violence that is increasing at an alarming rate. "Young men were resorting to violence after realizing that the 'principle of force' prevailed throughout society. The remedy is the supremacy of the law and a war against corruption in all its forms."[67]

Many reasons have been given for the phenomenon of women's turn to

Islamic garb and piety, including use of the veil as a political symbol, revival of Islamic traditions, and the security afforded by Islamic garb in the Middle East's overcrowded cities. One interesting explanation points to the uncertainty that women face as husbands become less available. Simply put, it is no longer easy to marry given the difficulty in finding housing and the financial burden of raising a family. According to a 1989 report, there were nine million unmarried men and women of marriageable age in Egypt. The median age of marriage for women was thirty and for men thirty-five. By 1997 the estimated number of young people who could not afford to marry had risen to ten million. The same study estimated the number of Egyptians living under the level of severe poverty at four and one-half million.[68] Unless married very young, middle-class and upper-working-class women in particular have found they might have to wait until their thirties to be married. This has encouraged early marriages for girls at the cost of educations and careers.[69]

Furthermore, it is not clear that growing paternalism is necessarily a sign of growing female servility to the wishes of a male-dominated society. Male members of the family are just as much victimized by this paternalism as are women. The proliferation of cases of husbands killed by wives, an ongoing phenomenon, is evidence of the lack of social and legal equality between men and women. Even though some of these murders are caused by infidelity, most have to do with women's despair against husbands who beat them and their children or wish to throw them out of the house so as to bring in younger wives, or occur because wives cannot be divorced from husbands against husbands' wishes. It should be remembered, however, that most cases involved poor, uneducated women who found no other recourse to save themselves and their children from marital abuse. The legal system differentiates according to wealth more than gender; the poor have little recourse to courts and law whether they are women or men.[70] The impact of new *khul'* laws is yet to be seen, but because gender problems involve much more than divorce, important changes have yet to be faced not only to discriminatory laws but also to the philosophy behind them.

The issue of sexual equality, which is used by feminists to gauge how equal women are to men within a particular society, may be of use here. Although legally Egyptian women still have a long way to go to achieve equal personal and human rights, the proliferation of Islamicist literature concerning sexual relations and the sexual rights of women indicates that women are gaining ground when it comes to the issue of women's sexual rights. Generally speaking, traditional culture is less puritan about relations between husband and wife than is middle-class morality. Interestingly, although state-sponsored religious leaders such as Sheikh Sha'rawi have come out with Islamic interpretations supporting the Nilotic practice of circumcising girls, conservative religious scholars, especially women, have spoken out loudly against the un-Islamicness of such practices. At the same time, it is curious that only a very few Westernized Egyptian feminists championed the subject of women's sexual rights. Those who did, such as Nawal Sa'dawi, were condemned by their peers. Angela Davis's visit to Egypt to investigate the phenomenon of revivalism persuaded her that Egyptian women, unlike their Western counterparts, did not regard their battle in achieving rights in sexual terms. "There is indeed a great danger of representing sexual liberation as women's liberation."[71] Although suffering from human rights abuses, in personal relationships women found themselves more confident within an Islamic environ. This was particularly so among classes of society that had previously experienced social mobility or had seen hopes of such mobility disappear.

Using drugs is another reaction to social dislocation. It has become one of the most serious problems in Egypt, afflicting old and young, men and women, rich and poor. Egypt went to war on drugs in the 1980s and 1990s; the death penalty become the punishment for importing, selling, manufacturing, cultivating, exporting, or dealing in drugs or in the seeds of drug plants.[72] Yet only a few drug dealers were ever brought to trial. One reason is that the drug trade worldwide is an important source of wealth for the informal market. Dealers in drugs enjoy great wealth and use it to buy goods, thus stimulating production and providing the population with cash liquidity. As elsewhere in the world, without the traffic in drugs the economy would worsen, a true contradiction symbolic of the "absurd" conditions under which parts of world society lives.

The frustrations of everyday life are worsened by fear for the future, particularly among the young. There is widespread unemployment and a belief that only those with the right connections can get good jobs. Every year about 450,000 new graduates expect to be given jobs by the government as promised by *Al-Mithaq,* and for years the government has hired graduates at the cost of bureaucratic inefficiency.[73] In 1989 an estimated 700,000 graduates with medium-level degrees in trade and commerce had been waiting for jobs since 1981 and 40,000 engineers were jobless.[74] Paradoxically, the educational system continued to graduate even larger numbers of students each year, and the government's obligation to provide jobs still stands as law. Rather than tackle the question of these socialist rights *(makasib ishtirakiya)* at its very roots, an action that could disturb the relationship between *khassa* and *'amma* that depends upon those rights as part of the formula, the government resorted to "no action" by simply slowing down hiring while encouraging young people to open their own businesses through training and bank loans, encouraging home-industries, and investing in a number of mega projects to provide employment. Thus various endeavors were attempted to solve the question of unemployment,[75] often with daring if short-lived solutions. For example, 28,000 1987–88 graduates were directed toward starting their own businesses. Banks were instructed to facilitate borrowing by new graduates, and the government announced that it would provide them with technical assistance. The president did his part by making public visits to new businesses, including small family "mom and pop" ventures. At the same time, megaprojects were launched by the government to build infrastructure, expand trade, and increase agricultural productivity. Increased job opportunities for youth and the unemployed were at the center of these projects, which cost the government billions and received extreme praise as well as criticism. Perhaps the most celebrated project is the Toshka land reclamation project in the south of Egypt. Begun in January 1977, the plan was to run a canal from Lake Nasser to the oases in the Western desert. Aims were similar to Nasser's Tahrir Project, that is, to create a New Nile Valley. But this project is much larger, with ambitions to reclaim half a million acres to agricultural production and build villages that would help ease population pressure from the Nile Valley in the future. Government estimates in 1977 were that the Toshka would provide three million new jobs. Another megaproject is that of Sharq al-'Uwaynat, with plans to reclaim a quarter-million acres and provide another half-million jobs.[76] Altogether the plan is to increase Egypt's 8 million feddans of agricultural land to 11.4 million feddans,[77] an ambitious plan that, if successful, would double Egypt's cultivable area before 1952.

Infitah was supposed to have solved the problem of slow productivity and with it unemployment. But the policy of *infitah* was implemented in a fashion that may have suited the *khassa* but did not bring about a free-market economy (see chap. 6) for some time. For example, liberalizing agricultural production and distribution were limited by Sadat's government. *Infitah* was applied to urban centers to benefit the *tujjar,* but the peasantry continued to be told what to produce, and government companies bought their crops for export at great profit. The same policy was continued for a while under Mubarak. While agricultural production and distribution were liberalized, vital hard-currency earning items, such as cotton, cane sugar, and rice, were excepted. Incentives were extended to quiet the protests of growers of these crops: government assistance in fighting soil erosion, raising the government price for a crop from year to year, extending financial assistance to farmers, inviting large-scale farmers to become members of the NDP, and NDP assistance for these farmers' bids for seats in the People's and Consultative Assemblies.

Under the controlling policies of Sadat and the early Mubarak, the peasantry continued to resist controls because market prices for their products were much higher than the government's. Canny and sophisticated in his own way, the peasant did not wish to see the value of his labor enjoyed elsewhere. The example of sugarcane is pertinent. Because Egyptian cane sugar is high in sweetness and brings high prices on world markets, government policy since Nasser had been to maximize sugarcane production, to export local sugar, and to import low-quality beet sugar for local consumption. The profit went to government-owned sugar-processing factories run by appointed officials and trading companies with monopolies over foreign trade in cash crops. The same policy applied to cotton: only the cheapest quality cotton fabric was manufactured for local consumption; high-quality, long-staple cotton was exported in raw and semi-finished condition. It was not until the 1990s that a free market for agricultural products became established and then mainly as a result of the changing economic atmosphere—increased entrepreneurial investments in exporting agricultural products such as onions, potatoes, and fruits to Arab and European countries. The economy also grew significantly as private manufacturing of cotton finished cloth and finished products—clothing and house furnishings—earned badly needed hard currency. With the changes in the makeup of the *khassa* and the pressures of a new world order, it was normal that the laws controlling production and distribution also would change.

Earlier, before Egypt became a signatory of the General Agreement on Tariffs and Trade (GATT) and made a free-market economy a state policy, resistance against *khassa* control of the economy took interesting forms. For example, although large-scale growers of sugarcane associated with the *khassa* and cooperated with them by delivering their product to government companies, smaller growers defied the government and sold their crops elsewhere. According to one 1989 report, government factories paid L.E. 1,064 for the production of one acre of sugarcane, but market prices reaching L.E. 3,000 were paid by fruit juice shops (sugarcane juice is a national drink) and *sirga*s (juicers) producing molasses. To stop the diversion of sugarcane from government-owned factories, executive laws on the governorate level forbade the sale of sugarcane outside the provinces in which it was grown. Because most juice shops are located in Lower Egypt and sugarcane is the cash crop of Upper Egypt, this administrative law was designed to stop the "smuggling" of sugarcane. Because the laws were illogical, they were disregarded, and the unofficial traffic increased to the point where government sugar factories worked at a fraction of their capabilities. Thus, a new factory at Girga in Upper Egypt was producing no more than seventy-seven days each year.[78] Furthermore, most peasants ordered by the government to plant a new unfamiliar brand of high-yielding sugarcane refused to do so because of the expenses involved.[79] Other crops that were restricted to public sector trading include wheat. Moving wheat from one governorate to the other was made illegal. The police were ordered to search and imprison all involved in "smuggling" wheat. The government's justification was that merchants were greedy and wanted to sell wheat at black-market prices because of expected shortages.[80]

Perhaps such situations formed an important point at which the government opted to end controls that were proving to be counterproductive and together with a changed world order pushed for unrestricted world markets across borders. Of course, as countries of the world signed such agreements, they also set rules that would restrict markets such as requiring exact descriptions, weights, measures, and freshness, health excuses that formed almost a barrier to imports from particular areas of the world. The free market finally meant an end to one of the most important socialist aims enjoyed by peasants—rent controls for agricultural land. Expectations were that peasant violence would ensue against landowners who canceled low-paying contracts as the final stages of the law were implemented in 1998. But the relative calm was an indication that the situation had changed in the countryside; most land belonged to the peasant and not to an absentee landlord.

The cost was heavy for large sectors of peasant society, however, particularly for landless peasants who could no long afford to pay the high price of rent reaching over a thousand pound per crop. Many left the village for Egypt's towns and cities in search of work, thereby increasing the number of unemployed by 17 percent, 75 percent of whom are young people.[81] While the growth in domestic production has reached 6 percent, according to the government, and the inflation rate dropped to less than 4 percent in 1997, the price paid by the poor for the success of the implementation of economic reform and Structural Adjustment Programmes—the development plan of the government—has been an even harder and more depressed life, according to Fatemah Farag's article in *Al-Ahram Weekly*. Farag compares two quarters of the city of Cairo. "Up on a hill is a lush golf course, the grass imported from Florida, complemented by a luxurious club house and an extensive complex of lavish villas—witness to the wealth creation generated by current policy. . . . Five minutes drive away is a district of low-grade housing, built to house those whose homes were destroyed by the 1992 earthquake. Here Fakiha lives in two small rooms with her five children, husband and mother-in-law."[82] Health concerns among the poor include widespread anemia and respiratory diseases, a major cause of death, which is not surprising given the air pollution. Bilharzia continues to be widespread among the peasantry, while hepatitis and cholera are increasing. Quoting a study by Heba Nassar, Farag details the fate of middle-class white-collar workers in the face of economic changes: "The former lower middle expenditure category moved to a status of long term or chronic poverty. The living conditions of this class, which depends mainly on employment as its source of income, were adversely affected by ERSAP due to the increase in the cost of living, removal of a significant share of food subsidies, changes in the employment policies, privatization as well as the limitation in the delivery of free social services." [83]

Generally speaking, the public sector had become an obsolete structure of bureaucratic supervision in which the bureaucracy represented a nonproductive giant obstructing the smooth operation of a market economy. Until the mid-1990s the constant losses suffered by the public sector were covered by the government budget, nearly bankrupting the state. Efforts to privatize the public sector under Sadat failed, fought all the way by members of the NDP. Businesses whose losses were covered by the government budget proved an excellent avenue for rewarding patronage. This is not unique to Egypt but seemed to have been a symptom in countries moving from socialist to capitalist economies.

Justifications for not liquidating the public sector included its importance in providing the public with subsidized goods that could become unaffordable in a free market economy.[84] Another reason was that the public sector provided guaranteed jobs for most blue-collar workers, who received not only salaries but a share in "profits" whether their productivity went up or down. Selling the public sector would mean the wholesale cancellation of the state's obligations to these workers. Therefore, labor continued to stand against such privatization, and, consequently, the state was in no hurry to tackle the issue: "Those policies which elicited, or threatened to elicit, the widest and most unified resistance from workers were the ones most readily abandoned by the government involved." [85] Up until the 1990s, the government's philosophical outlook toward public and private sectors was not liberal. As explained by a government official: "The affair is one of the development of our country, meaning that the money of the public sector and that of the private sector is the money of society, and we have to think of the ideal way to use it." [86] Thus, the government still viewed the economy with a collective outlook. The economy was directed according to established plans with the state acting as a big distributor within the economy.[87] Of course, the way the economy is directed ultimately benefits the *khassa*. Therefore, privatization of public sector companies moved ahead once interests shifted, and the power balance between *multazims* and *tujjar* became more equal as the *tujjar* began to ascend within the *khassa*. The shift in world capitalism and the aggressiveness of globalization with its emphasis on market forces all contributed to this process. Today Egypt is committed to privatization following Law 203 of 1991 establishing rules for privatizing 314 state-owned companies by the end of the millennium. The effort put into connecting Egypt with the internet and the expansion of the usage of computers is a sign of what is happening and of things to come. Given the names of companies doing business in Egypt, trade in the

Cairo Stock Exchange, and property purchases now open to foreigners, globalization has become a reality for the Egyptian upper classes. Even the government's megaprojects are open to foreign ownership. A Saudi prince, for example, "has invested in 432,000 feddans of desert near the eastern end of the project zone."[88] While this may be good business, what does it say to Egypt land-ownership control laws in effect since the Nasserist period, by which land ownership in the Nile Valley is set not to exceed one hundred acres per family? Reclaimable land could be owned in any quantity, but it is only those who are very rich—including foreigners—who have the financial ability to reclaim such land. Reclaimable land may be what Egypt needs, and perhaps those who finance such activity deserve to become great landowners, but in order for such land to be reclaimed, Nile water is being diverted to these mega-semi-international projects, even though Egypt potentially faces critical water shortages. There simply is not enough Nile water to go around, given these reclamation projects, industrial projects, and growth in population. Perhaps there is a new *khassa* combine coming into formation, with the country's limited resources being prioritized for their investments. This new combine seems to be international; the question is, are we seeing a new international "feudal" order appearing? If so, what about the *'amma*, nationally and internationally?

•   •   •

An interesting observation often made about Egypt is that here is a country whose government was at one point practically bankrupt, seeking loans everywhere and constantly demanding a rescheduling of existing loans in an active economy where money is readily available. Tourism, transfers from Egyptian workers in Arab countries, profits from private enterprises, and a healthy informal economy have contributed to this activity. Egypt seems to present two separate entities: an official "legal" structure with its economic and political edifice controlled by a national government, and an unofficial structure with its own legal traditions, customs, and economy. Discourses of nationalism, patriotism, and secularism, upheld by the first, are being replaced by sectarianism, parochialism, and communalism in the second. Culture is becoming the uniting factor rather than state-imposed secularism and nationalism. During the incredible reversal of Egypt's economy in the 1990s, a legacy for Mubarak and Ganzuri, basic structures still continue to hamper the takeoff that Egypt's economy is on the verge of making.

The official structure continued to depend on income from foreign trade, taxation, mercantilist controls of the economy, and, particularly, on foreign aid and borrowing. Thus, Mubarak continued Sadat's policy toward the United States by upholding the role outlined by the Rogers Plan and accepted by Sadat (see chap. 6). Even while trying to create some leverage in Egypt's relationship with the United States by warming up relations with Russia, Rumania, and other Eastern European countries, Mubarak became ever more dependent on the United States,[89] whose economic, military, and political aid is vital for today's *khassa* combine. Delegation after delegation after delegation is sent from Egypt to Washington, D.C., to facilitate the continuation of this aid. At the same time, the United States has increasingly turned to Egypt as an intermediary between it and the Arab world, particularly the Palestinians.[90] Egypt's role was cemented by joining the U.S.-led alliance against Iraq's Saddam Hussein in the Gulf War.

At the same time Egypt's leadership made great efforts to open up to Arab and African countries.[91] News of such exchanges were given prominent coverage in the Egyptian press, radio, and television.[92] The Arab Collective Economic Agreement, which involved Egypt, Jordan, Iraq, and North Yemen, and which failed because of the Gulf War, was meant to form a trade block similar to the EEC, in which Arab countries could complement each other through exchange of technical knowledge and industrial and agricultural commodities. Iraq had petroleum wealth and needed help in rebuilding its industrial infrastructure, devastated in its war with Iran. Yemen had good prospects for oil and was in the process of building a modern infrastructure. Jordan had close relations with Egypt and with the oil-rich Arab countries; it also had a viable industry and could contribute to active trade with the other three. Egypt had the manpower, as well as the skill and experience in certain industries, including construction and the military.[93] Egyptians also expected to play a leadership role in this new economic block.[94] The proposed activities fell within the development plan of the state and were part of the latent outlook that regarded collectivism as ideal for Egypt's situation. Today, yet another united Arab effort is underway. At the same time, failure of Arab cooperation has not stopped collectivist projects. Tushki, is today the most important desert land reclamation project in Egypt as it turns the desert into green cultivated fields. Similar projects at Nubariyya and 'Uwaynat have already proven their success. Desert reclamation is one area in which great strides have been made. One need but travel on the "desert" road from Cairo to Alexandria to see the successful progress of desert reclamation. The desert road is more a memory; today farmlands border the road nearly the full extent of the 220 kilometer ride. Drip-drop cultivation and other innovative methods were pioneered by Egyptian individuals and farmers. The phenomenon of apples growing in the desert is still quite surprising.

The unofficial structure depends on unreported transactions, petty capitalist enterprises such as vending, rental of furnished apartments, services of various types, crafts, and transportation, to mention a few. Good examples are taxis in service with their meters off, hairdressers going to their customers' homes rather than having them come to their shops, *ashab hirfa* (craftsmen) holding shop on street corners, and vendors carrying their foreign consumer items to customers' homes or selling them in their own homes to avoid tax officials.

Informality also takes place on a very large scale in transactions where no cash is involved. These range from exchanging real estate to not recording or registering sales of large consumer items or even of houses and land. The government's answer was to levy higher taxes and to hunt down tax evaders. Because big companies can afford to hire accountants to clear their books and can easily resort to bribery to end their tax troubles, it is really small and medium companies, and lately informal sectors of the economy that are hit by the taxes. Not only are taxes being levied on mechanics, electricians, and even peddlers, but these workers are being asked to pay exorbitant back taxes that they have no way of paying. Still, a great deal of wealth is held by the *'amma* today because however stringent tax collection is, individuals feel no moral qualms about evading taxes if they feel they are getting little in return.

Informality is tangible in illegal housing mushrooming on the periphery of Cairo and other cities without any particular plan. According to one study, "80 percent of all housing units built in Cairo since 1960 had been built without permits." [95] Because these settlements were established illegally, they often lack the most basic necessities such as schools, hospitals, running water, and electricity. Illegal communities have become the last resort for citizens with few other housing options because of the limited supply of legal building sites and the exorbitant price of land. Many of the informal communities began as villages whose closeness to the city meant that they were potential urban settlements. A study of Zenin, a "village" turned suburb, dated its history back 150 years and showed how its urbanization began slowly before the 1930s. [96] Because the state could not throw squatters off the land when they had nowhere else to go, it seemed logical to turn it into private property and have the squatters pay taxes on it. Thus, the government announced that all squatters had to come forward, pay a small price, and register the land they were cultivating or on which they had erected houses. [97] There was no enthusiasm on the people's part to do so, particularly among those who, according to the law, had usufruct rights to the land they were cultivating. They saw this not as a magnanimous gesture by the state, but as the act of a government using the issue of formality to collect the price on land already claimed by squatters and peasants. There was a strong basis for this argument; according to government figures, the first batch of land, 4,760 acres belonging to the Land Reform Authorities to be sold to those already in actual possession of it, was expected to bring in eighteen million pounds. [98] By ministerial decree 720 for the year 1989, governors of provinces were delegated to certify these ownership transactions. But executive action sometimes brought about different results. In one example the governor of Daqahl ya Province had the inhabitants of a community ejected, destroying ninety houses and making 180 families homeless in the process.[99]

The inconsistencies and contradictions that have been described in this chapter have led some to describe the Egyptian situation as "absurd." As one playwright explained: "The Theater of the Absurd is the best way to express some aspects of our contemporary Egyptian reality."[100] Frequently published short stories, plays, and songs that can be characterized as "absurd" mirror the perplexity of life and people's frustrations. Good examples are the short story collection written by Sonallah Ibrahim, *The Smell of It*,[101] and the award-winning play by Muhammad Tawfik, "The Day the Moon Fell," in which he mixes the traditional with the modern outlook of an Egypt trying to hold on to its roots and beliefs yet confronted with absurd situations.[102] The short stories written by young Egyptian intellectuals in the collection *Flights of Fantasy* are even more telling of the surrealistic way in which life is presenting itself in Egypt.

Popular songs in Egypt today put more emphasis on the tune than the content. Rather than the *tarab* (enrapturement) expected earlier from Um Kulthum, Farid al-Atrash, or 'Abd al-Halim Hafez, who continue to be popular but not as much as they used to be, today's songs are fast and loud and have the same beat and rhythm. The language spoken in the songs is an incomprehensible amalgamation of words originating in the idioms of Lower Egyptian peasants, Upper Egyptian *Si'idis*, the larger Arab world, and a spattering of foreign terms. Rather than the *qasida* of earlier times, the songs are made of disjointed meaningless rhyming words, the more absurd the more entertaining. The classical *qasa'id* and nationalist songs have been replaced by *mawwals* sung in colloquial idiom by *jalabiya*-garbed singers accompanied by *nayy* and *ribaba*. The *mawwal*, usually sung in popular weddings or *mawalid* (religious feasts), has become enjoyable to all classes. Singers from Upper Egypt such as Ahmed 'Adawiya have become popular among the more urban tastes of Cairo and Alexandria. 'Amr Diab, Egypt's "heartthrob" singer, holds mass beach concerts with loud crashing brass bands accompanying his Western-beat music. His concerts are sold out in Egypt, Europe, and America, where he entertains the young and old of Arab immigrant communities. Tastes and language are a good indication of the cultural diffusion taking place. Not only were general tastes taking a decidedly popular *(baladi)* turn, but both upward and downward social mobility was altering the social scene. Marriage between classes had become quite common, and money as a factor for marriage was replacing the earlier snobbism of the "children of the distinguished" class *(awlad al-dhawat)*, which was determined by the ability to speak languages and use the proper pronunciation for French or English. Mixing up the *b* with the *p* or saying *z* in place of "the" used to make outcasts of non-*dhawat* who were trying to make their way in. That used to be so important, and now it means less than nothing except for the few who remain from that class and those who were attached to it. That should have been expected; the mass media, particularly television, together with the population explosion and urbanization has done more for the spread of "Egyptian" revivalism than any other force, political and economic included.

The same can be said of the theater, where once classical *fusha* theater presented translations of world literature meant to entertain the educated and intellectuals; today it is popular commercial comedy *'ammiya* theater, often accompanied by light song and dance, that is predominantly watched by all sectors of society. There were two dominant forms of theater in Nasserist Egypt. The first was government-sponsored "highbrow" theater where "great" world drama translated into classical Arabic was produced. Aspiring intellectuals went to the Pocket Theater to watch avant-garde plays, one-person plays, and so on. Today that theater is mostly used as a warehouse. There are still classical Arabic theaters, but these are supported by the Ministry of Culture, which seems to be a leftover from the Nasser regime when the state planned to teach Egyptians what culture was. To the state, culture was not something practiced by the people, but a "high" culture into which people were to be "indoctrinated."

The second form of theater was popular comedy theater. Disdained by state elitist idiocrats, popular comedy theater is today the only form enjoyed by Egyptians. When a classical Arabic play is a success it is invariably a comedy dealing with or hinting at contemporary farces. Some comedies have continued fully booked for five and six years and are still running strong. People enjoy theater that talks about and to them, and Egyptian theater is quite good at doing so, realistically describing everyday life. There on the stage, jokes laughed at by audiences, reference to social groups, vices, corruption, and intersocial alliances did not need to be explained to those watching. References to mamluks, *tujjar, khassa, 'ammat al-sha'b,* to a public job as an *'izba* and to a man holding a parasitical position of relative influence as an *aldush,* were quite natural to daily conversations among Egyptians.

Popular theater has changed in the last few decades, demonstrating a distinct deterioration in the quality of language used to the point where vulgarities and obscenities are used. Yet the growing popularity of this form of theater among all classes is another sign of growing cultural homogeneity and similarities in taste and aesthetics. The same can be said about television and cinema. Two popular plays exemplify many of the points that have been raised in this study. The first, which continued to be shown for nearly six years, is Samir Ghanim's *Ana Layis w'Akhuya Hayis* (I am at a loss while my brother is having a ball), the story of orphan twins adopted at birth. The first was adopted by a poor man and became a nationalist writer, whereas the other was adopted by an American couple who were visiting Egypt and had now returned as a senator and his wife from the United States. The usual switch takes place, and each gets to learn about the other's life. Soon the senator is speaking the same language that his twin was using at the beginning of the story, and the terms he uses to describe the society in which he once lived but to which he is now denied access were specifically the *khassa* and mamluks. The second play, Lenin al-Ramli's *Bi'l-'Arabi al-Fasih*, a modernistic spoof on a disunited Arab world, ends with a scene in which a white-masked woman recites a long ballad to the loss of identity in the fight for grand national and collective schemes and then the search for personal identity, which she found in introspection and acceptance of self. She ends her ballad in a dramatic Fanonesque gesture by removing the white mask and showing a proud, happy, dark face.

Cultural revivalism is taking place for many reasons in Egypt. Social transformations, economic and political crises, and the direct involvement of the upper classes have been shown as important in this process. The significance of cultural revivalism should be seen in the growing homogeneity that is bringing about an end to the cultural duality that has been a basic reason for the division of Egyptian society into *khassa* and *'amma*. Intellectuals who may at one time have espoused forced cultural change as part of their worldview have shown an appreciation for the phenomenon of revivalism and its significance. Thus, even though Anouar 'Abdel-Malek still looks for Egypt's salvation in Chinese-style socialism, he sees revivalism as a phase during which the influence of the "Western wave" is ebbing, and the movement of indigenous civilizational imperative is beginning.[103] Galal Amin has become a critic of the view that considers Westernization and development as basic to Egypt's future and instead considers Wsternization as having led to economic impoverishment, political dependency, and feelings of inferiority. As Boullata describes Amin's thoughts, "He believes that half the battle is won if the Arabs are psychologically convinced that the invading civilization is not necessarily more advanced than theirs, and that Western values are not necessarily indicative of greater progress than theirs."[104] Muhammad Salmawy's plays emphasize the need for self-liberation and inherent human equality through themes of every man and every woman. Even though his plays have been described as being derived from Western sources, Salmawy is careful to emphasize the authenticity of his works. In his *A Concerto to a Nayy*, Salmawy uses the image of the reed pipe's failure to become a modern flute in a modern orchestra to illustrate the futility of trying to force one society to conform to the culture of another. Something important is lost in the process: "The reed flute singing plaintively of its native reed bank was one of the most popular images for the soul longing to return to God used by the great poet and mystic Rumi." [105] It is also the image of authentic music of the soul for Egyptians; the image of the *nayy* being played on the Nile as the sun is setting is a nostalgic image of Egyptianness. [106]

CONCLUSION

The mob, which had meanwhile become the people, or the mass, or the base
. . . history had expropriated them; the revolution had established them.[1]

During the ceremony held to celebrate the opening of the first national exhibition in Alexandria on April 22, 1894, the *khedive* of Egypt, 'Abbas II, and the governor of the city, addressed the public in French.[2] Egypt's rulers before him, Muhammad 'Ali, 'Abbas I, Isma'il, and Tawfiq all used Turkish in preference to Arabic. Even Sa'id, who spoke of himself as an Egyptian, used Turkish and French in preference to Arabic. The British consuls general did not bother to learn the Arabic language, nor did many of the bureaucrats, civil servants, and educators they brought with them to Egypt. Rather, the administration and the schools were forced to use English or French either exclusively or jointly with Arabic to suit the needs of Egypt's foreign and local elite.

Members of the royal family and the upper classes who spoke Arabic preferred to use French as the language of prestige and sophistication. Their families, particularly the women, were taught French rather than Arabic, which was a way of keeping the classes distinct one from the other. Being a member of the Egyptian *dhawat* meant being francophile. Using a foreign language in preference to Arabic mirrored a social structure in which a foreign elite and its indigenous allies were dominant. It was not until the time of Faruq (1936–52) that Arabic became the language used by rulers and not until 1952 that rulers identifying themselves as ethnically Egyptian ruled the country. During the early twentieth century, nationalist groups, including the Wafd, did use Arabic when addressing the public, a sign of the importance of the masses in the political picture, but their children continued to receive foreign education and were culturally Westernized.

With the 1952 revolution came the complete Arabization of the government and educational system and the Egyptianization of the ruling *khassa*.

216

This did not mean the end of foreign influence in the economic and political spheres, which continued to reflect the ideologies adopted by the Nasserists: nationalism, socialism, Arab unity, and nonalignment, which all stemmed from non-Egyptian concepts. The real revolution that occurred with the coming of Nasser had already been in the making since the time of 'Urabi and Zaghlul, that is, the rise of the Egyptian element to dominance within the *khassa*. It could be looked at as the coming of a new historical bloc, were it not for the paternalistic approach that the Wafdist and Nasserist leadership had toward the *'amma* (masses) and the fact that the cultural discourse of their respective periods was based on the establishment of culture from above, a culture through which they established their hegemonic rule.

The connection between language and social structure continues to illustrate social evolution today. Egypt's *dhawat* before Nasser spoke in foreign languages partly because they had no reason to communicate with the people at large. They employed the language through which they communicated with members of their own class and with other groups that made up the *khassa* at that particular time. As Lord Cromer observed regarding the perception of his class toward the role they were playing in Egypt: "One alien race, the English, have had to control and guide a second alien race, the Turks, by whom they are disliked, in the government of a third race, the Egyptians."[3]

Egypt's nationalist parties before 1952 used Arabic to communicate with the rising masses, who were making their presence known through such associations as the Muslim Brotherhood and through labor strikes and mass demonstrations. Nasser also followed this approach in response to the continued growth of the political role played by Egypt's masses. Like Nahhas before him, Nasser had an interesting way of communicating, depending on which audience he was addressing. When he addressed members of his own class or intellectuals he used *fusha* (classical Arabic). But when he made a public speech in the open, particularly if it was being delivered during the celebration of a national occasion, Nasser turned to *'ammiya* (colloquial Arabic), speaking in familiar idioms, making jokes, and appealing to general Egyptian sympathy and humor. In him was exemplified Gramsci's concept of passion as a basis for hegemony, "feeling the elementary passions of the people, understanding them and therefore explaining and justifying them in the particular historical situation."[4] Nasser easily created political hegemony in his support, which enabled him to wield coercive power effectively. Hence, he was feared by members of the *khassa*, obeyed by the bureaucracy, respected by intellectuals, and idolized by the masses because he appeared to be one of them.

With Sadat a big change in language took place, which went beyond his lack of charisma. Sadat spoke in *fusha* when he addressed the nation. Because most of his speeches were delivered indoors, in the People's Assembly or on television, he was really addressing the new *multazim*s and *tujjar* who appeared during his period of rule. When he did use *'ammiya,* his tone was usually one of bored paternalism or reprimand; he notified the people of what was wrong with their actions very much like a paternal figure scolding its wayward offspring. Sadat liked to describe himself as a father, but the country did not accept him as such. His lack of popularity was a reflection of his style of leadership, which emphasized his own importance and failed to recognize the social evolution that was taking place in the country; while exalting Egypt's traditions, he looked at its culture as an object to be transformed.

Mubarak's use of language took dramatic turns and shows the direction that Egypt is taking today. For some time after he came to power, he mixed the formulas used by Nasser and Sadat. Although talking in *fusha* most of the time, he mixed *'ammiya* with *fusha* in the same speech. Toward the end of his first term in office, the *'ammiya* that he used deteriorated and became increasingly coarse. His jokes, idioms, tone, and form of address became quite "popular."[5] Except for special political events, "meetings with youth" and "award-giving" days, when the president read speeches to particular sectors of society in their own familiar idioms, Mubarak's speeches were increasingly directed to the Egyptian *'amma,* not only the middle but also the lower strata, consisting of traditional elements of *hirafiyin,* peasants and labor. Obviously, these groups had become important to the political process; they needed to be addressed and in their own language.

Since the nineteenth century Egypt's *khassa* have supported a discourse of modernity based on a philosophy of *tanwir,* calling for plans to modernize, industrialize, and adopt all aspects of material progress. Various ideologies were imported with relative success in the impact they left on cultural consciousness: liberalism, socialism, Marxism, Nasserism, and Islamic fundamentalism. One important repercussion of the acceptance of *tanwir* as hegemonic discourse has been social duality in which *khassa* and *'amma* were divided not only by power and wealth but also by the underlying culture and perception of group roles. Although both the *khassa* and the *'amma* could be subdivided into numerous classes and orders, there were common denominators within each division. Thus, by establishing their hegemonic discourse over the *'amma,* the *khassa* were able to wield power that they used to obtain their own benefits. These benefits included wealth, but power in itself was a reward aspired to by groups making up the *khassa.* The military, government bureaucrats and public sector administrators, and businessmen were consistently part of Egypt's *khassa* during the last two hundred years. They cooperated to ensure their common welfare, but they were constantly struggling to achieve positions of predominance within the *khassa.* The particular group in ascendance changed from one period to the other and was somewhat hinged on foreign relations and Egypt's dependence on outside powers. There is evidence to support the idea that when an outside power had direct control over Egyptian affairs, such as when Britain ruled Egypt, or when Egypt was highly dependent on foreign aid, such as under Sadat and Mubarak, it was the nonmilitary *khassa*, that is, business classes or government beneficiaries, who were predominant. But when there was a certain amount of independence of action for Egypt, as in the case of the mamluks, Muhammad 'Ali Pasha, or Nasser, the military was the predominant power within the *khassa*.

The *khassa* of particular eras molded the political, economic, and legal systems to ensure their own power and wealth. Given the importance of foreign trade for the *khassa*, mercantilism proved to be the most useful method to ensure their control over the nation's wealth. As an economic system, mercantilism calls for government interference, whether overt or covert, and a policy designed to ensure that control of trade remained in an elite's hands.

> The term [mercantilism] is confusing, since it defines a historical period, an economic school, and a moral attitude. Here, "mercantilism" means a bureaucratized and law ridden state that regards the redistribution of national wealth as more important than the production of wealth . . . and "redistribution," as used here, means the concession of monopolies or favored status to a small elite that depends on the state and on which the state is itself dependent.[6]

In the Egyptian case, redistribution of wealth worked to the benefit of a *khassa* rather than the country in general, appearances or government intentions notwithstanding. To realize profit, Egypt's manufacturing, agricultural, and service capabilities were oriented toward import-substitution and the production of items for export. This has been the policy followed by Egypt's rulers since the time of Muhammad 'Ali Pasha, with the exception of the period between the end of his rule and the 1952 revolution, when mercantilist policies appeared in the guise of a liberal market economy, although its primary impact was to benefit foreign business interests.

For mercantilism to work, administrative structures and laws were needed to ensure the smooth operation of mercantile activity, which brought about a continuous growth in the bureaucracy. For the system to produce the intended results, the *khassa* had to wield enough authority to establish the needed institutions and to enforce the established laws. At the same time the *khassa* also had to gain the consensus of the people for the system to operate smoothly. The *khassa*'s hegemony was achieved by adopting various ideologies from liberalism to socialism, and the *khassa*'s nationalities changed from Turkish to British to Egyptian. The one constant was that the ideologies and the hegemony established worked to the one end of benefiting the particular *khassa* combination that was dominant.

The relationship between state and society has been the focus of scholarly interest in recent years. Thus, numerous studies have appeared dealing with the nature of the state, the makeup of its government and institutions, the source of a nation's state power, the nature and composition of ruling classes, the coercive powers at the state's disposal (including police and armed forces), and the hegemonies created by dominant classes to legitimize their rule. In some studies Egypt may appear as an absolutist state in which the rulers established their power through coercion and in which society was a recipient of change imposed from above, its people acting as observers to historical transformations. By defining Egyptian society on its own terms and developing a methodology that is more in accordance with the nature of that society, this study has attempted to show that, in fact, there were close alliances between state and society, that the state can be seen as a medium through which particular hegemonies worked, and that the laws and institutions comprising the state change with the changes in particular elite alliances and the accompanying hegemony. Most important, it shows that there is no great separation between the state and society, that coercion was the outward manifestation of control exercised in a situation largely based on consensus in which the tentacles of patronage allowed society as a whole to persist and benefit from the extant hegemony. By looking beyond the legal and formal structures of government and toward the informal culture, it is possible to uncover such patterns of patronage.

The *'amma*'s role and their perception of it has been undergoing transformation according to the changes experienced by the superstructure. Examining the particular hegemony being established is one interesting way of seeing the evolution of the *'amma* and their growing importance in the nation's affairs. Although it is generally true that creating hegemony by an elite "involves developing intellectual, moral and philosophical consent from all major groups in a nation,"[7] the case of Egypt, as demonstrated in this study, shows that the *khassa* did not direct their efforts to society at large but to particular sectors of society that would help them to create hegemony, depending on the superstructure extant at the time. One trend throughout Egypt's modern history has been the growing inclusion of wider strata of society into Egypt's civil society. With the politicization of various classes, the ideologies had to take them into consideration. Thus were brought into this hegemony the *'ulama'*, the landowners, the new *afandiya*, comprising the educated and professional classes, and then labor and peasantry under the rule of Nasser. Today the situation has reversed itself, and the elite are resorting to the ideology of the masses as a basis for hegemony. Thus, the hegemony being established is based on the ideology of the masses, who have become a veritable civil society that cannot be ignored by political society.

GLOSSARY
NOTES
BIBLIOGRAPHY
INDEX

GLOSSARY

'abd al-ma'mur: slave of God's slave

'abiri al-sabil: homeless persons; those in need

'ada: usual practice

'adat: customs

'adl: justice

afandiyya: civil servants; white collar workers

ahl al-hukm wa al-sultan: men of government and authority

ahliyya; ahliyya khassa: legal competence; necessary requirements

akhtar jasima: great dangers

aldush: a person who acts as a leach or parasite to another

alquwa al-jibriya: power to force

amanat: trusteeship

amin: guarantor; superintendent

amirs, **mamluks:** with authority to rule; leaders, princes

'amiya: colloquial Arabic

'amma; 'ammat al-sha'b: public; people; masses; general populace

ana bita'ak: I am your man

'asabiya: ethnic or clan pride

asala: authenticity

ashab hirfa: craftsmen

atawa: tribute

awlad al-dhawat: distinguished class; children of the distinguished class

awqaf: religious endowments

a'yan: landed gentry

'azabs: auxiliary garrison soldiers

baladi: old term for an unrefined or vulgar person

baligh, thayb: adult girl; adult previously married woman

bayt al-ta'a: House of Obedience

bi'a: environment; contemporary colloquial term for an unrefined or vulgar person

bitigra: colloquial for "Do you read?"

bulugh: puberty

burqu': net veil

225

dah taba'i: "He is with me"

da'i, da'is: missionary, missionaries

daman, damin: backer; sponsor; guarantor

dar al-Iftaa': high council for *fatwas*

darar: harm; mistreatment of a wife

daya: midwife

dhawat: people of refinement

dhawat hawanim: ladies of the finer classes

dhimmis: protected non-Muslims

dhira': about one foot

dictatoriya: dictatorship

dimocratoriya: democracy

diwan al-afranj wa'l-tijara: council for foreigners and foreign trade

diwan al-bahr: council of the navy

diwan al-fabriqat: council of industry

diwan al-iradat: treasury

diwan al-jihadiyya: military council

diwan al-madaris: council for education, schools

diwans: councils of state

diya: blood-price

al-fahisha: sin

fa'iz: surplus

fa'iz iltizam: leftover *iltizams*

fallahin: peasants

farfur: leech; protégé

fi'at: groups; classes

filaha: agriculture

fiqh: Muslim jurisprudence

firda: informal or unofficial exactions

firman: edict of the sultan

fuqaha: Islamic scholar

fusha: classical Arabic

futuwwat: vigilantes; thugs

ghufara': security guards

al-gib; wa'l-'isma; wa'l-khissa: types of excellence

girbah: water container, often made of leather

hadd al-shahwa: age of carnal awareness

hajana: camel-mounted soldiers

hajj: man who has undertaken pilgrimage; respected older person

hakima: doctoress

halal: permissible

hamam: Turkish bath

hara: town quarter; narrow alley

harafish: thugs

hawanim: ladies

hawanim khawagat: foreign-looking ladies

hijr: guardianship because of incompetency

hirafiyyin: skilled labor; craftsmen

hisba: medieval executive laws

hiyaza: control of property

al-hizb al-watani: National Party

huddud: crimes considered by Islamic law to be against God

hujja: plea; document

'iba: cloak

'ibadat: worship, veneration

ib'adiya: untaxed, usually uncultivated land

ihram: purification and being in a state of purity

ijtihad: religious interpretation

iltizam: tax farm

imam-khatib: preacher

infitah: open door policy

intifadah: Palestinian revolt against Israeli occupation of West Bank and Ghaza

iqta'; iqta' wa ra's al-mal: feudalism; feudalism and capitalism

'irban: Arab bedouins

isqat haqihi: dropping his right

istidafat: hosting government officials

'izba; 'izab: landed estate(s); small village(s)

'izwa: dignity; power

jalabiya: woman's garment that covers the whole body from neck to ankle

jama'at: Islamic fundamentalist groups

jarida: free of duty

jibba: outer garment open in front with wide sleeves

jinsiya siyasiya: political nationality

jinsiya ta'ifiya: sectarian, or religious, nationality

jizya: poll tax

kafa'a: social parity

karimi: merchants (traded in spices)

al-kashif: supervisor; inspector; provincial governor

kharaj: land tax

khassa: the establishment; people of distinction; people of power and wealth

khatt: road

khawaja: contemporary slang word for foreigner; earlier was reference to big merchants

khedive: king; ruler

al-khowli: overseer

khulkhal: anklet, usually made out of silver

kifaya: sufficiency

kinaya: nickname

kurbaj: whip
kushufiya: financial supervision
la'iha: code
madhhab, madhahib: Muslim legal school(s)
mahasib: protégé
ma'mur: police lieutenant
mahkama shar'iya: shari'a court
mahmal: procession carrying the new black embroidered clothing of the Ka'ba, which
      was sent yearly as a gift from Egypt at the time of pilgrimage
mahr: dowry
mahsub: protégé
mahsubiya: clientele
majlis al-ahkam: legal council
majlis al-a'la: high council of the state
majlis al-haqaniya: [ministry] of justice
majlis al-milli: council for non-Muslims
majlis al-sihha: health council
majlis hisbi: guardianship court
majlis qadaya al-ahkam: council for court cases and decision
majlis shar': law council
makasib ishtirakiya: socialist gains, rights
majalis al-'ulama': clergy seminars; meetings; councils
malfufat: graceful
malikan: long-term or permanent holding
maliya: finance department
malqata: easy woman
mamluk: slave soldiers owned by slave-households; slave princes
ma'mur: police lieutenant
manabir: political platforms
manfa'a: right of usage
maqbul: acceptable; equivalent; debt
al-mar'a wal-dhakira: Women and Memory Association
maristan: premodern hospital
markaz, marakiz: district(s)
mashayikh: elders
masmuh al-masatib: tax-free land allotted to village sheikhs
mastabas: stone benches located outside peasants' homes
mawlana al-sheikh: holy man; cleric
mawlid, mawalid: religious feast(s); saint's day
al-mawlid al-nabawi: feast celebrating the prophet Muhammad's birthday
mawwal: a poem in colloquial Arabic; a colloquial song
mihrim: sexually ineligible man; purified person on pilgrimage
milaya laff: long silky black cloth women wrapped around themselves before leaving
      the home

milk: property; ownership

milkiya kamila; milkiyat 'ayn: full ownership of a particular piece of land

milkiyat al-intifa': right of exploitation

milla: religious community

mi'mar basha: chief architect or engineer

misaharati: caller who wakes people at night to pray

mnigrashi: peasant colloquial for "we do not read"

mu'aamalat: social relations

mu'adhdhim: crier who summons Muslims to prayer

mu'akhar: agreed-upon delayed dowry paid at time of divorce or husband's death

mu'alim: master of a trade, craft

mudir: director

mudiriya: province; governerate; administration

mufti: deliverer of formal religious opinion

muhiba: sexually or romantically awakened

muhtassib: law keeper in medieval Egypt

mujtami'a: meeting together

mukhabarat: government secret service

multazim: tax farmer

mulukhiyya: a thick green soup, considered a national dish

muqata'a: land grant; tax farm

muqim sha'a'ir: ritual overseer found only in very large mosques

mushari': lawmaker

mushir: top rank in the Egyptian army

nafaqa: financial support

nafs: life; soul; living being

nahda: renaissance

nawahi: places; quarters of a town

nayy: reed pipe for playing music

niqab: full facial covering worn by fundamentalist Muslim women

nishan: medal

nishan al-rida: badge of commendation

nizam: regime

nizam jaded: modern Western-style army

nuwwab: deputies of *qadis*

odabashi: senior officers of a janissary corps

qadi: shari'a court judge

qanun: executive law

qanun al-'ayb: law of "shame" for insulting the person of the president

qanun al-fallah: law of the peasant

qasa'id, qasida: formal Arabic poetry

qasir: minor child

qati'a: a fief

qawamiha: its foundation

quftan: caftan

al-quwa al-jibriya: power to compel

quwat al-amn al-markazi: central security forces

raf'yadd: to remove control

rayyis: colloquial for boss, chief, president of republic

ribaba: a stringed instrument with one to three strings

ru'ah: citizens

rushd: age of rationality, majority

sab 'alani: public slander

safwa: elite

sahib al-dawla: honorary title for "presidency"

sahib al-'izza: salutation for a bey

sahib al-sa'ada: salutation for a pasha

sana'i': guilds of craftsmen

saqa: water carrier

saraf: cashier; treasurer

saraf bashi: chief treasurer

sar-tujjar: chief merchant

sha'b: populace; masses

shafalik: private estates

shahbandar al-tujjar: head *tajjir* or elected head of the merchants' guild

shahid: witness

shar', shari'a: law; Islamic law

shawla': a woman with a strong contrast between the whites and blacks of the eyes

sheikh, *shuyukh:* clergyman, clergymen; elder(s)

sheikh al-balad: village religious head

sheikh al-shuyukh: chief clergymen

shilla, shilal: groups of friends

shuhud: official court witnesses

shurta: police; peacekeeping forces

si'idis: people from Upper Egypt

sijill: volume (book); archival record; archive

sirdar, sirdariya: leader of the janissaries

sirga: juicer; factory where sugarcane is juiced and turned into molasses

sufi tariqa: mystical order

sunna: prophetic traditions

suq: marketplace

ta'a: obedience

tabi': crony (familiar or follower); *dah taba'i:* he is with me

tadhwib al-fawariq: melting class differences

tafsir: Qur'anic interpretation

tahmish: peripheralization

tajir: merchant

takamul: complementarity

tala'ub: corruption

talfiq: patching together

tamwin: supply agents

tanaqud: contradiction

tanwir: enlightenment

tarab: enrapturement

tarahil: mobile labor

tarbush: red brimless, high, skull-hugging hat

tas'ira: government-fixed price

tata'awad wa tatabakhar: sassy walk

al-tatalu'at al-tabaqiya: social climbing

tawa'if: guilds

tawkil: power of attorney

thaqafa: high culture; knowledge; intellectualism

ahl-thiqa: people of confidence

tijara: trade; commerce

tujjar: merchants; entrepreneurs; businessmen; investors

turath: heritage

'uber: the army's successful crossing of the Suez and Barlef line

'udul: honest, upright individuals of the court

'ulama': Islamic clergy

umana' al-shurta: police

umara': prince

'umda, 'umad: village chief(s)

umma: Islamic nation

'uqdat al-khawaja: inferiority complex from foreigners

'urf: traditional generalized laws

'ushr: one-tenth; tithe

wahhabism: Islamic enlightenment

wakil: deputy; guardian

waliy, waliy 'asib: governor or guardian; a guardian with the right to force a girl to marry

al-walliyy: holder of the *wilaya*

waqf: religious endowment

wasiy: legal guardian

wasiya: a will

wasta: intermediary; go-between

wikala: a *tajir's* headquarters

wilaya: historically, guardianship of an Islamic ruler over his people

wirash: workshops

wishah: badge

wizarat al-sha'b: people's ministry

yigaru al-mazahir: keeping up pretenses
al-za'im al-mu'min: the believing leader
zajal: popular style of poetry
zina: adultery
zubat al-ahrar: Free Officers

NOTES

Introduction

1. John Obert Voll, *Islam: Continuity and Change in the Modern World* (Syracuse: Syracuse Univ. Press), 1994.

2. Exceptionalism looks at the history of particular groups as unique and different from that of others. American cultural exceptionalism, for example, holds that because it was founded by immigrants—who were the most individualistic and were most imbued with a work ethic—who were escaping from European oppression, Americans will always be individualistic and will believe in liberal freedoms, oppose strong government, and fight against oppression. Exceptionalism, therefore, treats cultures as having a fundamental, unchanging essence. If exceptionalist discourses emphasize positive aspects of Western traditions, they continue to accept negative aspects of Arab and Islamic culture. See, for example, Seymour Martin Lipset, *American Exceptionalism: A Double-Edged Sword* (New York: W. W. Norton, 1996).

3. Gilles Kepel, *The Revenge of God: The Resurgence of Islam, Christianity, and Judaism in the Modern World* (University Park: Pennsylvania State Univ. Press, 1994).

4. P. J. Vatikiotis, *The History of Modern Egypt from Muhammad Ali to Mubarak,* 4th ed. (Baltimore, Md.: Johns Hopkins Univ. Press, 1991), 9.

5. Ibid., 17.

6. Samuel P. Huntington, *The Clash of Civilizations and the Remaking of the World Order* (New York: Simon and Schuster, 1996).

7. Anouar Abdel-Malek, *Egypt: Military Society: The Army Regime, the Left, and Social Change under Nasser* (New York: Random House, 1968).

8. *The Living Webster: Encyclopedic Dictionary of the English Language* (Chicago: English Language Institute of America, 1977), 246.

9. Renato Rosaldo, *Culture and Truth: The Remaking of Social Analysis* (Boston: Beacon Press, 1989), 107, discussing Raymond Williams, *Marxism and Literature* (Oxford: Oxford Univ. Press, 1977).

10. Walter Armbrust, *Mass Culture and Modernism in Egypt* (Cambridge: Cambridge Univ. Press, 1996), 25.

11. O. Dreyer, *Cultural Changes in Developing Countries, Progress,* Problems of the Third World Series (Moscow: Progress Publishers, 1976), 11.

12. Ibid.

13. Issa Boullata, *Trends and Issues in Contemporary Arab Thought* (Albany: State Univ. of New York Press, 1990), 117.

14.　See, for example, Mahmud 'Abd al-Fadil, *al-Tashkilat al-ijtima'iyya wa'l-taqwinat al-tabaqiya fi al-watan al-'arabi* (Beirut: Markaz Dirasat al-Wihda al-'Arabiya, 1988), 23.

15.　Fuad I. Khuri, *Imams and Emirs: State, Religion and Sects in Islam* (London: Saqi Books, 1990), 164. He quotes Muhammad Mahdi Shamsuddin, vice-president of the Shi'a High Council in Lebanon.

16.　For a good discussion of evolution of property *(milk)* in Egypt, see Ken M. Cuno, *Land, Society, and Economy in Lower Egypt, 1740–1858* (Cambridge: Cambridge Univ. Press, 1992).

17.　Hisham Sharabi, *Neopatriarchy: A Theory of Distorted Change in Arab Society* (Oxford: Oxford Univ. Press, 1988), 4.

18.　Robert Vitalis, *When Capitalists Collide: Business Conflict and the End of Empire in Egypt* (Berkeley: Univ. of California Press, 1995), 4–5.

19.　John Waterbury, *The Egypt of Nasser and Sadat: The Political Economy of Two Regimes* (Princeton: Princeton Univ. Press, 1983).

20.　Raymond Hinnebusch, *Egyptian Politics under Sadat: The Post-Populist Development of an Authoritarian-Modernizing State* (London: Lynne Reiner Publishers, 1988).

21.　Samir Amin, *The Arab Nation: Nationalism and Class Struggle* (London: Zed Press, 1978).

22.　'Abd Allah al-'Arawi, *Mafhum al-dawla* (Beirut: al-Markaz al-Thaqafi al-'Arabi, 1988).

23.　Carla Pasquinelli discussing Foucault's concepts about state. "Power Without the State," *TELOS* 68 (summer 1986), 85.

24.　Lawrence Kritsman, *Michel Foucault: Politics, Philosophy, Culture, Interviews and Other Writings, 1977–1984* (New York: Routledge, 1988), 102.

25.　Pasquinelli, "Power," 85, interpreting Michel Foucault's ideas on power in *Discipline and Punish.*

26.　John Kenneth Galbraith, *The Anatomy of Power* (Boston: Houghton Mifflin, 1983), 6–7.

27.　Ferdinand Braudel, *The Perspective of the World: Civilization and Capitalism 15th–18th Century,* vol. 3 (New York: Harper and Row, 1984), 287, 294.

28.　Robert B. Ekelund and Robert F. Hebert, *A History of Economic Theory and Method,* 3d ed. (New York: McGraw-Hill, 1990), 42–43.

29.　Ibid., 49.

30.　Ibid., 55.

31.　Ibid., 56.

32.　Afaf Lutfi al-Sayyid Marsot, *Egypt in the Reign of Muhammad Ali* (Cambridge: Cambridge Univ. Press, 1984), 162–95.

33.　Hernando Soto, *The Other Path: The Invisible Revolution in the Third World* (New York: Harper and Row, 1989), xvi.

34.　Braudel, *Perspective of the World,* 30–35.

35.　Partha Chatterjee, *Nationalist Thought and the Colonial World: A Derivative Discourse?* (London: Zed Books, 1986), 8. Chatterjee's comments on nationalism in India are relevant: "The new [nationalist] claimants to power in the nations of Asia and Africa constantly and profitably use this fallacy in a 'rhetoric of the heart,' a fervent, impassioned, romantic, and inherently false discourse."

36.　Pedro Cavalcanti and Paul Piccone, *History, Philosophy and Culture in the Young Gramsci* (Saint Louis, Mo.: Telos Press, 1975), 78.

37.　Peter Gran, "Historians, Historiography, and State Hegemony in India, Iraq, and Mexico," paper, 5.

38. Ibid., 13.

39. David Forgacs, ed., *An Antonio Gramsci Reader: Selected Writings, 1916–1935* (New York: Schoken Books, 1988), 200.

40. Antonio Gramsci, *Letters from Prison* (New York: Harper and Row, 1973), 44.

41. Ibid.

1. The Background

1. See Marsot, *Egypt,* chap. 1, about the competition Egyptian craftsmen and *tujjar* faced in the eighteenth century from European goods and merchants.

2. Daniel Crecelius, *The Roots of Modern Egypt* (Minneapolis, Minn.: Bibliotheca Islamica, 1981), 19–20.

3. Stanford Shaw, *Ottoman Egypt in the Eighteenth Century,* Harvard Middle Eastern Monograph Series (Cambridge, Mass.: Harvard Univ. Press, 1962), 5.

4. P. M. Holt, "The Last Phase of the Neo-*Mamluk* Regime," *L'Égypte au XIXᵉ siècle* (Aix-en-Provence: Centre National de la Recherche Scientifique, 1982), 147–48.

5. Abdel Aziz Ezz el Arab, "Notes on the Political Economy of Eighteenth Century Egypt: The Ruling Class and Its Socio-Economic Impact," in *Studies in Egyptian Political Economy: Methodology, Theory, and Case Studies,* ed. Herbert Thompson, vol. 2, American Univ. in Cairo Papers in Social Science, no. 3 (Cairo: American Univ. in Cairo, 1979), 54.

6. Alexandria, 1198 [1782], 100:137–208,137–209, 198–310.

7. Ramadan al-Khowli, "Observations on the Use of Shari'a Court Records as a Source of Social History," in *A History of Her Own: Deconstructing Women in Islamic Societies,* ed. Amira el-Azhary Sonbol and John Obert Voll (forthcoming).

8. Afaf Lutfi al-Sayyid Marsot, *Men and Women in Eighteenth Century Egypt* (Austin: Univ. of Texas Press, 1996).

9. Peter Gran, *The Islamic Roots of Capitalism* (Austin: Univ. of Texas Press, 1979).

10. Nelly Hanna, *Tujjar al-qahira fil-'asr al-'uthmani* (Cairo: al-Dar al-Misriya al-Libnaniya, 1997).

11. Tim Mitchell, *Colonizing Egypt* (Cambridge: Cambridge Univ. Press, 1988).

12. This is the description given by Afaf Marsot in *Egypt.*

13. Khaled Fahmy, *All the Pasha's Men: Mehmed Ali, His Army and the Making of Modern Egypt* (Cambridge: Cambridge Univ. Press, 1997), 11.

14. Rosaldo, *Culture and Truth,* 26.

15. See Islamic marriage contracts from the third to fifth century Egyptian courts published in Adolph Grohmann, *Awraq al-bardi al-'arabiyya bi dar al-kutub al-misriya,* vol. 1 (Cairo: Matba'at Dar al-Kutub al-Misriya, 1994).

16. Anne K. Capel and Glenn E. Markoe, eds., *Mistress of the House, Mistress of Heaven* (New York: Hudson Hills Express with Cincinnati Art Museum, 1996), 181.

17. Mohsen Shouman, *al-Yahud fi misr min al-fath al-'uthmani hatta awa'il al-qarn al-tasi' 'ashr* (al-Zaqaziq, 1996).

18. Amira el-Azhary Sonbol, "Questioning Exceptionalism: Islamic Law," *Journal of Middle East Studies* (summer 1998).

19. Dumyat, 1195 [1779], 279:95–116.

20. Alexandria, 1074 [1664], 51:114–278.

21. Shouman, *al-Yahud fi misr,* 350–410.

22. André Raymond, *Le Caire des janissaires* (Paris: CNRS Editions, 1995), 52–54.

23. Alexandria, 1074 [1664], 51:121–294.

24. Dumyat, 1195 [1684], 279:100–125.

25. 'Abdel-Rahman 'Abdel-Rehim, *Fusul min Tarikh Misr al-iqtisadi wal-ijtima'i fil-'asr al-'uthmani* (Cairo: al-Hay'a al-Misriyya al-'Amma lil-Kitab, 1990), 42.

26. Pascale Ghazaleh, "The Guilds: Between Tradition and Modernity," in *The State and Its Servants,* ed. Nelly Hanna (Cairo: American Univ. in Cairo Press, 1995), 61. Ghazaleh refers to Bernard Lewis, "The Islamic Guilds," *Economic History Review* 8 (1937): 20–37.

27. Ibid., 60.

28. Ibid., 64.

29. Alexandria 1130 [1714], 65:104–98.

30. Ibid.

31. Dumyat, 1120/1708, 176:130, 232–124.

32. Galal el-Nahhal, *Judicial Administration of Ottoman Egypt in the Seventeenth Century* (Minneapolis: Bibliotheca Islamica, 1979), 4.

33. Ibid.

34. See, for example, Salah Ahmad Haridi, *al-Hiraf wal sina'at fi al-qarn al-thamin 'ashar* (Cairo, 1974).

35. El-Nahhal, *Judicial Administration,* 54–57.

36. See his first article on the subject, Ramadan al-Khowli, "Archives as a Source of Women's History: Problems and Limitations," in *A History of Her Own,* ed. Amira el-Azhary Sonbol and John Obert Voll (forthcoming).

37. Michael Winter, *Egyptian Society under Ottoman Rule: 1517–1798* (London: Routledge, 1992).

38. Max Weber, *The Protestant Ethic and the Spirit of Capitalism* (New York: Charles Scribner's Sons, 1958), 52.

39. Oleg Grabar, *The Illustrations of the Maqamat* (Chicago: Univ. of Chicago Press, 1984).

40. Haim Gerber, *State, Society, and Law in Islam: Ottoman Law in Comparative Perspective* (Albany: State Univ. of New York Press, 1994).

41. Lawrence Rosen, *The Anthropology of Justice: Law as Culture in Islamic Society* (New York: Cambridge Univ. Press, 1989).

42. Ibid., 59.

43. Dumyat, 1011 [1602], 43:84–182.

44. Nikki R. Keddie and Beth Baron, eds., *Women in Middle Eastern History: Shifting Boundaries in Sex and Gender* (New Haven, Conn.: Yale Univ. Press, 1993).

45. Suraiya Faroqhi, *Making a Living in the Ottoman Lands: 1480–1820* (Istanbul: Isis Press, 1995), 132.

46. Dumyat, 1120 [1708], 176:252–40.

47. Alexandria 1130 [1714], 65:306–170.

48. John Benson, *The Penny Capitalists: A Study of Nineteenth-Century Working-Class Entrepreneurs* (New Brunswick, N.J.: Rutgers Univ. Press, 1983).

49. Alexandria 1130 [1714], 65:141–247.

50. Ballas, 1279 [1862], 24:8–12.

51. Ibid., 24:8–9.

52. Marriages of non-Muslims celebrated in *shari'a* court were often witnessed by Muslims. These witnesses may have accompanied the couple to court, but were most probably court assigned witnesses, *'udul.* Alexandria 973 [1565], 9:37–105.

53. Dumyat, 1170 [1754], 250:107–32.

54. Ibid., 1195 [1779], 279:325, 326–418.

55. Ibid., 1120 [1708], 176:84–82.

56. Ibid., 1120 [1708], 176 85–83.

57. Ibid., 1195 [1779], 279:265–38.

58. Ibid., 1171 [1775], 250:55–79, year A.H.1171.

59. Alexandria, sijillat, 1074 [1664], 51:35–82.

60. Bab al-'Ali, 1044 [1634], 116:216–1145.

61. Isna 1193 [1779], 30:11–40.

62. Dumyat, 1016 [1607], 47:368–750.

63. Cairo, Bab al-'Ali, 1044 [1634], 116:216–1145.

64. Ibid., 1031 [1621], 103:176–566.

65. Ibid., 1029 [1619], 102:312–1569.

66. Cairo, Misr, 1266 [1846], 23:101–285.

67. Alexandria, 1285–1293 [1868–1876], 3:90–92.

68. Cairo, Bab al-'Ali, 1034 [1624], 106:342–1229.

69. Assiut 1298 [1881], 19:49–98.

70. Alexandria 1281 [1864], 1:86–18.

71. Alexandria 1899, 38:1–329.

72. Abd al-Rahman al-Jabarti, *Napoleon in Egypt: al-Jabarti's Chronicle of the First Seven Months of the French Occupation, 1798*, trans. Shmuel Moreh (Princeton, N.J.: Markus Wiener Publishing, 1993), 3.

73. Laila 'Abdel-Latif, Dirasat fi tarikh wa mu'arikhi misr wa'l-sham iban al-'ahd al-'uthmani, Ph.D. diss., Cairo Univ., 1979.

74. Terence Walz, "Family Archives in Egypt: New Light on Nineteenth-Century Provincial Trade," in *L'Egypte au xixᵉ siecle* (Paris: Centre National de la Recherche Scientifique, 1982).

75. Laila 'Abdel Latif, *al-mujtama' al-misri fil 'asr al-'uthmani* (Cairo: Dar al-Kitab al-Jami'i, 1987), 29.

76. See Nelly Hanna, *Making Big Money in 1600: The Life and Times of Isma'il Abu Taqiyya, Egyptian Merchant* (Syracuse: Syracuse Univ. Press, 1998).

77. Abd al-Rahman al-Jabarti, *Tarikh 'aja'ib al-athar fi'l-tarajim wa'l-akhbar*, 3 vols. (Beirut: Dar al-Gil, n.d.), 1:204.

78. André Raymond, "The Residential Districts of Cairo During the Ottoman Period," in *The Arab City: Its Character and Islamic Cultural Heritage*, ed. Ismail Serageldin and Samir el-Sadek (Riyadh, Saudi Arabia: Arab Urban Development Institute, 1982), 104.

79. Nelly Hanna, *An Urban History of Bulaq in the Mamluk and Ottoman Periods* (Cairo: Institut Français d'Archeologie Orientale, 1982), 10.

80. Ibid.

81. Ibid., 22.

82. Ibid., 105.

83. Gran, *Islamic Roots*, 19.

84. Robert Tignor in Moreh, *Napoleon in Egypt*, 7.

85. James Harry Scott, "Diplomatic and Consular Corps: The Capitulations," in *Twentieth Century Impressions of Egypt* (London: Lloyd's Greater Britain Publishing, 1909), 111–12.

86. Ibid.

87. Stanford Shaw, *The Financial and Administrative Organization and Development of Ottoman Egypt* (Princeton: Princeton Univ. Press, 1962).

88. 'Abdel-Rehim, *Fusul*, 50, and Mohsen Shouman, "The Beginnings of Urban *Iltizam*" in *The State and Its Servants: Administration in Egypt from Ottoman Times to the Present*, ed. Nelly Hanna (Cairo: American Univ. in Cairo Press, 1995), 21. He refers to al-Qalqashandi, *Subh al-a'sha*, 10 vols. (Cairo: n.p.,1963), 446–47.

89. Shouman, "Beginnings of Urban *Iltizam*."

90. Charles Issawi, *The Economic History of the Middle East: 1800–1914* (Chicago: Univ. of Chicago Press, 1966), 80.

91. Ra'uf 'Abbas and 'Asim Disuqi, *Kibar al-mulak wal-falahin fi Misr: 1837–1952* (Cairo: Dar Qiba' lil-Tiba'a wal-Nashr wal-Tawzi', 1998), 14.

92. Farhat J. Ziadeh, *Property Law in the Arab World* (London: Graham and Trotman, 1979), 2.

93. 'Abbas and Disuqi, *Kibar,* 16.

94. Ibid.

95. Yusuf al-Malawani (Ibn al-Wakil, pseud.), *Tuhfat al-ahbab bi man malak Misr min al-muluk wal-nuwab,* ed. Abdel-Rahim 'Abdel-Rahman (Cairo: Dar al-Kitab al-Gami'i, 1998), p. y.

96. 'Abdel-Rehim, *Fusul,* 52.

97. Shouman, "Beginnings of Urban *Iltizam*," 24, refers to sub-*iltizam*s as *multazim al-batin;* the word *al-batin* today is used to mean "subletting."

98. Dumyat, 1120 [1612], 176:35–43.

99. Dishna, 1274 [1853] 1:15–90.

100. Ezz el Arab, "Political Economy," 59.

101. Roger Owen, *The Middle East in the World Economy: 1800–1914* (London: Methuen, 1981), 14, and Afaf Lutfi al-Sayyid Marsot, "The Role of the *'ulama'* in Egypt During the Early Nineteenth Century," in *Political and Social Change in Modern Egypt,* ed. P. M. Holt (London: Oxford Univ. Press, 1968), 264.

102. Winter, *Egyptian Society under Ottoman Rule,* 115.

103. Issawi, *Economic History of the Middle East,* 27.

104. Shaw, *Ottoman Egypt in the Eighteenth Century,* 23.

105. Ibid., 8.

106. Ibid., 23.

2. Building the Modern State: Mercantilism in a New Form

1. Braudel, *Perspective of the World,* 294.

2. John Waterbury, *Hydropolitics of the Nile Valley* (Syracuse: Syracuse Univ. Press, 1979). See also Anouar Abdel-Malek, *Civilizations and Social Theory* (Albany: State Univ. of New York Press, 1981), 67.

3. Karl A. Wittfogel, *Oriental Despotism: A Comparative Study of Total Power* (New Haven, Conn.: Yale Univ. Press, 1957), 101.

4. Samir Amin, *The Arab Nation: Nationalism and Class Struggle* (London: Zed Press, 1978), 18.

5. Owen, *Middle East,* 89.

6. Wittfogel, *Oriental Despotism,* 101.

7. Ibid.

8. Ibid.

9. Ibid.

10. Robort Bocock, *Hegemony* (London: Open Univ., 1986), 11.

11. Perry Anderson, *Emergence of the Absolutist State* (London: Humanities Press, 1974), 376.

12. Moustafa Fahmy, *La Revolution de l'industrie en Égypte et ses consequences sociales au 19ᵉ siècle (1800–1850)* (Leiden: E. J. Brill, 1954), 96.

13. Terence Walz, "Family Archives in Egypt: New Light on Nineteenth-Century Provincial Trade," in *L'Égypte au xixe siècle* (Paris: Centre National de la Recherche Scientifique, 1982), 30.

14. Ibid.

15. Susan Jane Staffa, *Conquest and Fusion: The Social Evolution of Cairo, 642–1850* (Leiden: E. J. Brill, 1977), 251–52.

16. Ibid.

17. Fred De Jong, *Turuq and Turuq-Linked Institutions in Nineteenth Century Egypt* (Leiden: E. J. Brill, 1978).

18. Braudel, *Perspective of the World*, 287.

19. Gaston Wiet, *Mohammed Ali et les beaux-arts* (Cairo: Dar al-Maaref, 1949), 41.

20. Alexandria 1074 H., 51:74–175.

21. Wiet, *Mohammed Ali et les beaux-arts*, 17.

22. Ibid., 83–84.

23. Hanna, *Urban History*, 16–17.

24. Ibid.

25. 'Ali al-Giritli, "The Commercial, Financial, and Industrial Policy of Muhammad Ali," in *The Economic History of the Middle East: 1800–1914*, ed. Charles Issawi (Chicago: Univ. of Chicago Press, 1966), 390.

26. Muhammad Fu'ad Shukri, 'Abd al-Maqsud al-'Anani, and Sayyid Muhammad Khalil, *Bina' dawlat Misr Muhammad 'Ali: al-Siyasa al-dakhiliya* (Cairo: Dar al-Fikr al-'Arabi, 1948), 778.

27. J. A. Hobson, *Imperialism: A Study* (London: George Allen and Unwin, 1902).

28. Afaf Lutfi al-Sayyid Marsot, *Egypt in the Reign of Muhammad Ali* (Cambridge: Cambridge Univ. Press, 1984).

29. M. Fahmy, *La Revolution de l'industrie en Égypte*, 24–29.

30. Fred Lawson, "Provincial Society in Egypt, 1820–1824," *International Journal of Middle East Studies* 13 (1981): 131.

31. Ibid.

32. Ibid., 131, 147–48.

33. al-Giritli, "Policy of Muhammad Ali," 390. See also *Wasf Misr*, vol. 6 (Cairo: Maktabat al-Khanji, 1979), chaps. 1, 13.

34. al-Giritli, "Policy of Muhammad Ali," 390.

35. al-Jabarti, *Tarikh*, 3:451–55.

36. Ibid., 471.

37. Ibid., 475.

38. Ibid., 1221–27.

39. Issawi, "Economic History of the Middle East," 396.

40. According to Sayyid Mar'i, *al-islah al-zira'i wa-mushkilat al-sukkan fi al-qutr al-misri* (Cairo: Kutub Qawmiya, 1965?), 19, the pasha's interest in controlling all agricultural production led him to promise a reward of a few acres for directions to land that was being cultivated outside government supervision.

41. al-Jabarti, *Tarikh*, 3:374–75.

42. Owen, *Middle East*, 68.

43. al-Jabarti, *Tarikh*, 3:455.

44. Ibid., 3:449.

45. Ibid., 3:457–59.

46. Afaf Marsot, "Muhammad 'Ali's Internal Politics," in *L'Égypte au XIXe siècle* (Paris: Centre National de la Recherche Scientifique, 1982), 155–58.

47. al-Jabarti, *Tarikh,* 3:356.

48. Ibid., 3:501.

49. Ibid., 3:502.

50. Ibid., 3:513.

51. Ibid., 3:475.

52. Labib Yunan Rizq, *Tarikh al-sahafah fi Misr* (Cairo, n.d.), 13.

53. Staffa, *Conquest and Fusion,* 251–52.

54. Ibid., 251.

55. *Qanun Namat Misr alathi asdarahu al-sultan al-qanuni li hukm Misr,* trans. Ahmad Fouad Mitwalli (Cairo, 1986), 22.

56. Ibid., 14.

57. Shukri, al-'Anani, and Khalil, *Bina' dawlat Misr,* 11.

58. Amin Sami Pasha, *Taqwim al-Nil wa 'asr Isma'il* (Cairo: Dar al-Kutub al-Misriya, 1936) 1: 395.

59. Shukri, al-'Anani, and Khalil, *Bina' dawlat Misr,* 11–14.

60. See Amira Sonbol, *The Creation of a Medical Profession in Egypt, 1800–1922* (Syracuse: Syracuse Univ. Press, 1992).

61. Shukri, al-'Anani, and Khalil, *Bina' dawlat Misr,* 25–27.

62. Report of W. B. Hodgson to the American State Department dating from March 1835, found in Shukri, al-'Anani, and Khalil, *Bina' dawlat Misr,* 272–73.

63. Ibid., 616.

64. Sami Pasha, *Taqwim al-Nil.*

65. Shukri, al-'Anani, and Khalil, *Bina' dawlat Misr,* 23.

66. al-Jabarti, *Tarikh,* 3:469.

67. Ibid.

68. Wiet, *Mohammed Ali et les beaux-arts,* 21–24.

69. Quoted in Shukri, al-'Anani, and Khalil, *Bina' dawlat Misr,* 15.

70. Ibid., 98.

71. Ibid., 617.

72. Staffa, *Conquest and Fusion,* 269.

73. Ibid.

74. Ibid., 157.

3. Imagining Duality: The Construction of Culture

1. Muhammad 'Abd al-Hamid, M.D., "Mushkilat tatbib wal-iltizam al-'ilagi," in *al-Majalat al-tibbiya al-misriya,* year 10, vol. 1, Jan. 1934 (Cairo: al-Jam'iya al-Tibiya al-Misriya, 1934), 237.

2. See, for example, Nabil al-Sayyid al-Tokhy, *Si'id Misr fi 'ahd al-hamla al-firinsiya 1798–1801* (Cairo: al-Hay'a al-Misriya al-'Amma li'l-Kitab, 1997), for the less-known resistance in Upper Egypt.

3. The architect Charles Norry, member of the savants, quoted in Robert Solé, *Les savants de Bonaparte* (Paris: Editions du Seuil, 1998), 25–26. "Nous cherchions l'Alexandrie d'Alexandre bâtie par l'architecte Dinocharàs, nous cherchions cette ville où sont nés, où se sont formés tant de grands hommes, cette bibliothèque où les Ptolémées avaient réuni le dépôt des connaissances humaines; nous cherchions enfin cette ville commerçante, son peuple actif, industrieux: nous ne trouvâmes que ruines, barbarie, avilissement et pauvreté de toute parts."

4. Edward Lane, *An Account of the Manners and Customs of the Modern Egyptians* (The Hague: East-West Publications, 1978).

5. Guillaume André Villoteau, musical expert attached to the savants of the Napoleonic army, quoted in Solé, *Les savants de Bonaparte,* 141. "Les Egyptiens . . . n'aimaient point notre musique et trovaient la leur délicieuse; nous, nous aimons la nôtre et trouvons la musique des Egyptiens détestable: chacun de son côté croit avoir raison."

6. Chabrol de Volvic, "Dirasat fi 'adat wa taqalid sukkan Misr al-muhdithin" in *Wasf Misr,* vol. 1, *al-Misriyun al-muhdithun* (Cairo: Maktabat Madbuli, 1989), 39–41.

7. Florence Nightingale, *Letters from Egypt: A Journey on the Nile, 1849–1850* (New York: Weidenfeld and Nicolson, 1987), 22.

8. Antoine-Barthélemy Clot, *Aperçu general sur l'Égypte,* 2 vols. (Paris: Fortin, Masson, 1840), 409. "Ils pretendirent que les Arabes n'avaient ni l'intelligence, ni l'aptitude des autres hommes."

9. Vatikiotis, *History of Modern Egypt,* 9.

10. Douglas Sladen, *Egypt and the English* (London: Hunst and Blackett, Ltd., 1908), preface and 73, is representative of the great pride the British took in their work in Egypt.

11. Moreh, *Napoleon in Egypt,* 28–29.

12. Taha Hussain, *Mustaqbal al-thaqafa fi Misr* (Cairo: al-Hay'a al-misriya al-'Amma li'l-Kitab, 1993), al-Tanwir series.

13. Frederick Oakley, *These Fifty Years: The Story of the Old Cairo Medical Mission from 1889 to 1939* (Old Cairo: Church Missionary Society, 1939), 1.

14. Vatikiotis, *History of Modern Egypt,* 208–9.

15. H. D. Terill, *Lord Cromer: A Biography* (New York: Edward Arnold, 1897), 330–51.

16. Egypt, Ministry of Education, Egyptian Government Schools, *Syllabus of the Primary Course of Study* (Cairo: National Printing Dept., 1907), 96, and Egypt, Ministère de l'Instruction Publique, *Programme de l'enseignement primaire et de l'enseignement secondaire* (Cairo: National Printing Dept., 1892), 137.

17. Egypt, Ministry of Education, *Regulations Relating to the Examination for the Secondary Education Certificate* (Cairo: National Printing Department, 1909), 16.

18. Egypt, Ministry of Education, *Secondary Education Certificate,* 5.

19. Latifa Muhammad Salim, *Faruq wa suqut al-malakiya fi Misr: 1936–1952* (Cairo: Maktabat Madbuli, 1989), 16.

20. "Il n'est admis à l'école de droit ni élèves boursiers ni élèves gratuits." Philippe Gelat Bey, *Répertoire général annoté de la législation et de l'administration égyptiennes* (Alexandria: J. C. Lagoudakis, 1908), 2:379.

21. Ibid., 356–57.

22. Ibid., 365.

23. Ibid. Article 10.

24. Ibid., 373.

25. Donald Malcolm Reid, *Cairo University and the Making of Modern Egypt* (Cairo: American Univ. in Cairo Press, 1990), 96.

26. Gelat Bey, *Répertoire,* 2:392–93.

27. Egypt, Department of Statistics, Population et mouvement de l'état civil, vol. 2, Étrangers établis en Égypte (Cairo, 1879).

28. Ahmad al-Shirbini, *Tarikh al-tigara al-misriyya fi 'asr al-hurriyya al-iqtisadiyya: 1840–1914* (Cairo: al-Hay'a al-Misriya al-'Amma li'l-Kitab, 1995), 40.

29. Ibid., 39–40.

30. Gelat Bey, *Répertoire,* 2:198–99.

31. Ibid., 2:250–51.

32. Gelat Bey, *Répertoire,* 6:231.

33. Ibid.

34. Gelat Bey, *Répertoire,* 6:5–7

35. Gelat Bey, *Répertoire,* 6:118.

36. Muhammad Qadai Pasha, ed., *al-Kitab al-dhahabi li'l-mahakim al-ahliyya, 1883–1933* (Cairo: Matabi' al-Amiriyya, 1938), 118, 124, 128. Maroni and Moriando, chief architects of mixed court laws, may have gone to the *shari'a* intentionally or may have simply used the Ottoman *majalla* that had begun to appear in 1869.

37. Read more about mixed courts in Byron Cannon, *Politics of Law and Courts in Nineteenth-Century Egypt* (Salt Lake City: Univ. of Utah Press, 1988), and Nathan Brown, *Rule of Law in the Arab World: Courts in Egypt and the Gulf* (Cambridge: Cambridge Univ. Press, 1997).

38. *The Egyptian Codes* (London: William Cowles and Sons, 1892), 1–2.

39. C. H. Perrott, "Law and Justice," in *Twentieth Century Impressions of Egypt* (London: Lloyd's Greater Britain Publishing, 1909), 96–109.

40. *al-Waqai' al-misriya,* no. 1186, Aug. 9, 1881.

41. Patrick Gaffney, "The Changing Voices of Islam in Egypt" (paper presented at the Middle East Studies Association Meeting, San Francisco, Calif., Nov. 1988).

42. Ibid.

43. Philippe Gallad, *Qamus al-idara wa'l-qada'* (Alexandria: Matba'at al-Qamus, 1895), 4:1954–55.

44. Sheikh Muhammad 'Abdu, "Taqrir islah al-mahakim al-shari'a (1899)," in *'al-A'mal al-kamila li'l-Sheikh Muhammad 'Abdu,* 5 vols., ed. Muhammad 'Imara, 2:217–90.

45. Sheikh Muhammad Abu Zahra, *al-Zawag wa'l-talaq al-madani fi'l-Qur'an* (Cairo, 1980), 1–3.

46. Muhammad 'Afifi, *al-Awqaf wa'l-hayat al-iqtisadiya fi Misr fi'l-'asr al-'uthmani* (Cairo: al-Hay'a al-Misriya al-'Amma li'l-Kitab, 1991), 151.

47. Alexandria, da'awi, 1275, 1:63, case 139.

48. Naqd court case 45/48, quoted in *al-Muhama al-shar'iya,* 31: 2115.

49. Manfalut 1229 [1814], 5: 26–122.

50. Misr 1266 [1850], 23: 237–635.

51. One such example from Aug. 8, 1926, is detailed in *Majalat al-Qada' al-Shar'i,* year 4, 443–34.

52. Emile Butaye and Gaston de Leval, *A Digest of the Laws of Belgium and the French Code Napoleon* (London: Stevens and Sons, Ltd., 1918), 132.

53. *al-Kitab al-dhahabi,* 1:234.

54. See Margaret Lee Meriwether, *The Kin Who Count: Family and Society in Ottoman Aleppo, 1770–1840* (Austin: Univ. of Texas Press, 1999).

55. Muhammad al-Bakri, *al-Ahwal al-shakhsiya,* 2 vols. (Cairo, 1991), 620–21.

56. Ibid., 623.

57. Ibid., 616–28.

58. *Bulletin de législation et de jurisprudence égyptiennes, 1914–1915* (Alexandria: Société de Publications Égyptiennes, 1915), 90.

59. *Majlis al-milli,* Damanhur, 27–11–1953, case 15.

60. See, for example, Mahkamat Masr al-Jadida al-Jus'iya, 23–7–1956, case 98.

61. Chris Eccels, *Egypt, Islam, and Social Change* (Berlin, 1984), 79: "The fees schedule issued as an appendix to the 1856 law was longer than the law itself."

62. Gelat Bey, *Répertoire,* 378–79.

63. Ibid., 378.

64. 'Abd al-'Azim Ramadan, *Mustafa Kamil fi mahkamat al-tarikh* (Cairo: al-Hay'a al-Misriya al-'Amma li'l-Kitab, 1994), 16.

65. Ibid.

66. Abd al-Rahman Fahmi, *Mudhakirat 'Abdal-Rahman Fahmi: yawmiyat Misr al-siyasiya,* ed. by Labib Yunan Rizq (Cairo: al-Hay'a al-Misriya al-'Amma li'l-Kitab, 1987), 1:117–18.

67. Ibid., 126.

68. Ibid., 119.

69. 'Abd al-Wahab Bakr, *al-Bulis al-misri: 1922–1952* (Cairo: Maktabat Madbuli, 1988), 68–78.

70. Ibid., 21.

71. Ibid., 270.

72. Ibid., 28–30.

73. Egypt, Ministry of Justice, "Prisons," *al-Majmu'a al-da'ima li'l-qawanin wa'l-qararat al-misriya,* pamphlet no. 106, p. 6, item 9, nos. 55 and 56, dated Feb. 9, 1901.

74. Egypt, Government, Dar al-Watha'iq, European Archives, Special Documents, Education, box 6, 1882–1922, 30.

75. See regulations for *ghufara'* in *al-Majmu'a al-kamila li'l-qawanin wa'l-qararat,* item 35, p. 5.

76. Bakr, *al-Bulis al-misri,* 123, quoting national security reports for 1927, 1928, 1929, and the Taqrir al-Sanawi for 1930–37.

77. Ibid., 129, quoting *al-Waqa'i' al-misriya,* no. 68 for 1923.

78. Ministry of Justice, the Judicial Adviser, *Report for the Year 1908* (Cairo: National Printing Department, 1909), 4.

79. Ibid., *Report for the Year 1912,* 9.

80. Ibid., *Report for the Year 1908,* 13–14.

81. Taqarir Amn (police records), Cairo and Alexandria, 1940, box 24, Sayyida Zaynab May 11; Alexandria, *zabt,* box 24, May 1940; Masr al-Gedida, Mar. 3, 1927, box 40, vol. 3, Oct. 15, 27.

82. Taqarir Amn (police records), Alexandria, vol. 3, 1927, file 40, Oct. 10; Cairo and Alexandria, hawadith, box 24, May 1940; Qism al-Darb al-Ahmar, Mar. 10, 1940; Batiniya, May 4, 1940.

83. Taqarir Amn (police records), Cairo and Alexandria, hawadith, box 24, 1940, qism Shubra, Mar. 11.

84. Taqarir Amn, (police records), Cairo, Oct. 1927, case 877, 2288 shooting of wife, 1026 husband throws wife out of window; Cairo and Alexandria, hawadith, box 24, May 1940.

85. Dumyat, ishadat, vol. 8, 1 al-Qi'da 975 to Rabi' al-awwal 975, p. 25, case 84; p. 61, case 237; p. 107, case 445.

86. Isna, ishadat, vol. 29, 1191–92, p. 22, case 41.

87. Taqarir Amn (police records), Cairo, Sept. 1927, case 1267.

88. Ibid., Oct. 1927, case 1349.

89. Taqarir Amn (police records), Cairo and Alexandria, hawadith, Mar. 1940, box 24, Bab al-Shi'riya.

90. Ibid., box 24, hawadith, 1940, qism al-Sayyida, Mar. 31; Feb. 2, 1940, Rawd al-Farag.

91. Taqarir Amn (police records), Cairo, ginayat, June 1927, case 2055.

92. Alexandria *shari'a* court, da'awi, 1285 [1867], 3:10; 1293, 92:95; Ma'iya, sadir, aqalim wa muhafazat, Arabi, 1272 [1856] pt. 4:1617, p. 29, case 38 from Qina, and p. 63, case 115 from Manfalut.

93. Dumyat, ishadat, 999 [1591], 30:17–50.

94. Ibid., 30:25–61.

95. Ibid., 30:25–62.

96. Ibid., 30:32–77.

97. Taqarir Amn (police records), Cairo, 1927, Oct. 20, case 2346.

98. Ibid., 1927, Oct. 6, case 1368.

99. Qism Misr al-Gadida, box 24, 1940, police report 1378, May 11.

100. Cairo and Alexandria, hawadith, box 24, 1940, Qism al-Khalifa, May 22; Qism Shubra, mahdar 19, May 2.

101. Cairo, Taqarir Amn (police records), Harat al-Nasara, 1927, Oct. 6, case 1368; Misr al-qadima, case 468, Feb. 22, 1940.

102. Taqarir Amn (police records), case 1498 ginayat, Mar. 3, 1940.

103. Taqarir Amn (police records), Cairo, Oct. 1927, case 2143, rape of a sixteen-year-old boy.

104. Mitchell, *Colonizing Egypt*.

105. Qasim Amin, "al-Misriyun," in *Qasim Amin: al-a'mal al-kamila*, ed. Muhammad 'Imara (Cairo: Dar al-Shuruq, 1989), 56.

106. Ibid., 59.

107. Ibid., 63.

108. Bayram al-Tunsi, *Maqamat Bayram* (Cairo: Maktabat Madbuli, 1985), 38–42, 153–54.

109. Ibid., 92–96.

110. Hussain Mu'nis, *Bashawat wa super bashawat* (Cairo: al-Zahra' li'l-I'lam al-'Arabi, 1988), 7.

111. Bayram al-Tunsi, *al-A'mal al-kamila*, vol. 10, *al-sayyid wi miratuh fi baris* (Cairo: al-Hay'a al-Misriya al-'Amma li'l-Kitab, 1995), 3.

4. Foreign Rule and the *Tujjar*

1. Hobson, *Imperialism*, 15.

2. Sobhi Wahida, *Fi usul al-mas'ala al-misriya* (Cairo, 1950), 202–3. Wahida points to the significance of particular details included in the treaty to the foreign *tujjar* who stood to gain from it.

3. Egypt, Government, Dar al-Watha'iq al-Qawmiya, 'Ahd Isma'il, box 24, files 50/5. Memorandum dated Oct. 17, 1871, from Minister of War Isma'il Pasha to the Khedive regarding General Stone's wish to bring American professors from West Point to teach at the new military school.

4. Ibid., concerning a Eugene O'Reilly, a British citizen exiled from England because of pro-Irish activities.

5. Ibid., Mar. 12, 1972, 4.

6. Egypt, Government, Dar al-Watha'iq al-Qawmiya, Foreign Section, Education, box 6: 1882–1922, 31.

7. Thomas Mayer, *The Changing Past: Egyptian Historiography of the Urabi Revolution, 1882–1983* (Gainesville: Univ. of Florida Press, 1988).

8. Quoted in ibid., 51.

9. 'Uthman Amin, *Muhammad 'Abdu* (Cairo: al-Maktab al-Misri al-Hadith, 1978).

10. Trevor Le Gassick, ed. and trans., *The Defense Statement of Ahmad 'Urabi the Egyptian* (Cairo: American Univ. in Cairo Press, 1982), 18.

11. 'Ali Barakat, *Tatawur al-milkiya al-zira'iya fi Misr wa-atharuha 'ala al-haraka al-siyasiya: 1813–1914* (Cairo: Dar al-Thaqafa al-Jadida, 1977), 421–23.

12. Mu'nis, *Bashawat wa super bashawat*, 1.

13. Sabri Abul-Magd, *Sanawat ma qabl al-thawra: 1930–1952* (Cairo: al-Hay'a al-Misriya al-'Amma li'l-Kitab, 1987), 69.

14. Sa'd Zaghlul, *Athar al-za'im Sa'd Zaghlul: 'ahd wizarat al-sha'b*, comp. Muhammad Ibrahim al-Hariri (1927; reprint, Cairo: Maktabat Madbuli, 1991), 1:118.

15. Ibid., 13.

16. *The Living Webster: Encyclopedic Dictionary of the English Language* (Chicago: English Language Institute of America, 1977), 1091.

17. Barakat, *Tatawwur al-milkiya al-zira'iya fi Misr*, 54–70.

18. Sayyid Mar'i, *al-Islah al-zira'i wa-mushkilat al-sukkan fi al-qutr al-misri* (Cairo: Kutub Qawmiya, 1965), 18–23.

19. Ibid., 24.

20. Ibid., 40.

21. Galal Yehya, *Misr al-haditha* (Alexandria: Mansha'at al-Ma'arif, n.d.), 24.

22. David Landes, *Bankers and Pashas* (Cambridge, Mass.: Harvard Univ. Press, 1979), 41–47.

23. Ibid., 43–45. The Credit Foncier's board included Jewish, French, Lebanese, German, Greek, Italian, and British members.

24. Jeffrey G. Collins, *The Egyptian Elite under Cromer, 1882–1907* (Berlin: Klaus Schwarz Verlag, 1984), 41–42.

25. Ibid., 46–47.

26. Yusif Idris, *The Sinners* (Washington, D.C.: Three Continents Press, 1984).

27. Issawi, *Economic History of the Middle East*, 365.

28. Collins, *Egyptian Elite under Cromer*, 28.

29. Collins, *Egyptian Elite under Cromer*, 64. British overseas interests commonly followed such strategies, as the case of India illustrates. There the British constructed railway networks related entirely to British commercial and strategic needs even though they expected the colony to pay the price for such construction. See Sumit Sarkar, *Modern India: 1885–1974* (London: Macmillan, 1989), 36, for comparison.

30. Gabriel Baer, "Social Change in Egypt: 1800–1914," in *Political and Social Change in Modern Egypt*, ed. P. M. Holt (London: Oxford Univ. Press, 1968), 140.

31. Barakat, *Tatawur al-milkiya al-zira'iya fi Misr*, 154.

32. Mar'i, *al-Islah al-zira'i*, 35.

33. Egypt, Government, Department of Justice, High order regarding the election and function of the *ghufara'*, the *tuwafa*, and their *mashayikh*, law no. 53, dated Nov. 10, 1884, article 6 reads, "Each village should have one or two *ghufara'* on condition that the elect[ed] one would be a relative of the *mashayikh* or an owner of property or [a member of] renown[ed] families." See also arts. 7 and 11. The law of 1884 was amended in 1984, 1909, 1924, and 1936. The essence of the original law remained the same.

34. Barakat, *Tatawur al-milkiya al-zira'iya fi misr*, 233.

35. Egypt, Ministry of Justice, *Faharis majmu'at al-qawanin wa'l-awamir al-malakiya l-muta'aliqa bi'l-shu'un al-'amma, Sanat 1928* (Cairo: al-Matba'a al-Amiriya, 1930), 35.

36. Ibid., 107–8; Gelat Bey, *Répertoire*, 2: 667–68.

37. Ma'iyya Saniya, 1282 [1864], 1:3–2 Saddir Awamir, Mudiriyyat Bani Suwaif and Fayum.

38. *Dictionnaire géographique de l'Égypte* (Cairo: Imprimérie Nationale, 1899), xix.

39. Egypt, Ministry of the Interior, *Annual Report for 1909*, 27.

40. Ibid.

41. F. Robert Hunter, "The Making of a Notable Politician: Muhammad Sultan Pasha (1825–1884)," *International Journal of Middle East Studies* 15 (1983): 538.

42. Ibid., 539.

43. Robert Springborg, *Family, Power, and Politics in Egypt: Sayed Bey Marei—His Clan, Clients, and Cohorts* (Philadelphia: Univ. of Pennsylvania Press, 1982).

44. See laws nos. 5 for 1926, 12 for 1943, 44 for 1946, and 61 for 1941 that determined the area to be planted with cotton for 1941–42, and laws 89 and 90 of 1945 and 121 of 1946, deciding the particular types of cotton to be planted in specific areas. Published in Egypt, Ministry of Justice, *Majmu'at al-watha'iq al-rasmiya* (Cairo: al-Matabi' al-Amiriya, 1951). The laws are also published in *al-waqa'i' al-misriya*, each under its own date.

45. *al-Waqa'i' al-misriya*, no. 10, Jan. 16, 1950. Egypt, Ministry of Justice, *Majmu'at al-watha'iq al-kamila, Jan.-Mar. 1950* (Bulaq: Matabi' al-Amiriya, 1951), 23.

46. Alan Riding, *Distant Neighbors: A Portrait of the Mexicans* (New York: Vintage Books, 1989), 114.

47. Sabri Abul-Magd, *Sanawat ma qabl al-thawra: 1930–1952* (Cairo: al-Hay'a al-Misriya al-'Amma li'l-Kitab, 1987), 158–66.

48. Bakr, *al-bulis al-misri*, 72–74.

49. Marius Deeb, *Party Politics in Egypt: Wafd and Its Rivals, 1919–1939* (London: Ithaca Press, 1979), 23.

50. Nabil 'Abd al-Hamid Sayyid Ahmad, *al-Nashat al-iqtisadi li'l-ajanib wa atharihi fi'l mujtama' al-misri: 1922–1952* (Cairo: al-Hay'a al-Misriya al-'Amma li'l-Kitab, 1982), 24.

51. Ralf Dahrendorf, *The Modern Social Conflict: An Essay on the Politics of Liberty* (New York: Weidenfeld and Nicolson, 1988), 23.

52. Soto, *Other Path*, 202.

53. Abbas Hilmi II, "Mémoires d'un souverain: Abbas Hilmi II khédive d'Égypte: Mon reigne, 1892–1914," MSS.

54. Cromer, *Abbas II*, vii.

55. Yehya, *Misr al-haditha*, 24.

56. Egypt, Government, Dar al-Watha'iq al-Qawmiya, 'Asr Isma'il, box 30, file 58/2, no. 16, "Cabinet de sa majesté le roi," 1876. This box contains elaborate plans of items to be constructed at his various palaces and the khedive's own comments regarding these plans.

57. Ibid., file 58/2, no. 22, 1875.

58. Earl of Cromer, *Modern Egypt* (London: Macmillan, 1908), 29–30.

59. This was the most prestigious address, reminiscent of the "Your Grace" reserved only for dukes in Britain.

60. Egypt, Government, Ministry of Justice, Royal Decree no. 3, Jan. 4, 1923, regarding civil titles.

61. Egypt, Government, Ministry of Justice, Royal Decree no. 95, Dec. 25, 1922, regarding establishing the "Sultan Fuad Military Star."

62. Egypt, Government, Royal Decrees nos. 4, 5, 6, and 7, Jan. 4, 1923; Royal Decrees nos. 7 and 9 for Jan. 6, 1923; and Royal Decree no. 80, Oct. 28, 1928.

63. Latifa Muhammad Salim, *Faruq wa suqut al-malakiyya fi misr: 1936–1952* (Cairo: Maktabat Madbuli, 1989), 16.

64. Trevor E. Evans, *Mission to Egypt (1934–1946): Lord Killearn, High Commissioner and Ambassador* (Cardiff: Univ. of Wales Press, 1971), 5.

65. Ibid.

66. Abul-Magd, *Sanawat,* 129.

67. Bakr, *al-bulis al-misri,* 140.

68. 'Abd al-Rahman al-Raf'i, *Fi a'qab al-thawra al-misriya,* pt. 1, p. 249.

69. Muhammad Hussain Haykal, *Mudhakirat fi'l-siyasa al-misriya,* 3 vols. (Cairo: Dar al-Ma'arif, 1977), 190–95, and Kamil Mursi, *Asrar majlis al-wizara'* (Cairo: al-Maktab al-Misri al-Hadith, 1985), 207–10.

70. 'Abdel-'Azim Ramadan, *Tatawur al-haraka al-wataniya fi misr min sanat 1918 ila sanat 1936,* 2d ed. (Cairo: Maktabat Madbuli, 1983), 678–79.

71. Mursi, *Asrar,* 221.

72. Charles D. Smith, "4 February 1942: Its Causes and Its Influence on Egyptian Politics and on the Future of Anglo-Egyptian Relations, 1937–1945," *International Journal of Middle East Studies* 10 (1979): 453–79.

73. Haykal, *Mudhakirat,* pt. 1, 55–109, discusses the expectations, anxieties, and the final disappointment with President Wilson's "defection" experienced by Egyptian nationalist elements.

74. Muhammad Farid, *Awraq Muhammad Farid,* pt. 1, *al-Murasalat,* comp. Mustafa al-Nahhas Gabr (Cairo: Markaz Watha'iq wa Tarikh Misr al-Mu'asir, 1986).

75. Abul-Magd, Sanawat, 106.

76. Fahmi, *Mudhakirat,* 1, 11–12.

77. Isma'il Sidqi, *Mudhakarati* (Cairo: Maktabat Madbuli), and Saniya Qura'a, *Nimr al-siyasa al-misriya* (Cairo: Dar al-Ma'arif al-Misriya, n.d.), 71–73.

78. Qura'a, *Nimr al-siyasa al-misriya,* 71–73.

79. Bakr, *al-Bulis al-misri,* 79–80.

80. Hobson, *Imperialism.*

81. Zaghlul, *Mudhakirat,* 2:638.

82. Ibid., 627–50.

83. The syndicate approached British cotton spinners in the International Cotton Conference in Liverpool and Manchester in June 1921. Deeb, *Party Politics,* 23.

84. Ibid., 23–24.

85. Sidqi, *Mudhakarati,* 51.

86. Ibid., 35, 48.

87. Sidqi tells the story of how Sa'id Pasha had imprisoned his grandfather for nine months and how it was suggested to Sidqi's father that he and his brother should approach the pasha and play upon his feelings for their father so that he would release him. They did so, and not only did it work but the apologetic pasha presented their father with a 900-acre estate. Sidqi, *Mudhakarati,* 6.

88. 'Abd al-'Aziz Ramadan, ed., *Mudhakirat Sa'd Zhaglul* (Cairo: al-Hay'a al-Misriya al-'Amma li'l-Kitab, 1987), 60.

89. Ibid., 52–54.

90. Ibid., 61–62.

91. 'Ali Amin, *al-Kitab al-mamnu',* 2 vols. (Cairo: al-Maktab al-Misri al-Hadith, 1978), 196. The name given in this case is that of Sayyid Muhammad Basha, who was involved in an assassination attempt on Prime Minister Muhammad Sa'id Pasha in 1919.

92. Ibid., 214, gives his name as Muhammad 'Uthman al-Tobgi.

93. Ibid., 205. The names given are those of Shaykh Gadallah and Ibrahim Musa who prepared bombs.

94. Ibid., 206, Muhammad Tewfiq.

95. Ibid.

96. Muhammad 'Ali 'Alluba, *Dhikrayat ijtima'iya wa siyasiya* (Cairo: al-Hay'a al-Misiriya al-'Amma li'l-Kitab, 1988), 86–88.

97. Ibid., 54–55.

98. 'Ali Amin, *al-Kitab al-mamnu'*, 1:5.

99. Antonio Gramsci, *Selections from the Prison Notebooks* (New York: International Publishers, 1971), 178.

100. David Forgacs, *An Antonio Gramsci Reader: Selected Writings, 1916–1935* (New York: Schocken Books, 1988), 201.

101. Ibid. I am drawing similarity between Gramsci's analysis of the 1870–71 Paris Commune as the culmination of the changes evident with 1789 and with the results of the 1919 revolution in Egypt as culminating with 1952.

102. Ramadan, *Tatawur al-haraka al-wataniya*, 23.

103. Rizq, *Tarikh al-sahafah fi Misr*, 14.

104. Barakat, *Tatawwur al-milkiya al-zira'iya fi misr*, 151–54.

105. Ibid., 23–31.

106. Ramadan, *Tatawur al-haraka al-wataniya*, 35, quoting a speech of Mustafa Kamil.

107. Derek Hopwood, *Egypt: Politics and Society, 1945–1981* (London: George Allen and Unwin, 1982), 22.

5. Socialism and Feudalism: The New Mamluks

1. Marc Bloch, *Feudal Society*, vol. 2, *Social Classes and Political Organization* (Chicago: Univ. of Chicago Press, 1961), 446.

2. Ibrahim Amer, "al-Ard wal-fallah, al-Masalah al-Zira'iya fi Misr," in *Contemporary Arab Political Thought*, ed. Anouar Abdel-Malek (London: Zed Press, 1983), 120.

3. Bloch, *Feudal Society*, 2:444: "The most distinctive characteristics of feudal societies [are] the virtual identity of the class of chiefs with the class of professional warriors."

4. De Soto, *Other Path*, 210.

5. Mikhail Gorbachev, *Perestroika: New Thinking for Our Country and the World* (New York: Harper and Row, 1987), 101.

6. Gamal Abdel Nasser, *The Philosophy of the Revolution* (Buffalo, N.Y.: Economica Books, 1959), 36.

7. Gorbachev, *Perestroika*, 29.

8. Ibid.

9. Nasser, *Philosophy*, 28–29.

10. Gamal Abdel Nasser, *al-Mithaq* (Beirut: Dar al-Massira, n.d.), 9.

11. Ibid., 10–11.

12. Gamal Abdel Nasser, *Alf su'al wa ajwibat al-qa'id al-mu'allim Jamal 'Abd al-Nasser* (Cairo: Arab Socialist Union, n.d.), 25.

13. Nasser, *al-Mithaq*, 14.

14. Nasser, *Philosophy*, 30.

15. Ibid., 31.

16. Mustafa Kamel, *Awraq Mustafa Kamel: al-Murasalat* (Cairo: Markaz Watha'iq wa Tarikh Misr al-Mu'assar, 1982), 104.

17. 'Abd al-'Azim Ramadan, *Mudhakirat al-siyasiyin wa'l zu'ama' fi Misr: 1891–1981* (Cairo: Maktabat Madbuli, 1989), 33.

18. Nasser, *Philosophy*, 50.

19. Girgis Salama, *Tarikh al-ta'lim al-agnabi fi Misr* (Cairo, 1963), 124.

20. Barbara Ehrenreich, *Fear of Falling: The Inner Life of the Middle Class* (New York: Pantheon Books, 1989), 12.

21. Hinnebusch, *Egyptian Politics under Sadat*, 3.

22. Nasser, *al-Mithaq*, 79.

23. Gamal Abdel Nasser, *al-Tanzim wa'l-haraka: al-muhadarat al-khassa b'il-tanzim al-tali'i* (Cairo: Arab Socialist Union, 1966), 15.

24. Kamal Rif'at, *Nasseriyun Na'am* (Cairo: Dar al-Mawqif al-'Arabi, 1976), 9.

25. It is said that when the revolution had proven a success, the leaders of the Wafd met with the Free Officers, congratulated them on the success of their coup, and asked them to step aside so that they could get on with the business of running the country. "*Sibuna nishtaghal*" were the words the Wafdists used, which were repeated by Nasser with sarcasm and reproduced in the headlines of the newspapers the following day.

26. Jeswald W. Salacuse, "Foreign Investment and Legislative Exemptions in Egypt: Needed Stimulus or New Capitulations?" in *Social Legislation in the Contemporary Middle East*, ed. Lawrence O. Michalak and Jeswald W. Salacuse (Berkeley and Los Angeles: Univ. of California Press, 1986), 244.

27. Mahmoud Hussein, *Class Conflict in Egypt: 1945–1970* (New York: Monthly Review Press, 1973), 17.

28. Nasser, *al-Mithaq*, 19.

29. Ibid., 20–21.

30. Abdel Majid Farid, *Nasser, A Reassessment*, Arab Papers, no. 8 (London: Arab Research Centre, 1981), 4.

31. Ahmed Abdalla, *The Student Movement and National Politics in Egypt* (London: al-Saqi Books, 1985), 101. Public expenditure on education rose from L.E. 2.5 million in 1965 to 33.3 million in 1972–73.

32. Ibid., 108.

33. Forgacs, *Antonio Gramsci Reader*, 301.

34. 'Abdallah Imam, *'Ali Sabri yatathakar* (Cairo: Roz al-Yusuf, 1987), 30.

35. Safinaz Kazim, *al-Khadi'a al-nasiriya* (Cairo: Dar al-I'tisam, 1984), 24–29.

36. Ibid., 30.

37. Rif'at al-Sa'id, *al-Garima: watha'iq 'amaliyat ightiyal Shuhdi 'Atiya* (Cairo: Dar Shuhdi li'l-Nashr, 1984), 176.

38. Mu'nis, *Bashawat wa super bashawat*, 98–102. Corruption and actions of the secret services are no secret in Egypt.

39. Bloch, *Feudal Society*, 1:165.

40. Ibid., 164.

41. Ibid.

42. Mu'nis, *Bashawat wa super bashawat*, 135–38.

43. Bloch, *Feudal Society*, 1:147.

44. Mu'nis, *Bashawat wa Super Bashawat*, 142–43.

45. Bloch, *Feudal Society*, 1:146.

46. Ibid., 145.

47. Yusuf Idris, *al-Farafir* (Cairo: Maktabat Gharib, 1977).

48. Hopwood, *Egypt: Politics and Society*, 3.

49. Nasser, *al-Mithaq*, 159–62.

50. Ibid., 164.

51. Ibid., 175.

52. Ibid., 117.

53. Ibid., 179.

54. Nasser, *Alf su'al*, 10.

55. 'Abdallah Imam, *'Ali Sabri yatathakar*, 30.

56. Nasser, *Alf su'al*, 35–41.

57. See Gamal Selim, *al-Tanzimat al-siriya li-thawrat 23 yulyu fi 'ahd Gamal 'Abd al-Nasser* (Cairo: Maktabat Madbuli, 1982).

58. Ibid., 8.

59. Ibid., back cover.

60. Anis Mansur, *'Abd al-Nasser: al-muftara 'alayhi wa'l-muftari 'alayna* (Cairo: al-Maktab al-Misri al-Hadith, 1988), 25. Mansur tells of his own experience after losing the favor of the regime and his position at *Akhbar al-yum*.

61. Springborg, *Politics in Egypt*.

62. Gamal Abdel Nasser, *Watha'iq 'Abdel Nasser: khutab, ahadith, tasrihat* (Cairo: Ahram Center for Political and Strategic Studies, 1973).

63. Springborg, *Politics in Egypt*, 108.

64. Hopwood, *Egypt: Politics and Society*, 38.

65. Ibid., 40.

66. Sami Gohar, *al-Samitun yatakalamun* (Cairo: al-Maktab al-Misri al-Hadith, 1975), 30.

67. Mahmud Fawzi, *Thuwar yulyu yatahadathun* (Cairo: al-Zahra' li'l-I'lam al-'Arabi, 1988), presents a collection of articles written by various members of the Revolutionary Council.

68. Faruq Fahmi, *Ightiyal 'Abd al-Hakim 'Amir* (Cairo: Mu'assasat Amun al-Haditha, 1988), 43. In the book various theories are discussed regarding the death of the *mushir* as are details regarding the specific instances in which he clashed with Nasser.

69. Abdel Majid Farid, Robert Stephens, and Muhamed Auda, *Nasser, A Reassessment*, Arab Papers (London: Arab Research Center, 1981), 4.

70. 'Abdallah, *'Ali Sabri yatadhakar*, 87.

71. Mu'nis, *Bashawat wa super bashawat*, 2.

72. Gohar, *al-Samitun yatakalamun*, 38. This was based on an interview with al-Baghdadi.

73. Ibid.

74. For a comprehensive study of Sanhuri's significance, see Enid Hill, *Al-Sanhuri and Islamic Law*, vol. 10, American Univ. in Cairo Papers in Social Science, no. 1 (Cairo: American Univ. in Cairo, 1987).

75. John Kenneth Galbraith, *Economics in Perspective* (Boston: Houghton Mifflin, 1987), 30.

76. Nasser, *al-Mithaq*, 121.

77. Ibid., 117–19.

78. Ibid., 126–27.

79. Ibid., 121.

80. 'Ali 'Abdel-Razik, *al-Islam wa usul al-hukm: bahth fi'l-khilafa wa'l-hukuma fi'l-Islam* (Beirut: Dar Maktabat al-Hayat).

81. 'Imad Gum'a Imam, *al-Baquri bayn al-ikhwan wa'l-thawra* (Cairo, 1992), 59–80.

82. Lam'i al-Muti'i, *Ha'ula' al-rijal min al-Azhar* (Cairo: Anglo-Egyptian Bookshop, 1989), 241.

83. Maraghi held the position of Sheikh al-Azhar twice, in 1928 and 1935.

84. Fakhr-aldin al-Ahmadi al-Zawahri, *al-Siyasa wa'l-Azhar: min mudhakirat sheikh al-Islam al-zawahri* (Cairo: Matba'at al-I'timad, 1945), 289–90.

85. Rif'at Sayyid Ahmad, *al-Din wa'l-dawla wa'l-thawra* (Cairo: al-Dar al-Sharqiya, 1989), 241.

86. Saniya Qura'a, *Tarikh al-Azhar fi alf 'am* (Cairo: Maktabat al-Sahafa al-Dawli, 1968), 357–60.

87. Ibid., 359.

88. "Surat al-Ahqaf," 9. *The Holy Qur'an*, trans. Yusuf Ali (Brentwood, Md.: Amana Corp., 1983).

89. Rif'at, *Nasseriyun na'am*, 40.

90. *Qur'an,* "Surat al-Safat," 39.

91. *Qur'an,* "Surat al-Baqara," 143.

92. Rif'at, *Nasseriyun na'am*, 17.

93. Ibid., 16.

94. Anouar Abdel-Malek, *Rih al-sharq* (Cairo: Dar al-Mustaqbal, 1983), 259.

95. Ibid.

6. The New *Tujjar* and *Infitah*

1. Sheikh 'Ashur Muhammad Nasr, delegate to the Assembly from Alexandria, while defending himself in front of the Assembly during the meetings held to have him expelled for acts considered insulting to Sadat. Quoted in Gamal Selim, *Dictatoriyat al-Sadat: 'Asr al-dimoktatoriya* (Cairo: Maktabat Madbuli, 1983), 95.

2. "U.S. Objectives in the Middle East," Department of State Bulletin 63 [hereafter cited as DSB 63] (Aug. 10, 1970): 175–78.

3. Richard Nixon, "U.S. Foreign Policy for the 1970s: Building for Peace," a report to Congress Feb. 25, 1971, Department of State Bulletin 64 [hereafter cited as DSB 64] (Mar. 22, 1971): 389–91.

4. "On June 19th the USA launched an initiative to get both sides to re-establish the ceasefire, observe a military standstill in an agreed zone on both sides of the Israel-UAR ceasefire line, agree on a set of principles as the basic starting point for Arab-Israeli talks under the auspices of Ambassador Jarring." This description of the Rogers plan was given by Nixon. Ibid.

5. DSB 63 (Jan. 11, 1970): 44.

6. Walter Laqueur, *Confrontation: The Middle East and World Politics* (New York: Bantam Books, 1974), 6; "The Middle East: Statesmen Speak and Guns Answer," *Time* 96 (July 6, 1970): 7.

7. DSB 63 (Aug. 10, 1970): 178.

8. DSB 63 (Aug. 3, 1970): 130.

9. "Supplemental Assistance and Basic U.S. Policy in the Middle East and East Asia," statement by Secretary Rogers to the Senate Committee on Foreign Relations, Dec. 10, 1970, DSB 64 (Jan. 4, 1971), 19.

10. "Rogers News Conference, July 15," DSB 63 (Aug. 3, 1970): 132. "I think what he (Nixon) was referring to was that if there was a political settlement in the Middle East, then it would be our hope that the Soviet troops would be removed from the UAR."

11. "Secretary Rogers' News Conference, March 16," DSB 64 (Apr. 5, 1971): 482.

12. Don Peretz, "Peace Efforts of Kennedy, Johnson and Nixon," *Annals of the American Academy of Political and Social Science: America and the Middle East* 401 (May 1972): 124.

13. "Secretary Rogers' News Conference, December 23," DSB 64 (Jan. 11, 1971): 44.

14. Hinnebusch, *Egyptian Politics under Sadat*, 51.

15. Anwar Sadat, *In Search of Identity: An Autobiography* (New York: Harper Colophon Books, 1978), 221–24.

16. Abdalla, *Student Movement*, 140.

17. Malak Zaalouk, *Power, Class and Foreign Capital in Egypt: The Rise of the New Bourgeoisie* (London: Zed Books, 1989), 77.

18. John Waterbury, *The Egypt of Nasser and Sadat: The Political Economy of Two Regimes* (Princeton: Princeton Univ. Press, 1983), 373.

19. See the memoirs of Hussain Muhammad Hamuda, *Asrar harakat al-zubat al-ahrar wa'l-Ikhwan al-Muslimun* (Cairo: al-Zahra' li'l-I'lam al-'Arabi, 1989).

20. See Selim, *Dictatoriyat al-Sadat,* for the various members of the National Assembly who were expelled for voicing opposition to Sadat.

21. Mark N. Cooper, "The Demilitarization of the Egyptian Cabinet," *International Journal of Middle East Studies* 14 (1982): 20–255.

22. Ibid., 204.

23. Riding, *Distant Neighbors,* 116.

24. Waterbury, *Egypt of Nasser and Sadat,* 247.

25. Ibid.

26. Milovan Djilas, *The New Class: An Analysis of the Communist System* (New York: Praeger, 1957), 47.

27. Waterbury, *Egypt of Nasser and Sadat,* 247.

28. Ibid.

29. Ehrenreich, *Fear of Falling,* 144.

30. Zaalouk, *Power, Class and Foreign Capital,* 11.

31. For a survey of women entrepreneurs in contemporary Egypt see Earl L. Sullivan, *Women in Egyptian Public Life* (Syracuse: Syracuse Univ. Press, 1986).

32. See Zaalouk, *Power, Class and Foreign Capital,* 132–140, for further discussion of this group.

33. Selim, *Dictatoriyat al-Sadat.*

34. Anwar Sadat, "The October Paper," in *The Public Diary of President Sadat,* ed. Raphael Israeli, vol. 3, *The Road of Pragmatism* (Leiden: E. J. Brill, 1979), 470.

35. Part of an address delivered by Sadat to the Central Committee of the Arab Socialist Union, Cairo, Mar. 27, 1976, in Israeli, *Public Dairy of President Sadat,* vol. 3: 1239.

36. Hinnebusch, *Egyptian Politics under Sadat,* 57.

37. Ibid.

38. Ibid., 58.

39. Ibid., 59.

40. Israeli, *Public Diary of President Sadat,* 1198, from a speech delivered by Sadat to the People's Assembly abrogating the Treaty of Friendship and Cooperation with the Soviet Union, Mar. 14, 1976.

41. Ibid., 1239,

42. Gorbachev, *Perestroika,* 17.

43. Ibid., 22.

44. Ibid., 57.

45. Nicholas Hopkins, *Agrarian Transformation in Egypt* (Boulder, Colo.: Westview Press, 1987), 143–45.

46. Ibid., 144.

47. Arthur Goldschmidt, *Modern Egypt* (Boulder, Colo.: Westview Press, 1988), 164.

48. Heba Handousa (presentation at Georgetown Univ. Symposium *Egypt: '88,* Apr. 1988).

49. Israeli, *Public Diary of President Sadat,* vol. 2: 485.

50. Ibid., 532.

51. Ibid., 533.

52. Nasser, *al-Mithaq,* 101.

53. De Soto, *Other Path,* xvi.

54. Ibid.

55. Ibid.

56. Ibid., xvi–xvii.

57. Ibid., vi.

58. Goldschmidt, *Modern Egypt,* 151.

59. Ibid., 167.

60. Salacuse, "Foreign Investment and Legislative Exemptions," 241.

61. Ibid., 245–46.

62. Ibid., 243.

63. Israeli, *Public Diary of President Sadat,* vol. 3: 1286.

64. Jehan Sadat, *A Woman of Egypt* (New York: Simon and Schuster, 1987), 34.

65. Ibid., 39.

66. Ibid., 45, 53, 64, 336–37.

67. Anwar Sadat, from an address to delegations of Egyptian scholars and students in America delivered in Ras al-Tin Palace, Alexandria, Aug. 3, 1976, in Israeli, *Public Diary of President Sadat,* vol. 3: 1355.

68. Selim, *Dictatoriyat al-Sadat,* 9.

69. Ghali Shoukri, *Egypt: Portrait of a President, 1971–1981* (London: Zed Press, 1981), v.

70. Anwar Sadat, from address to People's Assembly, Mar. 14, 1976, in Israeli, *Public Diary of President Sadat,* vol. 3: 1199.

71. Anouar Abdel-Malek, *Rih al-sharq* (Cairo: Dar al-Mustaqbal, 1983), 65.

72. Anwar Sadat, address commemorating the twenty-fourth anniversary of the revolution, Univ. of Alexandria, July 26, 1976, in Israeli, *Public Diary of President Sadat,* vol. 3: 1343.

73. Sayyid 'Ashmawi, *al-'Ayb fi al-dhat al-masuna: inhiyyar haybat hukm al-fard al-mutlaq, al-khidiwi, al-sultan, al-malik 1882–1952* (Cairo: Kitab al-Mahrusa: 1999), 19.

74. Selim, *Dictatoriyat al-Sadat,* 7.

75. Ni'mat Ahmad Fu'ad, *Sina'at al-gahl: kitab fi'l-siyasa* (Cairo: Dar al-Mustaqbal al-'Arabi, 1985), 46.

76. Muhammad Hassanein Heikal, *Kharif al-ghadab* (Cairo, 1983), 381–86.

77. Fu'ad, *Sina'at al-gahl,* 41 and 39.

78. Ibid., 20.

79. P. J. Vatikiotis, *History of Egypt,* 292.

80. Gilles Kepel, *Muslim Extremism in Egypt: The Prophet and Pharaoh* (Berkeley and Los Angeles: Univ. of California Press, 1986), 226–31.

81. See Ahmad Ra'if, *al-Bawaba al-sawda': safahat min tarikh al-ikhwan al-muslimin* (Cairo: al-Zahra' li'l-I'lam al-'Arabi, 1988), for a description of the treatment of the Ikhwan.

82. Shoukri, *Egypt,* 443–51.

83. Waterbury, *Egypt of Nasser and Sadat,* 365.

84. Ibid., 370.

85. Ibid., 368.

86. Selim, *Dictatoriyat al-Sadat,* 141.

87. Shoukri, *Egypt,* v.

88. Fu'ad Sirag al-Din, *Limadha al-hizb al-jadid* (Cairo: Dar al-Shuruq, 1977).

89. Ibid., 58–59.

7. An End to Duality?

1. Forgacs, *Antonio Gramsci Reader,* 56–57.

2. Mohammed Arkoun, *Rethinking Islam Today* (Washington, D.C.: Georgetown Univ. Center for Contemporary Arab Studies, 1987), 3.

3. Eric Hobsbawm and Terence Ranger, *The Invention of Tradition* (Cambridge: Cambridge Univ. Press, 1984), 2.

4. Ibid., 8.

5. Forgacs, *Antonio Gramsci Reader,* 56–57.

6. *al-Taqrir al-istiratiji al-'Arabi: 1988* (Cairo: Ahram Political and Strategic Center, 1989), 574.

7. *al-Liwa' al-islami,* Dec. 22, 1988.

8. Hill, *Al-Sanhuri and Islamic Law,* 128.

9. Tahani Rached, director, *Quatre femmes d'Égypte,* produced by Éric Michel, Canadian Television, 1997.

10. *al-Ahram,* Aug. 19, 1998, 27.

11. *al-Ahram Weekly,* Feb. 3–9, 2000, 1.

12. Ibid., Jan. 27-Feb. 2, 2000, 1.

13. *al-Sha'b,* Jan. 28, 2000, 3.

14. B. J. Fernea has written a comprehensive and insightful study of Islamic feminism that shows how different it is from Western feminism, yet its dynamism and ambitions are very much within the struggle for women's rights in other parts of the world. Elizabeth Warnock Fernea, *In Search of Islamic Feminism: One Woman's Global Journey* (New York: Doubleday, 1998).

15. Amina Elbendary, "Conditional Surrender," *al-Ahram Weekly,* Jan. 13–19, 2000, 1.

16. Ibid., 20–26, 2000, 1.

17. *al-Ahram,* Feb. 11, 2000, 1.

18. *al-Hayat,* May 1, 1999, 17.

19. See various issues of *al-Jarida al-Rasmiya* issued by the Egyptian government. For example, see the Nov. 23, 1989, issue.

20. Enid Hill, *Mahkama! Studies in the Egyptian Legal System* (London: Ithaca Press, 1979), 82–86.

21. *al-Mugahid,* Jan. 1989, 21. This monthly magazine is published by the religious affairs section of the "psychological affairs" department of the military forces.

22. *al-Nur,* Jan. 11, 1989, 1.

23. Ibid., 1.

24. See, for example, issues of the *al-Liwa' al-Islami* during August and September 1989.

25. *al-Liwa' al-Islami,* Aug. 17, 1989, 3.

26. *al-Mugahid,* Jan. 1989, 4.

27. *al-Ahram,* Feb. 12, 1999, 7. "*Wilaya* of Mubarak for a fourth term, an indispensable national demand."

28. Galal Amin, "Social Mobility in Egypt," *Business Monthly* (Cairo: American Chamber of Commerce in Egypt, July 1989), 22.

29. Muhammad Husni Mubarak, *Khutab wa ahadith al-ra'is Muhammad Husni Mubarak: January–June 1985* (Cairo: Ministry of Information, 1987), 168. Egyptian workers in Arab states numbered 2.5 million in 1984.

30. John Esposito, *Islam: The Straight Path* (New York: Oxford Univ. Press, 1991), 172.

31. Jacques Berque, *Egypt: Imperialism and Revolution* (New York: Praeger, 1972), 93–94.

32. Linda Oldham, Haguer el Hadidi, and Hussein Tamaa, *Informal Communities in*

Cairo: The Basis of a Typology, vol. 10, American Univ. in Cairo Papers in Social Science, no. 4 (Cairo: American Univ. in Cairo Press, 1987).

33. See *al-Ahram* for article on migrant labor.

34. Naguib Mahfouz, *Midaq Alley* (Washington D.C.: Three Continents Press, 1980).

35. Elizabeth Warnok Fernea and Robert A. Fernea, *The Arab World: Personal Encounters* (New York: Anchor Books, 1987), 233, 239.

36. Berque, *Egypt: Imperialism and Revolution*, 84.

37. Ibid., 466.

38. Nicholas Hopkins, *Agrarian Transformation in Egypt*, 1.

39. Myrette Ahmed el-Sikkari, *Basic Needs, Inflation and the Poor of Egypt, 1970–1980*, vol. 7, American Univ. in Cairo Papers in Social Science, no. 2 (Cairo: American Univ. in Cairo, 1984), 19–26.

40. Ibid., 26.

41. *al-Ahram*, Aug. 5, 1989, 3.

42. *al-Ahram*, July 21, 1989, 6.

43. 'Izzat al-Sa'dani, "Rihlat al-ahwal wa'l-akhtar fi ghazw al-sahari wa'l-qifar," *al-Ahram*, Aug. 5, 1989, 3.

44. Yusuf Idris, "Innana Nakhtaniq . . . Nakhtaniq," *al-Ahram*, Feb. 1, 1988, 11.

45. *Cairo Times*, Jan. 20–26, 2000, 2.

46. *Akhbar al-Yom*, Oct. 30, 1999, 14.

47. *al-Ahram* report, 588. The danger level reached was 150.62 meters.

48. *al-Taqrir al-sanawi: 1988*, 591.

49. Ibid., 587–89.

50. Fu'ad, *Sina'at al-gahl*, 104–11.

51. Yunan Labib Rizk, "Al-Ahram: A Diwan of Contemporary Life," in *al-Ahram Weekly*, Jan. 13–19, 2000, 1.

52. *al-Ahram Weekly*, July 1–7, 1999, 1.

53. See Amira Sonbol, "Egyptian Society and Sectarian Strife." In *The Political Economy of Modern Egypt*, ed. Ibrahim Oweiss (Washington, D.C.: Center of Contemporary Arab Studies, Georgetown University, 1990).

54. *al-Ahram Weekly*, Jan. 28-Feb. 3, 1999, 1.

55. *al-Ahram*, Feb. 3, 1989, 15.

56. *Akher Sa'a*, Aug. 9, 1989, 3–8.

57. *al-Ahram* report, 576.

58. Neamat Fouad, "Law and the Egyptian Cultural Heritage: The Pyramids Plateau Project," in *Law and Social Change: Problems and Challenges in Contemporary Egypt*, ed. Cynthia Nelson, vol. 2, American Univ. in Cairo Papers in Social Science, no. 4 (Cairo: American Univ. in Cairo, 1983), 138–61. See also issues of Egyptian newspapers during 1987 and 1988 for a description of the problem and the extent of anger among various sectors of society.

59. Ahmed Gami, "Pyramids Plateau Project," in *Law and Social Change, Problems and Challenges in Contemporary Egypt*, ed. Cynthia Nelson, vol. 2, American Univ. in Cairo Papers in Social Science, no. 4 (Cairo: American Univ. in Cairo, 1983), 162–76.

60. Fouad, "Law and the Egyptian Cultural Heritage," 150.

61. Nadia Ramsis Farah, *Religious Strife in Egypt: Crisis and Ideological Conflict in the Seventies* (New York: Gordon and Breach Science Publishers, 1986), 30.

62. Amin, "Social Mobility in Egypt," 23.

63. Farah, *Religious Strife in Egypt*, 33.

64. Kepel, *Muslim Extremism in Egypt*, 219–21.

65. Nemat Guenena, *The "Jihad": An "Islamic Alternative" in Egypt,* vol. 9, American Univ. in Cairo Papers in Social Science, no. 2 (Cairo: American Univ. in Cairo Press, 1988), 89–95.

66. *Akhir Sa'a,* Aug. 9, 1989, 3.

67. *al-Ahram Weekly,* Jan. 28–Feb. 3, 1999, 1.

68. *Qadaya,* Aug. 18, 1997, 6.

69. *al-Wafd,* Nov. 23, 1989.

70. Hill, *Mahkama!* 83.

71. Angela Davis, *Women, Culture and Politics* (New York: Vintage Books, 1990), 136.

72. *al-Ahram,* July 21, 1989, 6. The law was passed on July 4, 1989.

73. *al-Ahram,* Feb. 9, 1988, 3; 120,000 had university degrees, and 230,000 had degrees from specialized agricultural, industrial, trade, and teachers' schools.

74. *al-Ummah,* Aug. 13, 1989, 3.

75. Ibid.

76. *al-Ahram,* Apr. 6, 1999, 13.

77. *Egypt: The Stable Emerging Market, A Report on the Egyptian Economy* (Cairo: American Chamber of Commerce, 1999), 20.

78. *al-Wafd,* Aug. 13, 1989, 1.

79. *al-Ahram,* July 7, 1989, 1.

80. *al-Ahram,* Aug. 13, 1989, 9.

81. *al-Ahram Weekly,* Jan. 20–26, 2000, 1.

82. Ibid.

83. Ibid., 2–3.

84. Heba Ahmad Handoussa, "Time for Reform: Egypt's Public Sector Industry," in *Studies in Egyptian Political Economy: Methodology, Theory and Case Studies,* ed. Herbert Thompson, vol. 2, American Univ. in Cairo Papers in Social Science, no. 3 (Cairo: American Univ. in Cairo, 1979).

85. Marsha Pripstein Posusney, "Labor as an Obstacle to Privatization: The Case of Egypt 1974–1987" (paper presented at the 1989 Annual Meeting of the American Political Science Association, Atlanta Hilton, Aug. 31, 1989), 4.

86. *al-Ahram,* Aug. 3, 1989, 9.

87. *al-Ahram,* July 21, 1989, 1.

88. *Cairo Times,* Feb. 11, 2000, 5.

89. *al-Ahram,* Mar. 15, 1989, 6.

90. See items on Bush turning toward Mubarak as an intermediary for the hostage situation. See also Mubarak's role in the dialogue between the United States and the Palestine Liberation Organization (PLO).

91. *al-Ahram,* Feb. 15, 1989, 1.

92. *al-Gumhuriya,* Aug. 6, 1989, 1, and *al-Ahram,* July 26, 1989, 1, are two good examples.

93. *al-Ahram,* Feb. 15, 1989.

94. *al-Ahram,* Feb. 3, 1989, 3.

95. Oldham, el Hadidi, and Tamaa, *Informal Communities in Cairo,* xvii.

96. Ibid., 1.

97. *al-Gumhuriya,* Aug. 3, 1989, 1. The government decided to give one hundred thousand acres in ownership to those who had claimed usufruct rights to it.

98. *al-Wafd,* Aug. 13, 1989, 1.

99. *al-Haqiqa,* Aug. 12, 1989, 1.

100. Muhammad Salmawy, *Come Back Tomorrow and Other Plays* (Washington, D.C.: Three Continents Press, 1984), 11.

101. Sonallah Ibrahim, *The Smell of It: Short Stories of Egypt and Cairo* (London: Heinemann, 1978).

102. Muhammad Tawfik, "The Day the Moon Fell," play MSS.

103. Abdel Malek, *Rih al-Sharq*, 13.

104. Issa Boullata, *Trends and Issues in Contemporary Arab Thought* (Albany: State Univ. of New York Press, 1990), 117.

105. Salmawy, *Come Back Tomorrow*, 8.

106. Ibid.

Conclusion

1. Jacques Berque, *Cultural Expression in Arab Society Today* (Austin: Univ. of Texas Press, 1978), 14.

2. Ramadan, *Mudhakirat al-siyasiyin wa'l zu'ama'*, 54.

3. Cromer, *Modern Egypt*, 5.

4. From Gramsci, *Selections from Prison Notebooks*, 418, quoted in Bocock, *Hegemony*.

5. Mubarak, *Khutab wa Ahadith*.

6. De Soto, *Other Path*, xvi.

7. Bocock, *Hegemony*, 37.

BIBLIOGRAPHY

Unpublished Sources

Abbas Hilmi II. "Mémoires d'un souverain: Abbas Hilmi II khédive d'Égypte: Mon reigne, 1892–1914." Durham, England: Durham Univ. Library, Abbas-Hilmi Collection.

Cairo. National Archives:
  Dar al-Watha'iq al-Qawmiya:
    Shari'a court records: Alexandria; Assiut; Bab al-'Ali; Ballas; Dishna; Dumyat; Isna; Manfalut.
    Taqarir Amn (Police records): Cairo and Alexandria. Ma'iyya Saniya records, Arabic.
    Arabic and Foreign sections: Asr Isma'il, Special Documents, Schools.

Gaffney, Patrick. "The Changing Voices of Islam in Egypt." Paper presented at the Middle East Studies Association Meeting, San Francisco, Calif., Nov. 1988.

Gran, Peter. "Historians, Historiography, and State Hegemony in India, Iraq, and Mexico." Unpublished paper.

Tawfik, Muhammad. "The Day the Moon Fell." Unpublished play.

Published Government Reports

Egypt. Department of Statistics. *Population et mouvement de l'état civil.* Vol. 2, *Étrangers établis en Égypte.* Cairo, 1879.

———. Egyptian Government Schools. *Syllabus of the Primary Course of Study.* Cairo: National Printing Department, 1907.

———. Judicial Advisor. *Report for the Year 1908.* Cairo: National Printing Department, 1909.

———. *Majmu'at al-watha'q al-kamila.* Bulaq: Matabi' al-Amiriya, Jan.–Mar. 1951.

———. *Majmu'at al-watha'iq al-rasmiya.* Cairo: al-Matabi' al-Amiriya, 1951.

———. Ministère de l'Instruction Publique. *Programme de l'enseignement primaire et de l'enseignement secondary.* Cairo: National Printing Department, 1892.

———. Ministry of Education. *Regulations Relating to the Examination for the Secondary Education Certificate.* Cairo: National Printing Department, 1909.

————. Ministry of the Interior. *Annual Report for 1909*. Cairo: Egyptian Government, 1909.

————. Ministry of the Interior. *Census of Egypt 1917*. Cairo: Egyptian Government, 1917.

————. Ministry of Justice. *Faharis majmuat al-qawanin wa'l-awamir al-malakiya al-muta'aliqa bi'l-shu'un al-'amma*. Year 1928. Cairo: al-Matba'a al-Amiriya, 1930.

————. Ministry of Justice. "Prisons." al-Majmu'a al-da'ima li'l qawanin wa'l-qararat al-misriya.

————. Presidency. *al-Jarida al-rasmiya*. Cairo: Arab Republic of Egypt.

United States. Department of State. Department of State Bulletin 63 (Jan. 11, 1970): 44; 63 (Aug. 3, 1970): 130; 63 (Aug. 10, 1970): 175–78; 64 (Jan. 4, 1971): 19; 64 (Jan. 11, 1971): 44; 64 (Mar. 22, 1971): 389–91; 64 (Apr. 5, 1971): 482.

al-Waqai' al-misriya.

Primary Sources

'Abdel-Razik, 'Ali. *al-Islam wa usul al-hukm: Bahth fi'l-khilafa wa'l-Hukuma fi'l-Islam*. Beirut: Dar Maktabat al-Hayat, n.d.

'Abdu, Sheikh Muhammad. "Taqrir islah al-mahakim al-shar'iya (1899)." In *'Imara al-a'mal al-kamila li'l-Sheikh Muhammad 'Abdu*, edited by Muhammad 'Imara. 5 vols, 2:217–90, n.d.

Abu Zahra, Sheikh Muhammad. *al-Zawag wa'l-talaq al-madani fi'l-Qur'an*. Cairo, 1980.

'Alluba, Muhammad 'Ali. *Dhikrayat ijtima'iya wa siyasiya*. Cairo: al-Hay'a al-Misriya al-'Amma li'l-Kitab, 1988.

'Ashmawi, Sayyid. *al-'ayb fi al-dhat al-masuna: inhiyyar haybat hukm al-fard al-mut-laq, al-khidiwi, al-sultan, al-malik 1882–1952*. Cairo: Kitab al-Mahrusa, 1999.

Fahmi, 'Abd al-Rahman. *Mudhakirat 'Abdal-Rahman Fahmi: yawmiyat misr al-siyasiya*. Edited by Labib Yunan Rizk, 2 vols. Cairo: al-Hay'a al-Misriya al-'Amma li'l-Kitab, 1987.

Farid, Muhammad. *Awraq Muhammad Farid*. Compiled by Mustafa al-Nahhas Gabr. Part 1, *al-Murasalat*. Cairo: Markaz Watha'iq wa Tarikh Misr al-Mu'asir, 1986.

Fernea, Elizabeth Warnock, and Robert A. Fernea. *The Arab World: Personal Encounters*. New York: Anchor Books, 1987.

Gorbachev, Mikhail. *Perestroika: New Thinking for Our Country and the World*. New York: Harper and Row, 1987.

Gramsci, Antonio. *Letters from Prison*. New York: Harper and Row, 1973.

————. *Selections from the Prison Notebooks*. New York: International Publishers, 1971.

Haridi, Salah Ahmad. *al-Hiraf wal sina'at fi al-qarn al-thamin 'ashar*. Cairo, 1974.

The Holy Qur'an. Translated by Ali Yusuf. Brentwood, Md.: Amana Corp., 1983.

Hussain, Taha. *Mustaqbal al-thaqafa fi Misr*. al-Tanwir Series. Cairo: al-Hay'a al-Misriya al-'Amma li'l-Kitab, 1993.

Ibrahim, Sonallah. *The Smell of It: Short Stories of Egypt and Cairo*. London: Heinemann, 1978.

Idris, Yusuf. *The Sinners*. Washington D.C.: Three Continents Press, 1984.

al-Jabarti, 'Abd al-Rahman. *Tarikh 'aja'ib al-athar fi'l-tarajim wa'l-akhbar*. 3 vols. Beirut: Dar al-Gil, n.d.

al-Kitab al-Dhahabi li'l-Mahakim al-Ahliyya, 1883–1933. Boulaq, Cairo: Matabi' al-Amiriyya, 1938.

Mahfouz, Naguib. *Midaq Alley*. Washington, D.C.: Three Continents Press, 1980.

al-Malawani, Yusuf (Ibn al-Wakil, pseud.). *Tuhfat al-ahbab bi man malak misr min al-muluk wal-nuwab*. Edited by Abdel-Rahim 'Abdel-Rahman. Cairo: Dar al-Kitab al-Gami'i, 1998.

Mubarak, Muhammad Husni. *Khutab wa ahadith al-ra'is Muhammad Husni Mubarak*. Cairo: Ministry of Information, 1987.

Mustafa Kamel. *Awraq Mustafa Kamel: al-murasalat*. Cairo: Markaz Watha'iq wa Tarikh Misr al-Mu'assar, 1982.

Nasser, Gamal Abdal. *Alf su'al wa ajwibat al-qa'id al-mu'allim Jamal 'Abd al-Nasir*. Cairo: Arab Socialist Union, n.d.

———. *al-Mithaq*. Beirut: Dar al-Massira, n.d.

———. *The Philosophy of the Revolution*. Buffalo, N.Y.: Economica Books, 1959.

———. *al-Tanzim wa'l-haraka: al-muhadarat al-khassa b'il-tanzim al-tali'i*. Cairo: Arab Socialist Union, 1966.

———. *Watha'iq 'Abdel Nasser: Khutab, ahadith, tasrihat*. Cairo: Ahram Center for Political and Strategic Studies, 1973.

Qanun Namat Misr alathi asdarahu al-sultan al-qanuni li hukm Misr. Translated by Ahmad Fouad Mitwalli. Cairo, 1986.

Rif'at, Kamal. *Nasseriyun Na'am*. Cairo: Dar al-Mawqif al-'Arabi, 1976.

Sadat, Anwar. *In Search of Identity: An Autobiography*. New York: Harper Colophon Books, 1978.

Sadat, Jehan. *A Woman of Egypt*. New York: Simon and Schuster, 1987.

Salmawy, Muhammad. *Come Back Tomorrow and Other Plays*. Washington, D.C.: Three Continents Press, 1984.

Sidqi, Isma'il. *Mudhakarati*. Cairo: Maktabat Madbuli, n.d.

Sirag al-Din, Fu'ad. *Limadha al-hizb al-jadid*. Cairo: Dar al-Shuruq, 1977.

Smith, Adam. *Wealth of Nations*. London: Penguin Books, 1974.

al-Tunsi, Bayram. *al-A'mal al-kamila*. Vol. 10, *al-Sayyid wi miratuh fi Baris*. Cairo: al-Hay'a al-Misriya al-'Amma li'l-Kitab, 1995.

———. *Maqamat Bayram*. Cairo: Maktabat Madbuli, 1985.

Wasf Misr. Cairo: Maktabat al-Khanji, 1979.

Zaghlul, Sa'd. *Athar al-za'im Sa'd Zaghlul: 'Ahd wizarat al-sha'b*. Compiled by Muhammad Ibrahim al-Hariri. 3 vols. Cairo: Maktabat Madbuli, 1991.

Periodicals

al-Ahram (daily newspaper)
al-Ahram Weekly (weekly newspaper)
Akhbar al-Yom (daily newpaper)
Akhir Sa'a (weekly magazine)
Business Monthly (magazine)
Cairo Times (monthly magazine)
al-Gumhuriya (daily newspaper)
al-Haqiqa (weekly newspaper)
al-Hayat (daily newspaper)
al-Liwa' al-Islami (weekly newspaper)
Majalat al-qada' al-shari'i (monthly/yearly journal)
al-Muhama al-shari'iya (quarterly/yearly journal)
al-Mujahid (monthly magazine)
al-Nur (daily newspaper)
Qadaya (weekly newspaper)
Roz al-Yusuf (weekly magazine)
al-Sha'b (daily newspaper)
al-Shabab (weekly newspaper)
Time (weekly magazine)
al-Umma (daily newspaper)
al-Wafd (daily newspaper)

Secondary Sources in Arabic

'Abbas, Ra'uf, and 'Asim Disuqi. *Kibar al-mulak wal-falahin fi misr: 1837–1952.* Cairo: Dar Qiba' lil-Tiba'a wal-Nashr wal-Tawzi', 1998.

'Abd al-Fadil, Mahmud. *al-Tashkilat al-ijtima'iyya wa'l taqwimat al-tabaqiya fi'l-watan al-'arabi.* Beirut: Markaz Dirasat al-Wihda al-'Arabiya, 1988.

'Abd al-Hamid, Muhammad, M.D. "Mushkilat al-tatbib wal-iltizam al-'ilagi." In *al-Majalat al-tibbiya al-Misriya,* year 10, vol. 1, Jan. 1934. Cairo: al-Jam'iya al-Tibiya al-Misriya, 1934.

'Abdel Latif, Laila. *al-Mujtama' al-misri fil 'asr al-'uthmani.* Cairo: Dar al-Kitab al-Jami'i, 1987.

Abdel-Malek, Anouar. *Rih al-Sharq.* Cairo: Dar al-Mustaqbal, 1983.

'Abdel-Rehim, 'Abdel-Rahman. *Fusul min Tarikh Misr al-iqtisadi wal-Ijtima'i fil-'asr al-'uthmani.* Cairo: al-Hay'a al-Misriya al-'Amma li'l-Kitab, 1990.

Abul-Magd, Sabri. *Sanawat ma qabl al-thawra: 1930–1952.* Cairo: al-Hay'a al-Misriya al-'Amma li'l-Kitab, 1987.

'Afifi, Muhammad. *al-Awqaf wa'l-hayat al-iqtisadiya fi Misr fi'l-'asr al-'uthmani.* Cairo: al-Hay'a al-Misriya al-'Amma li'l-Kitab, 1991.

Ahmad, Nabil ʿAbd al-Hamid Sayyid. *al-Nashat al-iqtisadi liʾl-ajanib wa atharihi fiʾl-mujtamaʿ al-misri: 1922–1952*. Cairo: al-Hayʾa al-Misriya al-ʿAmma liʾl-Kitab, 1982.

Ahmad, Rifaʿat Sayyid. *al-Din waʾl-dawla waʾl-thawra*. Cairo: al-Dar al-Sharqiya, 1989.

ʿAmil, Mahdi. *Fi ʿilmyat al-fikr al-khalduni*. Beirut: Dar al-Farabi, 1986.

Amin, ʿAli. *al-Kitab al-mamnuʿ*. 2 vols. Cairo: al-Maktab al-Misri al-Hadith, 1978.

Amin, Qasim. *al-Misriyun*. In *Qasim Amin: al-aʿmal al-kamila*, edited by Muhammad ʿImara. Cairo: Dar al-Shuruq, 1989.

Amin, ʿUthman. *Muhammad ʿAbdu*. Cairo: Dar Ihyaʾ al-Kutub al-ʿArabiya, 1944.

———. *Muhammad ʿAbdu*. Cairo: al-Maktab al-Misri al-Hadith, 1978.

al-ʿArawi, ʿAbd Allah. *Mafhum al-dawla*. Beirut: al-Markaz al-Thaqafi al-ʿArabi, 1988.

Bakr, ʿAbd al-Wahab. *al-Bulis al-misri: 1922–1952*. Cairo: Maktabat Madbuli, 1988.

al-Bakri, Muhammad. *al-Ahwal al-shakhsiya*. 2 vols. Cairo, 1991.

Barakat, ʿAli. *Tatawur al-milkiya al-ziraʿiya fi Misr wa-atharuha ʿala al-haraka al-siyasiya: 1813–1914*. Cairo: Dar al-Thaqafa al-Jadida, 1977.

Chabrol de Volvic, "Dirasat fi ʿadat wa taqalid sukkan Misr al-muhdithin." In *Wasf Misr*, vol. 1, *al-Misriyun al-muhdithun*, edited by Chabrol de Volvic, 39–41. Cairo: Maktabat Madbuli, 1989.

Elbendary, Amina. "Conditional Surrender," *al-Ahram Weekly*, Jan. 13–19, 2000, 1.

Fahmi, Faruq. *Ightiyal ʿAbd al-Hakim ʿAmir*. Cairo: Muʾassasat Amun al-Haditha, 1988.

Farahat, Muhammad Nur al-Din. *al-Qadaʾ al-sharʿi fi Misr fiʾl-ʿasr al-ʿuthmani*. Cairo: al-Hayʾa al-Misriya al-ʿAmma liʾl-Kitab, 1988.

Fawzi, Mahmud. *Thuwar yulyu yatahadathun*. Cairo: al-zahraʾ liʾl-Iʿlam al-ʿArabi, 1988.

Fuʾad, Niʿmat Ahmad. *Sinaʿat al-gahl: kitab fiʾl-siyasa*. Cairo: Dar al-Mustaqbal al-ʿArabi, 1985.

Gallad, Philippe. *Qamus al-idara waʾl-qadaʾ*. 6 vols. Alexandria: Matbaʿat al-Qamus, 1895.

Gohar, Sami. *al-Samitun yatakalamun*. Cairo: al-Maktab al-Misri al-Hadith, 1975.

Grohmann, Adolph. *Awraq al-bardi al-ʿarabiyya bi dar al-kutub al-misriya*. Vol. 1. Cairo: Matbaʿat Dar al-Kutub al-Misriya, 1994.

Hamuda, Hussain Muhammad. *Asrar harakat al-zubat al-ahrar waʾl-ikhwan al-muslimun*. Cairo: al-Zahraʾ liʾl-Iʿlam al-ʿArabi, 1989.

Hanna, Nelly. *Tujjar al-qahira filʾ-ʿasr al-ʿuthmani*. Cairo: al-Dar al-Misriya al-Libnaniya, 1997.

Haykal, Muhammad Hussain. *Mudhakirat fiʾl-siyasa al-misriya*. 3 vols. Cairo: Dar al-Maʿarif, 1977.

Heikal, Hassanein. *Kharif al-ghadab*. Beirut: Sharikat al-Matbuʿat, 1984.

Idris, Yusuf. *al-Farafir*. Cairo: Maktabat Gharib, 1977.

———. "Innana nakhtaniq . . . nakhtaniq." *al-Ahram*, Feb. 1, 1988, 11.

Imam, 'Abdallah. *'Ali Sabri yatathakar.* Cairo: Roz al-Yusuf, 1987.

Imam, 'Imad Gum'a. *al-Baquri bayn al-Ikhwan wa'l-thawra.* Cairo, 1992.

'Imara, Muhammad. *Qasim Amin: al-a'mal al-kamila.* Cairo: Dar al-Shuruq, 1989.

Kazim, Safinaz. *al-Khadi'a al-nasiriya.* Cairo: Dar al-I'tisam, 1984.

al-Kitab al-dhahabi lil-mahakim al-ahliyya: 1883–1933. Vol. 1. Cairo: al-Matabi'
al-Amiriya, 1937.

Mansur, Anis. *'Abd al-Nasser: al-muftara 'alayhi wa'l-muftari 'alayna.* Cairo: al-Maktab al-Misri al-Hadith, 1988.

Mar'i, Sayyid. *al-islah al-zira'i wa-mushkilat al-sukkan fi al-qutr al-misri.* Cairo:
Kutub Qawmiya, 1965.

Mu'nis, Hussain. *Bashawat wa super bashawat.* Cairo: al-Zahra' li'l-I'lam al-'Arabi,
1988.

Mursi, Kamil. *Asrar majlis al-wuzara'.* Cairo: al-Maktab al-Misri al-Hadith, 1985.

al-Muti'i, Lam'i. *Ha'ula' al-rijal min al-Azhar.* Cairo: Anglo-Egyptian Bookshop,
1989.

Qadri Pasha, Muhammad, ed. *al-Kitab al-dhahabi li'l-mahakim al-ahliyya,
1883–1993.* Cairo: Matabi' al-Amiriya, 1938.

Qura'a, Saniya. *Nimr al-siyasa al-misriya.* Cairo: Dar al-Ma'arif al-Misriya, n.d.

———. *Tarikh al-Azhar fi alf 'Am.* Cairo: Maktabat al-Sahafa al-Dawli, 1968.

al-Raf'i, 'Abd al-Rahman. *Fi a'qab al-thawra al-misriya.* 3 vols. Cairo: Dar al-Ma'arif
al-Misriya, 1989.

Ra'if, Ahmad. *al-Bawaba al-sawda': safahat min tarikh al-Ikhwan al-Muslimin.* Cairo:
al-Zahra' li'l-I'lam al-'Arabi, 1988.

Ramadan, 'Abdel 'Azim. *Mudhakirat al-siyasiyin wa'l zu'ama' fi Misr: 1891–1981.*
Cairo: Maktabat Madbuli, 1989.

———. *Mustafa Kamil fi mahkamat al-tarikh.* Cairo: al-Hay'a al Misriya al-'Amma
li'l-Kitab, 1994.

———. *Tatawur al-haraka al-wataniya fi Misr min sanat 1918 ila sanat 1936.* 2d ed.
Cairo: Maktabat Madbuli, 1983.

———, ed. *Mudhakirat Sa'd Zhaglul.* Cairo: al-Hay'a al-Misriya al-'Amma li'l-Kitab,
1987.

Rizk, Labib Yunan. *Tarikh al-sahafah fi Misr.* Cairo, n.d.

al-Sa'dani, 'Izzat. "Rihlat al-ahwal wa'l-akhtar fi ghazw al-sahari wa'l-qifar." *al-
Ahram,* Aug. 5, 1989, 3.

al-Sa'id, Rif'at. *al-Garima: watha'iq 'amaliyat ightiyal shuhdi 'atiya.* Cairo: Dar
Shuhdi li'l-Nashr, 1984.

Salama, Girgis. *Tarikh al-ta'lim al-Agnabi fi Misr.* Cairo, 1963.

Salim, Latifa Muhammad. *Faruq wa suqut al-malakiya fi Misr: 1936–1952.* Cairo:
Maktabat Madbuli, 1989.

Sami Pasha, Amin. *Taqwim al-Nil wa 'asr Isma'il.* Cairo: Dar al-Kutub al-Misriya,
1936.

al-Sanhuri, Nadia, and al-Shawi, Tawfiq. *'Abd al-Raziq al-Sanhuri min khilal
awraqihi al-shakhsiya.* Cairo: al-Zahra li'l-I'lam al-'Arabi, 1988.

Selim, Gamal. *Dictatoriyat al-Sadat: 'asr al-dimoqtatoriya.* Cairo: Maktabat Madbuli, 1983.

———. *al-Tanzimat al-siriya li-thawrat 23 yuliyo fi 'Ahd Gamal 'Abd al-Nasser.* Cairo: Maktabat Madbuli, 1982.

al-Shirbini, Ahmad. *Tarikh al-tigara al-misriyya fi 'asr al-huriya al-iqtisadiya: 1840–1914.* Cairo: al-Hay'a al-Misriya al-'Amma li'l-Kitab, 1995.

Shouman, Mohsen. *al-Yahud fi Misr min al-fath al-'uthmani hatta awa'il al-qarn al-tasi' 'ashr.* al-Zaqaziq, 1996.

Shukri, Muhammad Fu'ad, 'Abd al-Maqsud al-'Anani, and Sayyid Muhammad Khalil. *Bina' dawlat Misr Muhammad 'Ali: al-Siyasa al-dakhiliya.* Cairo: Dar al-Fikr al-'Arabi, 1948.

al-Taqrir al-istiratiji al-'Arabi: 1988. Cairo: al-Ahram Political and Strategic Center, 1989.

al-Tokhy, Nabil al-Sayyid. *Si'id Misr fi 'ahd al-hamla al-firinsiyya 1798–1801.* Cairo: al-Hay'a al-Misriya al-'Amma li'l-Kitab, 1997.

Wahida, Sobhi. *Fi usul al-mas'ala al-misriya.* Cairo, 1950.

Waqidi, Muhammad. *Bina' al-nazariya al-falsafiya: dirasat fi al-falsafa al-'arabiya al-mu'asara.* Beirut: Dar al-Tali'a, 1990.

Yehya, Galal. *Misr al-haditha.* Alexandria: Mansha'at al-Ma'arif, n.d.

al-Zawahri, Fakhr-aldin al-Ahmadi. *al-Siyasa wa'l-Azhar: Min mudhakirat Sheikh al-Islam al-Zawahri.* Cairo: Matba'at al-I'timad, 1945.

Secondary Sources in Western Languages

Abdalla, Ahmed. *The Student Movement and National Politics in Egypt.* London: Al Saqi Books, 1985.

Abdel-Malek, Anouar. *Civilizations and Social Theory.* Albany: State Univ. of New York Press, 1981.

Amer, Ibrahim. "al-Ard wal-fallah al-masaleh al-zira'iyya fi Misr." In *Contemporary Arab Political Thought,* edited by Anouar Abdel-Malek. London: Zed Press, 1983.

Amin, Galal. "Social Mobility in Egypt." *Business Monthly* (Cairo), July 1989.

Amin, Samir. *The Arab Nation: Nationalism and Class Struggle.* London: Zed Press, 1978.

Anderson, Perry. *Emergence of the Absolutist State.* London: Humanities Press, 1974.

Arkoun, Mohammed. *Rethinking Islam Today.* Washington, D.C.: Georgetown Univ. Center for Contemporary Arab Studies, 1987.

Armbrust, Walter. *Mass Culture and Modernism in Egypt.* Cambridge: Cambridge. Univ. Press, 1996.

Baer, Gabriel. "Social Change in Egypt, 1800–1914." In *Political and Social Change in Modern Egypt,* edited by P. M. Holt. London: Oxford Univ. Press, 1968.

Benson, John. *The Penny Capitalists: A Study of Nineteenth-Century Working-Class Entrepreneurs.* New Brunswick, N.J.: Rutgers Univ. Press, 1983.

Berque, Jacques. *Cultural Expression in Arab Society Today.* Austin: Univ. of Texas Press, 1978.

———. *Egypt, Imperialism and Revolution.* New York: Praeger, 1972.

Berger, Peter. *The Capitalist Revolution: Fifty Propositions about Prosperity, Equality and Liberty.* New York: Basic Books, 1986, 19.

Bloch, Marc. *Feudal Society.* Chicago: Univ. of Chicago Press, 1961.

Bocock, Robert. *Hegemony.* London: Open Univ., 1986.

Boullata, Issa. *Trends and Issues in Contemporary Arab Thought.* Albany: State Univ. of New York Press, 1990.

Braudel, Ferdinand. *The Perspective of the World: Civilization and Capitalism, 15th–18th Century.* New York: Harper and Row, 1984.

Brown, Nathan. *Rule of Law in the Arab World: Courts in Egypt and the Gulf.* Cambridge: Cambridge Univ. Press, 1997.

Bulletin de législation et de jurisprudence égyptiennes, 1914–1915. Alexandria: Société de Publications Égyptiennes, 1915.

Butaye, Emile, and Gaston de Leval. *A Digest of the Laws of Belgium and the French Code Napoléon.* London: Stevens and Sons, Ltd., 1918.

Cannon, Byron. *Politics of Law and Courts in Nineteenth-Century Egypt.* Salt Lake City: Univ. of Utah Press, 1988.

Capel, Anne K., and Glenn Markoe, eds. *Mistress of the House, Mistress of Heaven.* New York: Hudson Hills Express with Cincinnati Art Museum, 1996.

Cavalcanti, Pedro, and Paul Piccone. *History, Philosophy and Culture in the Young Gramsci.* Saint Louis, Mo.: Telos Press, 1975.

Chatterjee, Partha. *Nationalist Thought and the Colonial World: A Derivative Discourse?* London: Zed Books, 1986.

Clot, Antoine-Barthélemy. *Aperçu general sur l'Égypte.* 2 vols. Paris: Fortin, Masson, 1840.

Collins, Jeffrey G. *The Egyptian Elite under Cromer, 1882–1907.* Berlin: Klaus Schwarz Verlag, 1984.

Cooper, Mark N. "The Demilitarization of the Egyptian Cabinet." *International Journal of Middle East Studies* 14 (1982): 20–255.

Crecelius, Daniel. *The Roots of Modern Egypt.* Minneapolis, Minn.: Bibliotheca Islamica, 1981.

Cromer, Earl of. *Abbas II.* London: Macmillan, 1915.

———. *Modern Egypt.* London: Macmillan, 1908.

Cuno, Ken M. *Land, Society, and Economy in Lower Egypt, 1740–1858.* Cambridge: Cambridge Univ. Press, 1992.

Dahrendorf, Ralf. *The Modern Social Conflict: An Essay on the Politics of Liberty.* New York: Weidenfeld and Nicolson, 1988.

Davis, Angela. *Women, Culture and Politics.* New York: Vintage Books, 1990.

De Jong, Fred. *Turuq and Turuq-Linked Institutions in Nineteenth Century Egypt.* Leiden: E. J. Brill, 1978.

Deeb, Marius. *Party Politics in Egypt: The Wafd and Its Rivals, 1919–1939.* London: Ithaca Press, 1979.

De Soto, Hernando. *The Other Path: The Invisible Revolution in the Third World*. New York: Harper and Row, 1989.

Dictionnaire géographique de l'Égypte. Cairo: Imprimerie Nationale, 1899.

Djilas, Milovan. *The New Class: An Analysis of the Communist System*. New York: Praeger, 1957.

Dreyer, O. *Cultural Changes in Developing Countries. Progress*. Problems of the Third World Series. Moscow: Progress Publishers, 1976.

Dwyer, Kevin. *Arab Voices: Human Rights Debate in the Middle East*. Berkeley: Univ. of California Press, 1991.

Eccel, Chris. *Egypt, Islam and Social Change*. Berlin, 1984.

Egypt: The Stable Emerging Market, A Report on the Egyptian Economy. Cairo: Chamber of Commerce, 1999.

The Egyptian Codes. London: William Cowles and Sons, 1892.

Ehrenreich, Barbara. *Fear of Falling: The Inner Life of the Middle Class*. New York: Pantheon Books, 1989.

Ekelund, Robert B., and Robert F. Hebert. *A History of Economic Theory and Method*. 3d ed. New York: McGraw-Hill, 1990.

Esposito, John. *Islam: The Straight Path*. New York: Oxford Univ. Press, 1991.

———, ed. *Voices of Resurgent Islam*. New York: Oxford Univ. Press, 1983.

Evans, Trevor E. *Mission to Egypt (1934–1946): Lord Killearn, High Commissioner and Ambassador*. Cardiff: Univ. of Wales Press, 1971.

Ezz el Arab, Abdel Aziz. "Notes on the Political Economy of Eighteenth Century Egypt: The Ruling Class and Its Socio-Economic Impact." In *Studies in Egyptian Political Economy: Methodology, Theory and Case Studies*, edited by Herbert Thompson, 101–25. Vol. 2, American Univ. in Cairo Papers in Social Science, no. 3. Cairo: American Univ. in Cairo, 1979.

Fahmy, Khaled. *All the Pasha's Men: Mehmed Ali, His Army and the Making of Modern Egypt*. Cambridge: Cambridge Univ. Press, 1997.

Fahmy, Moustafa. *La Revolution de l'industrie en Égypte et ses consequences sociales au 19ᵉ siècle (1800–1850)*. Leiden: E. J. Brill, 1954.

Farah, Nadia Ramsis. *Religious Strife in Egypt: Crisis and Ideological Conflict in the Seventies*. New York: Gordon and Breach Science Publishers, 1986.

Farid, Abdel Majid, Robert Stephens, and Muhamed Auda. *Nasser, A Reassessment*. London: Arab Research Center, 1981.

Faroqhi, Suraiya. *Making a Living in the Ottoman Lands: 1480–1820*. Istanbul: Isis Press, 1995.

Fernea, Elizabeth Warnock. *In Search of Islamic Feminism: One Woman's Global Journey*. New York: Doubleday, 1998.

Forgacs, David, ed. *An Antonio Gramsci Reader: Selected Writings, 1916–1935*. New York: Schocken Books, 1988.

Fouad, Neamat. "Law and the Egyptian Cultural Heritage: The Pyramids Plateau Project." In *Law and Social Change: Problems and Challenges in Contemporary Egypt*, edited by Cynthia Nelson, 138–61. Vol. 2, American Univ. in Cairo Papers in Social Science, no. 4. Cairo: American Univ. in Cairo, 1983.

Foucault, Michel. *The Order of Things: An Archaeology of the Human Sciences.* New York: Vintage Books, 1970.

Galbraith, John Kenneth. *The Anatomy of Power.* Boston: Houghton Mifflin, 1983.

———. *Economics in Perspective.* Boston: Houghton Mifflin, 1987.

Gami, Ahmed. "Pyramids Plateau Project," *Law and Social Change.* In *Law and Social Change: Problems and Challenges in Contemporary Egypt,* edited by Cynthia Nelson, 162–71. Vol. 2, American Univ. in Cairo Papers in Social Science, no. 4. Cairo: American Univ. in Cairo, 1983.

Geertz, Clifford. *Works and Lives: The Anthropologist as Author.* Stanford, Calif.: Stanford Univ. Press, 1988.

Gelat Bey, Philippe. *Répertoire général annoté de la législation et de l'administration égyptiennes, 1840–1908.* 6 Vols. Alexandria: J. C. Lagoudakis, 1908.

Gerber, Haim. *State, Society, and Law in Islam: Ottoman Law in Comparative Perspective.* Albany: State Univ. of New York Press, 1994.

Ghazaleh, Pascale. "The Guilds: Between Tradition and Modernity." In *The State and Its Servants,* edited by Nelly Hanna, 61–74. Cairo: American Univ. in Cairo Press, 1995.

al-Giritli, 'Ali. "The Commercial, Financial, and Industrial Policy of Muhammad Ali." In *The Economic History of the Middle East: 1800–1914,* edited by Charles Issawi. Chicago: Univ. of Chicago Press, 1966.

Goldschmidt, Arthur. *Modern Egypt.* Boulder, Colo.: Westview Press, 1988.

Grabar, Oleg. *The Illustrations of the Maqamat.* Chicago: Univ. of Chicago Press, 1984.

Gran, Peter. *The Islamic Roots of Capitalism: Egypt, 1760–1840.* Austin: Univ. of Texas Press, 1979.

Guenena, Nemat. *The "Jihad": An "Islamic Alternative" in Egypt.* Vol. 9, American Univ. in Cairo Papers in Social Science, no. 2. Cairo: American Univ. in Cairo.

Guha, Ranajit. "On Some Aspects of the Historiography of Colonial India." In *Subaltern Studies,* vol. 1. Delhi: Oxford Univ. Press, 1987.

Handoussa, Heba Ahmad. Presentation at Georgetown Univ. Symposium *Egypt: '88,* Apr. 1988.

———. "Time for Reform: Egypt's Public Sector Industry." In *Studies in Egyptian Political Economy: Methodology, Theory and Case Studies,* edited by Herbert Thompson, 101–25. Vol. 2, American Univ. in Cairo Papers in Social Science, no. 3. Cairo: American Univ. in Cairo, 1979.

Hanna, Nelly. *Making Big Money in 1600: The Life and Times of Isma'il Abu Taqiyya, Egyptian Merchant.* Syracuse: Syracuse Univ. Press, 1998.

———. *An Urban History of Bulaq in the Mamluk and Ottoman Periods.* Cairo: Institut Français D'Archeologie Orientale, 1982.

Hill, Enid. *Mahkama! Studies in the Egyptian Legal System.* London: Ithaca Press, 1979.

———. *Al-Sanhuri and Islamic Law.* Vol. 10, American Univ. in Cairo Papers in Social Science, no. 1. Cairo: American Univ. in Cairo, 1987.

Hinnebusch, Raymond. *Egyptian Politics under Sadat: The Post-Populist Development of an Authoritarian-Modernizing State*. London: Lynne Reiner Publishers, 1988.

Hobsbawm, Eric, and Terence Ranger. *The Invention of Tradition*. Cambridge: Cambridge Univ. Press, 1984.

Hobson, J. A. *Imperialism: A Study*. London: George Allen and Unwin, 1902.

Holt, P. M. "The Last Phase of the Neo-Mamluk Regime." In *L'Egypte au XIX\u1d49 siecle*. Aix-en-Provence: Centre National de la Recherche Scientifique, 1982.

Hopkins, Nicholas. *Agrarian Transformation in Egypt*. Boulder, Colo.: Westview Press, 1987.

Hopwood, Derek. *Egypt: Politics and Society, 1945–1981*. London: George Allen and Unwin, 1982.

Hunter, F. Robert. *Egypt under the Khedives, 1805–1879: From Household Government to Modern Bureaucracy*. Pittsburgh, Pa.: Univ. of Pittsburgh Press, 1984.

———. "The Making of a Notable Politician: Muhammad Sultan Pasha (1825–1884)." *International Journal of Middle East Studies* 15 (1983).

Huntington, Samuel P. *The Clash of Civilizations and the Remaking of the World Order*. New York: Simon and Schuster, 1996.

Hussein, Mahmoud. *Class Conflict in Egypt: 1945–1970*. New York: Monthly Review Press, 1973.

Israeli, Raphael, ed. *The Public Diary of President Sadat*. Vol. 3, *The Road of Pragmatism*. Leiden: E. J. Brill, 1979.

Issawi, Charles. *The Economic History of the Middle East: 1800–1914*. Chicago: Univ. of Chicago Press, 1966.

Keddie, Nikki R., and Beth Baron, eds. *Women in Middle Eastern History: Shifting Boundaries in Sex and Gender*. New Haven, Conn.: Yale Univ. Press, 1993.

Kepel, Gilles. *Muslim Extremism in Egypt: The Prophet and Pharaoh*. Berkeley and Los Angeles: Univ. of California Press, 1986.

———. *The Revenge of God: The Resurgence of Islam, Christianity, and Judaism in the Modern World*. University Park: Pennsylvania State Univ. Press, 1994.

al-Khowli, Ramadan. "Archives as a Source of Women's History: Problems and Limitations." In *A History of Her Own*, edited by Amira el-Azhary Sonbol and John Obert Voll. Forthcoming.

Khuri, Fuad I. *Imams and Emirs: State, Religion and Sects in Islam*. London: Saqi Books, 1990.

Kritsman, Lawrence. *Michel Foucault: Politics, Philosophy, Culture, Interviews and Other Writings, 1977–1984*. New York: Routledge, 1988.

Landes, David. *Bankers and Pashas*. Cambridge, Mass.: Harvard Univ. Press, 1979.

Lane, Edward. *An Account of the Manners and Customs of the Modern Egyptians*. The Hague: East West Publication, 1978.

Laqueur, Walter. *Confrontation: The Middle East and World Politics*. New York: Bantam Books, 1974.

Lawson, Fred H. "Rural Revolt and Provincial Society in Egypt, 1820–1824." *International Journal of Middle East Studies* 13 (1981): 131–53.

Le Gassick, Trevor, ed. and trans. *The Defense Statement of Ahmad 'Urabi the Egyptian.* Cairo: American Univ. in Cairo Press, 1982.

Lewis, Bernard. "The Islamic Guilds." *Economic History Review* 8 (1937): 20–37.

Lipset, Seymour Martin. *American Exceptionalism: A Double-Edged Sword.* New York: W. W. Norton, 1996.

The Living Webster: Encyclopedic Dictionary of the English Language. Chicago: English Language Institute of America, 1977.

Marsot, Afaf Lutfi al-Sayyid. *Egypt in the Reign of Muhammad Ali.* Cambridge: Cambridge Univ. Press, 1984.

———. *Men and Women in Eighteenth Century Egypt.* Austin: Univ. of Texas Press, 1996.

———. "Muhammad 'Ali's Internal Politics." In *L'Égypte au XIXᵉ siècle.* Paris: Centre National de la Recherche Scientifique, 1982.

———. *Protest Movements and Religious Undercurrents in Egypt: Past and Present.* Washington, D.C.: Georgetown Univ. Center for Contemporary Arab Studies, 1984.

———. "The Role of the *'Ulama'* in Egypt During the Early Nineteenth Century." In *Political and Social Change in Modern Egypt,* edited by P. M. Holt. London: Oxford Univ. Press, 1968.

Mayer, Thomas. *The Changing Past: Egyptian Historiography of the Urabi Revolution, 1882–1983.* Gainesville: Univ. of Florida Press, 1988.

Meriwether, Margaret Lee. *The Kin Who Count: Family and Society in Ottoman Aleppo, 1770–1840.* Austin: Univ. of Texas Press, 1999.

"The Middle East: Statesmen Speak and Guns Answer," *Time* 96 (July 6, 1970): 7.

Mills, C. Wright. *The Power Elite.* London: Oxford Univ. Press, 1959.

Mitchell, Timothy. *Colonizing Egypt.* Cambridge: Cambridge Univ. Press, 1988.

Moreh, Shmuel, trans. *Napoleon in Egypt: al-Jabarti's Chronicle of the First Seven Months of the French Occupation, 1798.* Princeton, N.J.: Marcus Wiener Publishing, 1993, 28–29.

el-Nahhal, Galal. *Judicial Administration of Ottoman Egypt in the Seventeenth Century.* Minneapolis: Bibliotheca Islamica, 1979.

Nightingale, Florence. *Letters from Egypt: A Journey on the Nile, 1849–1850.* New York: Weidenfeld and Nicolson, 1987.

Nixon, Richard. "U.S. Foreign Policy for the 1970's: Building for Peace." Report to Congress, Feb. 25, 1971. Department of State Bulletin 64 (Mar. 22, 1971): 389–91.

Oakley, Frederick. *These Fifty Years: The Story of the Old Cairo Medical Mission from 1889 to 1939.* Old Cairo: Church Missionary Society, 1939.

Oldham, Linda, Haguer el Hadidi, and Hussein Tamaa. *Informal Communities in Cairo: The Basis of a Typology.* Vol. 10, American Univ. in Cairo Papers in Social Science, no. 4. Cairo: American Univ. of Cairo Press, 1987.

Owen, Roger. *The Middle East in the World Economy: 1800–1914.* London: Methuen, 1981.

Pasquinelli, Carla. "Power Without the State." *TELOS* 68 (summer 1986).

Peretz, Don. "Peace Efforts of Kennedy, Johnson and Nixon." *Annals of the American Academy of Political and Social Science: America and the Middle East* 401 (May 1972): 124.

Perrott, C. H. "Law and Justice." In *Twentieth Century Impressions of Egypt,* 96–109. London: Lloyd's Greater Britain Publishing, 1909.

Petry, Carl F. *The Civilian Elite of Cairo in the Later Middle Ages.* Princeton: Princeton Univ. Press, 1981.

Posusney, Marsha Pripstein. "Labor as an Obstacle to Privatization: The Case of Egypt 1974–1987." Paper presented at the Annual Meeting of the American Political Science Association, Atlanta Hilton, Aug. 31, 1989.

Quatre femmes d'Égypte. Produced by Éric Michel, directed by Tahini Rached, for Canadian Television, 1997.

Raymond, André. *Artisans et commerçants au Caire au XVIIIe siècle.* Vol. 1. Damascus: Institut Français de Damas, 1973–74.

———. *Le Caire des janissaires.* Paris: CNRS Editions, 1995.

———. "The Residential Districts of Cairo During the Ottoman Period." In *The Arab City: Its Character and Islamic Cultural Heritage,* edited by Ismail Serageldin and Samir el-Sadek. Riyadh, Saudi Arabia: Arab Urban Development Institute, 1982.

Reid, Donald Malcolm. *Cairo University and the Making of Modern Egypt.* Cairo: American Univ. in Cairo Press, 1990.

Riding, Alan. *Distant Neighbors: A Portrait of the Mexicans.* New York: Vintage Books, 1989.

Rizk, Yunan Labib. "al-Ahram: A Diwan of Contemporary Life." *al-Ahram Weekly,* Jan. 13–19, 2000, 1.

Rosaldo, Renato. *Culture and Truth: The Remaking of Social Analysis.* Boston: Beacon Press, 1989.

Rosen, Lawrence. *The Anthropology of Justice: Law as Culture in Islamic Society.* New York: Cambridge Univ. Press, 1989.

Sadat, Anwar. "The October Paper." In *The Public Diary of President Sadat,* edited by Raphael Israeli. Vol. 3, *The Road of Pragmatism.* Leiden: E. J. Brill, 1979.

Salacuse, Jeswald W. "Foreign Investment and Legislative Exemptions in Egypt: Needed Stimulus or New Capitulations?" In *Social Legislation in the Contemporary Middle East,* edited by Lawrence O. Michalak and Jeswald W. Salacuse. Berkeley and Los Angeles: Univ. of California Press, 1986.

Sarkar, Sumit. *Modern India: 1885–1974.* London: Macmillan, 1989.

Scott, James Harry. "Diplomatic and Consular Corps: The Capitulations." In *Twentieth Century Impressions of Egypt,* edited by Arnold Wright, 109–17. London: Lloyd's Greater Britain Publishing Company, 1909.

Sen, Asok. "Subaltern Studies: Capital, Class and Community," In *Subaltern Studies,* vol. 5. Delhi: Oxford Univ. Press, 1987.

Sharabi, Hisham. *Neopatriarchy: A Theory of Distorted Change in Arab Society.* New York: Oxford Univ. Press, 1988.

Shari'ati, 'Ali. *Man and Islam.* Mashhad, Iran: Univ. of Mashhad Press, 1982.

Shaw, Stanford. *The Financial and Administrative Organization and Development of Ottoman Egypt.* Princeton: Princeton Univ. Press, 1962.

—. *Ottoman Egypt in the Eighteenth Century.* Harvard Middle Eastern Monograph Series. Cambridge, Mass.: Harvard Univ. Press, 1962.

Shoukri, Ghali. *Egypt: Portrait of a President, 1971–1981.* London: Zed Press, 1981.

Shouman, Mohsen. "The Beginnings of Urban Iltizam." In *The State and Its Servants: Administration in Egypt from Ottoman Times to the Present,* edited by Nelly Hanna, 17–32. Cairo: American Univ. of Cairo Press, 1995.

el-Sikkari, Myrette Ahmed. *Basic Needs, Inflation and the Poor of Egypt, 1970–1980.* Vol. 7, American Univ. in Cairo Papers in Social Science, no. 2. Cairo: American Univ. in Cairo, 1984.

Sladen, Douglas. *Egypt and the English.* London: Hunst and Blackett, Ltd., 1908.

Smith, Adam. *Wealth of Nations.* London: Penguin Books, 1974.

Smith, Charles D. "4 February 1942: Its Causes and Its Influence on Egyptian Politics and on the Future of Anglo-Egyptian Relations, 1937–1945." *International Journal of Middle East Studies* 10 (1979).

Solé, Robert. *Les savants de Bonaparte.* Paris: Editions du Seuil, 1998.

Sonbol, Amira el-Azhary. *The Creation of a Medical Profession in Egypt: 1800–1922.* Syracuse: Syracuse Univ. Press, 1991.

—. "Egyptian Society and Sectarian Strife." In *The Political Economy of Contemporary Egypt,* edited by Ibrahim Oweiss. Washington, D.C.: Center for Contemporary Arab Studies, Georgetown Univ., 1990.

—. "Questioning Exceptionalism: Islamic Law." *Journal of Middle East Studies* (summer 1998).

Springborg, Robert. *Family, Power, and Politics in Egypt: Sayed Bey Marei—His Clan, Clients, and Cohorts.* Philadelphia: Univ. of Pennsylvania Press, 1982.

Staffa, Susan Jane. *Conquest and Fusion: The Social Evolution of Cairo, 642–1850.* Leiden: E. J. Brill, 1977.

Sullivan, Earl L. *Women in Egyptian Public Life.* Syracuse: Syracuse Univ. Press, 1986.

Terill, H. D. *Lord Cromer: A Biography.* New York: Edward Arnold, 1897.

Vatikiotis, P. J. *The History of Modern Egypt from Muhammad Ali to Mubarek.* Baltimore, Md.: Johns Hopkins Univ. Press, 1991.

Vitalis, Robert. *When Capitalists Collide: Business Conflict and the End of Empire in Egypt.* Berkeley: University of California Press.

Voll, John Obert. *Islam: Continuity and Change in the Modern World.* Syracuse: Syracuse Univ. Press, 1994.

Walz, Terence. "Family Archives in Egypt: New Light on Nineteenth-Century Provincial Trade." In *L'Égypte au xixe siècle.* Paris: Centre National de la Récherche Scientifique, 1982.

Waterbury, John. *The Egypt of Nasser and Sadat: The Political Economy of Two Regimes.* Princeton: Princeton Univ. Press, 1983.

—. *Hydropolitics of the Nile Valley.* Syracuse: Syracuse Univ. Press, 1979.

Weber, Max. *The Protestant Ethic and the Spirit of Capitalism.* New York: Charles Scribner's Sons, 1958.

Wehr, Hans. *Dictionary of Modern Written Arabic.* Ithaca, N.Y.: Spoken Language Services, 1976.

Wiet, Gaston. *Mohammed Ali et les beaux-arts.* Cairo: Dar al-Maaref, 1949.

Williams, Raymond. *Marzism and Literature.* Oxford: Oxford Univ. Press, 1977.

Winter, Michael. *Egyptian Society under Ottoman Rule: 1517–1798.* London: Routledge, 1992.

Wittfogel, Karl A. *Oriental Despotism: A Comparative Study of Total Power.* New Haven, Conn.: Yale Univ. Press, 1957.

Youssef, Magdy. "Preliminary Reflections on the Congress Theme: The Socio-Cultural Interaction Processes Between the Arab World and the West in Modern Times." *Intercultural Studies* (1983), 16.

Zaalouk, Malak. *Power, Class and Foreign Capital in Egypt: The Rise of the New Bourgeoisie.* London: Zed Books, 1989.

Ziadeh, Farhat J. *Property Law in the Arab World.* London: Graham and Trotman, 1979.

INDEX

obstacles to, 203; polygamy, 184–85; registrations ceasing during French invasion, 2; *'urfi* marriages, 186; weddings of the wealthy, 201

marriage contracts, 4

Marsot, Afaf, 2, 13

Marx, Karl, xxxix

masmuh al-masatib, 119

masses. *See 'amma*

mass media: in Egyptian revivalism, 213; magazines, 86, 201; television, 193, 213. *See also* press, the

al-mawlid al-nabawi, 54

mawlids, 54, 212

Mawsu'at Nasser li'l-Fiqh al-Islami, 148

mawwal, 212

Ma'ya, 72

Medal of Agriculture, 107

Medal of Industry and Trade, 107

Medal of Knowledge, 107

Medal of Perfection, 107

medals, 106, 107, 170

media. *See* mass media

Medical School for Girls, 63

medicine: health concerns of the poor, 207; Islamic conferences on, 189–90; medical infrastructure provided by *majlis al-sihha,* 49; water purification, 56

mercantilism, 32–55; *'amma* influenced by, xxxvii; classical definition of, xxxv; as continuing until recent crisis, xxv, xxxvi; different forms in different times and places, xxxvii; *diwan al-bahr* as central to, 50; and fiscal policy, 41, 166; versus free market, xxxv, 104; *infitah* policy as, 166; *khassa* favored by, 104, 180, 219–20; under Muhammad 'Ali, xxxvi, 34, 35, 38, 46, 51; in Nasser regime, 122–23; two approaches to, xxxv–xxxvi

merchants: class distinctions among, 22; mamluks extorting from, 24; ruling class connections of wealthy, 23; wealth and importance of, 21. *See also* foreign merchants; *tujjar*

Mexico, 156

Midaq Alley (Mahfuz), 191

middlemen, 38

mihrim, 185–86

military, the: under British rule, 90–93; economic activities of, 197–98; in the *khassa,* xxviii, xxix, xxxi, 198; Nasser on social role for the army, 125–26; 1967 defeat undermining legitimacy of, 153; Sadat as wary of, 175; Sadat supported by, 153; status changing under Sadat, 155–56. *See also* Free Officers

military school, 90–91

milkiyyat 'ayn, 119

milkiyyat al-intifa', 119

milla courts, 68, 69–70, 77

millet system, 5

Misr (newspaper), 61

Misr al-Fatat (Young Egypt), 121, 132, 171

Misr Group, 102

al-Misri, 'Aziz, 92

Mitchell, Tim, 3, 84

Mit Ghamr, 6

Al-Mithaq al-Watani (National Charter): on citizens' rights, 136–37; on confiscation of wealth, 144–45; on government jobs for graduates, 204; in al-Jazzar's "The Charter," 149–50; on labor, 165; Nasserist feudalism based on, 122, 129; women's rights under lost, 185

Mitri, Widad, 184

mixed courts, 68–69, 103, 242n. 36

monopolies: of Ibrahim Pasha over sugar, 46; mamlukid, 23, 38; of the modern state, 98; of Muhammad 'Ali, 34–35, 36, 37, 39, 40, 41, 90

Montreaux, Treaty of (1937), 103

morality, public, 17–18, 168

mozza, 202

al-Mu'alim Ghali, 45–46

mu'amalat, 183

Mubarak, 'Ali, 119

Mubarak, Hosni: appealing to the *'amma,* 190; Arabic as used by, 218; on birth rate, 194; as cautious about benefits, 167; in elections of 1984, 182; initial caution of, 181; *khul'* law supported by, 186; *kinayas* of, 190; middle-class frustration expressed by, 201; as military man, 155; and *mukhabarat,* 133; and new *tujjar,* xxxi, 200; private entrepreneurs under, 158;